THE BEST
PUB
QUIZ
BOOK

THE BEST PUB QUIZ BOOK

Ever!

CARLTON

Contents

INTRODUCTION

Over the past decade snugs and lounges in pubs the length and breadth of the country have become, if not seats of learning at least seats of intellect. Which makes a change from seats of worn leatherette (although these still prevail in some areas). The pub quiz has transformed the bar into an arena of knowledge where beery brethren battle to the final bell. The format is simple; some friends, acquaintances even complete strangers will do, a questioner, some paper, a collection of ragged Biros and a surfeit of beer and questions are all that is needed to create the perfect evening's entertainment. Wits are challenged, heads are huddled and patience is tested as teams attempt to outdo each other in their show of trivia retention. At these events you will learn that no fact is too small, no sport star too obscure and no war too insignificant to test the pub crowd's grey matter. In fact, the more obscure and wide-ranging the questions the greater the chance of involving the entire barroom – nothing will gain the pub idiot greater respect than showing that they have the entire cast, storyline and signature tune of Emergency Ward 10 lodged in their head, except perhaps their switching from slip-ons to lace ups. So take heart, and a copy of *The Best Pub Quiz Book Ever* to the boozer and have a few warm up sessions and see if you can't organise your own pub quiz. You know it makes sense; it's the only way you'll know all the answers.

The main aim of *The Best Pub Quiz Book Ever* is to entertain, so it is important that you retain a sense of humour and good sportsmanship as you play along, whether you are testing friends at home or setting a quiz for your local hostelry. That aside you also have to ensure that you are fully in control of your questions and players; remain calm, speak in a steady voice and be constantly unflapped when challenged by any of the more heavily imbibed, as indeed you will be.

If the locals do get testy your best bet is to head for the door while throwing beer nuts in the air to confuse them, though this should happen in only the roughest pubs or on outings with the extended family – in which case you should attempt to rescue your spouse, if you can do so without spilling your drink and it isn't them causing the trouble.

The Best Pub Quiz Book Ever is divided into three sections of Easy, Medium and Hard questions, which are all subdivided by specialist and pot-luck rounds. The former can be chosen either to help or hinder your players, giving Easy sports questions to the literature fanatics is bound to reveal some interesting answers but it is possibly more challenging to tailor your questions so that the experts receive the brain-wracking Hard questions and the novice the stupefyingly simple Easy questions. nothing hurts a fanatic more than being beaten on their specialist subject and the division of questions gives you the chance to employ a handicap system. Other handicap systems will also become apparent as you continue as quiz master, the team that wins the Sunday afternoon quiz will doubtless fail when it comes to Sunday night although if you want to set a quiz on Friday night you should check pupil dilation first, as on that evening of great relaxation you may find your teams asleep or brawling before calling the whole thing quits and joining them in a drink... or three.

In the interest of further clarification there follows a brief run down of each section:

Easy
In this primary round the main objective is to keep breathing, these questions are so easy that even the most docile pub idiot could gurgle his way through them in the time it takes to down a pint and still have time left to knock over the stack of pennies on the bar.

Medium
On your toes people, things are getting tricky. By now even the ringers on the out-of-towner's team will be sweating. These questions make for a challenge but you are bound to get the odd smug bar steward who will fancy his chances, for which you should continue on to section three.

Hard
Ask a full 30 of these questions and only the shrill wail of the pub cat fighting in the yard will be heard, brows will be furrowed, glances exchanged and beer stared into. To set an entire quiz using just these questions is a form evil so dark-hearted Fu Manchu would blanche.

All that is left to say is good luck with your testing and if you can't keep your spirits up at least try to keep them down.

The Easy Questions

If you think that Louis Armstrong was the first man on the moon or that Uri Geller was the first man in space then you will no doubt struggle through the next few questions terribly. For the rest of us though these are the EASY questions, so called because if the quizzee falters on these they are either three sheets to the wind or far too young to be in the pub – either state rendering them toddling buffoons whose social graces will equal their breadth of knowledge. So beware their flailing arms as you attempt to collect the answers.

These questions are perfect when used in the first round of an open entry quiz as they lull everyone into a false sense of security although you must beware that contestants don't shout answers out which creates a problematic precedent for the later, harder questions. Another way of placing these questions is to dot them about throughout the quiz thus making sure that on every team everyone should know the answer to at least one question despite their age.

If you are running a league quiz then some of your team members may heap derision on such obvious questions but don't worry even the cleverest quiz team member can come a cropper, as was noted in a championship final when a contestant was asked to name the continents he deliberated before eventually beaming out the answer, "A, E, I, O, U!".

Quiz 1 Pot-Luck 1

Answers - see page 11

Level 1

1 What was the original name of Drake's ship "The Golden Hind"?
2 What is the term for a positive electrode?
3 In "Last Of The Summer Wine" what was Nora's husband called?
4 Which swimming stroke is named after an insect?
5 Which English queen has the same name as a type of plum? *VICTORIA*
6 Which Rovers does veteran cartoon character Roy play for? *MELCHESTER*
7 How many dots are used in each letter in the Braille system?
8 Who won the Oscar for best actor in both 1993 and 1994? *Tom HANKS*
9 What is a female deer called?
10 Who was the first player to score a maximum 147 break in World Championship snooker? *CLIFF THORBURN*
11 What can be an island, a sweater or a potato? *JERSEY*
12 What unit is used to measure horses? *HANDS*
13 Who is Reg Dwight better known as? *ELTON JOHN*
14 Who is the lead singer with folk-rock group Steeleye Span?
15 In "Red Dwarf" what was the ranking of Technician Dave Lister?
16 How many tenpin bowling skittles need knocking down for a strike? *10*
17 How is 77 represented in Roman numerals?
18 Who is the patron saint of music?
19 What are birds of a feather said to do?
20 "Kiss Me Kate" is a musical version of which play by Shakespeare?
21 The single "Papa Don't Preach" came from which Madonna album?
22 Betz cells are found in which part of the body?
23 What is the only bird that can hover in the air and also fly backwards? *HUMMING*
24 Who earned the nickname "Slow-hand"?
25 In the Bible who goes after Mark and before John? *LUKE*
26 Which country does opera singer Pavarotti come from?
27 Which is the third largest of the Channel Islands?
28 Who was Liverpool manager for the '84 European Cup triumph?
29 In which Puccini opera does Mimi appear?
30 How many sides has an octagon?

Answers

Pot-Luck 2 (see Quiz 3)
1 Gregorian. 2 Guitar. 3 They abdicated. 4 October. 5 Seven. 6 Rome.
7 Goat. 8 25. 9 John Sullivan. 10 Four. 11 Australia. 12 Cher.
13 Waterloo. 14 The Diddymen. 15 Thursday. 16 John Betjeman.
17 Lilliput. 18 Dish. 19 Aardvark. 20 Seven. 21 Dirty. 22 George Best.
23 Siesta. 24 Edgar Allan Poe. 25 One minute. 26 Harrow. 27 M.
28 Badger. 29 Meg Mortimer. 30 "I'm free".

9

Quiz 2 Sport: The 50s

Answers - see page 12

 Level 1

1 Which two table sports was Joe Davis famous for?
2 Which athlete was the first to run a mile in under four minutes?
3 What nationality were tennis stars Lew Hoad and Ken Rosewall?
4 In which sport did Ben Hogan win the British championship?
5 Which Stirling driver won his first Grand Prix in 1955?
6 Which South American country gave a soccer debut to Pele?
7 In which steeplechase did Devon Loch fall when victory was in sight?
8 Which Rocky boxer retired undefeated in 1956?
9 In which country south of the Equator were the 1956 Olympics held?
10 What was the nationality of boxer Sugar Ray Robinson?
11 What was the first name of boxer La Motta known as the 'Bronx Bull'?
12 Which sport did Maureen 'Little Mo' Connolly play?
13 In which sport was Freddie Mills a star during the decade?
14 The opening of the 1952 Olympics was in which Finnish city?
15 What was the nationality of athlete Emil Zatopek?
16 Two famous Stanleys starred when Blackpool won the 1953 FA Cup Final. Mortensen was one. Who was the other?
17 Which honour did Gordon Richards get just before his first Derby win?
18 Which race was Lester Piggott the youngest-ever winner of in June 1954?
19 The Empire and Commonwealth Games were held in Canada in 1954. What are the games known as today?
20 What was the first name of Yorkshire-born Surrey off-spinner Laker?
21 Which football team were known as 'The Busby Babes'?
22 Where in Germany were this team involved in an air crash in 1958?
23 What was the first name of world mile record holder Ibbotson?
24 In 1957 Althea Gibson was the first black woman to win which tennis tournament?
25 Which soccer player received his 100th England cap in April 1959?
26 What nationality was the world heavyweight boxer Ingemar Johansson?
27 In which sport was Len Hutton the first professional to captain an England team?
28 Which race did Jim Peters run in under 2 hours 20 minutes?
29 In 1955, what was used for the first time in a Wembley international?
30 Which sportsmen asked for extra fees for televised matches in 1956?

Answers

TV: The 50s (see Quiz 4)
1 A dog. 2 Come Dancing. 3 Panorama. 4 The Good Old Days. 5 Sooty. 6 Opportunity Knocks. 7 The Sky At Night. 8 This Is Your Life. 9 Blue Peter. 10 Grandstand. 11 What The Papers Say. 12 Billy Bunter. 13 Tony Hancock. 14 10. 15 Lucille Ball. 16 First night of ITV. 17 Armchair. 18 Zoo Time. 19 Magician. 20 Dock Green. 21 Bill and Ben. 22 Palladium. 23 Billy Cotton. 24 Queen Elizabeth II. 25 Advertisements. 26 Tonight. 27 Richard. 28 What's My Line? 29 Army. 30 Westerns.

Quiz 3 Pot-Luck 2

Level 1

Answers - see page 9

1 Which type of calendar is used today in the western world? *GREGORIAN*
2 What instrument can be bass, electric or Spanish?
3 What special thing did Edward II, Richard II and Edward VIII all do while they were monarchs?
4 In which month of the year would you go to Munich for the beer festival? *OCTOBER*
5 What do the numbers add up to on the opposite sides of a dice?
6 Which city is said to have been founded by Romulus and Remus?
7 In the zodiac, which animal is linked with Capricorn?
8 How many years are involved in a silver anniversary?
9 Who scripted "Only Fools And Horses"? *JOHN SULLIVAN*
10 In music, how many quavers equal a minim?
11 Which country originated the term 'plonk' for wine?
12 How did Cherilyn Sarkasian LaPierre become better known?
13 What was the final battle that Napoleon fought in?
14 Which men used to perform with Ken Dodd?
15 On which day are British elections held? *THURSDAY*
16 Which poet wrote about the charms of Miss Joan Hunter Dunn?
17 What was the name of the land where Gulliver met the Little People?
18 In the nursery rhyme, who ran away with the spoon?
19 Which animal's name comes first in the dictionary? *AARDVARK*
20 How many sides has a 20-pence piece?
21 What is Den's nickname in "EastEnders"?
22 In the 1960s which footballer was called 'The Fifth Beatle'?
23 In Spain what is the word for an afternoon nap?
24 Who wrote "The Pit and the Pendulum"?
25 How long is there between rounds in boxing? *1 MINUTE*
26 Which public school did Sir Winston Churchill go to?
27 What is the thirteenth letter of the English alphabet?
28 Which is the largest land carnivore in Britain?
29 In "Crossroads" what part did Noele Gordon play?
30 In "Are You Being Served?" what was John Inman's catchphrase?

Quiz 4 TV: The 50s

Answers - see page 10

1   What kind of creature was Lassie?
2   Which series began in 1950 and has since been presented by Terry Wogan, David Jacobs and Rosemarie Ford?
3   Which current BBC current affairs programme began in 1953?
4   Which programme recreated Old Time Music Hall?
5   Which TV puppet appeared with his creator Harry Corbett?
6   Which much-knocked talent show began its 20-year run in 1956?
7   Which series about astronomy started with Patrick Moore?
8   Which programme surprised its 'victims' with a big red book?
9   Which kid's series coined the phrase, "Here's one we made earlier"?
10 Which sports programme, begun in 1958, can still be seen on Saturday afternoons?
11 Which long-running series from 1956 looks at the week's press?
12 Gerald Campion played which overweight pupil of Greyfriars school?
13 Which comedian had a half hour show with his name in the title?
14 What was the number of the emergency ward in the hospital drama?
15 Who played the title role in "I Love Lucy"?
16 What major TV event happened in 1955 on the night Grace Archer died on radio?
17 Where were you invited to sit in to watch some theatre?
18 Desmond Morris presented which natural history programme?
19 What type of entertainer was David Nixon?
20 Where was PC George Dixon's 'patch'?
21 What were the names of the Flowerpot Men?
22 Which London theatre staged a Sunday night variety show?
23 Which bandleader's catchphrase was "Wakey Wakey!"?
24 Whose coronation was televised in 1953?
25 What was ITV given permission to include with its programmes that BBC could not?
26 Cliff Michelmore presented which nightly information programme?
27 What was the first name of eminent broadcaster Dimbleby?
28 In which programme did a panel try to guess someone's occupation?
29 In which game did a group of National Service soldiers appear?
30 "Laramie" and "Maverick" were what types of series?

Quiz 5 Pot-Luck 3

Level 1

Answers - see page 15

1 Which actor played Jim Hacker in TV's "Yes Prime Minister"?
2 How many children were there in Enid Blyton's Famous Five? *Four*
3 Who appeared with The Coconuts? *KID CREOLE*
4 What kind of animal was Phillip Schofield's puppet pal Gordon?
5 What is the stage name of Harry Webb?
6 What was Conrad Phillips most famous TV role?
7 Which film gave Jack Nicholson his first Oscar? *ONE FLEW OVER*
8 Which season do Americans call the Fall?
9 The fabled bird the griffin had the head of which real bird?
10 On which Common would you find the Wombles?
11 Whose catchphrase is, "Nice to see, to see you nice"?
12 Who was the first Labour MP? *KEIR HARDIE*
13 Who at the age of fourteen became Britain's youngest chess International Master?
14 Which country does Bryan Adams come from?
15 Who was known as the lady with the lamp?
16 What is the plural of the word sheep?
17 How is Rebecca Rolfe better known?
18 What is the symbol for the Gemini sign of the zodiac?
19 Where in a horse is the coffin joint?
20 What word can go before cheese, plant and roll?
21 Which Simon and Garfunkel song features the words "Jesus loves you more than you can say"? *MRS ROBINSON*
22 Which 'famous first' is attributed to asparagus in Britain?
23 Which substance is most used for pencil lead?
24 To ten years either way, in which year did Charles Dickens die?
25 Which long-running radio programme was devised by Roy Plomley?
26 Which Lloyd Webber musical does the song "Memory" come from?
27 What drink does pear juice make?
28 What name can be a lettuce or a mass of floating frozen water? *ICEBERG*
29 Which vegetable did Sir Walter Raleigh bring to England?
30 In the strip cartoon, what is the name of Snoopy's brother?

Answers

Pot-Luck 4 (see Quiz 7)
1 Kipps. 2 Ascot. 3 Union. 4 Eddie Waring. 5 Gilbert and Sullivan. 6 Lucy Locket. 7 Edward Fox. 8 Blue. 9 Right. 10 Peter and Gordon. 11 The General Lee. 12 Desdemona. 13 15. 14 Motor racing. 15 Japan. 16 Turkey. 17 The Doors. 18 12. 19 Uganda . 20 Maria Callas. 21 Quarto. 22 Even numbers. 23 Two. 24 Hangman. 25 Kidneys. 26 Knot garden. 27 Billy J. Kramer. 28 17th. 29 Greta Garbo. 30 None.

1   What was the name of Bill Haley's backing group?

2   Which shoes did Elvis warn you not to step on 1956?

3   What kind of doll was Cliff Richard's first No 1?

4   Which blonde film star sang about her Secret Love?

5   Where was the Doggie when Lita Roza asked how much it was?

6   What relation to each other were Don and Phil Everly?

7   Where were the tulips from, which Max Bygraves sang about?

8   According to Connie Francis where did she find lipstick?

9   Whom did the Beverley Sisters see kissing Santa Claus?

10   How were the Balls of Fire described by Jerry Lee Lewis?

11   According to Frank Sinatra how do Love and Marriage go together?

12   Which Buddy was killed in a plane crash?

13   What did Perry Como ask you to catch and put in your pocket?

14   Which Biblical Garden did Frankie Vaughan sing about?

15   Who sang "Oh Carol" about fellow singer/songwriter Carole King?

16   Who's Boy Child did Harry Belafonte sing about in 1958?

17   Which line follows "Be Bop A Lula" at the start of the Gene Vincent hit?

18   Which 1950s pop star is Kim Wilde's father?

19   Who had hits with "When I Fall In Love" and "Stardust"?

20   Where did the Lace which the Big Bopper sang about come from?

21   Who asked "What do you want, if you don't want money"?

22   Where did Pat Boone write his Love Letters?

23   Which late soul singer had a hit with "Reet Petite" in 1957?

24   How many steps are there to heaven?

25   What Blues ain't there no cure for, according to Eddie Cochran?

26   In the song title, what did Shirley Bassey ask her Honey Honey to do?

27   Which record machine appeared in coffee bars in the 1950s?

28   According to Lonnie Donegan what might lose its flavour on the bedpost overnight?

29   How many tons did Tennessee Ernie Ford sing about?

30   According to The Platters what gets in your eyes?

Quiz 7 Pot-Luck 4

Level 1

Answers - see page 13

1 "Half A Sixpence" is based on which story by H.G. Wells?
2 At which course are the Coventry Stakes run?
3 Soyuz was the name of a Russian spacecraft, but what does the name mean?
4 Who talked of an "early bath" and an "up and under"?
5 Who wrote the Savoy operas?
6 Who lost her pocket?
7 In the film "The Day of the Jackal", who played the Jackal?
8 What colour is a sapphire?
9 Does Elizabeth II face to the left or right on a British coin?
10 How were the musical duo Asher and Weller better known?
11 What did Bo and Luke Duke call their car?
12 In Shakespeare's "Othello", who is the female lead?
13 In the pirate song, how many men were on the dead man's chest?
14 Mike Hawthorne was the first Briton to win the World Champion in which sport?
15 Venetian blinds originated in which country?
16 A poult is the young of which creature?
17 Which group recorded the original of "Light My Fire"?
18 In an English trial, how many people sit on the jury?
19 Where - apart from the Moon - are the Mountains Of The Moon?
20 Which great soprano earned the name of 'La Divina'?
21 What measure of paper is 8 by 10 inches?
22 On a standard roulette wheel which numbers appear on the black?
23 What number is *dos* in Spanish?
24 In which game do you draw part of a gallows for every wrong answer?
25 Bright's disease affects which organs of the body?
26 What name is given to a garden with geometrically arranged beds and small hedges?
27 Who sang with The Dakotas?
28 In which century was 1658?
29 Which actress said, "I want to be alone"?
30 How many kings of England have been called Philip?

Answers

Pot-Luck 3 (see Quiz 5)
1 Paul Eddington. 2 Four – one was a dog. 3 Kid Creole. 4 Gopher. 5 Cliff Richard. 6 William Tell. 7 One Flew over the Cuckoo's Nest. 8 Autumn. 9 Eagle. 10 Wimbledon. 11 Bruce Forsyth. 12 Keir Hardie. 13 Nigel Short. 14 Canada. 15 Florence Nightingale. 16 Sheep. 17 Pocahontas 18 Twins. 19 Foot. 20 Swiss. 21 Mrs Robinson. 22 First frozen food. 23 Graphite. 24 1870. 25 Desert Island Discs. 26 Cats. 27 Perry. 28 Iceberg. 29 Potato. 30 Spike.

Quiz 8 The Royal Family

Answers - see page 14

Level 1

1 How many daughters does Queen Elizabeth II have?
2 Who is the father of Princes William and Harry?
3 What is the Duchess of York's nickname?
4 Which member of the royal family was married to Lord Snowdon?
5 What is the Queen Mother's first name?
6 What is the Queen's residence in Scotland called?
7 Which Prince is Duke of Edinburgh?
8 Which Prince was a helicopter pilot in the Falklands War?
9 Who is the Princess Royal?
10 On which programme did the Princess of Wales give her first solo TV interview?
11 Which school did Prince William start at in 1995?
12 What is the Queen's favourite breed of dog?
13 What was the name of the woman for whom Edward VIII abdicated?
14 Which Queen was married to Prince Albert?
15 What is the name of the Queen's London residence?
16 How many English kings have been called George?
17 What was the Princess of Wales' maiden name?
18 What was Princess Anne's first husband called?
19 Who is the father of Princesses Beatrice and Eugenie?
20 Who is Queen Elizabeth II's youngest son?
21 Who interviewed Prince Charles on ITV and wrote a revealing biography about him?
22 What type of operation did the Queen Mother have in December 1995?
23 Which castle was badly damaged by fire in 1992?
24 What is Prince Harry's proper first name?
25 Which Royal survived a kidnap attempt in 1974?
26 Who had her jewels stolen at an airport in 1995?
27 Prince Charles is Duke of which county of southwest England?
28 Which title did Edward VIII take after he abdicated?
29 What is the name of the Queen's residence in Norfolk?
30 What is the Royal Yacht called?

Answers

Sounds Of The 50s (see Quiz 6)
1 The Comets. 2 Blue Suede. 2 Livin'. 4 Doris Day. 5 In The Window. 6 Brothers. 7 Amsterdam. 8 On Your Collar. 9 Mommy. 10 Great. 11 Like A Horse and Carriage. 12 Holly. 12 A Falling Star. 14 Eden. 15 Neil Sedaka. 16 Mary's. 17 "She's My Baby". 18 Marty Wilde. 19 Nat King Cole. 20 Chantilly. 21 Adam Faith. 22 In the Sand. 23 Jackie Wilson. 24 Three. 25 Summertime. 26 Kiss Me. 27 Jukebox. 28 Chewing Gum. 29 16. 30 Smoke.

Answers - see page 19

1 What do the letters AIDS stand for?
2 How many stomachs has a cow?
3 With which swimming stroke do races begin in the water?
4 What have you been doing if you finish by casting off?
5 How is the Roman city of Verulamium known today?
6 Roy Jenkins was a founder of which political party?
7 What does Susan Hampshire suffer from?
8 Film star Roy Scherer died in 1985. What was his screen name?
9 Which city in the world has the largest population?
10 Whose ship was the first to sail round the world?
11 In music hall, who was the 'Prime Minister of Mirth'?
12 Who composed "The Flight Of The Bumble Bee"?
13 Which actor can be found in The Nag's Head and The Royal Oak?
14 What is the full name of BBC Radio 5?
15 What was invented by Lewis Waterman in the 1880s?
16 Which illustrator was famous for detailed drawings of weird and wonderful mechanical inventions?
17 Who appears with Lamb Chop?
18 Following the 1963 Peerage Act, who was the first peer to disclaim his title?
19 What was "Prisoner: Cell Block H" originally called?
20 Which instrument usually has 47 strings?
21 What is the name of Dennis the Menace's dog?
22 For over a quarter of a century, which tobacco company has produced a football yearbook?
23 Who wrote "Help Me Make It Through The Night"?
24 Moving anti-clockwise on a dartboard what is the number next to 4?
25 Who created the detective Paul Temple?
26 Who pricked her finger on a spinning wheel and slept for 100 years?
27 Who became Earl of Stockton on his 90th birthday?
28 Which traffic light follows green?
29 In "My Friend Flicka" who or what was Flicka?
30 Which is the first month of the year to have exactly 30 days?

Answers

Pot-Luck 6 (see Quiz 11)
1 The Late, Late Breakfast Show. 2 Two. 24 Greek, 26 English. 3 Pancakes. 4 Leaves. 5 Perseus. 6 Noah. 7 Kojee Bear. 8 John Curry. 9 1986. 10 Eight. 11 First test tube baby. 12 Excalibur (also referred to as Caliburn). 13 Russell Harty. 14 Desert island. 15 Tongue. 16 Richard Nixon. 17 Quentin Crisp. 18 Bob Hope. 19 Harry Palmer. 20 Private Eye. 21 Grasshopper. 22 18. 23 West Germany. 24 88. 25 Eight. 26 Pavement. 27 Crocodile. 28 Sarah Kennedy. 29 Fifty years. 30 Three.

Quiz 10 Around England

Answers - see page 20

1 The Severn, the Trent and the Ouse are all what?
2 In which county are all ten of England's highest peaks?
3 Which is the second largest city in England?
4 Which London station was named after a long-reigning Queen?
5 In which county are the seaside resorts of Clacton and Southend?
6 Leeds Castle is in Kent. Where is Leeds?
7 Which seaside resort is famous for its Tower and its Golden Mile?
8 What might you see at Regent's Park, Chester and Whipsnade?
9 What is the name of the famous cathedral in York?
10 Which is the largest island in England?
11 What did Sunderland become in 1992 which Manchester, Liverpool and Birmingham became in the 19th century?
12 Which river runs through London?
13 Which is further north, Southport or Northampton?
14 Which stretch of water divides England and France?
15 What do the letters NEC stand for?
16 What is the area around Stoke-on-Trent known as?
17 Which northern city is served by Ringway airport?
18 Which motorway starts south of Birmingham and goes northwest towards Scotland?
19 Which part of the country would a Geordie come from?
20 Near which large city would you find the Wirral?
21 Which two cities are the home of England's two oldest universities?
22 Which range of northern hills is called the backbone of England?
23 Which moorland area of southwest Devon is the site of a high-security prison?
24 What are Dagenham, Luton and Cowley famous for producing?
25 Where would a Manx person come from?
26 Which famous stones can be seen on Salisbury Plain?
27 Whose birthplace might you be visiting in Stratford-on-Avon?
28 In which county is the English terminal of the Channel Tunnel?
29 How many square miles is the City of London?
30 Which was England's smallest county before the 1974 changes?

Answers

40s and 50s Films (see Quiz 12)
1 Bambi. 2 80 days. 3 Over the River Kwai. 4 White Christmas. 5 Tramp. 6 Ben Hur. 7 Fantasia. 8 Gone With The Wind. 9 Bob Hope. 10 Casablanca. 11 Laurence Olivier. 12 Brief Encounter. 13 Hitchcock. 14 Welles. 15 Alec Guinness. 16 Ealing Comedies. 17 In The Rain. 18 Hot. 19 Genevieve. 20 James Dean. 21 Grace Kelly. 22 Brigitte Bardot. 23 Ten. 24 At The Top. 25 Elizabeth Taylor. 26 Rogers. 27 Brando. 28 Arsenic. 29 Love. 30 Eternity.

Quiz 11 Pot-Luck 6

Level 1

Answers - see page 17

1 In which TV show did the 'Mr Puniverse' contest take part?
2 How many more letters are there in the English than the Greek alphabet?
3 Which food item is used in an annual race at Olney?
4 Which part of the mint plant is used to make mint sauce?
5 In legend, who slew the gorgon Medusa?
6 Who had sons called Ham, Shem and Japheth?
7 What was the name of Rolf Harris's puppet koala bear?
8 Which British olympic gold ice skating medallist died in 1995?
9 When did Halley's Comet last appear?
10 How many legs has a lobster?
11 Louise Brown will always hold which famous first?
12 What was the name of King Arthur's sword?
13 Who on TV often used the phrase "you are, are you not..."?
14 On the radio where are you sent with eight records of your choice?
15 Which part of its body does a snake use to detect noise?
16 Who was the first American president to resign from office?
17 In "The Naked Civil Servant" who did John Hurt portray?
18 "Thanks For The Memory" is the theme song of which comedian?
19 Who did Michael Caine play in "The Ipcress File"?
20 Which magazine has been edited by Richard Ingrams and Ian Hislop?
21 In "Kung Fu" what name do the Buddhist priests give to Kwai Chang Caine?
22 In Australian football, how many players are there on a side?
23 In which country was Checkpoint Charlie located?
24 What number in bingo is two fat ladies?
25 How many notes are there in an octave?
26 What is it that Americans call the sidewalk?
27 Which creature links Jimmy Nail's Shoes and Elton John's Rock?
28 Who on TV has been "Game For A Laugh" and on "A Busman's Holiday"?
29 How many years are involved in a golden celebration?
30 How many faults are incurred for a refusal in showjumping?

Answers

Pot-Luck 5 (see Quiz 9)
1 Acquired Immune Deficiency Syndrome. 2 Four. 3 Backstroke. 4 Knitting. 5 St Albans. 6 Social Democrat Party. 7 Dyslexia. 8 Rock Hudson. 9 Tokyo. 10 Ferdinand Magellan. 11 George Robey. 12 Rimsky-Korsakov. 13 Nicholas Lyndhurst. 14 Radio Five Live. 15 Fountain Pen. 16 Heath Robinson. 17 Shari Lewis. 18 Tony Benn. 19 Prisoner. 20 Harp. 21 Gnasher. 22 Rothmans. 23 Kris Kristofferson. 24 18. 25 Francis Durbridge. 26 Sleeping Beauty. 27 Harold Macmillan. 28 Amber. 29 Horse. 30 April.

Level 1

Answers - see page 18

1 Which Disney film released in 1942 was about a little fawn?
2 How many days did it take David Niven to go Around the World?
3 In the 1957 film about Japanese prisoners of war, where was the Bridge?
4 Which yuletide classic was first sung by Bing Crosby in "Holiday Inn"?
5 If Lady is a pedigree spaniel what is the name of the mongrel?
6 Which Ben won 11 Oscars in 1959?
7 In which 1940 film did Mickey Mouse conduct the orchestra?
8 In which film did Vivien Leigh play Scarlett O'Hara?
9 Who starred in the Road films with Dorothy Lamour and Bing Crosby?
10 Which film set in Rick's Café starred Humphrey Bogart and Ingrid Bergman?
11 Which distinguished actor, later a Lord, played the lead in "Henry V"?
12 Which film starred Celia Johnson, Trevor Howard and a train station?
13 Which Alfred directed the thrillers "Rebecca" and "Notorious"?
14 Which actor Orson starred in "Citizen Kane" and "The Third Man"?
15 Who played eight different characters in "Kind Hearts and Coronets"?
16 What was the series of comedies made in West London studios called?
17 Where was Gene Kelly Singin' in 1952?
18 How did Some Like It in the film with Jack Lemmon, Tony Curtis and Marilyn Monroe?
19 What was the name of the car that involved Kenneth More and Dinah Sheridan in the London to Brighton road run?
20 Which young star of "East of Eden" died in a car crash aged 24?
21 Which actress married Prince Rainier of Monaco?
22 Which French 'sex kitten' starred with Dirk Bogarde in "Doctor at Sea"?
23 In the Charlton Heston film how many commandments were there?
24 Where was there Room in the film starring Laurence Harvey?
25 Who was the young star of "National Velvet" in 1945?
26 Which dancer/actress Ginger won an Oscar in 1940?
27 Which actor Marlon starred in "On the Waterfront"?
28 What goes with Old Lace in the title of the Cary Grant film?
29 What is A Many Splendored Thing in the film about the Korean War?
30 From Here to where is the Oscar-winning movie with Deborah Kerr, Burt Lancaster and Frank Sinatra?

Quiz 13 Pot-Luck 7

Answers - see page 23

1 What does an arctophile collect?
2 Which of Verdi's operas is set in Ancient Egypt?
3 What gives red blood cells their colour?
4 Who has had hits with "Tutti Frutti" and "Rip It Up"?
5 On TV, what kind of creature was Flipper?
6 Which animals took Hannibal over the Alps?
7 How is the auracaria tree more commonly known?
8 In which team game do you try to move backwards all the time?
9 Which situation comedy had Wendy Craig and Geoffrey Palmer as a married couple?
10 Who was the first British monarch to visit New Zealand?
11 Who recorded the albums "John Wesley Harding" and "Nashville Skyline"?
12 Who does The Beast fall in love with?
13 What is the main ingredient in a brick?
14 What hangs down from the roof of cave – a stalagmite or a stalactite?
15 What is the body of a penguin covered with?
16 How does Saturday's child work for a living?
17 Who appeared with Keith Chegwin on "Multi Coloured Swap Shop" and later married him?
18 Which musical direction means at ease, at a slow comfortable pace?
19 Which bell said, "You owe me five farthings"?
20 Which king is said to have burnt the cakes?
21 Which British national daily newspaper ceased publication in 1995?
22 Which girl shares her name with a Christmas song?
23 How many edges in a cube?
24 Which dance comes from "Orpheus In The Underworld"?
25 At what age does a filly become classified as mare?
26 What type of creature is a Pacific sea wasp?
27 Who had a No 1 in 1995 with "You Are Not Alone"?
28 How many are there in a baker's dozen?
29 George Harrison's "My Sweet Lord" was claimed to sound like which other song?
30 Is the South Pole at the Arctic or the Antarctic?

Quiz 14 Football

Answers - see page 24

1 Who plays home games at Ewood Park?
2 Which team are known as the Gunners?
3 What colour are Manchester United's home shirts?
4 Which footballer made a record with Lindisfarne?
5 Who was England's manager for the 1990 World Cup in Italy?
6 Which city has teams called Wednesday and United?
7 Which ground hosts the FA Cup Final?
8 Who plays against Rangers in an Auld Firm derby match?
9 How many minutes in the second half of a Premier League match?
10 What name is shared by Birmingham, Coventry and Leicester?
11 Which colour card is used to send a player off?
12 Who joined Liverpool from Nottingham Forest for £8 million plus in 1995?
13 Which country does Ryan Giggs play for?
14 Who was Ian St John's partner on TV?
15 Which East Anglian team is nicknamed The Canaries?
16 How many players should be on the pitch at the start of a game?
17 Who won the World Cup in 1958, 1962, 1970 and 1990?
18 Which team plays home games at Villa Park?
19 What is the name of BBC 1's long-running Saturday night soccer show?
20 Hearts and Hibs come from which Scottish city?
21 What number is traditionally worn on the goalie's shirt?
22 Which Geordie played for England and managed the Republic of Ireland?
23 Which country does Jurgen Klinsmann come from?
24 If you were at Goodison Park who would be playing at home?
25 Which London team earned the nickname "The Crazy Gang"?
26 Which Nottingham club was managed by Brian Clough?
27 What is the colour of the home strip of both Everton and Chelsea?
28 Which country do Hendry, Goram and McCoist play for?
29 Can a goalkeeper score a goal for his own team?
30 At which Lane do Spurs play when at home?

Soaps (see Quiz 16)
1 Queen Victoria. 2 Curly Watts. 2 The patio. 4 Ramsay. 5 Joan Collins. 6 Emmerdale. 7 Southfork. 8 Falcon. 9 Casualty. 10 Home and Away. 11 H. 12 Peyton. 12 Crossroads. 14 A magazine. 15 The Colbys. 16 Knot's. 17 Brookside. 18 Jason Donovan. 19 Jack and Vera Duckworth. 20 Angie Watts. 21 J.R. 22 Carrington. 23 Girl. 24 Emmerdale. 25 Melbourne. 26 The Bill. 27 Rita Sullivan. 28 Ena. 29 America. 20 Barbara Windsor.

Answers

Quiz 15 Pot-Luck 8

Level 1

Answers - see page 21

1 Thomas Arnold was headmaster of which public school?
2 What kind of creature was Rikki-Tikki-Tavi?
3 In the story, how many men were in Jerome K. Jerome's boat?
4 In which town do the Flintstones live?
5 In 1930, which country did Amy Johnson fly to from England?
6 When "Coronation Street" moved from two to three programmes a week in 1989, what was the new day for transmission?
7 Who wrote "Watership Down"?
8 Which animal is regarded as the one with the longest life span?
9 Who in the Bible had a coat of many colours?
10 What is the outer layer of skin called?
11 What meat appears in a Punch and Judy show?
12 Who left "Take That" in July 1995?
13 What does an invertebrate not have?
14 Who was the tallest of Robin Hood's Men?
15 Who wrote "The Female Eunuch"?
16 In "Countdown" how many letters are selected for the letters game?
17 What was the actual first name of Hopalong Cassidy?
18 Della Street was secretary to which famous legal character?
19 What did Constantinople become known as in March 1930?
20 Who did Sri Lanka beat in the quarter finals of the '94 cricket World Cup?
21 Who wrote the song "White Christmas"?
22 Which star sign has the bull as its symbol?
23 What was special about the meeting of Sue Middleton and Alex Tatham who married in 1991?
24 In a tennis tie-break, what is the largest winning margin?
25 Who won the Eurovision Song Contest in bare feet?
26 What do philatelists collect?
27 Rudolf Hess was the last prisoner in which jail?
28 Who composed "Peter Grimes"?
29 What does PAYE stand for?
30 Who played student Alan Moore in "Rising Damp"?

Answers

Pot-Luck 7 (see Quiz 13)
1 Teddy bears. 2 Aida. 3 Haemoglobin. 4 Little Richard. 5 Dolphin. 6 Elephants. 7 Monkey puzzle. 8 Tug of War. 9 Butterflies. 10 Elizabeth II. 11 Bob Dylan. 12 Beauty. 13 Clay. 14 Stalactite. 15 Feathers. 16 Hard. 17 Maggie Philbin. 18 Adagio. 19 St Martins. 20 Alfred. 21 "Today". 22 Carol. 23 12. 24 The can-can. 25 Five. 26 Jellyfish. 27 Michael Jackson. 28 33. 29 He's So Fine recorded by the Chiffons. 30 Antarctic.

Quiz 16 Soaps

Answers - see page 22

1 What is the name of the pub in Albert Square?
2 Whom did Raquel marry in secret in December 1995?
3 What was Trevor Jordache buried under in "Brookside"?
4 In which street is "Neighbours" set?
5 Which British actress played Alexis in "Dynasty"?
6 In which soap is there a pub called The Woolpack?
7 What is the name of the ranch in "Dallas"?
8 Which bird added to a Crest completes a soap series?
9 Which hospital soap is set in Holby City Hospital?
10 Which Australian soap is set in Summer Bay?
11 On which Cell Block might there be a Prisoner in an Australian soap?
12 Which Place was the the name of the first major US soap?
13 Which British soap was set in a motel?
14 In the 1960s series "Compact", what was Compact?
15 Which soap was a spin-off of "Dynasty"?
16 In which Landing did some members of Dallas's Ewing family settle?
17 Which soap has featured the Corkhills, the Grants and the Dixons?
18 Who left his role as Scott Robinson and became a West End Joseph?
19 Which couple took over The Rovers' Return after Bet Gilroy left?
20 Who was Sharon's mum in "EastEnders"?
21 By what initials was actor Larry Hagman known as in "Dallas"?
22 What was Blake and Krystle's surname in "Dynasty"?
23 In "Home and Away" was Bobby Simpson a boy or a girl?
24 Where was there a horrific air crash in December 1993?
25 In which Australian city is "Neighbours" set?
26 Which police series is based at Sun Hill police station?
27 In "Coronation Street" who owns The Kabin?
28 What was the first name of legendary Street character Mrs Sharples?
29 Which country did Michelle go to when she left Albert Square?
30 Which Carry On star became Phil and Grant's mum in "EastEnders"?

Quiz 17 Pot-Luck 9

Answers - see page 27

1 What colour is pure molten gold?
2 What is the zodiac sign of Pisces?
3 Whose face is on an American five-dollar bill?
4 Who had a No 1 hit with the song "Wuthering Heights"?
5 With which branch of medicine is Mesmer associated?
6 Who sang on a "Showboat" and ended up in "Dallas"?
7 In the nursery rhyme, what did Tom, Tom the piper's son steal?
8 Who wrote "Where Have All The Flowers Gone"?
9 In "HMS Pinafore" who did Sir Joseph Porter bring on boat along with his sisters?
10 According to the proverb, what begins at home?
11 Which birds are traditionally used by Japaneses fishermen to help them catch fish?
12 Who plays TV's Inspector Morse?
13 Called chequers in America, what's the name of this game in Britain?
14 Who was the last queen of England by succession before Elizabeth II?
15 What is the term for fear of enclosed spaces?
16 Name the consortium that runs the National Lottery?
17 What was the name of the Big River sung about by Jimmy Nail?
18 What is the name of the person who delivers the mail in Greendale?
19 Which city is the setting for "Saturday Night Fever"?
20 What was the No 1 recording made by Matthews Southern Comfort?
21 Which food item is most consumed by humans throughout the world?
22 Who says, "Know what I mean, 'Arry"?
23 Which day of the week is named after the god Thor?
24 Who first recorded "A Whiter Shade Of Pale"?
25 What is Sweden's national flower?
26 What do entomologists study?
27 What tree does a date grow on?
28 In the song, what did my true love send to me on the seventh day of Christmas?
29 Who was the famous son of Uther Pendragon?
30 Who has been world darts champion a record five times?

Quiz 18 Theatre and Musicals

Answers - see page 28

Level 1

1 Which musical is based on the story of Romeo and Juliet?
2 Who wrote the long-running play "The Mousetrap"?
3 Complete the title of the comedy: "No Sex Please ____"
4 In "Starlight Express" what do the performers wear on their feet?
5 What was Jesus Christ according to Tim Rice and Andrew Lloyd Webber?
6 According to the comedy, There's a what in My Soup?
7 Where is the Fiddler in the musical which starred Topol?
8 Which London theatre's motto was, "We never closed"?
9 Which New York street is famous for its theatres?
10 Which musical about Professor Higgins and Eliza Doolittle is based on "Pygmalion"?
11 Who wrote the music in the comic operas for which Gilbert wrote the words?
12 What do the initials RSC stand for?
13 Which musical is based on T. S. Eliot's poems?
14 Who first played the title role in "Evita" in the West End?
15 Which musical is the name of a US state?
16 Which show includes "Climb Ev'ry Mountain"?
17 Which musical is the name of a fairground ride?
18 Which musical is about a circus impresario?
19 In which musical does Fagin appear?
20 Which Boulevard is the title of a musical?
21 Which part of the Pacific is the setting for a popular musical?
22 Which class of Society is a musical based on "The Philadelphia Story"?
23 Oh which Indian city appears in the title of a controversial show?
24 The Importance of Being what is the name of an Oscar Wilde play?
25 Who are with the Guys in the show about gangsters?
26 Which girl is the lecturer Educating in the play by Willy Russell?
27 Which Miss is a musical set in Vietnam?
28 What is the full name of the show often just referred to as Les Mis?
29 What do you say to Dolly in the title of the show?
30 Aspects of what are the theme of which Lloyd Webber musical?

Quiz 19 Pot-Luck 10

Answers - see page 25

Level 1

1 On the radio, what did ITMA stand for?
2 What was the most famous group managed by Andrew Loog Oldham?
3 Which character had a sister Petra and a niece Dawn?
4 Who recorded the album "Brothers In Arms"?
5 In which sport is the Davis Cup played for?
6 Which English king was said to be Unready?
7 In song, what colour toothbrush was Max Bygraves?
8 Which veteran entertainer brought his 'odd odes' to TV?
9 Which US president was assassinated in a Washington theatre?
10 Who had a rifle called "Old Betsy"?
11 David Lean's film was about a passage to which country?
12 Which city was "so good they named it twice"?
13 In song, where do the deer and the antelope play?
14 Which planet is fourth from the sun?
15 According to a Nick Berry song title every loser does what?
16 How many sides has a parallelogram?
17 Which film star dog had three names each containing three letters?
18 Where did Larry the Lamb live?
19 In which country did the Thuggee - from which we derive the word thug - operate?
20 What part did Joan Collins play in "Dynasty"?
21 Which country did Juan Perón rule?
22 Is it the male or female cuckoo that makes the "cuck-oo" call?
23 Which jockey was knighted in 1953?
24 On TV, what's the name of Edina's daughter?
25 What can be a box or part of the body?
26 What nationality was the notorious murderer Dr Crippen?
27 Which Brian appeared in "Z Cars" and "Cats" and is an authority on Mount Everest?
28 Which holy sounding character was created by Leslie Charteris?
29 Which insects live in apiaries?
30 What does WRAF stand for?

Pot-Luck 9 (see Quiz 17)

Answers

1 Green. 2 Fish. 3 Abraham Lincoln. 4 Kate Bush. 5 Hypnotism. 6 Howard Keel. 7 A pig. 8 Pete Seeger. 9 His cousins and his aunt. 10 Charity. 11 Cormorants. 12 John Thaw. 13 Draughts. 14 Queen Victoria. 15 Claustrophobia. 16 Camelot. 17 Tyne. 18 Postman Pat. 19 New York. 20 Woodstock. 21 Rice. 22 Frank Bruno. 23 Thursday. 24 Procol Harum. 25 Lily of the valley. 26 Insects. 27 Palm. 28 Seven swans a-swimming. 29 King Arthur. 30 Eric Bristow.

Quiz 20 40s and 50s Newsround

Level 1

1 Which Winston took over as prime minister in 1940?
2 Who was the German leader throughout World War II?
3 What name was given to the persistent air attack on London?
4 What does POW stand for?
5 Who was known as the Forces' Sweetheart?
6 What was the popular name for the Home Guard ?
7 Which country was Stalin leader of?
8 Which continent was El Alamein in?
9 In which country did the D Day landings take place?
10 V-E Day commemorated victory on which continent?
11 World War II ended in which year?
12 Whose engagement to Philip Mountbatten was announced in 1947?
13 Which Jewish state was founded in 1948?
14 Which competition did Miss Sweden win the first of in 1951?
15 Which type of denim trousers took Britain by storm in 1955?
16 Which future US president did Jacqueline Bouvier marry in 1953?
17 Which country launched the first satellite – Sputnik 1 – in space?
18 What was climbed by Edmund Hillary and Tensing in 1953?
19 Which craft which floats on an air cushion was invented in 1958?
20 What type of prize-winning Bonds were introduced?
21 Which large plastic hoop became a sports craze in the 1950s?
22 Which small car did Austin and Morris launch in 1959?
23 What was the name of the London to Birmingham motorway?
24 Which word for 13- to 19-year olds was first coined in the 1950s?
25 A frothy version of which non-alcoholic drink became popular in this era?
26 What did Billy Butlin found in the 1950s?
27 What type of parking payment machine was introduced in London?
28 Where did spies Burgess, Maclean and Philby defect to?
29 Which type of 1950s music used a washboard?
30 What did CND marchers on the way to Aldermaston want to ban?

Quiz 21 Pot-Luck 11

Answers - see page 31

Level 1

1 Which creatures did St Patrick drive out of Ireland?
2 In which TV programme do Patsy and Edina appear?
3 A 1990 ad for jeans helped put which early 70s Steve Miller Band song to the top of the charts?
4 In which month does the grouse shooting season start in Britain?
5 What type of racing has only two cars competing on the track at the same time?
6 How many years are celebrated by a platinum anniversary?
7 What is an oblong bar of gold called?
8 Who has played Lord Peter Wimsey and Bertie Wooster on TV?
9 Which European soccer trophy did Spurs become the first British team to win?
10 In the Paul McCartney/Stevie Wonder hit what went with ebony?
11 In which month is Twelfth Night?
12 In which city is the Whitney art gallery?
13 In which soap do the Sugdens appear?
14 What are the initials of thriller writer James?
15 Who recorded the album "The Immaculate Collection"?
16 In the book title, who did writer Laurie Lee have cider with?
17 Which musical does "I Know Him So Well" come from?
18 Which fictional Scottish doctor kept a casebook?
19 Who made up Abba with Benny, Bjorn and Annifrid?
20 Which traveller had the unusual first name of Lemuel?
21 Who wrote the words to "The Boxer"?
22 In which country is Hampden Park Stadium?
23 What can be upside down, ginger or Dundee?
24 Who was presenter of the 60s pop show "Saturday Club"?
25 Who was the lead singer with Culture Club?
26 What do the French words *au revoir* mean ?
27 Who said, "Am I dying beyond my means?"?
28 Who played the character of Mrs Fawlty?
29 Which Marie is supposed to have said, "Let them eat cake"?
30 What do the initials TB stand for?

Answers

Pot-Luck 12 (see Quiz 23)
1 Mobile Army Surgical Hospital. 2 300. 3 Spain. 4 Edward VIII. 5 The Life And Loves Of A She Devil. 6 Valhalla. 7 Iron. 8 Rommel. 9 Mrs Dale's Diary. 10 January. 11 Reg Varney. 12 Piano. 13 Dusty Springfield. 14 Haddock. 15 Avocado. 16 Austria. 17 Plimsoll Line. 18 Soup. 19 Lorna Doone. 20 Vivaldi. 21 Dublin. 22 Richmal Crompton. 23 XIV. 24 Chair. 25 Alexander the Great. 26 Karen. 27 Intelligence. 28 Spencer. 29 Jerusalem. 30 Bonsai.

Quiz 22 Geography

Answers - see page 32

 Level 1

1 Is Australia in the northern or the southern hemisphere?
2 What does each star on the flag of the United States stand for?
3 Which country does the holiday island of Ibiza belong to?
4 Which island would you visit to kiss the Blarney Stone?
5 In which country would you be if you were visiting the Taj Mahal?
6 The south of which continent is closest to the Falkland Islands?
7 In which mountain range would you find Mount Everest?
8 Which country is Luxembourg the capital of?
9 What colour is the spot in the middle of the Japanese flag?
10 The island of Sicily is at the toe of which country?
11 Which country is also known as The Netherlands?
12 In which country are Maoris the indigenous population?
13 In which Scandinavian country would you find fjords?
14 Which country's languages include English, Zulu and Afrikaans?
15 Which country's name could be part of a Christmas dinner?
16 In which city is the Vatican City?
17 What is K2?
18 In which country is the Yellow River, also known as Huang He?
19 Which country has four letters, the last one q?
20 Which country, capital Bangkok, used to be called Siam?
21 Which ocean lies between Europe and America?
22 Which European country has an area called Flanders?
23 Is the South Pole in the Arctic or the Antarctic?
24 Which Rock is on the south coast of Spain?
25 Which isle lies between England and Northern Ireland?
26 Which island to the south of India used to be called Ceylon?
27 Which sea separates Europe and Africa?
28 In which ocean is Fiji?
29 Which island, in the Arctic Ocean, is the largest in the world?
30 In which continent is the world's longest river, the Nile?

Answers

Sounds of the 60s (see Quiz 24)
1 Happiness. 2 Blue Jeans. 3 Dustman. 4 Downtown. 5 Congratulations. 6 Sonny. 7 Diana Ross. 8 Pins. 9 Whiter. 10 The Pacemakers. 11 24. 12 Freddie. 13 Herman. 14 Roy Orbison. 15 Go. 16 Lollipop. 17 Fashion. 18 Billy J. Kramer. 19 The Rising Sun. 20 Lulu. 21 Four. 22 Cilla Black. 23 The Monkees. 24 Nights. 25 Dusty Springfield. 26 The Who. 27 Yellow. 28 The Shadows. 29 The Beach Boys. 30 Papas.

Quiz 23 Pot-Luck 12

Level 1

Answers - see page 29

1 What do the letters in M*A*S*H actually stand for?
2 How many minutes in five hours?
3 A car with the international registration letter E comes from where?
4 Who came first King Edward VIII or George VI?
5 Ruth and Bobbo Patchett appear in which novel?
6 Where were Norse gods said to live?
7 Fe is the symbol of which chemical element?
8 Which army commander was known as "The Desert Fox"?
9 In which early radio soap was Mary worried about Jim?
10 What is the first month of the year to have exactly 31 days?
11 On TV, who worked in "The Rag Trade" and "On The Buses"?
12 Which musical instrument has dampers, hammers and strings?
13 "You Don't Have To Say You Love Me" was which singer's first No 1?
14 Which fish is smoked and cured and called 'finnan'?
15 Which pear-shaped tropical fruit has given its name to a bathroom suite colouring?
16 The Spanish Riding School is in which country?
17 What was the original name of the line on a ship showing the level to which it could be loaded?
18 Bouillabaisse is what kind of fish dish?
19 John Ridd is the male lead in which book with a girl's name as its title?
20 Who wrote the music "The Four Seasons"?
21 In which city in 1916 was the Easter Rising?
22 Who wrote the stories about a schoolboy named William Brown?
23 Which King Louis built the palace at Versailles?
24 Sedan, arm and high are all types of what?
25 Who had a horse called Bucephalus?
26 What was the first name of the female singer in The Carpenters?
27 In the USA what does the I stand for in CIA?
28 What was the surname of Frank in "Some Mothers Do 'Ave 'Em"?
29 "Walk upon England's mountains green" is the second line of which rousing song?
30 What name is given to the Japanese skill of growing miniature trees?

Answers

Pot-Luck 11 (see Quiz 21)
1 Snakes. 2 Absolutely Fabulous. 3 The Joker. 4 August. 5 Drag Racing.
6 70. 7 Ingot. 8 Ian Carmichael. 9 European Cup Winners' Cup. 10
Ivory. 11 January. 12 New York. 13 Emmerdale. 14 P.D. 15 Madonna.
16 Rosie. 17 Chess. 18 Doctor Finlay. 19 Agnetha. 20 Gulliver. 21
Paul Simon. 22 Scotland. 23 Cake. 24 Brian Matthew. 25 Boy George.
26 Until we meet again. 27 Oscar Wilde. 28 Prunella Scales. 29
Antoinette. 30 Tuberculosis.

Quiz 24 Sounds of the 60s

Level 1

Answers - see page 30

1 What was Helen Shapiro Walking Back to in 1961?
2 What was Venus wearing in 1962 according to Mark Wynter?
3 What was the occupation of Lonnie Donegan's old man?
4 In which part of town was Petula Clark in the 1960s?
5 What was the title of Cliff Richard's 1968 Eurovision song?
6 Who was Cher's first singing partner with a hit song?
7 Who was lead singer with The Supremes?
8 What did The Searchers sing about along with Needles?
9 What shade of Pale did Procol Harum sing about?
10 Who was Gerry's backing group?
11 How many Hours was Gene Pitney from Tulsa?
12 Who sang with The Dreamers?
13 Who had Hermits?
14 Who was known as 'The Big O'?
15 What followed Ready, Steady in the title of the pop show?
16 My Boy, according to Millie, is called what?
17 What were The Kinks Dedicated Followers of in 1966?
18 Who sang with The Dakotas?
19 According to The Animals, what was the name of The House in New Orleans?
20 Who was heard to "Shout" in 1964?
21 How many were there in the Tops, Pennies and Seasons?
22 Which Liverpool lady took "Anyone Who Had a Heart" to No 1?
23 Which US band 'aped' The Beatles and sang "Daydream Believer"?
24 What was in White Satin according to The Moody Blues?
25 Who left her two group members and sang "I Only Want to Be With You"?
26 Which group wrote the rock opera "Tommy"?
27 What colour was The Beatles' Submarine?
28 Who was Cliff Richard's backing group?
29 Who felt "Good Vibrations" in 1966?
30 Who sang with The Mamas?

Answers

Geography (see Quiz 22)
1 Southern. 2 A state. 3 Spain. 4 Ireland. 5 India. 6 South America. 7 Himalayas. 8 Luxembourg. 9 Red. 10 Italy. 11 Holland. 12 New Zealand. 13 Norway. 14 South Africa. 15 Turkey. 16 Rome. 17 Mountain. 18 China. 19 Iraq. 20 Thailand. 21 Atlantic. 22 Belgium. 23 Antarctic. 24 Gibraltar. 25 Isle of Man. 26 Sri Lanka. 27 Mediterranean. 28 Pacific. 29 Greenland. 30 Africa.

Quiz 25 Pot-Luck 13

Level 1

Answers - see page 35

1 What is the boiling point of water?
2 Alphabetically, which is the second sign of the zodiac?
3 What is Goldfinger's first name?
4 Who had a No 1 hit with the song "I Just Called To Say I Love You"?
5 Who wrote "The Owl and The Pussycat"?
6 What are beds of snooker tables traditionally made of?
7 By what name was travelling show tap dancer Luther Robinson known?
8 What was the name of the "Neighbours" character played by Kylie Minogue?
9 What word describes the permanent disappearance of a species?
10 The Star of Africa is what type of gem?
11 In education, what does BA stand for?
12 In the human body, what has four chambers?
13 Which creature can turn its stomach inside out?
14 There are 78 cards in which type of pack?
15 What is arachnophobia the fear of?
16 Which two writers created "Auf Wiedersehen, Pet"?
17 How many cards of the same suit are needed for a flush in poker?
18 What name is given to an athletics event such as running or hurdling?
19 Which war in Europe took place between 1936–9?
20 Under what name did Samuel Clemens write?
21 Who recorded the album "Tubular Bells"?
22 In which city is the Obelisk of Luxor?
23 Which day of the week is named after the moon?
24 In the USA what is a greenback?
25 Who composed the tune to "Twinkle Twinkle Little Star"?
26 Which Charles wrote "The Origin Of Species"?
27 Donnerstag is German for which day?
28 Jennyanydots was what kind of cat?
29 What is the federal republic of Switzerland divided into?
30 Who wrote "Rebecca"?

Answers

Pot-Luck 14 (see Quiz 27)
1 The Scarecrow. 2 Schilling. 3 Measles. 4 Oasis. 5 Alma. 6 Cabriolet. 7 Clock. 8 Cilla Black. 9 Scott Joplin. 10 Bell. 11 Jacobs. 12 1931. 13 Bread. 14 Cabbage. 15 Allan Sherman. 16 Three. 17 Radioactivity. 18 Larry Grayson. 19 Tyne. 20 Anthony Quinn. 21 Sex change. 22 Blue. 23 Lawson. 24 Cruet. 25 Nap. 26 The Blue Angel. 27 Tom Waits. 28 Captain W. E. Johns. 29 Fifty. 30 World Boxing Association.

Quiz 26 Sport: The 60s

Answers - see page 36

Level 1

1 In which Italian city were the 1960 Olympic Games held?
2 What nationality were 1961 Wimbledon finalists Christine Trueman and Angela Mortimer?
3 What was the first name of heavyweight boxing champion Liston?
4 Who won the FA Cup for the first time, under Bill Shankly?
5 What was the surname of cricketer Fiery Fred who retired in 1968?
6 What nationality was 1962 Wimbledon champion Rod Laver?
7 In what kind of racing was Jim Clark world champion?
8 Which Stanley retired from playing football aged 50?
9 Who won the World Cup in 1966?
10 Which Glasgow soccer team were the first British side to win the European Cup?
11 In 1969 Tony Jacklin was US Open Champion in which sport?
12 What was the surname of boxer Cassius?
13 What was the first name of British Wimbledon champion Mrs Jones?
14 What was the first name of US golfer Palmer?
15 Which Henry was British heavyweight champion in 1963?
16 Which father of Damon won the World Driver's championship in 1962?
17 What was the surname of Wimbledon singles champion Billie-Jean?
18 Which country does 1969 motor racing champion Jackie Stewart come from?
19 What is the surname of former Manchester United legend George?
20 How did Anita Lonsborough win an Olympic gold medal in 1960?
21 Which country was banned from the Olympics because of apartheid?
22 Which jump won Mary Rand a gold medal at the 1964 Olympics?
23 What was the surname of international footballers Jackie and Bobby?
24 Which international football trophy was stolen in 1966?
25 At which sport were Margaret Court and Maria Bueno champions?
26 Who were the runners-up in the 1966 World Cup?
27 What sport was Jack Brabham famous for?
28 Which England manager Alf received a knighthood?
29 Which UK tennis championship was the first to be seen on TV in colour in 1967?
30 Sir Matt Busby retired as manager of which football club?

Answers

TV: The 60s (see Quiz 28)
1 Coronation Street. 2 Z Cars. 3 Forsyte Saga. 4 University Challenge. 5 Your Lucky Stars. 6 Dr Who. 7 Dr Finlay. 8 Flintstones. 9 Liver Birds. 10 Magic Roundabout. 11 Man From UNCLE. 12 Match of the Day. 13 Horse. 14 Adam. 15 The Avengers. 16 Home. 17 That Was The Week That Was. 18 Mason. 19 Peyton Place. 20 The Saint. 21 Songs of Praise 22 Star Trek. 23 Till Death Us Do Part. 24 Tomorrow's. 25 Top of the Pops. 26 Williams. 27 England, West Germany. 28 Dudley Moore. 29 Winters. 30 The Beatles.

1 Which part did Michael Jackson play in "The Wiz"?
2 What is the currency of Austria?
3 Which childhood disease is also known as rubella?
4 Who recorded the album "Definitely, Maybe"?
5 In "Coronation Street", what is the name of Mike Baldwin's wife?
6 Cab is a shortening of which word?
7 In rhyming slang what is meant by dickory dock?
8 How is Priscilla White better known?
9 Who wrote "Maple Leaf Rag"?
10 The Tsar Kolokol is the biggest what in the world?
11 Which David presented "Juke Box Jury"?
12 To five years either way, when was the Empire State Building finished?
13 Which comedy series featured the Boswell family?
14 *Brassica oleracea* is better known as what?
15 Who wrote home from Camp Grenada?
16 How many sides has an isosceles triangle?
17 What does a Geiger counter detect?
18 Whose catchphrase was, "Shut that door!"?
19 Which major river flows through Newcastle?
20 Who was the star of "Zorba The Greek"?
21 Which much publicized operation did Doctor Richard Raskind undergo?
22 In the song, what colour are Crystal Gale's brown eyes made?
23 Which Nigel is a former Chancellor of the Exchequer?
24 What is the word for a condiment container?
25 What can be a sleep or how fabric lies?
26 In which film did Dietrich sing "Falling In Love Again"?
27 Which actor/songwriter is closely linked to Jim Jarmusch?
28 Who created Biggles?
29 According to Paul Simon, how many ways are there to leave your lover?
30 In boxing, what does WBA stand for?

Quiz 28 TV: The 60s

Level 1

1 Which soap, which started in 1960, tells of life in Weatherfield?
2 Which Cars were at the heart of a long-running police drama series?
3 Which family Saga spanned the Victorian and Edwardian eras?
4 Which university quiz was hosted by Bamber Gascoigne?
5 What did you Thank in the ITV Saturday evening pop show?
6 Which Doctor arrived on our screens in the Tardis in 1963?
7 Whose Casebook was based in a Scottish village surgery?
8 Which cartoon series had a Stone Age setting with Fred and Wilma?
9 Which Birds were flatmates in Liverpool?
10 Which Roundabout was about Dougal, Florence and Zebedee?
11 How was the the Man from the United Network Command for Law and Enforcement better known?
12 Which show began broadcasting highlights of the day's football?
13 What kind of animal was Mr Ed who was able to talk?
14 What was the first name of sci-fi adventurer Adamant?
15 Which series included Emma Peel and Steed?
16 Where was Cathy told to Come in the 1966 play about homelessness?
17 Which satirical programme was abbreviated to TW3?
18 What was the surname of Los Angeles defence lawyer Perry?
19 Which Place was the setting for the early soap with Mia Farrow and Ryan O'Neal?
20 What was the nickname of amateur sleuth Simon Templar?
21 What is TV's long-running hymn singing programme, begun in 1961?
22 Which programme saw the first adventures of the starship Enterprise?
23 Which series starred the controversial Alf Garnett?
24 Which World about new inventions and discoveries began in 1965?
25 Which chart music show started in 1964?
26 Which American Andy hosted a long running easy music show?
27 Who played in the football match watched by 32 million in 1966?
28 Who starred with Peter Cook in "Not Only... But Also"?
29 What was the surname of comedy duo Mike and Bernie?
30 In 1963 which Fab Four were all four panellists on "Juke Box Jury"?

Quiz 29 Pot-Luck 15

Level 1

Answers - see page 39

1 Red, yellow and blue are what type of colour?
2 In which TV programme does Hyacinth Bucket appear?
3 Which John was Labour leader before Tony Blair?
4 Which soccer side has Alexandra in its name?
5 The Acol system is used in which game?
6 How many years are celebrated by a ruby anniversary?
7 What three colours are in the flag of Belgium?
8 Which Leo plays Rumpole?
9 What number does the Roman numeral C stand for?
10 What was the name of Miss Rigby in the song by the Beatles?
11 In which month is Valentine's Day?
12 Which Ron played Fagin on film?
13 Roberta Flack had a No 1 with a song about the First Time I Saw Your what?
14 What are the initials of the poet Eliot?
15 What did Polly Flinders do?
16 Which Frederick wrote "The Day Of the Jackal"?
17 Which term means related to the moon?
18 Which Roger has played James Bond?
19 What are John, Paul, George and Ringo better known as?
20 On what part of your body would you wear a muff?
21 Which Wendy starred in "Butterflies"?
22 In which city is The Oval cricket ground?
23 Which Florence was known as the lady with the lamp?
24 What is a young fox called?
25 On which course is the Derby run?
26 Which special name is given to a group of ravens?
27 Who recorded the album "Thriller"?
28 On TV, is "Brookside" a close, an avenue or a drive?
29 Grandfather, cuckoo and carriage are types of what?
30 RoSPA is the Royal Society for the Prevention of what?

Answers

Pot-Luck 16 (see Quiz 31)
1 Curly 2 Florence Nightingale. 3 Germany. 4 Dr Doolittle. 5 Wendy Richard. 6 HMV - His Master's Voice. 7 Carbon. 8 Popeye. 9 Red and white. 10 November. 11 Dublin. 12 Arnold Layne. 13 Poker. 14 Geometry. 15 Simple Minds. 16 13. 17 Five. 18 Limbo. 19 Eight. 20 Grimm. 21 Heidi. 22 Temple. 23 Heifer. 24 Natalie. 25 Godiva. 26 Midas. 27 Domesday. 28 Frankie Laine. 29 Eye. 30 Briers.

Quiz 30 60s Films

Answers - see page 40

1 On which Side of New York was the musical Story about rival gangs?
2 Who starred as Cleopatra and married co-star Richard Burton?
3 With which country is Lawrence associated in the film with Peter O'Toole?
4 Which role did Warren Beatty play to Faye Dunaway's Bonnie?
5 What type of Cowboy was Jon Voight in the 1969 film?
6 Who was The Graduate in the film of the same name?
7 Who won an Oscar as Professor Higgins in "My Fair Lady"?
8 Which musical by Lionel Bart was based on a Dickens novel?
9 Which western actor won his only Oscar for "True Grit"?
10 Which actress Mia starred in the controversial "Rosemary's Baby"?
11 What were the hills alive with in the musical set in Austria?
12 What was the nationality of Zorba in the film with Anthony Quinn?
13 Guess Who's Coming to which meal in the Katharine Hepburn film?
14 Which nanny did Julie Andrews win an Oscar for playing?
15 Who played Alfie?
16 Which blonde Julie was a Darling?
17 Who played Fanny Brice in "Funny Girl"?
18 Which Doctor did Omar Sharif play in the film set in the USSR?
19 Which Gregory won an Oscar for "To Kill A Mockingbird"?
20 Which Miss was Maggie Smith whose Prime won an Oscar in '69?
21 Which actor Paul played Thomas More in "A Man For All Seasons"?
22 How many Dalmatians starred in the 1961 Disney film?
23 Who was Butch Cassidy's partner?
24 In the 1968 film when was "The Space Odyssey"?
25 Which 1960 Hitchcock film has the most famous shower scene ever?
26 Which meal was taken at Tiffany's in the film with Audrey Hepburn?
27 Who played James Bond in "Dr No"?
28 What accompanied the Bad and The Ugly in the Clint Eastwood film?
29 Which Sweet girl was played by Shirley Maclaine in the 1968 musical?
30 Which film with Vanessa Redgrave was about King Arthur's court?

Answers

Hi-Tech: Transport (see Quiz 32)
1 M1. 2 Right. 3 Essex. 4 Ford. 5 Hot Air Balloon. 6 Wright. 7 Queen Elizabeth II. 8 France. 9 Rolls Royce. 10 Atlantic. 11 Train. 12 English Channel. 13 Jet. 14 Concorde. 15 Black. 16 M25. 17 Manchester. 18 Jaguar. 19 Queen Mary. 20 M11. 21 Waterloo. 22 Germany. 23 Underground. 24 Paris. 25 Lorry. 26 Railway. 27 Folkestone. 28 1995. 29 Moscow. 30 Dartford.

Quiz 31 Pot-Luck 16

Answers - see page 37

Level 1

1 What is Norman Watts' nickname in "Coronation Street" ?
2 In 1907, who was the first woman to receive the Order of Merit?
3 Which country does a car come from if it has the international registration letter D?
4 Which doctor had a pet chimp called Chee Chee?
5 Who played Miss Brahms?
6 Which company had Nipper the dog as its trade mark?
7 C is the symbol of which chemical element ?
8 Which cartoon character has Bluto as his arch rival?
9 Which two colours appear on the flag of Denmark?
10 What is the last month of the year to have exactly 30 days?
11 In which city was the 1994 Eurovision Song Contest held?
12 In a Pink Floyd song who had the strange hobby of collecting clothes?
13 If you are playing Southern Cross you are playing a form of which game?
14 Euclid is associated with which branch of mathematics?
15 Which group had a No 1 with "Belfast Child"?
16 How many players are in a Rugby League team?
17 In the UK what is the maximum number of years between General Elections?
18 What type of dance involves moving under a low horizontal pole?
19 How many pints in a gallon?
20 Which brothers, Jacob and Wilhelm, wrote fairy tales?
21 Johanna Spyri created which little girl?
22 Which child star Shirley won an Oscar at the age of six?
23 What name is given to a cow that has not had a calf?
24 What is the first name of Nat King Cole's singing daughter?
25 Which Lady rode naked through the streets of Coventry?
26 In legend, which king turned everything he touched into gold?
27 William the Conqueror ordered which Book to be compiled?
28 Who sang the theme song to "Rawhide"?
29 REM stands for rapid movement of what?
30 Which Richard starred in "Ever Decreasing Circles"?

Answers

Pot-Luck 15 (see Quiz 29)
1 Primary. 2 Keeping Up Appearances. 3 Smith. 4 Crewe. 5 Bridge. 6 40. 7 Black, red and yellow. 8 McKern. 9 100. 10 Eleanor. 11 February. 12 Moody. 13 Face. 14 T.S. 15 Sat among the cinders. 16 Forsyth. 17 Lunar. 18 Moore. 19 The Beatles. 20 Hands. 21 Craig. 22 London. 23 Nightingale. 24 Cub. 25 Epsom. 26 Unkindness. 27 Michael Jackson. 28 Close. 29 Clock. 30 Accidents.

Quiz 32 HI-Tech: Transport

Answers - see page 38

1 Which motorway runs from London to Leeds?
2 Do more countries drive on the left or on the right?
3 In which county is Stansted airport?
4 Which company made the first production-line car, the Model T?
5 What did the Mongolfier brothers fly in in 1783?
6 What was the surname of aviation pioneers Orville and Wilbur?
7 What is the full name of the QE2?
8 Which country do Renault cars come from?
9 Who produced the luxury Silver Ghost?
10 Over which ocean did Alcock and Brown fly in 1919?
11 What would you be travelling in if you were in a Pullman?
12 Under which stretch of water would you be if you were on Le Shuttle?
13 Which engine for aircraft was patented by Frank Whittle in 1930?
14 Which Anglo-French supersonic aircraft made its first flight in 1969?
15 What is the traditional colour for a London taxi?
16 Which motorway circles London?
17 Which city is served by Ringway Airport?
18 Which type of sports car is also the name of a big cat?
19 What was the Queen Elizabeth's luxury sister ship?
20 Which motorway runs from London to Cambridge?
21 Which London railway station is named after a battle with Napoleon?
22 Which country do Volkswagen cars originate in?
23 How would you be travelling if you were taking the Jubilee line?
24 In which city is Charles de Gaulle airport?
25 What type of vehicle is a juggernaut?
26 Which type of transport is George Stephenson famous for?
27 Near which Kent port is the English opening of the Channel Tunnel?
28 In which year did Nigel Mansell last race Formula 1 cars?
29 The Trans-Siberian railway runs from Vladivostock to which Russian city?
30 At which Thames crossing is there a tunnel and the Queen Elizabeth Bridge?

Quiz 33 Pot-Luck 17

Level 1

1 Which motorway was the first to be built in Britain?
2 What is the zodiac sign of the Bull?
3 On a dart board, which number is bottom centre?
4 Who had a No 1 hit with the song "Dancing Queen"?
5 Born Arthur Jefferson in 1890, what was this comic better known as?
6 What profession did Hillary Clinton previously practise?
7 Which character was played on TV by both Julie Walters and Lulu?
8 In which sport are there madisons and pursuits?
9 Who is the only singer to have No 1 hits in the 50s, 60s, 70s, 80s and 90s?
10 According to proverb, what does the hand that rocks the cradle do?
11 What was founded in 859 at Fez, Morocco, that is reckoned to be the oldest of its type in the world?
12 Which writer established the Three Laws of Robotics?
13 Called hood in America, what's this part of the car called in the UK?
14 Titan is a moon of which planet?
15 What is hydrophobia the fear of?
16 How many furlongs in a mile?
17 On TV, what is the name of Mavis Wilton's husband?
18 Which annual race was first held in 1829?
19 What type of animal is a Lhasa Apso?
20 Garibaldi, Nice and Ginger Nut are all types of what?
21 In the USA, which are the two main political parties?
22 Which Noel said, "Television is something you appear on: you don't watch it"?
23 What was the trade of Thomas Wolsey's father?
24 What did Siam change its name to?
25 Who recorded the album "Hold Me, Thrill Me, Kiss Me"?
26 Which Bay housed the island prison Alcatraz?
27 What colours are on the flag of Argentina?
28 In which town did Jesus grow up?
29 Who set up Biba?
30 If a triangle has an angle of 58 degrees and an angle of 77 degrees, what is the third angle?

Answers

Pot-Luck 18 (see Quiz 35)
1 Russia. 2 John Osborne. 3 Altimeter. 4 George Michael. 5 Burt Reynolds. 6 Edward VIII. 7 Talk. 8 Fred Astaire. 9 Six. 10 Leviticus. 11 Housemaid's Knee. 12 Milan. 13 Captain. 14 Black. 15 The Kabin. 16 Seven. 17 Fish. 18 On the face. It's a nose. 19 Mersey. 20 Dana. 21 Basil Brush. 22 Huey Lewis. 23 Prue. 24 Thompson Twins. 25 School. 26 Cairo. 27 Porridge. 28 Cricket. 29 Aubergine. 30 Ronald Reagan.

Quiz 34 Hollywood

Answers - see page 44

1 Which tough guy star of "Casablanca" married Lauren Bacall?
2 Who co-starred with Bob Hope in the Road films and died playing golf?
3 Which actress was shunned by Hollywood when she left her husband and children for director Roberto Rossellini?
4 What is the first name of actor Curtis, father of Jamie Lee?
5 Which Officer and a Gentleman married supermodel Cindy Crawford?
6 How was Ruth Elizabeth Davis better known?
7 Which director Cecil B. was famous for epic movies?
8 Which Kops were the creation of director Mack Sennett?
9 Which daughter of Judy Garland won an Oscar for "Cabaret"?
10 Who is Kirk Douglas's famous son?
11 Which actress Ava was Frank Sinatra's second wife?
12 What relation is Shirley Maclaine to fellow star Warren Beatty?
13 Which Katharine had a long relationship with Spencer Tracy?
14 Which actress Grace became Princess of Monaco?
15 Which British suspense film director worked in Hollywood from 1939?
16 Which actress daughter of Henry was known as Hanoi Jane because of her anti-Vietnam war activities in the 1970s?
17 Who co-starred with Vivien Leigh in "Gone With the Wind"?
18 How is Jack Lemmon's co-star in "The Odd Couple", Walter Matasschanskavasky better known?
19 Who was Fred Astaire's most frequent dancing partner?
20 Which child star Shirley went on to be a US Ambassador?
21 Which silent movie star Rudolph died at an early age?
22 Hollywood legends Lionel, Ethel and John share what surname?
23 Which actor Paul is the husband of actress Joanne Woodward?
24 Who was married to Sean Penn and was chosen for the role of Evita?
25 Who was born Doris Kappelhoff and co-starred with Rock Hudson?
26 Which star of "Top Gun" married Nicole Kidman?
27 Which actor James, famous for gangster roles, is credited with the catchphrase "You dirty rat!"?
28 Why was Jimmy Durante nicknamed Schnozzle?
29 Who married Richard Burton twice?
30 Which actress Demi married Bruce Willis?

Answers

Around Scotland (see Quiz 36)
1 East. 2 John o' Groat's. 3 Edinburgh. 4 Yes. 5 Hadrian. 6 St Andrews. 7 Whisky. 8 Balmoral. 9 Highland Games. 10 Skiing. 11 Mountains. 12 Aberdeen. 13 Shetland. 14 Ness. 15 Skye. 16 Kintyre. 17 Clyde. 18 Edinburgh. 19 Haggis. 20 Gretna Green. 21 Lake. 22 Ben Nevis. 23 Dundee. 24 Perth. 25 Tweed. 26 North Sea. 27 Valley. 28 Glasgow. 29 Dundee. 30 St Andrew.

42

Quiz 35 Pot-Luck 18

Answers - see page 41

Level 1

1 Which country is Aeroflot from?
2 Who created Jimmy Porter?
3 Which instrument measures a plane's height above sea level?
4 Who recorded the album "Listen Without Prejudice"?
5 Who played the Bandit in "Smokey and The Bandit"?
6 Which king of England abdicated and was succeeded by his younger brother?
7 In rhyming slang what is meant by rabbit and pork?
8 How is Frederick Austerlitz better known?
9 How many players are there in a volleyball team?
10 What is the third book of the Old Testament?
11 What is the common name for the complaint bursitis?
12 In which city is La Scala opera house?
13 In the British army which rank comes between Lieutenant and Major?
14 What colour is the gem jet?
15 What is the name of the newsagent's in "Coronation Street"?
16 How many sides has a heptagon?
17 What type of creature is used for the dish Bombay duck?
18 Where on your body is your olfactory organ?
19 Which major river flows through Liverpool?
20 Which singer had a No 1 with "All Kinds Of Everything"?
21 Rodney Bewes, Derek Fowlds and Roy North have all been straight men to which character?
22 Who sings with the News?
23 What is the first name of TV cook Leith?
24 Which trio took their name from characters in the Tintin cartoons?
25 What can be a group of fish or a place of education?
26 What is the capital of Egypt?
27 Which Ronnie Barker comedy was set inside a prison?
28 In which sport might you see a Chinaman and a maiden?
29 Which vegetable is also known as the egg plant?
30 Jane Wyman was the first wife of which famous American?

Answers

Pot-Luck 17 (see Quiz 33)
1 M1. 2 Taurus. 3 3. 4 Abba. 5 Stan Laurel. 6 Lawyer. 7 Pauline Mole Adrian's mum. 8 Cycling. 9 Cliff Richard. 10 Rule the world. 11 University. 12 Isaac Asimov. 13 Bonnet. 14 Saturn. 15 Water. 16 Eight. 17 Derek. 18 Oxford and Cambridge boat race. 19 Dog. 20 Biscuit. 21 Democrats and Republicans. 22 Coward. 23 Butcher. 24 Thailand. 25 Gloria Estefan. 26 San Francisco. 27 Blue and white. 28 Nazareth. 29 Barbara Hulanicki. 30 45 degrees.

Quiz 36 Around Scotland

Answers - see page 42

1 Is Dundee on the east or west coast of Scotland?
2 Which is the most northerly point on the British mainland?
3 Which city is Scotland's capital?
4 Are Scottish banknotes legal tender in England?
5 Who built a wall to divide Scotland from England?
6 Where is the Royal and Ancient Golf Club?
7 The name of which Scottish product means 'water of life'?
8 Where is the Queen's Scottish residence?
9 What is the name of the Games held at Braemar?
10 Which sport is Aviemore particularly famous for?
11 What are the Cairngorms?
12 Which east coast port is known as The Granite City?
13 Which islands give their name to ponies and wool?
14 In which Loch is there said to be a monster?
15 Which Isle was linked to the mainland by a bridge in 1995?
16 Which Mull was the title of a song by Paul McCartney?
17 Which river flows through Glasgow?
18 Which city holds an annual Arts Festival?
19 Which speciality's ingredients include sheep's stomach and oatmeal?
20 Which village was a popular destination for runaway couples?
21 What does the word 'loch' mean?
22 What is Scotland's highest mountain?
23 Which city gives its name to a rich fruit cake?
24 Which city shares its name with a city in Australia?
25 Which river in The Borders gives its name to a woollen fabric?
26 Which sea is to the east of the Scottish mainland?
27 What is a glen?
28 In which city is Hampden Park Stadium?
29 Which is further north, Edinburgh or Dundee?
30 Who is Scotland's patron saint?

Answers

Hollywood (see Quiz 34)

Quiz 37 Pot-Luck 19

Answers - see page 47

1 Dr John Pemberton invented which drink in 1886?
2 Usually called by his last name, what was Steed's first name in the "Avengers"?
3 Which Fleet Street church has the tallest steeple designed by Christopher Wren?
4 Victor Barna was five times world champion in which sport?
5 What is the Welsh name for Wales?
6 How many years are celebrated by an emerald anniversary?
7 In which village is "Emmerdale" set?
8 What three colours are on the flag of Australia?
9 What number does the Roman numeral L stand for?
10 Who recorded the album "Everything Changes"?
11 In cartoons, who 'kept on walking'?
12 What do you suffer from if you have coryza?
13 What is the first name of TV cook Tovey?
14 What are the initials of comic writer Wodehouse?
15 Who directed the film "Tommy"?
16 The Haka is a dance performed by which rugby union team?
17 Which George wrote "Porgy And Bess"?
18 Snooker's Eddie Charlton comes from which country?
19 In which year were women first given the vote?
20 On what part of your body would you wear an espadrille?
21 Which of the following can vote in a general election: the mentally ill, criminals, people under 18?
22 In which country is the Curragh racecourse?
23 Which element is used in computer chips?
24 To five years either way, when was the GLC formed?
25 Which planet is 4,500 million years old?
26 What does the French word *pomme* mean?
27 What trees belong to the genus *Quercus*?
28 Which village is the setting for "Noel's House Party"?
29 Who wrote the poem "Anthem For Doomed Youth"?
30 Who scored a century in the 1996 cricket World Cup Final?

Quiz 38 Animals

Answers - see page 48

Level 1

1 Where does a kangaroo keep its young?
2 Which black and white mammal lives in China's bamboo forests?
3 Where do koalas live?
4 How many legs does an adult insect have?
5 What type of creature is a black widow?
6 Which animal's nickname is 'ship of the desert'?
7 Which breed of spaniel shares its name with a king?
8 Which sea creature is known as a Portuguese man-of-war?
9 What is a female sheep called?
10 What do carnivorous animals live on?
11 Which animals are described as canine?
12 What is a fox's tail called?
13 Which saint is the heaviest breed of dog named after?
14 What is special about a guinea pig's tail?
15 What are pigs' feet called?
16 Which elephants have the smaller ears, African or Indian?
17 What are edible sturgeon eggs called?
18 What name is given to the period of winter sleep by some animals?
19 What does an invertebrate animal not have?
20 What would a billy and a nanny produce?
21 Which black and white mammal sprays a foul smelling liquid when attacked?
22 How does a boa constrictor kill its prey?
23 Why does a fish need gills?
24 What does a scorpion have at the end of its tail?
25 What does a chameleon change to camouflage itself?
26 What does an Isle of Man Manx cat not have?
27 What type of insect is a Red Admiral?
28 What is another name for an Alsatian dog?
29 What kind of animal is a Suffolk Punch?
30 A lynx is a member of which family group?

Answers — **Cricket** (see Quiz 40)
1 Australia and England. 2 Manchester. 3 Before. 4 Cork. 5 Essex. 6 Jack Russell. 7 Lords. 8 Randall. 9 Warwickshire. 10 England. 11 Two. 12 Yorkshire. 13 Wicket keeper. 14 Nottingham. 15 None. 16 India. 17 W.G. 18 Northamptonshire. 19 Stewart. 20 Caught and bowled. 21 Left. 22 Lancashire. 23 Sunday. 24 Six. 25 Brian Johnson. 26 Terence. 27 Australia. 28 Six. 29 Middlesex. 30 Ted Dexter.

46

Quiz 39 Pot-Luck 20

Answers - see page 45

1 Which Order did Edward III found in 1350?
2 Which tavern was the favourite of Falstaff?
3 Which actor talked to a six-foot high, invisible rabbit in the film "Harvey"?
4 Which England soccer skipper was injured in both the 1986 and 1990 World Cup final stages?
5 Which Harold said, "Most of our people have never had it so good."
6 Cliff Richard and Marty Robbins had different songs that shared which title?
7 Which writer featured Jonathan Harker in his most famous novel?
8 Myosotis is more commonly known as which flower?
9 Which Tropic is further north, Capricorn or Cancer?
10 To ten years either way, when did Thomas Cook organize his first continental holiday?
11 Which orange seller became mistress of Charles II?
12 Who recorded the album "Shepherd Moons"?
13 What is the word for a group of hounds?
14 Which sport is a mixture of map reading and cross country running?
15 Which actor recorded that he "was born under a wand'rin' star"?
16 How many legs has a spider?
17 In music, name the horizontal lines around which notes are written?
18 Which New England poet had "miles to go before I sleep"?
19 Which work does Anitra's Dance come from?
20 Who made his last stand at Little Bighorn?
21 Which sport awards the Harmsworth Trophy?
22 What is the Paris underground called?
23 Which is the largest of the apes?
24 Who did Morecambe and Wise not want to sing on their show?
25 Which Alfred mapped out moorland routes in northern England?
26 Which Italian saint was born at the town of Assisi?
27 Who captained England in the 1991 Rugby World Cup?
28 Which planet does Superman come from?
29 Who took "Africa" into the record charts?
30 What name is given to an adult male seal?

Pot-Luck 19 (see Quiz 37)
1 Coca Cola. 2 John. 3 St Bride's. 4 Table tennis. 5 Cymru. 6 55. 7 Beckindale. 8 Blue, red and white. 9 50. 10 Take That. 11 Felix the Cat. 12 Common cold. 13 John. 14 P.G. 15 Ken Russell. 16 All Blacks. 17 Gershwin. 18 Australia. 19 1918. 20 Feet. 21 None. 22 Ireland. 23 Silicon. 24 1965. 25 Earth. 26 Apple. 27 Oaks. 28 Crinkley Bottom. 29 Wilfred Owen. 30 Aravinda de Silva.

Quiz 40 Cricket

Answers - see page 46

1 Which international teams contest The Ashes?
2 In which city is the ground Old Trafford?
3 In LBW what does the B stand for?
4 Which bowler Dominic took a Test hat-trick in 1995?
5 Which county was captained by Graeme Gooch?
6 Which English wicket keeper shares his name with a breed of dog?
7 The Nursery End, The Pavilion End and St John's Road are all linked with which ground?
8 Which former England batsman Derek was known as 'Rags'?
9 Which team won the County Championship in 1994 and 1995?
10 Robin Smith is an international for which country?
11 How many bails are there on a set of wickets?
12 Which county does Geoff Boycott come from?
13 What was the specialist position of Australia's Rodney Marsh?
14 Trent Bridge is in which English city?
15 How many runs are scored in a maiden over?
16 Which country was captained by Kapil Dev?
17 What were the initials of legendary Victorian cricketer Dr Grace?
18 Which county side was captained by Allan Lamb?
19 In the 1990s, which Alec has opened and kept wicket for England?
20 In scoring, what does c & b stand for?
21 Was David Gower a left- or right-handed batsman?
22 Which English county did West Indies skipper Clive Lloyd play for?
23 On which day of the week were John Player League games played?
24 How many valid deliveries are sent down in a Test cricket over?
25 Which cricket commentator on radio was known as 'Johnners'?
26 What does the initial T stand for in I. T. Botham's name?
27 In which country do Sheffield Shield games take place?
28 What does the batsman score for a shot that sends the ball over the boundary without touching the ground?
29 England skippers Brearley and Gatting have both captained which county?
30 Who was known as "Lord Ted"?

Quiz 41 Pot-Luck 21

Answers - see page 51

1 What is the name of the computer game hedgehog?
2 What is the zodiac sign of the Crab?
3 Which Alan wrote "Boys From the Blackstuff"?
4 Who had a No 1 hit with the song "Maggie May"?
5 In golf what is the term for two over par?
6 The initials TC stand for which cartoon character?
7 What were followers of John Wycliffe called?
8 Which country's national flag is a green rectangle?
9 Which group consists of twins Maurice and Robin and older brother Barry?
10 Who said - though not in English - "I think therefore I am"?
11 In education, what does GCSE stand for?
12 Which rock superstar is a former chairman of Watford football club?
13 Called a trailer in America, what's the name of this vehicle in the UK?
14 In which month is Royal Ascot horse-racing season?
15 What is agoraphobia a fear of?
16 What do the initials RAM stand for in computing?
17 Which village does Jane Marple live in?
18 How many kilogrammes make one metric ton?
19 Which comedian uses the catchphrase,"Rock on, Tommy"?
20 What type of food is dill?
21 Which Scottish soccer team are known as 'The Dons'?
22 Who says, "Hi-Yo Silver!"?
23 Which day of the week is named after the Anglo-Saxon god Tiw?
24 On what date is American Independence Day?
25 What kind of animal is a seahorse?
26 The failure to produce enough insulin leads to which medical condition?
27 Which soccer side play at a Cottage?
28 Which insect transmits malaria?
29 In the fable, what did the boy cry to trick the villagers?
30 What does Norman Painting write and appear in?

Answers

Pot-Luck 22 (see Quiz 43)
1 Germany. 2 Drachma. 3 Mother of Pearl. 4 Simply Red. 5 Bianca. 6 O. 7 Eyes. 8 Judy Garland. 9 Terms at Oxford. 10 Samson. 11 Music. 12 Zither. 13 Blue Whale. 14 Red. 15 Morris. 16 Ten. 17 Numbers. 18 Walpurgis. 19 Peter Wright. 20 Swan. 21 Interpol. 22 Milligan. 23 Black Beauty. 24 Sturgeon. 25 Tony Hatch and Jackie Trent. 26 Brussels. 27 Blue. 28 Olympus. 29 Squash. 30 Very High Frequency.

Quiz 42 TV Sitcoms

Answers - see page 52

Level 1

1 What is the first name of Mrs Bucket of "Keeping Up Appearances"?
2 Which actress Joanna played Patsy in "Absolutely Fabulous"?
3 Who was the café owner, played by Gorden Kaye, in "Allo Allo"?
4 In which sitcom does grumpy Victor Meldrew appear?
5 What is the surname of Del Boy and Rodney of "Only Fools and Horses"?
6 Which sport is the sitcom "Outside Edge" centred on?
7 What kind of Life did Jerry and Margo's neighbours Tom and Barbara lead?
8 What was the profession of Steptoe and Son?
9 In the sitcom title how many Children did Bill and Ben Porter have?
10 Which of Nora Batty's wrinkled garments turned on Compo?
11 Which two characters were "Just Good Friends"?
12 During which war was "Dad's Army" set?
13 Which senior political position did James Hacker MP reach?
14 In what type of establishment was "Are You Being Served?" set?
15 In which northeast city was "Auf Wiedersehen Pet" set?
16 Who is Tracey's sister in "Birds of a Feather"?
17 Whose servant was Baldrick?
18 Which sitcom was about the Boswell family from Liverpool?
19 At which hotel was Manuel the waiter?
20 In which series would you meet the Yellowcoats from Maplin's?
21 How were the Lads Terry Collier and Bob Ferris known?
22 What did H stand for in the series M*A*S*H?
23 What is the profession of Alec Callender in "May to December"?
24 How were the Men Behaving in the series about Gary and Tony ?
25 Which sitcom was set in a bar in Boston?
26 Who were Tom and Diana Waiting for at the Bayview Retirement Home?
27 What sort of Statesman was Alan B'Stard MP?
28 Where were the characters in "Porridge"?
29 Which country is Rab C. Nesbitt from?
30 Who was Frank Spencer's wife in "Some Mothers Do 'Ave 'Em"?

Answers

60s Newsround (see Quiz 44)
1 John F. Kennedy. 2 6. 3 Berlin. 4 Eichmann. 5 Marilyn Monroe. 6 Wilson. 7 Beeching. 8 Martin Luther King. 9 Harold Macmillan. 10 Shrimpton. 11 Eagle. 12 India. 13 Moors. 14 Smith. 15 Wight. 16 Russia. 17 Manson. 18 West Germany. 19 Garland. 20 Edward. 21 Prince Charles. 22 The Moon. 23 Kray. 24 Israel. 25 Economics. 26 Flower. 27 Campbell. 28 Mini. 29 Czechoslovakia. 30 The Beatles.

1 Which country is Lufthansa from?
2 What is the currency of Greece?
3 What is another word for nacre?
4 Who recorded the album "Stars"?
5 In "EastEnders" what is the name of Carol's red-haired daughter?
6 In Morse Code what letter is represented by three dashes?
7 In rhyming slang what are mince pies?
8 How is Frances Gumm better known?
9 What are Trinity and Hilary?
10 In the Bible, who was betrayed by Delilah?
11 In which branch of the arts is the metronome used?
12 Which musical instrument featured in the theme of "The Third Man"?
13 What type of whale is the largest?
14 What colour is vermilion?
15 Which Desmond wrote "The Naked Ape"?
16 How many sides has a decagon?
17 What is the fourth book of the Old Testament ?
18 Which night is April 30th?
19 "Spycatcher" was the controversial memoirs of which former intelligence officer?
20 A cob is a male of which creature?
21 Hello, hello, hello, what was founded in Vienna in 1923?
22 Which Spike said, "Money can't buy friends, but you can get a better class of enemy"?
23 What was the horse in the title of Anna Sewell's novel?
24 From which fish is caviar obtained?
25 Who composed the theme for "Neighbours"?
26 What is the capital of Belgium?
27 What colour is the dye obtained from the plant woad?
28 Which mountain was said to be home of the Greek gods?
29 Which game is played in an enclosed space with both players hitting the ball in the same direction?
30 What does VHF stand for?

Answers

Pot-Luck 21 (see Quiz 41)
1 Sonic. 2 Cancer. 3 Bleasdale. 4 Rod Stewart. 5 Double bogey. 6 Top Cat. 7 Lollards. 8 Libya. 9 The Bee Gees. 10 René Descartes. 11 General Certificate of Secondary Education. 12 Elton John. 13 Caravan. 14 June. 15 Open spaces. 16 Random Access Memory. 17 St Mary Mead. 18 One thousand. 19 Bobby Ball. 20 Herb. 21 Aberdeen. 22 The Lone Ranger. 23 Tuesday. 24 4th July. 25 Fish. 26 Diabetes. 27 Fulham. 28 Mosquito. 29 Wolf. 30 The Archers.

Quiz 44 60s Newsround

Answers - see page 50

1 Who defeated Richard Nixon to become US president in 1960?
2 James Hanratty was charged with a murder on which A road?
3 Which European city was divided into East and West by a Wall?
4 Which Adolf was executed in May 1962 for his part in the Holocaust?
5 Which screen sex symbol was found dead in a bungalow near Hollywood in August 1962?
6 Which Harold became leader of the Labour Party in 1963?
7 Which Doctor wielded his axe on the railway network?
8 Who made a speech proclaiming, "I have a dream"?
9 Which Conservative resigned as prime minister in 1963?
10 Which model Jean was known as "The Shrimp"?
11 What type of creature was Goldie who made the headlines by escaping from London Zoo?
12 Mrs Indira Gandhi was appointed prime minister of which country?
13 Which notorious Murders involved Myra Hindley and Ian Brady?
14 Which Ian declared independence for Rhodesia?
15 On which Isle was there a 1969 rock festival featuring Bob Dylan?
16 Leonid Brezhnev became leader of which country?
17 Which Charles led "The Family" in the Sharon Tate murder?
18 Willi Brandt became chancellor of which country?
19 In 1969 which actress and singer Judy died at the age of 47?
20 Which Kennedy was involved in the car accident at Chappaquiddick?
21 Which member of the royal family was invested as Prince of Wales?
22 Neil Armstrong became the first man to set foot where?
23 Which gangland twins Ronald and Reginald were jailed?
24 Golda Meir became the first woman prime minister of which country?
25 LSE, the scene of student protest, was the London School of what?
26 What type of Power symbolized the 1967 peace and love festivals?
27 Which Donald was killed trying to break the world water speed record?
28 Which type of skirt was the main fashion of the 1960s?
29 Soviet tanks moved to crush the Dubcek reforms in which country?
30 Brian Epstein was the manager of which pop group?

Answers

TV Sitcoms (see Quiz 42)
1 Hyacinth. 2 Lumley. 3 René. 4 One Foot in the Grave. 5 Trotter. 6 Cricket. 7 The Good Life. 8 Rag and bone men. 9 2 Point 4. 10 Stockings. 11 Vince and Penny. 12 Second World War. 13 Prime Minister. 14 Department store. 15 Newcastle. 16 Sharon. 17 Blackadder. 18 Bread. 19 Fawlty Towers. 20 Hi de Hi! 21 Likely Lads. 22 Hospital. 23 Solicitor. 24 Badly. 25 Cheers. 26 God. 27 New. 28 Prison. 29 Scotland. 30 Betty.

Quiz 45 Pot-Luck 23

Answers - see page 55

1 If it rains on St Swithin's Day, how many more days is it supposed to rain?
2 In which TV programme did Bruce Forsyth and Rosemarie Ford appear?
3 Who played Robin Hood in the original British TV series?
4 Which composer wrote "The Marriage of Figaro"?
5 What is a low, shallow basket used by gardeners called?
6 How many years are celebrated by a golden anniversary?
7 In "David Copperfield" what was the surname of Uriah?
8 What name is shared by TV presenter Zoe and singer Michael?
9 What number does the Roman numeral M stand for?
10 What sort of creature is a capercaillie?
11 In which month is Remembrance Day?
12 What type of vehicle provided a 50s hit for Nancy Whiskey?
13 How many faces has an icosahedron?
14 What are the initials of "Lady Chatterley" author Lawrence?
15 What name is given to a litter of piglets?
16 What type of dancing is associated with Margot Fonteyn?
17 Which soap pub sells Churchill Strong?
18 Who recorded the album "Both Sides"?
19 How many children did Queen Victoria have?
20 Who is the resident Lord in "Private Eye"?
21 What are paper measures called equal to 500 sheets?
22 In which country is Flushing Meadow tennis stadium?
23 What is the domed recess at the east end of a church called?
24 What is a young goat called?
25 How did master escapologist Harry Houdini die?
26 After which George was the American state of Georgia named?
27 Which viral disease is also called grippe?
28 Who said, "Anyone can get old. All you have to do is live long enough"?
29 In what game do you peg, and score for pairs and fifteens?
30 What does PYO stand for?

Answers

Pot-Luck 24 (see Quiz 47)
1 Scapegoat. 2 300. 3 Bayern Munich. 4 20 franc. 5 Warhol. 6 Eight.
7 Lead. 8 Slade. 9 Intestate. 10 A pig. 11 Annie Oakley. 12 Meatloaf.
13 Swarm. 14 Clarinet. 15 Coyote. 16 Seven. 17 Natural. 18 Susan.
19 72. 20 Grape. 21 2 Point 4 Children. 22 Parental Guidance. 23 The
Queen Mother. 24 Flute. 25 Mrs Hudson. 26 Beaufort. 27 Paris. 28
Pictionary. 29 The Red Crescent. 30 Six.

Quiz 46 Geography

Answers - see page 56

1 In which Swiss mountain range is the Jungfrau?
2 Which is the next largest island in the world after Australia?
3 Which seaside resort is Super-Mare?
4 On which continent is the Kariba Dam?
5 What are Lakes Michigan, Superior, Huron, Erie and Ontario known as collectively?
6 If the southern limit of the tropics is Capricorn what is the northern limit called?
7 Which island is to the south of Australia?
8 In the south of which country was Saigon?
9 If you were in Benidorm in which country would you be?
10 Which London palace has a maze?
11 Which isle off the west coast of England has three legs as its symbol?
12 Which country is connected to Wales by the Severn Bridge?
13 Which US state is a collection of islands in the Pacific?
14 Which language do natives of Hamburg speak?
15 Which county has a red rose as its symbol?
16 Which Queen gave her name to the capital of Hong Kong?
17 Which Bank is made of sand in the North Sea?
18 In which county is Penzance?
19 Which islands are Sark and Alderney part of?
20 Greece is in which continent?
21 What are the counties of Essex, Suffolk, Norfolk and Cambridgeshire collectively known as?
22 Is Japan in the northern or the southern hemisphere?
23 What is the name of the biggest Canyon in Arizona?
24 Which country is Santa Claus said to live in?
25 Is the Arctic Circle near the north or the south pole?
26 On the south of which continent are the Andes?
27 If you were looking at the Ganges which country would you be in?
28 Which country do the Scilly Isles belong to?
29 Which country originally produced Fiat cars?
30 What is the most westerly point of England?

Level 1

1 What animal-linked name describes someone who always gets blamed?

2 How many seconds in five minutes?

3 Which German side won the European Cup in 1974, 1975 and 1976?

4 Debussy appears on which French bank note?

5 Which Andy said, "In the future everyone will be famous for 15 minutes?"

6 In snooker what is the score for potting a black?

7 Pb is the symbol of which chemical element?

8 Who recorded the seasonal song "Merry Xmas Everybody"?

9 Which term means dying without having made a will?

10 Who or what was the Empress of Blandings?

11 Who was Little Sure Shot according to Sitting Bull?

12 Who recorded the album "Bat Out Of Hell"?

13 What is the word for a group of bees?

14 Which musical instrument is played by Acker Bilk?

15 What is another name for the prairie wolf?

16 How many colours are there in the rainbow?

17 In music, what is a note if it is neither sharp nor flat?

18 Who was Madonna desperately seeking in her first feature film?

19 How many inches in two yards?

20 What type of fruit is dried to produce a sultana?

21 Apart from "The Flowerpot Men" in which show do Bill and Ben appear?

22 In films what do the letters PG stand for ?

23 Who lives at Clarence House in London?

24 What instrument does James Galway play?

25 What is the name of Sherlock Holmes's housekeeper?

26 Which Admiral gave his name to a weather measurement scale?

27 Where was Glenn Miller flying to when his plane disappeared?

28 In which game do players have to guess a word from a drawing?

29 What is the Muslim equivalent of the Red Cross?

30 How many squares on a Rubik Cube never move?

Quiz 48 Sounds of the 70s

Answers - see page 54

Level 1

1 Which Brotherhood had a Eurovision winner in 1976?
2 Peters and who said "Welcome Home" in 1973?
3 Which Gary was Leader of the Gang?
4 Which City Rollers had a hit with "Bye Bye Baby"?
5 A "Ballroom Blitz" came from which sugary-sounding group?
6 What had the T originally stood for in T Rex?
7 Which group led by Noddy Holder sang "Weer All Crazee Now"?
8 Who sang "Do Ya Think I'm Sexy"?
9 Who sang with Elton John on "Don't Go Breaking My Heart"?
10 "Bohemian Rhapsody" was recorded by which group?
11 Who helped Gladys Knight 'make it through the night' in 1972?
12 "Sugar Baby Love" and "Jukebox Jive" were hits for which group?
13 What was the capacity of the group who said "I'm Not in Love"?
14 How many Jacksons were there when they sang "I Want You Back"?
15 What did the New Seekers say they would like to teach the world to do?
16 Fair-haired Debbie Harry sang with which group?
17 What did Gloria Gaynor say she would do in 1979?
18 Which Harry was "Without You" in 1972?
19 Which Swedish group met their Waterloo in 1974?
20 Which band has the same name as the first book in the Bible?
21 What does ELO stand for?
22 What joins Earth and Wind in a group's name?
23 Which bird of prey sang about the Hotel California?
24 What sort of feet did Mud sing about?
25 Showaddywaddy were Under the Moon of what in 1976?
26 Which singer Art had a solo No 1 after duo success with Paul Simon?
27 Which TV tech David charted with his ballads?
28 Who were "Stayin' Alive" with "Night Fever" in 1978?
29 Which Jerry sang "In The Summertime"?
30 What day did the Boomtown Rats not like?

Geography (see Quiz 46)
1 Alps. 2 Greenland. 3 Weston. 4 Africa. 5 Great Lakes. 6 Tropic of Cancer. 7 Tasmania. 8 Vietnam. 9 Spain. 10 Hampton Court. 11 Isle of Man. 12 England. 13 Hawaii. 14 German. 15 Lancashire. 16 Victoria. 17 Dogger Bank. 18 Cornwall. 19 Channel Islands. 20 Europe. 21 East Anglia. 22 Northern. 23 Grand Canyon. 24 Lapland. 25 North. 26 America. 27 India. 28 United Kingdom. 29 Italy. 30 Land's End.

Answers

Quiz 49 Pot-Luck 25

Answers - see page 59

1 What colour is a peridot stone?
2 What is the zodiac sign of the Twins?
3 In which part of the body is the patella?
4 Who had a No 1 hit with the song "Bachelor Boy"?
5 What is the second letter of the Greek alphabet?
6 What is the nest of an eagle called?
7 Which film star has a statue in Leicester Square?
8 In which month is Queen Elizabeth II's official birthday?
9 Who was lead singer with Dawn?
10 What did the Rochdale Pioneers pioneer?
11 Which 1995 movie starred a wet Kevin Costner?
12 Which board game involves moving through rooms to solve a murder?
13 Called a tuxedo in America, what's this garment called in the UK?
14 What type of jewels are traditionally associated with Amsterdam?
15 What is zoophobia a fear of?
16 In which programme did Rab C. Nesbitt first appear on TV?
17 What was Charon's job?
18 Which Edith sang "Je ne regrette rien" (No Regrets)?
19 What colour is the Central Line on a London Underground map?
20 What type of food is a bagel?
21 What sits on a dolly in a television studio?
22 Who says, "You'll like this – not a lot!"?
23 Which day of the week is named after the god Woden?
24 Who recorded the album "From The Cradle"?
25 Which "Coronation Street" supermarket employed Reg and Vera?
26 What is the claw of a bird of prey called?
27 What type of sport took place in the 'Frying Pan'?
28 Dr Stephen Hawking wrote a brief history of what?
29 Which Club is concerned with pedigree in the dog world?
30 Which English king was painted by Hans Holbein?

Quiz 50 Sport: the 70s

Answers - see page 60

1 Bobby Moore captained which country in the 1970 World Cup?
2 Which British golfer Tony won the US Open Championship?
3 In 1970 Margaret Court won four major tournaments in which sport?
4 Which horse-riding princess was voted Sportswoman of the Year?
5 At which Scottish stadium was there a crowd disaster in 1971?
6 Which Sebastian completed a hat-trick of running records in 1979?
7 John Conteh became a champion in which sport?
8 Which London team won the League and FA Cup double in 1971?
9 What was the sport of Britain's David Wilkie?
10 In 1976 which cricketer Viv hit 291 runs in an innings against England?
11 Which 19-year-old Evonne triumphed at Wimbledon in 1971?
12 Which Ray was the most successful snooker player of the 70s?
13 Which soccer team won the Scottish League every season from 1970 to 1974?
14 Which horse won the Grand National three times?
15 Who was manager of Nottingham Forest when they won the European Cup?
16 Which Brendan won the only British track and field medal of the 1976 Olympic Games?
17 Bjorn Borg comes from which country?
18 Which Barry became world 500cc motor-cycling champion?
19 Which Daley became the youngest ever athlete to represent Britain in the decathlon?
20 Which British player won the 1977 women's singles at Wimbledon?
21 Which English soccer side twice won the European Cup?
22 In which sport was Mike Brearley an England captain?
23 Which country outside the UK won the Grand Slam in 1977?
24 Which Suffolk soccer side won the FA Cup in 1978?
25 Which team won the 1978 soccer World Cup staged in Argentina?
26 In 1978–9 Hull Kingston Rovers were champions in which sport?
27 Which Niki was badly burnt in the 1976 German Grand Prix?
28 Which TV mogul started his own cricket unofficial test series?
29 Which Jackie was world champion motor racing driver in 1971 and 1973?
30 Ally MacLeod was manager of which national soccer side?

Answers

70s Films (see Quiz 52)
1 Star Wars. 2 The Godfather. 3 A car. 4 A shark. 5 Saturday. 6 Kramer. 7 Superman. 8 Cuckoo's. 9 Grease. 10 Third. 11 Nile. 12 Rocky. 13 Kermit. 14 Eagle. 15 King Kong. 16 Towering Inferno. 17 M*A*S*H. 18 Orange. 19 Jackal. 20 Bugsy. 21 Clint Eastwood. 22 Diamonds. 23 Deer. 24 Beverly Hills. 25 Dog. 26 Robert Redford. 27 Great and Small. 28 Now. 29 Moon. 30 Poseidon.

58

Quiz 51 Pot-Luck 26

Level 1

Answers - see page 57

1 Which country are All Nippon Airways from?
2 What is the currency of India?
3 On TV, what are the names of Pauline Fowler's two sons?
4 How many squares are there on a chess board?
5 James I and Charles I were members of which royal dynasty?
6 How many lanes are there in an Olympic swimming pool?
7 Who is the sister of Joey Boswell?
8 How is Gordon Sumner better known?
9 What name links singer Kate and former USA President George?
10 In the Bible, who was famous for his wisdom?
11 What was the secret state police of Nazi Germany called?
12 In which country is Schiphol airport?
13 What is Kevin Webster's job in "Coronation Street"?
14 What colour is heliotrope?
15 Which tree family includes the sycamore and maple?
16 How many sides has a dodecagon?
17 Which event did the first popular greeting card celebrate?
18 What is the home of a beaver called?
19 Who wrote of "Season of mists and mellow fruitfulness'?
20 What name is given to an extension of a stage in front of a curtain?
21 Of which country was Golda Meir prime minister?
22 Who recorded the album "Divine Madness"?
23 Which short-legged dog is named after the 18th-century parson who bred them?
24 Which vegetable is the main ingredient in coleslaw?
25 What was the profession of Hedda Hopper and Louella Parsons?
26 Which element has the atomic number 1 in the periodic table?
27 What is the first name of gardener and presenter Titchmarsh?
28 Who created Chief Inspector Alleyn?
29 How many legs has a daddy-long-legs?
30 What does VDU stand for?

Answers

Pot-Luck 25 (see Quiz 49)
1 Green. 2 Gemini. 3 Knee. 4 Cliff Richard. 5 Beta. 6 Eyrie. 7 Charlie Chaplin. 8 June. 9 Tony Orlando. 10 The Co-op. 11 Waterworld. 12 Cluedo. 13 Dinner jacket. 14 Diamonds. 15 Animals. 16 Naked Video. 17 Ferryman who, in Greek mythology, takes the dead to the underworld. 18 Piaf. 19 Red. 20 Bread roll. 21 A camera. 22 Paul Daniels. 23 Wednesday. 24 Eric Clapton. 25 Bettabuys. 26 Talon. 27 Horse racing. 28 Time. 29 Kennel. 30 Henry VIII.

Quiz 52 70s Films

Answers - see page 58

Level 1

1 Which Wars were there in 1977?
2 Which 1972 film, with Marlon Brando, was about the Mafia?
3 What was Herbie?
4 Which creature took a starring role in "Jaws"?
5 What Night was there Fever in the movie with John Travolta?
6 Who was versus Kramer in the Dustin Hoffman film?
7 Who is Clark Kent better known as?
8 Which bird's Nest did One fly over in 1975?
9 In which film did John Travolta and Olivia Newton-John sing "You're the One That I Want"?
10 What Kind of Close Encounters were there in 1977?
11 On which Egyptian river was there Death in the Agatha Christie film?
12 Which boxer did Sylvester Stallone play?
13 Name the frog in "The Muppet Movie"?
14 Which bird of prey Landed in the war movie based on Jack Higgins' novel?
15 Which 1970s film about a giant ape was a remake of a 1933 movie?
16 Which disaster movie was about a fire in the world's tallest building?
17 Which film told of a mobile hospital in the Korean War?
18 Which fruit was Clockwork in the Stanley Kubrick film?
19 Which animal's Day was it in the film about an assassin based on the Frederick Forsyth novel?
20 What was the first name of gangster Malone?
21 Who starred in the western "Every Which Way But Loose"?
22 What were Forever in the James Bond movie?
23 What sort of Hunter was Robert de Niro in the film with Meryl Streep?
24 Where was Eddie Murphy a Cop in the film series?
25 Digby was the biggest what in the world?
26 Who starred with Paul Newman in "The Sting"?
27 How were All Creatures described in the 1974 film about a vet?
28 When was Apocalypse in the 1979 film?
29 Which planet features in the title of a 1979 Bond movie?
30 Which Adventure was about a disaster on a luxury liner?

Quiz 53 Pot-Luck 27

Answers - see page 63

1 Catherine Parr survived which royal husband?
2 Which programme features Jilly Goolden, Oz Clarke and Michael Barry?
3 What is meant by the Latin phrase *caveat emptor*?
4 Which English club did soccer TV pundit Alan Hansen play for?
5 What spirit is made from fermented sugar cane?
6 How many years are celebrated by a silver anniversary?
7 Which Phil became famous for presenting "One Man And His Dog"?
8 What is the capital of the Isle of Man?
9 How did Yetta Feldman die in "So Haunt Me"?
10 Which Tom starred in "Magnum"?
11 Which word meaning letter is in titles of books of the Bible?
12 Who recorded the album "Simply The Best"?
13 What paper is used to test acid and alkali?
14 What are the initials of English writer Priestley?
15 Who presented the first ever edition of "Mastermind"?
16 How many seconds in quarter of an hour?
17 Which special day follows Shrove Tuesday?
18 Who came first as US President, Washington or Lincoln?
19 Diana Ross, Florence Ballard and Mary Wilson formed what?
20 How is the UK golfing term albatross known in America?
21 Which social security benefit was introduced in 1909?
22 What name is adopted by Don Diego de la Vega?
23 What were the first three Eddystone lighthouses lit by?
24 What is a young hare called?
25 At what degree celsius does water freeze?
26 Which animal's name means river horse?
27 What is the first name of TV cook Carrier?
28 Which day of the week is *dimanche* in French?
29 What nickname was given to winter sportsman Eddie Edwards?
30 In "The Colbys" what is Sable short for?

Quiz 54 Pot-Luck 28

Answers - see page 64

Level 1

1 Which soap has the pub The Malt Shovel?
2 How many minutes in two and a half hours?
3 Which country is a car from if it has the international registration letters CH?
4 In CB terminology, what is a water hole?
5 Which Harold said, "A week is a long time in politics!"?
6 In darts, what is the lowest score for three trebles?
7 N is the symbol of which chemical element ?
8 Who recorded the album "Parklife"?
9 Which actress Jane developed her fitness programmes?
10 What is the last month of the year to have exactly 31 days?
11 Which Australian bird does not fly?
12 Which veteran DJ Tony was the first voice on Radio 1?
13 In geometry, how many minutes are there in a degree?
14 What is a segment of garlic called?
15 Which Barbra sang "A Woman In Love"?
16 What is the first letter on the bottom line of a keyboard?
17 Where is the surgery of Dr Richard Locke?
18 What is 'black gold'?
19 How many feet are there in ten yards?
20 What is Edward Woodward's only hit single?
21 Which Henry started the Promenade Concerts?
22 Which composer wrote the Water Music?
23 What word means dry on a bottle of Italian wine?
24 Which garden shrub is known as the butterfly bush?
25 Who is Debbie McGee married to?
26 Which 1960s pop star played the lead in "Love Hurts"?
27 Which Dustin starred in "The Graduate"?
28 In the 1850s a Singer sewing machine became the first item to be sold under which trading terms?
29 Starting in March, in which month does the coarse fishing close season end in British rivers?
30 Which word can be someone in an army or a piece of toast?

Answers

Pot-Luck 29 (see Quiz 56)
1 The Dubliners. 2 Leo. 3 Chris de Burgh. 4 Marks and Gran. 5 Head. 6 Harry Enfield. 7 The Goon Show. 8 Ronnie Barker, Ronnie Corbett. 9 Baldrick. 10 Deep. 11 Independent Television News. 12 Flamingo. 13 Music hall. 14 Ian McShane. 15 Horses. 16 Sweet Charity. 17 Dane. 18 Ruth. 19 Madonna. 20 Loaf of bread. 21 Polo. 22 Michael Barrymore. 23 Friday. 24 Frank. 25 Sri Lanka. 26 Hairdresser. 27 Spector. 28 Japanese flower arranging. 29 Lord Scarman. 30 Pace.

Quiz 55 Food and Drink

Answers - see page 61

Level 1

1 What is the main ingredient in an omelette?
2 Which animal does venison come from?
3 Which garden herb is made into a sauce often eaten with lamb?
4 In which country did the word biscuit originate?
5 What is traditionally eaten on Shrove Tuesday?
6 What is another name for French fries?
7 What is a slice of bacon called?
8 Which edible sugary substance do bees make?
9 What is done to a herring to make it into a kipper?
10 Which vegetable can be King Edward or Desirée?
11 Which country does Edam cheese originate from?
12 What do you add to milk to make porridge?
13 What is minestrone?
14 What is bottled tomato sauce called?
15 What colour is vodka?
16 Where did the dish *paella* originate?
17 Which fruit is covered with toffee at a fairground?
18 Which nuts are used to make marzipan?
19 Is a Spotted Dick usually eaten hot or cold?
20 What meat dish is Cumberland famous for?
21 Which pudding is eaten with roast beef?
22 Which vegetables can be French, runner or baked?
23 What colour is piccalilli?
24 What sort of food is a rollmop?
25 Is wholemeal bread brown or white?
26 If something is cooked *'au gratin'* what must it contain?
27 Petits pois are small what?
28 In which country is Peroni beer bottled?
29 What are the two main ingredients of a shandy?
30 Who hosts "Masterchef" on TV?

Answers

Pot-Luck 27 (see Quiz 53)
1 Henry VIII. 2 Food and Drink. 3 Buyer beware. 4 Liverpool. 5 Rum.
6 25. 7 Drabble. 8 Douglas. 9 Choked on a chicken bone. 10 Selleck.
11 Epistle. 12 Tina Turner. 13 Litmus. 14 J.B. 15 Magnus Magnusson.
16 900. 17 Ash Wednesday. 18 Washington. 19 The Supremes. 20
Double eagle. 21 Old age pension. 22 Zorro. 23 Candles. 24 Leveret.
25 0. 26 Hippopotamus. 27 Robert. 28 Sunday. 29 The Eagle. 30
Sabelia.

Quiz 56 Pot-Luck 29

Level 1

Answers - see page 62

1 Who joined forces with The Pogues on "Jack's Heroes"?
2 What is the zodiac sign of the Lion?
3 Who recorded the album "Spark To A Flame"?
4 Which duo created "Birds Of A Feather"?
5 In the Bible, what part of John the Baptist's anatomy did Salome demand as a reward for her dancing?
6 Which comedian talked about "Loadsamoney"?
7 Which radio show was originally called "Crazy People"?
8 Which two TV comedians say "It's goodnight from me..." "...And it's goodnight from him"?
9 Who did Tony Robinson play in the "Blackadder" series?
10 According to proverb, how do still waters run?
11 In the broadcasting sector, what does ITN stand for?
12 Which exotic bird stands on one leg?
13 The Americans call it vaudeville, what is it called in Britain?
14 Which actor plays the title role in "Lovejoy"?
15 What is hippophobia a fear of?
16 Which musical does "Hey Big Spender" come from?
17 Which Great breed of dog sounds like it comes from Scandinavia?
18 What is the first name of TV cook Mott?
19 Which singer's name is Ciccone?
20 What type of food is a bloomer?
21 Chukkas are the playing periods in which sport?
22 Who says, "All wight?"?
23 Which day of the week is named after the goddess Frigg?
24 Which Anne kept a diary while in hiding during the Second World War?
25 What was Ceylon renamed as?
26 What is Fiona's job in "Coronation Street"?
27 Which record producer Phil produced a 'wall of sound' in the 1960s?
28 What is ikebana?
29 Who headed the report into the 1981 Brixton riots?
30 Who is Hale's comic partner?

Quiz 57 TV: The 70s

Answers - see page 67

Level 1

1 Which Irish comedian held a cigarette, sat on a bar stool and chatted?
2 What was the profession of the Angels?
3 Which poetess Pam won "Opportunity Knocks" in 1975?
4 What made up the Bouquet in the series with Susan Penhaligon?
5 Whose Angels were undercover detectives?
6 The Duchess of which street was part of a 1970s drama series?
7 Which king and son of Queen Victoria was the subject of a TV serial?
8 Which Tudor queen was played by Glenda Jackson?
9 The Fall and Rise of which Perrin was played by Leonard Rossiter?
10 What was the first name of Basil Fawlty's wife?
11 How were Bill Oddie, Tim Brooke-Taylor and Graeme Garden known?
12 Which children's series told of life in a London comprehensive?
13 In which series did The Fonz appear?
14 Who was told It Ain't Half Hot in the sit com set in India?
15 When will it be Alright in the Denis Norden series begun in 1977?
16 Which Jim fixed it?
17 Which series about three delinquent OAPs began in the 1970s?
18 Whose Flying Circus was a big 1970s hit?
19 Which early evening news magazine was transmitted throughout the country?
20 Which series about sheep dog trials began in the 1970s?
21 What was the nationality of detective Van Der Valk?
22 Which Liverpool shipping Line was an extremely popular long-running series?
23 In which part of the country was the Poldark series set?
24 Which building moisture problem was the title of the series about Rigsby and Miss Jones?
25 Who was Starsky's police partner?
26 Who started presenting "That's Life" in 1974?
27 Who starred in their Christmas Show watched by 28 million in 1977?
28 To what was Audrey Fforbes-Hamilton born?
29 If Lord Bellamy was Upstairs, where were Hudson and Mrs Bridges?
30 In which part of England was "When the Boat Comes In" set?

Literature (see Quiz 59)

Answers

Literature (see Quiz 59)
1 The Bible. 2 Agatha Christie. 3 Brontë. 4 Wodehouse. 5 Adrian Mole. 6 Vet. 7 Cartland. 8 Rumpole. 9 Lady Chatterley. 10 Horse racing. 11 Archer. 12 Collins. 13 Rendell. 14 Peace. 15 Treasure. 16 Twist. 17 Pan. 18 Eagle. 19 Catherine. 20 James. 21 Alice. 22 Three. 23 Crusoe. 24 The Willows. 25 Scrooge. 26 Cooper. 27 Daffodils. 28 Poetry. 29 Belgian. 30 Monk.

Quiz 58 Pot-Luck 30

Level 1

Answers - see page 68

1 Which country are KLM from?
2 What is the currency of the Netherlands?
3 What is the first name of TV cook Dimbleby?
4 Which birds congregate in a gaggle?
5 On TV, what is the first name of Alf Roberts' wife?
6 What was Tony Hancock's address in East Cheam?
7 In rhyming slang what is the Sweeney Todd?
8 How is Robert Zimmermann better known?
9 Who punched Russell Harty during a chat show?
10 In the Bible, what was the name of the first garden?
11 How many minutes in four and three quarter hours?
12 What is the name of 'She Who Must Be Obeyed'?
13 Which cartoon character says, "Smarter than the average bear"?
14 What colour do you get if you mix red and yellow?
15 Which sport does Sam Torrance play?
16 How many sides has a rhombus?
17 In which children's TV show did Bungle, George and Zippy appear?
18 What colour was the Pimpernel in Baroness Orczy's novel?
19 Which major river flows through Vienna?
20 Which song was a hit for both Buddy Holly and Mud?
21 What can dogs do that wolves cannot?
22 In the film "Free Willy" what was Willy?
23 Where in the body is the cranium?
24 Which rock guitarist had a band called the Experience?
25 What can be planes or sprays of water?
26 What is the capital of Norway?
27 Grant and Truman have been presidents of which country?
28 Which name is shared by model Cindy and actor/singer Michael?
29 Who recorded the album "A Night At The Opera"?
30 What does VCR stand for?

Pot-Luck 31 (see Quiz 60)
1 Tuesday. 2 Jeux Sans Frontières. 3 Paddington. 4 Danny McGlone.
5 Alaska. 6 30. 7 Endive. 8 Tank. 9 Simon Preston. 10 Tracy.
11 December. 12 Madness. 13 Badminton. 14 1878. 15 Wizzard.
16 Puffin. 17 Lenin. 18 Maureen Lipman. 19 T. Rex. 20 By sense of
smell. 21 Suez. (The opera was Aida.) 22 Chestnut. 23 Kissin' Cousins.
24 Foal. 25 Jimmy Nail. 26 The Queen Mother. 27 Surprise, Surprise.
28 Pepys. 29 Fish. 30 Open University.

Answers

Quiz 59 Literature

Answers - see page 65

Level 1

1 What is the best selling book of all time?
2 Who created the character of Miss Marple?
3 Which Emily wrote "Wuthering Heights"?
4 Which creator of Jeeves and Wooster is known by his initials P.G.?
5 Whose first Secret Diary was written when he was 13 3/4?
6 What was the profession of James Herriot?
7 What is the surname of romantic novelist Dame Barbara?
8 Which London barrister was created by John Mortimer?
9 Whose Lover was the subject of a book by D.H. Lawrence?
10 Which sport are Dick Francis' novels about?
11 Which politician Jeffrey wrote "Kane and Abel"?
12 Which novelist Jackie has an actress sister called Joan?
13 Which Ruth created Inspector Wexford?
14 What did Tolstoy write about together with War?
15 What was on the Island Robert Louis Stevenson wrote about?
16 What was the surname of the Dickens character Oliver?
17 Which Peter took the Darling children to Never Never Land?
18 Which bird of prey Has Landed, in the book by Jack Higgins?
19 What is the first name of novelist Miss Cookson?
20 Which detective novelist is known by her initials P.D.?
21 Which little girl had Adventures Through the Looking Glass?
22 How many Musketeers were there in the title of the book by Dumas?
23 Which Robinson was shipwrecked on a desert island?
24 Where is the Wind in the story about Toad and Badger?
25 What was the surname of Ebenezer in "A Christmas Carol"?
26 Which Jilly wrote about Polo and Riders?
27 Which popular yellow spring flower did Wordsworth write about?
28 What type of writing is John Betjeman famous for?
29 What is the nationality of Agatha Christie's detective Poirot?
30 What is the religious occupation of medieval detective Cadfael?

Quiz 60 Pot-Luck 31

Answers - see page 66

 Level 1

1 On which day of the week is the Budget usually presented?
2 What was the French title of "It's A Knockout"?
3 Which fictional bear is named after a London station?
4 Who did Robbie Coltrane play in "Tutti Frutti"?
5 What is the largest state of the USA?
6 How many years are celebrated by a pearl anniversary?
7 Which curly-leaved salad plant is a member of the chicory family?
8 Which armoured combat vehicle was first used in World War I?
9 Which doctor does Simon Shepherd play in "Peak Practice"?
10 In "Coronation Street" what is the name of Deirdre's daughter?
11 In which month is the shortest day?
12 Who recorded "Michael Caine"?
13 In which sport is the Thomas Cup awarded?
14 To ten years either way, when were women first allowed to take degrees at British universities?
15 Which group had a No 1 with "See My Baby Jive"?
16 Which bird is associated with Lundy Island?
17 How is Russian revolutionary Vladimir Ilyich Ulyanov better known?
18 Who played Beattie Bellman in the TV commercials?
19 What are Marc Bolan and Micky Finn better known as?
20 How do male moths find female moths in the dark?
21 Which canal had an opera written especially for its opening?
22 What type of nut is a marron glacé?
23 In which film did Elvis Presley play a double role?
24 What is a young horse called?
25 Who recorded the album "Crocodile Shoes"?
26 Who became Lord Warden of the Cinque ports in 1978?
27 Which show has featured Christopher Biggins, Bob Carolgees and Gordon Burns?
28 Which Samuel kept a famous diary in the seventeenth century?
29 What is a coley?
30 In education, what does OU stand for?

Answers

Pot-Luck 30 (see Quiz 58)
1 Netherlands. 2 Guilder. 3 Josceline. 4 Geese. 5 Audrey. 6 23 Railway Cuttings. 7 Flying Squad. 8 Bob Dylan. 9 Grace Jones. 10 Eden. 11 285. 12 Hilda Rumpole. 13 Yogi Bear. 14 Orange. 15 Golf. 16 Four. 17 Rainbow. 18 Scarlet. 19 Danube. 20 Oh Boy. 21 Bark. 22 A whale. 23 The head. 24 Jimi Hendrix. 25 Jets. 26 Oslo. 27 USA. 28 Crawford. 29 Queen. 30 Video Cassette Recorder.

Quiz 61 Around Wales

Answers - see page 71

Level 1

1 What is Wales' highest mountain?
2 Which Welshman wrote "Portrait Of The Artist As A Young Dog"?
3 Which Sea is to the north of Wales?
4 What are the Brecon Beacons?
5 Which island lies off the north west coast of Wales?
6 Which spring flower is a Welsh emblem?
7 What is the capital of Wales?
8 Which Channel is to the south of Wales?
9 Is Caernarvon Castle in the north or south of Wales?
10 Caerphilly is a town and also what type of food?
11 Which creature of legend is seen on the Welsh flag?
12 Which city in the south of the country is its second largest?
13 Which sport is played at Cardiff Arms Park?
14 Which wild cat gives its name to a Bay on Cardiff's quayside?
15 The production of which fuel affected the Welsh landscape until its decline in recent years?
16 Who was invested as Prince of Wales in 1969 at Caernarvon Castle?
17 Which vegetable is a Welsh emblem?
18 Which country lies to the east of Wales?
19 Who is the patron saint of Wales?
20 What is the mountainous area around Snowdon called?
21 Which Welsh Bay shares its name with a woollen jacket?
22 Which is the only Welsh county to have a first class cricket team?
23 What is the currency of Wales?
24 Wales has the highest density in the world of which farm animal?
25 Which Welsh Secretary challenged John Major for the Tory Party leadership in the summer of 1995?
26 Which county is further north, Clwyd or Gwent?
27 Which Strait separates Anglesey from the mainland?
28 Which North Wales university town shares its name with a resort of Northern Ireland?
29 The UK's longest river rises in Wales. What is it called?
30 Which town is further south, Aberystwyth or Swansea?

Answers

Football (see Quiz 63)
1 Newcastle. 2 Platt. 3 Blue and white. 4 Two. 5 USA. 6 Bristol. 7 Goal. 8 Scotland. 9 Leicester. 10 Blackpool. 11 Royle. 12 Spain. 13 Rangers. 14 Manchester United. 15 Northern Ireland. 16 Red. 17 France. 18 Tottenham. 19 Southampton. 20 As hosts they automatically qualified. 21 Pleat. 22 Own goal. 23 Graham Taylor. 24 Scotland. 25 Bramall. 26 Liverpool. 27 3.00pm. 28 Stuart Pearce. 29 Wales. 30 Chelsea.

Quiz 62 Pot-Luck 32

Answers - see page 72

Level 1

1 How did Van Gogh commit suicide?
2 What is the upper age limit for being an MP in the UK?
3 Who spent most weeks in the singles' charts in 1994?
4 Who was the first reigning British monarch to visit a Communist country?
5 Which opera features the song "Take A Pair Of Sparkling Eyes"?
6 In snooker, how many points are scored for potting the green ball?
7 S is the symbol of which chemical element?
8 Who recorded the album "Music Box"?
9 Which card game is another name for a prison van?
10 What is the second month of the year to have exactly 31 days?
11 In the Bible, who led the children of Israel to the Promised Land?
12 What goes before 'mantle', 'slipper' and 'smock' in flower names?
13 Where in Indiana was actor Gary Cooper born?
14 Who played Rowdy Yates in "Rawhide"?
15 Which horse won the English Triple Crown in 1970?
16 Timperley Early and Cawood Castle are types of what?
17 In the solar system which is the third planet from the sun?
18 What has subdivisions comprising 12, 52 and 365 units?
19 How many sides in four oblongs?
20 According to proverb, a little what is a dangerous thing?
21 What would you be playing if you were talking about spares and strikes?
22 In rugby, what name is given to a forward on either end of the front row of a scrum?
23 Whose catchphrase was, "Heavens to Murgatroyd"?
24 What is the first name of TV cook Harriott?
25 What is the least valuable piece on a chessboard?
26 What was the name of Barnum's famous giant elephant?
27 What is the first name of Mr Sugden of "Coronation Street"?
28 How many pieces of silver did Judas get for betraying Christ?
29 Which food is made from the lining of a cow's stomach?
30 What collective name is used for items made from precious gems?

Answers *Pot-Luck 33* (see Quiz 64)
1 Two. 2 Virgo. 3 Han Solo. 4 Clog. 5 Microsoft. 6 Kent. 7 Table Mountain. 8 On the BBC colour test card. 9 Rick. 10 Simple Minds. 11 Robert Kennedy. 12 Conservative. 13 Monaco. 14 Maud Grimes. 15 Vodka and tomato juice. 16 Sparrow. 17 Squash. 18 Celine Dion. 19 Billy Joe McAllister. 20 Soup. 21 Rolls Royce. 22 Michael Caine. 23 Saturday. 24 As Time Goes By. 25 Outside. 26 Marilyn Monroe. 27 Blue. 28 Light flyweight. 29 500. 30 Cher.

Quiz 63 Football

Answers - see page 69

1 Which team is known as The Magpies?
2 Which David has played for Aston Villa, Milan, Sampdoria and Arsenal?
3 What two colours are in Blackburn's home strip?
4 How many linesmen are there in an international match?
5 In which country was the 1994 World Cup finals held?
6 Which city has teams called Rovers and City?
7 What position did Peter Shilton play?
8 Tommy Docherty and Jock Stein have both managed which country?
9 Who plays home games at Filbert Street?
10 Which club is linked with the playing career of Jimmy Armfield?
11 Which Joe managed Everton when they won the 1995 FA Cup?
12 Which country do Real Madrid come from?
13 In QPR what does the letter R stand for?
14 Which club did Steve Bruce play for in a Premiership winning season?
15 Which country did George Best play for?
16 What is the home colour of Nottingham Forest?
17 Which country does David Ginola come from?
18 At which club did Terry Venables and Alan Sugar clash?
19 Who did Alan Shearer play for before he joined Blackburn?
20 Why did France not play in qualifying games for the '98 World Cup?
21 Which David has managed Spurs, Luton and Sheffield Wednesday?
22 What do the letters o.g. stand for?
23 Who was the England manager when the side failed to reach the 1992 World Cup finals?
24 Which country does Gary McAllister play for?
25 Which Lane do Sheffield United play at?
26 Which club is associated with the song "You'll Never Walk Alone"?
27 What is the traditional kick-off time for Saturday League games?
28 Which English fullback is known as "Psycho"?
29 Which country does Neville Southall play for?
30 Which London side did Ruud Gullit join in 1995?

Answers

Around Wales (see Quiz 61)
1 Snowdon. 2 Dylan Thomas. 3 Irish Sea. 4 Mountains. 5 Anglesey. 6 Daffodil. 7 Cardiff. 8 Bristol Channel. 9 North. 10 Cheese. 11 Dragon. 12 Swansea. 13 Rugby. 14 Tiger. 15 Coal. 16 Prince Charles. 17 Leek. 18 England. 19 St David. 20 Snowdonia. 21 Cardigan. 22 Glamorgan. 23 Pound sterling. 24 Sheep. 25 John Redwood. 26 Clwyd. 27 Menai Strait. 28 Bangor. 29 Severn 30 Swansea.

Quiz 64 Pot-Luck 33

Answers - see page 70

Level 1

1 How many packs of cards are needed for a game of Canasta?
2 What is the zodiac sign of the Virgin?
3 Which character did Harrison Ford play in "Star Wars"?
4 What is a sabot?
5 Bill Gates founded which computer corporation?
6 Which Clark was a journalist on "The Daily Planet"?
7 Where would you see fog called the Tablecloth?
8 Carol Hersey is reckoned to be the most seen person on British television. Where does she appear?
9 What is the first name of TV cook Stein?
10 Who recorded the album "Once Upon A Time"?
11 Who did Sirhan Sirhan assassinate?
12 In 1995 which political party leadership was contested by two Johns?
13 What is ruled by the House of Grimaldi?
14 In "Coronation Street" what is Maureen Holdsworth's mother called?
15 What are the two main ingredients of a Bloody Mary?
16 In the rhyme, who killed Cock Robin?
17 What is a world sport, an American vegetable and a British soft drink?
18 Who recorded the album "The Colour Of My Love"?
19 Who jumped off the Tallahatchee Bridge?
20 What type of food is consommé?
21 The 'Silver Ghost' was what type of car?
22 Who says, "Not many people know that!"?
23 Which day of the week is named after the god Saturn?
24 What was Sam asked to play by Rick in "Casablanca"?
25 Where would you eat if you were eating *al fresco*?
26 How is Norma Jean Baker better known?
27 What colour features in the title of George Gershwin's Rhapsody?
28 What is the lowest weight in boxing?
29 How many sheets of paper are there in a ream?
30 Who was Sonny's singing partner?

Answers

Pot-Luck 32 (see Quiz 62)
1 He shot himself. 2 There isn't one. 3 Mariah Carey. 4 Elizabeth II (1972 Yugoslavia). 5 The Gondoliers. 6 Three. 7 Sulphur. 8 Mariah Carey. 9 Black Maria. 10 March. 11 Moses. 12 Lady's. 13 Gary. 14 Clint Eastwood. 15 Nijinsky. 16 Rhubarb. 17 Earth. 18 A year. 19 16. 20 Knowledge. 21 Ten-pin bowling. 22 Prop. 23 Snagglepuss. 24 Ainsley. 25 Pawn. 26 Jumbo. 27 Percy. 28 30. 29 Tripe. 30 Jewellery.

Quiz 65 Pot-Luck 34

Answers - see page 75

1   Which country are Qantas airlines from?
2   What is the currency of Russia?
3   What type of plant grows from seed, flowers and dies in a year?
4   Helen Sharman was the first Briton to go where?
5   What is Andy Capp's wife called?
6   Which British monarch was the husband of Queen Elizabeth the Queen Mother?
7   In rhyming slang what is Barnet Fair?
8   How is Declan McManus better known?
9   What animal is shown in the painting "The Monarch Of The Glen"?
10 Where would you look to discover the Mount of the Moon and the Girdle of Venus?
11 Which insect might be used by a snooker player?
12 In Roman numerals what is MD + MD?
13 What is the first name of Polish film director Polanski?
14 What colour is saffron?
15 What was Al short for in Al Capone's name?
16 How many sides has a trapezium?
17 In which Olympic event would the competitor use ribbons and hoops?
18 Which metal is an alloy of copper and zinc?
19 Which major river flows through Cairo?
20 What is a Blenheim Orange?
21 Which country did Prime Minister Bhutto rule?
22 In which film did John Travolta play Vincent Vega?
23 What number is opposite a one on a dice?
24 Who recorded the album "Made In England"?
25 Charlie Hungerford was ex-father in law of which law enforcer?
26 What is the capital of Sweden?
27 Which title gave hits to both Jennifer Rush and Frankie Goes To Hollywood?
28 What is Roget's word book known as?
29 Ed Koch was the mayor of which town?
30 In which round was the Bruno v Tyson 1996 fight stopped?

Answers

Pot-Luck 35 (see Quiz 67)
1 Basil Spence 2 A Question of Sport. 3 Nudist. 4 Niven. 5 Weathering.
6 Mario Lanza. 7 Wolves. 8 Mexico. 9 500. 10 Elly May. 11 March.
12 Paul McCartney. 13 Exit. 14 C.S. 15 Manuel. 16 Accidentally shot
himself dead. 17 Calcium. 18 Jethro Tull. 19 Take That. 20 Sleeve. 21
Beaufort. 22 South Africa. 23 J.R. Ewing. 24 Colt. 25 Aer Lingus. 26
Holidays. 27 Anton. 28 Deuce. 29 Shark. 30 Mineworkers.

Quiz 66 70s Newsround

Answers - see page 76

Level 1

1 Which Edward became prime minister in 1970?
2 What type of currency was introduced to Britain in 1971?
3 Idi Amin seized power in which country?
4 Henry Cooper retired from which sport?
5 What type of short pants became the fashion craze for women?
6 Bangladesh was formed from the eastern part of which country?
7 Which Sir Anthony was declared to be a Russian spy?
8 Which Mother won a Nobel Peace Prize?
9 Which Conservative leader became prime minister in 1979?
10 The Shah of which country was forced into exile?
11 The strike-bound months of 1978 and 1979 became known as the Winter of what?
12 Which Liberal leader resigned after allegations about his private life?
13 Which princess sought a divorce from the Earl of Snowdon?
14 In which sea off the British coastline was oil discovered?
15 Under Patrick Steptoe's guidance what was produced from a test tube for the first time in July 1978?
16 Whose shroud went on display at St John's Cathedral in Turin?
17 Steve Biko died in a cell in which country?
18 What sport did Kerry Packer try to take over with his cash offers?
19 Which king of rock died in Tennessee in 1977?
20 Freddie Laker brought cut-price travel in what type of transport?
21 Which Jubilee did Queen Elizabeth II celebrate in 1977?
22 The Sex Pistols were the leaders of the movement known as what kind of rock?
23 Which leader of Communist China died in 1976?
24 Which 'Lucky' Lord vanished after the murder of his child's nanny?
25 Which scandal forced Richard Nixon to resign as US President?
26 Which countries fought in the 1973 Yom Kippur War?
27 What did the Amoco Cadiz spill off the Brittany coastline?
28 How many days were in a working week during the 1974 power shortage?
29 Which earl was murdered by the IRA in 1979?
30 Which Labour MP James became prime minister?

Answers

Geography (see Quiz 68)
1 Spain. 2 India and Pakistan. 3 Northumberland. 4 Peking. 5 Buckingham Palace. 6 Austria. 7 Devon. 8 Red. 9 Derbyshire. 10 Italy. 11 Africa. 12 West. 13 Argentina. 14 Paris. 15 Portugal. 16 Algeria. 17 Thailand. 18 Scotland. 19 Oslo. 20 Africa. 21 Netherlands. 22 Florida. 23 France. 24 Birmingham. 25 Washington. 26 Pacific. 27 Brazil. 28 Europe. 29 Sweden. 30 Belgium.

Quiz 67 Pot-Luck 35

Answers - see page 73

1 Who designed Coventry cathedral?
2 In which TV programme do Ian Botham and Bill Beaumont appear as team captains?
3 In 1979, Brighton Council decided to allow what type of beach?
4 Which David told his life story in "The Moon's a Balloon"?
5 Rocks are broken down by the elements by what gradual process?
6 Which tenor took the title role in "The Great Caruso"?
7 The word lupine relates to which animals?
8 In which country is the volcano Popocatépetl?
9 What number does the Roman numeral D stand for?
10 What was Jed Clampett's daughter called in "The Beverley Hillbillies"?
11 In which month is the first day of spring?
12 Who co-wrote a "Liverpool Oratorio" with Carl Davis?
13 Which stage direction means to go off stage?
14 What are the two initials of Narnia creator Lewis?
15 What was the name of the Spanish waiter in "Fawlty Towers"?
16 What dramatic event happened to Terry Kath of rock group Chicago at a party in 1978?
17 Which element is found in bones, shells and teeth?
18 In the early 1700s who invented a seed drill?
19 What are Gary Barlow, Howard Donald, Jason Orange and Mark Owen better known as?
20 What part of a garment is a raglan?
21 What scale is used to measure wind velocity?
22 In which country is the Table Mountain?
23 Which soap character had a secretary called Sly?
24 What is a young stallion called?
25 What is the Republic of Ireland's airline called?
26 What does the French word *vacances* mean?
27 What is the first name of TV cook Mosimann?
28 In tennis, what is a score of 40 all called?
29 Threshers and hammerheads are types of what?
30 The NUM is the National Union of what?

Quiz 68 Geography

Answers - see page 74

Level 1

1 Which country can you easily walk to from Gibraltar?
2 Urdu is an important language in which two Asian countries?
3 Which is England's most northerly county?
4 What did Bejing used to be called?
5 Which is the Queen's London home?
6 In which European country is Salzburg?
7 Which county divides Cornwall from Somerset?
8 What 'colour' is the Sea between Egypt and Saudi Arabia?
9 In which county is the Peak District?
10 In which country is the resort of Rimini?
11 Madagascar is to the east of which continent?
12 Is California on the east or west coast of the USA?
13 Which is the nearest country to the Falkland Islands?
14 Near which French city is the Disney Theme Park?
15 In which country is the Algarve?
16 Which is further west Algeria or Ethiopia?
17 Which country used to be called Siam?
18 In which country is the county of Tayside?
19 Which Scandinavian capital begins and ends with the same letter?
20 Chad is in which continent?
21 What is Holland also known as?
22 In which US holiday state is Miami?
23 Which country is divided from Spain by the Pyrenees?
24 What is the largest city in the West Midlands?
25 Which town of Tyne and Wear shares its name with the US capital?
26 The Philippines are in which Ocean?
27 What is the largest country of South America?
28 In which continent is Slovenia?
29 Which country originally produced Volvo cars?
30 In which country do most Flemish speakers live?

Answers

70s Newsround (see Quiz 66)
1 Heath. 2 Decimal. 3 Uganda. 4 Boxing. 5 Hot. 6 Pakistan. 7 Blunt
8 Teresa. 9 Margaret Thatcher. 10 Iran. 11 Discontent. 12 Jeremy
Thorpe. 13 Margaret. 14 North Sea. 15 A baby. 16 Jesus Christ. 17
South Africa. 18 Cricket. 19 Elvis Presley. 20 Aircraft. 21 Silver. 22
Punk. 23 Mao Tse-tung. 24 Lucan. 25 Watergate. 26 Egypt, Syria and
Israel. 27 Oil. 28 Three. 29 Mountbatten. 30 Callaghan.

Quiz 69   Pot-Luck 36

Answers - see page 79

Level 1

1 Which extra title was given to Catherine II of Russia?
2 Which constituency returned the MP with the highest majority in the 1992 General Election?
3 Which country is a car from if it has the international registration letter H?
4 Which came first the House of Tudor or the House of Stuart?
5 Which Norman said, "He got on his bike and looked for work."
6 What was the name of the witch played by Agnes Moorhead in "Bewitched"?
7 Zn is the symbol of which chemical element?
8 In "Coronation Street" what is Ken Barlow's job?
9 According to proverb, one man's meat is another man's what?
10 Which radio DJ urged listeners to 'fight the flab'?
11 Williams and Conference are types of what?
12 Who recorded the album "Medusa"?
13 How many times did Will Carling skipper England before giving up the captaincy in '96?
14 What is capital of Afghanistan?
15 Who was the female lead in the TV sitcom "Terry and Junc?"
16 In which country was "The Flame Trees of Thika" set?
17 What's the link between Shag, The Weatherman and Sakkarin?
18 Which Irish entertainer Val used to sing in a rocking chair?
19 How many yards in a mile?
20 Who was the only British female singer to have three UK No 1s in the 60s?
21 What was the name of the Ewing ranch in "Dallas"?
22 The USA government is nicknamed which relative?
23 What name is given to poisonous fluid from a snake?
24 Which Biblical town was destroyed with Gomorrah?
25 On what type of farm are horses bred?
26 What famous first in TV advertising is held by Bird's Eye frozen peas?
27 What number is Beethoven's concerto known as the "Emperor"?
28 Which River provided hits for Andy Williams and Danny Williams?
29 What name is given to a baby elephant?
30 What colour pottery is Josiah Wedgwood noted for?

Pot-Luck 37 (see Quiz 71)
1 Spring. 2 Libra. 3 Madagascar. 4 Rolling Stones. 5 Flat. 6 Walt Disney. 7 Plum. 8 Carburettor. 9 Tongue. 10 A rest. 11 Greenwich Mean Time. 12 Black. 13 Waistcoat. 14 May. 15 Badminton. 16 An ear. 17 Miser. 18 Norma. 19 Orwell. 20 Sugar. 21 Jenny. 22 Fred Flintstone. 23 January. 24 Fleetwood Mac. 25 Lincoln. 26 Labour. 27 Friar. 28 Wall Street. 29 Australia. 30 Ronnie Corbett.

Answers

Level 1

1 What was invented by Lazlo and Georg Biro?
2 Which fashion item is Oscar Levi Strauss responsible for?
3 What nationality was motor vehicle pioneer Gottlieb Daimler?
4 What was developed by André and Edouard Michelin?
5 What type of pen did Lewis Waterman invent?
6 Which air cushion vehicle was invented by Christopher Cockerell?
7 Which engine used in aircraft was invented by Sir Frank Whittle?
8 What did John Logie Baird invent, first called 'seeing by wireless'?
9 Which communication system is Alexander Graham Bell famous for?
10 Who invented a code made up of dots and dashes?
11 For whom did Louis Braille develop his writing system?
12 Which method of food preservation did Clarence Birdseye invent?
13 What type of lamp is Humphry Davy famous for?
14 Which predecessor of the CD player did Thomas Edison create?
15 Which breakfast food was developed by Will Keith Kellogg in 1898?
16 Which invention is Marconi known for?
17 Which company, motto 'Small is beautiful', was founded in the late 1940s and developed the Walkman?
18 Which explosive was invented by Alfred Nobel?
19 What type of milk did Louis Pasteur give his name to, because of the treatment it undergoes?
20 In which source of power were Volta and Ampère pioneers?
21 What powered James Watt's engine in 1765?
22 What would you use Isaac Singer's invention for?
23 In which room would you be most likely to use the inventions of Kenneth Wood – known to his friends as Ken?
24 At what sort of party might you see the invention of Earl W. Tupper?
25 Which frozen confection was originally called Eskimo pie?
26 Which Earl invented a snack of meat between two slices of bread?
27 What was special about the fabric Charles Macintosh invented?
28 Which essential for foreign tourists was invented by American Express?
29 What type of camera did George Eastman invent?
30 What type of aircraft is Sikorsky famous for?

Answers

TV: The 80s (see Quiz 72)
1 All Creatures Great and Small. 2 Allo Allo. 3 Jersey. 4 Boys from the Blackstuff. 5 Brideshead. 6 Lacey. 7 Fame. 8 French. 9 A Laugh. 10 Grant. 11 Highway. 12 The Galaxy. 13 Boats. 14 Oxford. 15 India 16 Fire Brigade 17 Lovejoy. 18 Miami. 19 Not The Nine o'Clock News. 20 All Hours. 21 Spitting Image. 22 Michael Aspel. 23 Dogs. 24 Roland. 25 Holland. 26 Barrister. 27 Japanese. 28 J.R. 29 Watchdog. 30 Sir Humphrey Appleby.

Quiz 71 Pot-Luck 37

1 Which season does the word vernal relate to?
2 What is the zodiac sign of the Balance?
3 On which island are most lemurs found?
4 Who had a No 1 hit with the song "(I Can't Get No) Satisfaction"?
5 What type of horse racing does not include fences and obstacles?
6 Who created Mickey Mouse?
7 In nursery rhyme, what did Little Jack Horner pull out of a pie?
8 Which device produces the mix of air and petrol in internal combustion engines?
9 What is a butterfly's proboscis?
10 According to proverb, what is a change as good as?
11 What does GMT stand for?
12 What name is shared by athlete Roger and TV presenter Cilla?
13 Called a vest in America, what's the name of this garment in the UK?
14 Hawthorn traditionally blooms in which month?
15 Which game is played with rackets and shuttlecocks?
16 Which part of his anatomy did Van Gogh cut off?
17 What word describes someone mean with money, like Scrooge?
18 What is the first name of John Major's wife?
19 Which George wrote "Animal Farm"?
20 What type of food is Demerara?
21 What name is given to a female donkey?
22 Who says, "Yabbadabba Doo!"?
23 Which month is named after the god Janus?
24 Who recorded the album "Rumours"?
25 Which city of central England gave its name to a shade of green?
26 Was Clement Attlee a Conservative or Labour politician?
27 What was the profession or calling of Tuck in Sherwood Forest?
28 Where is the New York Stock Exchange?
29 In which country would you see wild wombats?
30 Who was Ronnie Barker's comic partner?

Answers

Pot-Luck 36 (see Quiz 69)
1 The Great. 2 Huntingdon (J. Major 36,320). 3 Hungary. 4 The House of Tudor. 5 Tebbit. 6 Endora. 7 Zinc. 8 Teacher. 9 Poison. 10 Terry Wogan. 11 Pear. 12 Annie Lennox. 13 57. 14 Kabul. 15 June Whitfield. 16 Kenya. 17 All guises of Jonathan King. 18 Doonican. 19 1,760. 20 Sandie Shaw. 21 South Fork. 22 Uncle Sam. 23 Venom. 24 Sodom. 25 Stud. 26 First product advertised in colour. 27 Fifth. 28 Moon. 29 Calf. 30 Blue.

Quiz 72 TV: The 80s

Answers - see page 78

1 Which series was about Yorkshire vet James Herriot?
2 In which series would you find the Fallen Madonna with the Big Boobies?
3 On which island was "Bergerac" set?
4 Which programme gave the catchphrase 'Gissa job'?
5 What was Revisited in the series with Jeremy Irons?
6 Who was Cagney's police partner?
7 What were students at the New York High School of Performing Arts seeking?
8 Which Fields did Hester and William go to after "Fresh Fields"?
9 What was Jeremy Beadle Game for?
10 Which Russell was astrologer on "Breakfast Time"?
11 Which religious programme did Harry Secombe start to present?
12 What was the Hitch Hiker's Guide to?
13 What was being built in the yards in "Howard's Way"?
14 In which university city was Inspector Morse based?
15 In which eastern country was "The Jewel in the Crown" set?
16 Which emergency service is featured in "London's Burning"?
17 Which series featured Ian McShane as an antiques dealer?
18 In which city did Sonny Crockett investigate Vice?
19 What wasn't a news bulletin but did feature Pamela Stephenson and Rowan Atkinson?
20 When was the shop with David Jason and Ronnie Barker Open?
21 Which satirical programme featured latex puppets?
22 Who began presenting "This Is Your Life" in 1987?
23 Which pets featured on the programmes with Barbara Woodhouse?
24 Which Rat revived the flagging fortunes of TV-am?
25 Which Jools presented "The Tube"?
26 What was the profession of claret-swigging Horace Rumpole?
27 Who were the women prisoners of in "Tenko"?
28 Whose shooting in November 1980 was watched by 27 million?
29 What sort of dog became a consumer's champion in the 1980s?
30 Who was MP Jim Hacker's Permanent Under Secretary?

Quiz 73 Pot-Luck 38

Level 1

Answers - see page 83

1 Which country does the airline Iberia come from?
2 What is the currency of South Africa?
3 What was seemingly fearless "A-Team" member B. A. Baracus very frightened of?
4 Who wrote the Aldwych farces, including "Rookery Nook"?
5 What year is included in the name of the group who recorded "Simon Says"?
6 Which school did Queen Elizabeth II attend as a youngster?
7 In rhyming slang what is dog and bone?
8 What was Frederick Bulsara better known as?
9 On TV, Danny Kane is co-owner of which club?
10 In the Bible, which book follows Matthew?
11 What famous first did Edward White achieve for America?
12 In which country is the Matterhorn?
13 Who was the first female DJ on Radio 1?
14 What colour is associated with an Oxford or Cambridge sports award?
15 Which rock forms the greater part of the White Cliffs of Dover?
16 Which food was advertised to the tune of "I Can't Let Maggie Go"?
17 In tennis, what name is given to a serve which cannot be returned?
18 Who recorded the album "Bad"?
19 Which major river flows through Gloucester?
20 Who created "Dalziel and Pascoe"?
21 According to Rhoda, in which year was she born in the Bronx, New York?
22 Which card game has the same name as a horse-racing town?
23 Who founded the Rocket record label?
24 What was the first name of Burgess, the spy who defected to Russia?
25 How was Eric Bartholomew better known?
26 What is the capital of Denmark?
27 In which series did a Flood become a Tipple?
28 "Just when you thought it was safe to go back in the water..." was the advertising line for which film?
29 In which street is the Bank of England?
30 What does TUC stand for?

Answers

Pot-Luck 39 (see Quiz 75)
1 Keystone. 2 Are You Being Served? 3 Salamander. 4 The Dail. 5 REM. 6 Kuwait City. 7 John Masefield. 8 Bygraves. 9 Bournemouth. 10 Parcel. 11 October. 12 Enya. 13 Matinee. 14 W.B. 15 Heather. 16 Dodd. 17 Bongos. 18 The Bar. 19 Shadows. 20 Head. 21 Dick Dastardly. 22 Much Binding in the Marsh. 23 Hamburg. 24 Filly. 25 Status Quo. 26 New Orleans. 27 Whitelaw. 28 Slob. 29 Fiddler on the Roof. 30 Mick Jagger.

Quiz 74 Jet Setters

Answers - see page 84

Level 1

1 What is the first name of supermodel Evangelista?
2 Which veteran Scottish rock star is married to model Rachel Hunter?
3 Princess Caroline is a member of which royal family?
4 What was the surname of Jackie Onassis's first husband?
5 What is the first name of actress/presenter Ms de Cadenet?
6 Lady Helen, daughter of the Duke and Duchess of Kent, named her son after which famous explorer?
7 What was the first name of tycoon Donald Trump's former wife?
8 What is the first name of actress and model Miss Hurley?
9 Who is the magician partner of model Claudia Schiffer?
10 Which Texan model married Mick Jagger?
11 Which Swedish actress is a former wife of the late Peter Sellers?
12 What is the surname of eight-times married actress Zsa Zsa?
13 What is the first name of celebrity photographer Bailey?
14 Which LA Hills are the home of many of the rich and famous?
15 What is the first name of kilt-wearing designer Gaultier?
16 How is skinny 1960s model Lesley Hornby better known?
17 What is the surname of celebrity sisters Joan and Jackie?
18 What is the first name of actress/model Miss Seymour?
19 Who is the head of the Virgin group?
20 What is the first name of gossip columnist Dempster?
21 Which ski resort is a favourite for Prince Charles for his Xmas break?
22 What is the nationality of Sophia Loren?
23 Which TV show made Pamela Anderson famous?
24 Which princess is known by her husband's first name?
25 Which Royal has a home on the island of Mustique?
26 What is the first name of fashion designer Westwood?
27 Of which country is Juan Carlos king?
28 What is the profession of the Queen's cousin Lord Lichfield ?
29 Which Pakistani cricketer married heiress Jemima Goldsmith?
30 Which fuel did the Getty family make their fortune from?

Answers

Sport: The 80s (see Quiz 76)
1 Lineker. 2 Bob Champion. 3 Geoff Boycott. 4 Ovett. 5 Liverpool. 6 Davis. 7 Australia. 8 Hailwood. 9 Watson. 10 Everton. 11 Navratilova. 12 Bolero. 13 Italy. 14 Zola Budd. 15 Los Angeles. 16 Lyle. 17 Brazil. 18 Dennis Taylor. 19 Belgium. 20 Javelin. 21 Boxing. 22 Boris Becker. 23 Maradona. 24 Flo Jo. 25 Bryan Robson. 26 Somerset. 27 France. 28 Czechoslovakia. 29 Rangers. 30 Jack Charlton.

Quiz 75 Pot-Luck 39

Answers - see page 81

1 Which knockabout Kops were created by Mack Sennett?
2 In which TV programme did the staff of Grace Brothers appear?
3 What is another name for the creature the axolotl?
4 What is the name of the Irish Parliament?
5 Which band features the lyrics of Michael Stipe?
6 What city is the capital of Kuwait?
7 Who wrote the poem "Sea Fever"?
8 Which Max recorded sing-a-long records?
9 Where is the fictional Bayview Retirement Home?
10 In the children's party game, what is passed around and unwrapped?
11 In which month is Halloween?
12 Who recorded the album "Watermark"?
13 What word taken from the French describes an afternoon show?
14 What are the initials of Irish poet Yeats?
15 Which moorland shrub is said to bring good luck?
16 Which comic Ken says, "How tickled I am"?
17 Which instrument is traditionally held between the knees?
18 What name is given to barristers collectively?
19 What are Hank Marvin, Brian Bennett and Bruce Welch better known as?
20 On what part of your body would you wear a homburg?
21 Which cartoon villain exclaimed, "Drat and double drat!"?
22 In the classic comedy, Kenneth Horne and Richard Murdoch brought which village to radio?
23 In which city did the hamburger originate?
24 What is a young mare called?
25 Which rock group's name is the Latin for the existing state of things?
26 In the song, the House Of The Rising Sun is in which city?
27 Which Conservative politician William spoke of a "short, sharp, shock"?
28 What is the surname of the decidedly anti-social TV characters Wayne and Waynetta?
29 The village of Anatevka appears in which musical?
30 Who played Ned Kelly in the 1970 film of the same name?

Answers

Pot-Luck 38 (see Quiz 73)
1 Spain. 2 Rand. 3 Flying. 4 Ben Travers. 5 1910 (Fruitgum Co.) 6 None at all. 7 Phone. 8 Freddie Mercury. 9 The Paradise Club. 10 Mark. 11 First to walk in space. 12 Switzerland. 13 Annie Nightingale. 14 Blue. 15 Chalk. 16 Bread (Brand was Nimble). 17 Ace. 18 Michael Jackson. 19 Severn. 20 Reginald Hill. 21 1941. 22 Newmarket. 23 Elton John. 24 Guy. 25 Eric Morecambe. 26 Copenhagen. 27 May to December. 28 Jaws II. 29 Threadneedle Street. 30 Trades Union Congress.

Quiz 76 Sport: The 80s

Level 1

Answers - see page 82

1 Which Gary was England's top soccer marksman of the 1980s?
2 Who fought back from cancer to win the Grand National?
3 Which English batsman became the highest run getter in Test history?
4 Which Steve was Sebastian Coe's great rival in mid-distance races?
5 Which club were English soccer champions six times in the 80s?
6 Which Steve became snooker World Champion in 1981?
7 The America's Cup left home for the first time ever to go to where?
8 Which motor-cycle legend Mike was killed in a motor accident in 1981?
9 Which Tom won both the US and British Opens in the same year?
10 Which team were English soccer champions under Howard Kendall?
11 Which Martina dominated Wimbledon in the 1980s?
12 Which piece of music by Ravel did Torvill and Dean use in winning an Olympic gold for ice dancing?
13 Which country beat West Germany to win the 1982 soccer World Cup?
14 The Daily Mail ran a campaign to get which South African athlete to receive a British passport?
15 Where in the USA was the centre for the 1984 Olympic Games?
16 In golf, which Sandy won the 1988 US Masters?
17 Which country is motor racing's Nelson Piquet from?
18 Who became a world snooker champion wearing 'upside-down' glasses?
19 In which country was the 1985 Heysel Stadium soccer tragedy?
20 In which event did Tessa Sanderson win Olympic gold?
21 What was Barry McGuigan's sport ?
22 Which 17-year-old German won the Wimbledon men's singles?
23 Which Diego benefited from "The hand of God"?
24 What was the nickname of sprinter Florence Griffith-Joyner?
25 Who in soccer was known as 'Captain Marvel'?
26 Viv Richards and Ian Botham played together for which county?
27 Which team won the Five Nations tournament from 1986 to 1989?
28 Which country does Ivan Lendl originate from?
29 Which Scottish soccer team was managed by Graeme Souness?
30 Which Englishman became soccer boss of the Republic of Ireland?

Quiz 77 Pot-Luck 40

Answers - see page 87

1 What is another name for the rowan tree?
2 How many hours in four days?
3 Which country is a car from if it has the international registration letter J?
4 Who provided the voice of The Book in "The Hitch-Hiker's Guide To The Galaxy"?
5 Which Oscar said, "I have nothing to declare except my genius."
6 In darts, what is the lowest score from three different trebles?
7 Au is the symbol of which chemical element?
8 Which soap features The Woolpack pub?
9 What subject does Geoff Hamilton deal with?
10 What name is given to the vast grassy plains of Russia?
11 Who has been married to Gemma Craven and Liz Hobbs?
12 Who recorded the album "Steam"?
13 Bovine relates to which kind of animals?
14 What is the chief ingredient in the production of glass?
15 Which creatures sang, "We All Stand Together"?
16 Which composer had the Christian names Johann Sebastian
17 Which monster of the horror genre was created by Mary Shelley?
18 Who forms a trio with Clegg and Foggy?
19 How many sides in three rectangles?
20 On which river does Stoke stand?
21 Which word could go before cab, skirt and van?
22 Six is the lowest of what type of number?
23 Which month is said to come in like a lion and go out like a lamb?
24 What is the name of Bill Clinton's daughter?
25 What did the navigator Amerigo Vespucci give his name to?
26 "Have I Got News For You" is the TV version of which radio show?
27 Who wrote "A Brief History Of Time"?
28 How many cards are there in each suit?
29 In "EastEnders" what was Sam's surname before she married Ricky?
30 What sort of bird is a muscovy?

Quiz 78 80s Films

Answers - see page 88

1 What relation was Danny de Vito to Arnold Schwarzenegger in their 1988 film?
2 Which Bruce starred in "Die Hard"?
3 Which singer won an Oscar for "Moonstruck"?
4 Out of which continent were Meryl Streep and Robert Redford in 1985?
5 In which film did Dustin Hoffman dress up as a woman to get a job as a soap star?
6 What was Richard Gere in the film with Debra Winger?
7 What does an inventor tell Honey he has Shrunk in the 1989 movie?
8 What does ET stand for in the 1982 film?
9 What sort of Attraction was there between Michael Douglas and Glenn Close?
10 Which bored housewife Shirley had an unforgettable Greek holiday?
11 Which disfigured Man did John Hurt portray in the 1980 film?
12 Which film told the story of two athletes in the 1924 Olympics?
13 What is Australian adventurer Mick Dundee's nickname?
14 Which adventurer Indiana was played by Harrison Ford?
15 Which Indian leader was played by Ben Kingsley?
16 What sort of Busters were Dan Aykroyd and Sigourney Weaver?
17 Which composer did Tom Hulse play in "Amadeus"?
18 Which film with Bob Hoskins is also the name of a painting?
19 Which former actor became president of the USA in 1980?
20 What was the Fish Called in the 1988 movie?
21 Which Naked film was the first in the series with Leslie Nielsen?
22 Who played James Bond in "For Your Eyes Only"?
23 What Strikes Back in the 1980 film?
24 Where was Eddie Murphy a Cop in the film series?
25 Where was Michael J. Fox Back to in 1985?
26 The Return of what in 1983 was the sixth film in the "Star Wars" series?
27 Which US pop superstar starred in "Moonwalker"?
28 Which cartoon Rabbit was Framed in 1988?
29 Which famous ship did they try to Raise in the 1980 film?
30 How many Men looked after Baby in 1987?

Quiz 79 Pot-Luck 41

Answers - see page 85

 Level 1

1 Which swimmer won seven gold medals at the 1972 Olympics?
2 What is the zodiac sign of the Archer?
3 Which Palace in London started a television service?
4 Who had a No 1 hit with the song "Imagine"?
5 Which brass musical instrument shares its name with an ice-cream?
6 What is another name for the plant woodbine?
7 Which university featured Hugh Laurie, Tony Slattery and Emma Thompson in its 1981 revue?
8 What type of pre-wedding party is for women only?
9 What is the cord high above the ground which acrobats perform on?
10 What are pipistrelles?
11 Which nickname did saxophonist Julian Adderley acquire?
12 Who wrote "Solo", "Butterflies" and "Luv"?
13 It's a tail lamp in the USA, what's this part of the car called in the UK?
14 Who wrote "Lord Jim"?
15 St Albans started and Bosworth finished which hostilities?
16 Which Concern is a charity about the needs of the elderly?
17 In which police drama was Stick a source of information on criminal activity?
18 Which group recorded "I'm The Urban Spaceman"?
19 In which part of Germany might you find a chocolate gâteau with cream and cherries?
20 What type of food is canneloni?
21 How many laps are completed in a speedway race?
22 What was the title of Pearl Jam's first album?
23 In which TV series did Marilyn have an Uncle Herman?
24 Where are the headquarters of the Rugby Union?
25 Which fictional pirate had a bosun named Smee?
26 What is the theme song in the cartoon "The Snowman"?
27 Which bird has the Latin name *Troglodytes troglodytes*?
28 Who gives his name to Radio 2's "News Huddlines"?
29 In which sport did Neal Adams win Olympic medals?
30 Who is Victoria Wood's comic partner?

Answers

Pot-Luck 40 (see Quiz 77)
1 Mountain ash. 2 96. 3 Japan. 4 Peter Jones. 5 Wilde. 6 18. 7 Gold. 8 Emmerdale. 9 Gardening. 10 Steppes. 11 Frazer Hines. 12 East 17. 13 Oxen. 14 Sand. 15 Frogs. 16 Bach. 17 Frankenstein. 18 Compo. 19 12. 20 Trent. 21 Mini. 22 Perfect number (It is equal to the sum of its divisions.) 23 March. 24 Chelsea. 25 America. 26 The News Quiz. 27 Stephen Hawking. 28 13. 29 Mitchell. 30 Duck.

87

Quiz 80 Sounds of the 80s

Answers - see page 86

Level 1

1 Which Triangle did Barry Manilow sing about in 1981?
2 Which 'well preserved' group had a hit with "Going Underground"?
3 Who did Dexy's Midnight Runners tell to Come On?
4 What relation were the Thompsons who had hits with "Love on Your Side" and "We Are Detective"?
5 Which orange juice/champagne mix were Eurovision winners in 1981?
6 Andrew Ridgeley and George Michael were which group?
7 Who was Like A Virgin in 1984?
8 What colour was Chris de Burgh's Lady in, in 1986?
9 Which type of dance completes the Spandau group's name?
10 Which law enforcers sent a Message in a Bottle?
11 Which band shares its name with a form for the unemployed?
12 Who was a Jealous Guy with Roxy Music in 1981?
13 Where was Billy Joel's Girl in his 1983 Number 1?
14 Which Genesis drummer had three No 1 vocal hits in the 1980s?
15 Where does Gloria Estefan's Sound Machine come from?
16 Which Scottish Modern Girl Sheena had a hit with US singer Prince?
17 Which group did Simon Le Bon sing with?
18 Who Just Called to Say I Love You in 1984?
19 Who sang with Barbara Dickson on the hit "I Know Him So Well"?
20 What did Jennifer Rush sing about The Power of in 1985?
21 Where did Madness say they were Driving in 1982?
22 Which band headed by Mark Knopfler wanted "Money for Nothing"?
23 Band Aid asked Do They Know It's what?
24 What did Cyndi Lauper say Girls wanted to have more of?
25 Which group was Midge Ure chiefly associated with in the 80s?
26 Where were David Bowie and Mick Jagger Dancing in 1985?
27 Which former "EastEnders" and "Heartbeat" star had a hit with "Every Loser Wins" in 1986?
28 Which Shakin' star recorded "This Ole House"?
29 Where was the Ferry going across on the charity record in 1989?
30 Which two stars went from Ramsay Street to the top of the charts?

Answers

80s Films (see Quiz 78)
1 Twin. 2 Willis. 3 Cher. 4 Africa. 5 Tootsie. 6 An Officer and A Gentleman. 7 The Kids. 8 Extra Terrestrial. 9 Fatal. 10 Valentine. 11 Elephant Man. 12 Chariots of Fire. 13 Crocodile. 14 Jones. 15 Gandhi. 16 Ghost. 17 Mozart. 18 Mona Lisa. 19 Ronald Reagan. 20 Wanda. 21 Naked Gun. 22 Roger Moore. 23 The Empire. 24 Beverly Hills. 25 The Future. 26 The Jedi. 27 Michael Jackson. 28 Roger. 29 The Titanic. 30 Three.

Quiz 81 Pot-Luck 42

Level 1

1 "I Got Plenty of Nuthin'" comes from which Gershwin work?
2 Who answers the phone by saying, "the lady of the house speaking"?
3 What would you find in an arboretum?
4 Who recorded the album "12 Deadly Cyns ... And Then Some"?
5 Which record label turned down The Beatles?
6 In which country is the dong used as currency?
7 What line goes before the line, "In the windmills of you mind"?
8 What is the antirrhinum more commonly known as?
9 Who was Queen of England for nine days before she was beheaded?
10 Which country has had two kings called Carol on the throne this century?
11 On TV, what type of shop does Des Barnes work in?
12 Who created the series "Prime Suspect"?
13 What's the surname of cartoon hero Quick Draw?
14 What colour is muscovado sugar?
15 In which unusual way does Yorick first appear on stage in "Hamlet"?
16 How many sides has a cube?
17 What is the currency of Israel?
18 Who created the crazy Captain Kremmen?
19 Which major river flows through Bristol?
20 What is the surname of rugby players Tony and Rory?
21 Which character has been played by Albert Finney, Peter Ustinov and David Suchet?
22 What is the nationality of Chris de Burgh?
23 Which term means that material can be decomposed by natural means?
24 What sort of vehicle is a limousine?
25 In which TV series was a teacher nicknamed 'Privet'?
26 Who fronted the Tijuana Brass?
27 What is the largest wild member of the dog family?
28 Who is Magnus Magnusson's TV presenter daughter?
29 Ed Koch was the mayor of which town?
30 What does SNP stand for?

Pot-Luck 43 (see Quiz 83)
1 Edelweiss. 2 Piers Brosnan. 3 Virgo. 4 Cape Kennedy. 5 Cars. 6 Henry VIII. 7 Dando. 8 Holly. 9 240. 10 The Saint. 11 March. 12 Vincent Van Gogh (By Don McLean). 13 Ha'penny. 14 Pie In the Sky. 15 Fuchsia. 16 West Indies. 17 Taylor. 18 Shorthand. 19 Wet Wet Wet. 20 Be prepared. Motto of the Boy Scouts, song of Scar. 21 Hops. 22 Arthur Hailey. 23 Colin Cowdrey. 24 Joey. 25 British Open. 26 The Outer Limits. 27 Samurai. 28 Cycling. 29 Kylie Minogue. 30 Dungeons and Dragons.

Answers

Quiz 82 Bird Brains

Answers - see page 92

Level 1

1 Which bird has a red breast?
2 Which birds can be barn, tawny or snowy?
3 What two colours is a magpie?
4 Which birds are associated with the Tower of London?
5 What colour is a female blackbird?
6 The teal belongs to which family group?
7 What word can go in front of sparrow or martin to name a bird?
8 Which bird lays its eggs in the nests of others?
9 Which bird has the same name as a chess piece?
10 Which bird featured in the film "Kes"?
11 Which part of the golden eagle is gold?
12 Which part of a bird was used as a pen?
13 An early riser is said to be up before which bird?
14 What colour is the plumage on the head of a male mallard?
15 What is special about a swallow's tail?
16 Which bird starts its name with the word "Bull"?
17 The jay is a member of which family?
18 Which seashore bird has a colourful triangular bill?
19 Which reddish brown songbird sings just before dawn or after dusk?
20 What colour is a tufted duck?
21 Which game bird is a word meaning grumble?
22 Which bird is the symbol of peace?
23 Which bird was said to deliver babies?
24 Which bird is so called because of its fast flight?
25 What is the largest bird in the world?
26 Which flying toy shares its name with a bird?
27 What is a baby swan called?
28 Which letter of the alphabet sounds like a bird's name?
29 What is Britain's smallest bird?
30 Is a fledgling a young or old bird?

Quiz 83 Pot-Luck 43

Answers - see page 89

1 What is the national flower of Austria?
2 Who played Remmington Steele?
3 Which John plays snooker in "Big Break"?
4 What was the earlier name of Cape Canaveral?
5 What does the "EastEnders" Deals On Wheels sell?
6 Which monarch is credited with writing "Greensleeves"?
7 Which Jill teamed up with Nick Ross to present "Crimewatch UK"?
8 Which spiky tree has the scientific name *Ilex aquifolium*?
9 How many old pence were there in £1?
10 Which TV sleuth has the car registration number ST1?
11 In which month is St Patrick's Day?
12 The song starting, "Starry, starry night" is about whom?
13 Which pre-decimal coin do you shove in a table game?
14 Which is the most famous restaurant in the fictitious town of Middleton?
15 What did German botanist Leonhard Fuchs give his name to?
16 Curtly Ambrose plays international cricket for which team?
17 Which name is shared by actress Elizabeth and snooker star Dennis?
18 What sort of quick writing did Pitman invent?
19 What are Marty Pellow, Graeme Clark, Tom Cunningham and Neil Mitchell better known as?
20 What's the link between the Boy Scouts and Uncle Scar?
21 What is dried in an oast house?
22 Who wrote "Hotel"?
23 Which great English batsmen had the initials M.C.C.?
24 What is a young kangaroo called?
25 Which major golf championship is decided by a four-hole playoff?
26 Which programme started with the words, "There is nothing wrong with your television set...."?
27 Historically, what is the name of Japan's warrior class?
28 Which sport is Chris Boardman famous for?
29 Which Australian had a hit with "I Should Be So Lucky"?
30 Which fantasy game has its name made up of places of imprisonment and legendary creatures?

Quiz 84 80s Newsround

Answers - see page 90

Level 1

1 Which Alfred, a master film maker, died in 1980?
2 What was Southern Rhodesia renamed?
3 Which crack force stormed the Iranian Embassy in London in 1980?
4 Lech Walesa led strikers in which country?
5 Which Beatle was shot dead in New York?
6 What name was given to murderer Peter Sutcliffe?
7 Which former Hollywood actor became US President?
8 Which MP Edwina became "Eggwina" after a salmonella scare?
9 Over 250 people died in an air crash at which Scottish border town?
10 What was Lester Piggott sent to jail for avoiding?
11 What natural disaster hit Armenia in 1988?
12 What topped 3,000,000 in Britain for the first time since the 1930s?
13 Who became a princess by marrying Prince Charles?
14 In which city did the Barbican arts centre open?
15 Which Islands were the cause of a war between Britain and Argentina?
16 Whose London bedroom did Michael Fagin break into?
17 What was "The Mary Rose" which saw sunlight after 400 years?
18 Which Neil became leader of the Labour Party in 1983?
19 In 1988 François Mitterrand was re-elected president of which country?
20 What name was given to young upwardly mobile persons?
21 Which Colonel Oliver starred in the US "Irongate" court hearing?
22 How many general elections did Margaret Thatcher win in the 1980s?
23 What was the "The Herald Of Free Enterprise" which met disaster in 1987?
24 Which company, famed for stout, was implicated in a share scandal?
25 President "Baby Doc" fled from which country?
26 Which Mikhail became Soviet leader in 1985?
27 Bob Geldof organized Live Aid to provide food for which country?
28 What was Piper Alpha, scene of a deadly fire?
29 Which George was elected US president?
30 Which cabinet minister Cecil was forced to resign after his jilted mistress told her side of events to the press?

Quiz 85 Pot-Luck 44

Level 1

Answers - see page 95

1 What is a smolt?
2 Which song contains the words,"If you lose your teeth when you're out to dine borrow mine!"
3 Which country is a car from if it has the international registration letters MEX?
4 Who came first as monarch, Queen Elizabeth I or Henry II?
5 The Charge of the Light Brigade took place during which battle?
6 In snooker, how many points are scored by potting the yellow ball?
7 Cu is the symbol of which chemical element?
8 Which soap pub sells Newton and Ridley?
9 What is the first month of the year to have exactly 31 days and follow a month of 31 days?
10 What are dried plums called?
11 In the past, which animal did doctors use to drain blood from the sick?
12 Who recorded the album "Post"?
13 What is the word for a group of porpoises?
14 What are the two main flavours in a banoffee pie?
15 What sort of bird was Edd, the 1992 British Olympic mascot?
16 What is the medical name for dizziness due to heights?
17 Which county shares its name with a make-up selling lady?
18 On a map, what are lines called that join places of equal height above sea level?
19 How many pints in three quarts?
20 What is the name of TV cook Floyd?
21 What is a male goose called?
22 In which county is Land's End?
23 Who was in Wings and The Moody Blues?
24 'Phiz' illustrated works by which famous writer?
25 What sort of Pie provided a classic hit for Don McLean?
26 Which animals are a favourite of investigator Jemima Shore?
27 How many do you get if you add a baker's dozen to a score?
28 Was 1994 a leap year?
29 In the comic strip who was Blondie's husband?
30 From which plant is linen obtained?

Pot-Luck 45 (see Quiz 87)

Answers

1 Tiny. 2 Capricorn. 3 Fish. 4 Chris de Burgh. 5 Scar. 6 Black and white. 7 School. 8 It was the setting for BBC's El Dorado. 9 Jerome. 10 Popes. 11 Member of the European Parliament. 12 The Stingers. 13 Turkey. 14 John Wesley. 15 Blocks. 16 Elizabeth I. 17 Hands. 18 Idle hands. 19 South Africa. 20 Fruit. 21 Guinea pig. 22 John McEnroe. 23 October. 24 Diving. 25 Led Zeppelin. 26 Ascot. 27 D. 28 Soup. 29 John Wayne. 30 Mel Smith.

1 Which game show is based on snooker?
2 Where are prizes passed through on a conveyor belt?
3 Which show's biggest prizes are on the gold run?
4 Which word and numbers game show was the first programme on Channel 4?
5 Who preceded Les Dawson as host of "Blankety Blank"?
6 Which Cilla Black show has girls and guys choosing unseen partners?
7 Which show is based on a game of darts?
8 Which show has famous folk answering questions sitting in boxes?
9 Which board game inspired a TV whodunnit show?
10 What type of Maze was presented by Richard O'Brien?
11 Whose Fortunes are won in the show presented by Les Dennis?
12 Which Factor is a contest of physical and mental agility?
13 Who followed Bruce Forsyth as host of "You Bet!"?
14 Which DJ Nicky hosts "Wheel of Fortune"?
15 Which personality, always ready for a Challenge, took part in a helicopter-oriented "Treasure Hunt"?
16 What must celebrities look through in the show with David Frost?
17 Which Addicts are quizzed by Noel Edmonds?
18 Which Michael presents "Strike It Lucky"?
19 Which show tests contestants on what things cost in the shops?
20 What must you Play Right in the show with Bruce Forsyth?
21 Which international show was also called "Jeux Sans Frontières"?
22 Which show was based on the parlour game charades?
23 Which Roy presents "Catchphrase"?
24 What must Every Second do in the show with Paul Daniels?
25 In which show might you compete with Amazon, Rhino, Jet and Wolf?
26 What might you Raise in the show with Bob Holness?
27 Which Phillip presents "Talking Telephone Numbers"?
28 Who presents "Masterchef"?
29 Which Des presented the revamped "Take Your Pick"?
30 Chris Evans told his audience, Don't Forget Your what?

Quiz 87 Pot-Luck 45

Answers - see page 93

Level 1

1 What size was Tim in "A Christmas Carol"?
2 What is the zodiac sign of the Goat?
3 What is held in a creel?
4 Who had a No 1 hit with the song "Lady In Red"?
5 What did Al Capone have on his face that gave him his nickname?
6 What two colours are on the flag waved at the end of a motor race?
7 In nursery rhyme, where did Mary's little lamb follow her to?
8 In which way did the village of Los Barcos become famous?
9 Which half of Robson and Jerome played the part of Paddy Garvey?
10 What were Liberius, Sissinius and Constantine?
11 In the political sector, what does MEP stand for?
12 Who backed B. Bumble?
13 The ancient city of Troy is in which modern country?
14 Who founded the Methodist movement?
15 What do sprinters start from in a track race?
16 Who ordered the execution of Mary Queen of Scots?
17 What do volleyball players hit the ball with?
18 According to the proverb, what does the devil make work for?
19 Which rugby nation was readmitted to international competition in 1993?
20 What type of food is a pomelo?
21 What is another name for a cavy?
22 Who said, "You cannot be serious!"?
23 What was the eighth month of the Roman calendar?
24 Which Olympic water sport includes twists, tucks and pikes?
25 Who recorded the original track "Stairway To Heaven"?
26 Which race meeting is as famous for its hats as for its horses?
27 What letter features on a snooker table?
28 What type of food is gazpacho?
29 How is Western actor Marion Morrison better known?
30 Who is Griff Rhys-Jones' comic partner?

Answers

Pot-Luck 44 (see Quiz 85)
1 A young salmon. 2 Friendship (From Anything Goes). 3 Mexico. 4 Henry II. 5 Balaclava. 6 Two. 7 Copper. 8 Rovers' Return. 9 August. 10 Prunes. 11 Leech. 12 Björk. 13 School. 14 Banana and toffee. 15 Duck. 16 Vertigo. 17 Avon. 18 Contour lines. 19 Six. 20 Keith. 21 Gander. 22 Cornwall. 23 Denny Laine. 24 Charles Dickens. 25 American. 26 Cat. 27 33. 28 No. 29 Dagwood. 30 Flax.

Quiz 88 Cricket

Answers - see page 94

Level 1

1 Garner and Roberts were pacemen for which international team?
2 The Oval is the home of which county?
3 What bird is linked to a score of nought?
4 Which 1990s English Test pace bowler has the same first name as an English county?
5 Which county has been captained by Mike Atherton?
6 Which Donald became the first Australian to score 300 test runs in a day?
7 At most, how many wickets can fall in a two innings game?
8 Which former England all-rounder earned the nickname "Beefy"?
9 Which term describes a ball bowled out of the striker's reach?
10 Graeme Hick is an international for which country?
11 How many stumps are there on a set of wickets?
12 Which county side comes from Wales?
13 What term describes fielders positioned closely behind the batsmen?
14 Grace Road is the ground of which county?
15 What must an umpire raise to show that a player is out?
16 Which country did all rounder Richard Hadlee play for?
17 What is the surname of Australian brothers Gregg and Ian?
18 Which county side did Fred Trueman play most of his cricket for?
19 Which West Indian batsman Brian started rewriting the record books in 1994?
20 What is added to the scores of the batsmen to make the total?
21 What does the abbreviation "st" stand for?
22 Which country did Abdul Qadir play for?
23 If the umpire raises both arms above his head what is he signalling?
24 What is a batsman said to collect if he scores 0 twice in a match?
25 Which radio commentator is known as 'Aggers'?
26 Which Warwickshire ground hosts Test cricket?
27 Lillee and Thomson formed a deadly pace attack for which country?
28 Can a Test Match end in a tie?
29 Which country do Donald, McMillan and Cronje play for?
30 Which Australian tycoon started a 'circus' in the 1970s?

Answers

TV: The Game Shows (see Quiz 86)
1 Big Break. 2 The Generation Game. 3 Blockbusters. 4 Countdown. 5 Terry Wogan. 6 Blind Date. 7 Bullseye. 8 Celebrity Squares. 9 Cluedo. 10 Crystal. 11 Family. 12 Krypton. 13 Matthew Kelly. 14 Campbell. 15 Anneka Rice. 16 Keyhole. 17 Telly. 18 Barrymore. 19 The Price is Right. 20 Your Cards. 21 It's A Knockout. 22 Give Us A Clue. 23 Walker. 24 Count. 25 Gladiators. 26 Roof. 27 Schofield. 28 Loyd Grossman. 29 O'Connor. 30 Toothbrush.

Quiz 89 Pot-Luck 46

Level 1

Answers - see page 99

1 "Up Where We Belong" was the theme from which film?
2 What is the currency of Italy?
3 What is another name for the wildebeeste?
4 What word goes before glove, hound and trot?
5 What is Ryan O'Neal's actress daughter called?
6 Which English queen never married?
7 In rhyming slang what is a north and south?
8 How is Terry Nelhams better known?
9 What was the name of the Elephant Man?
10 To ten years either way, when was the Automobile Association formed?
11 In the plant world, what do the letters RHS stand for ?
12 Between which two African countries are the Victoria Falls?
13 Which country is golfer Ian Woosnam from?
14 Gemma Jones became the Duchess of where?
15 What does the word hirsute mean?
16 What word relates to Enya, The Wombles and Venezuela?
17 In feet how wide is a hockey goal?
18 Who wrote "Little Men"?
19 Which major river flows through New Orleans?
20 Whose last words were, "Thank God I have done my duty"?
21 Which country did General Franco rule?
22 Which sisters recorded "I'm In The Mood For Dancing"?
23 Which Hertfordshire town was Britain's first Garden City?
24 What can be HT, floribunda or a rambler?
25 Which word can mean suspicious or to do with seafood?
26 Where is the Sea of Showers?
27 Which king would have been blown up if the Gunpowder Plot had succeeded?
28 For which sport is Lennox Lewis famous?
29 Which purple precious gem is the birthstone for February?
30 Which game is connected with Boris Schapiro?

Answers

Pot-Luck 47 (see Quiz 91)
1 Get Smart. 2 Birds Of A Feather. 3 Prescott. 4 Rabbit. 5 Rose. 6 Banjos. 7 ET. 8 Sylvia's Mother. 9 Four. 10 Pressure of gases. 11 March. 12 Toad. 13 Flora. 14 J.R.R. 15 Spiderman. 16 Motor racing. 17 Birmingham. 18 Abbot and Costello Go To Mars. 19 Police. 20 Shoulders. 21 Emperor. 22 12. 23 Tin Pan Alley. 24 Three. 25 The clubhouse. 26 The first dog in space. 27 Eddie Calvert. 28 Fireball XL5. 29 Wembley. 30 Heavy Goods Vehicle.

1 The Bay of Biscay lies to the north of which country?
2 Which Gulf lies between Iran and Saudi Arabia?
3 Brittany is part of which country?
4 Which US city is known by its initials LA?
5 Which South American country shares its name with a nut?
6 Near which large city is the Wirral?
7 Which is Britain's most southerly point on the mainland?
8 In which country is Shanghai?
9 In which county is Lake Windermere?
10 To which country does the island of Bermuda belong?
11 The state of the Vatican is in which city?
12 Is San Francisco on the east or west coast of the USA?
13 Which Union was Ukraine once part of?
14 In which country is Zurich?
15 In which country is the holiday destination of Bali?
16 Which island lies to the south of India?
17 In which country would you hear the language Afrikaans?
18 Which group of islands does Gran Canaria belong to?
19 Where would you be if you had climbed Mount Olympus?
20 In which US state is Orlando?
21 Which Ocean is to the west of Portugal?
22 In which country is The Hague?
23 Monte Carlo is in which principality?
24 Which US state has the Arctic Circle running through it?
25 Which Land in Denmark is made up of bricks?
26 Which Falls are on the Canadian/US border?
27 Which country's women might wear a kimono?
28 Which Ocean's name means peaceful?
29 Which country originally produced Peugeot cars?
30 What is the English for what the French call an autoroute?

Answers

Scientists and Inventors (see Quiz 92)
1 Penicillin. 2 X-rays. 3 Greek. 4 Bunsen burner. 5 Curie. 6 Albert. 7 Temperature. 8 Halley. 9 Stephen. 10 Newton. 11 Italian. 12 The atom. 13 Nicotine. 14 Darwin. 15 Microscope. 16 Rutherford. 17 Temperature. 18 Leonardo Da Vinci. 19 Edison. 20 Grass. 21 Attenborough. 22 Atom. 23 Antiseptic. 24 Morris. 25 Blood. 26 Weaving. 27 Pea. 28 Africa. 29 Steam. 30 Spinning Jenny.

Quiz 91 Pot-Luck 47

Answers - see page 97

1 In which secret agent spoof did Agent 99 appear?
2 In which TV programme do Sharon, Tracey and Dorien appear?
3 Which John became deputy Labour leader under Tony Blair?
4 What kind of animal features in the book "Watership Down"?
5 What flower is the emblem of the Labour Party?
6 Which instruments were featured in the hit single that came from the film "Deliverance"?
7 Who used a children's computer to 'phone home'?
8 Who did Dr Hook speak to when trying to get through to Sylvia?
9 What number does the Roman numeral IV stand for?
10 What is measured by a manometer?
11 In which month is St David's Day?
12 What type of animal is a natterjack?
13 Which Roman goddess of flowers is the name of a brand of margarine?
14 What are the initials of writer Tolkien?
15 What superhero can Peter Parker turn into?
16 Which sport does Murray Walker comment on?
17 Which city do Aston Villa come from?
18 In which film do Abbott and Costello land on Venus?
19 What are Sting, Stewart Copeland and Andy Summers better known as?
20 On what part of your body would you wear a stole?
21 What is the world's largest species of penguin called?
22 In a pack of cards how many jacks' eyes can be seen?
23 London's Denmark Street acquired which nickname?
24 In "Fifteen To One" how many contestants take part in the final round?
25 Where is the 19th hole on an 18 hole golf course?
26 Who or what was Laika?
27 Who was the man with the golden trumpet?
28 Which spacecraft was commanded by Steve Zodiac?
29 In which stadium did England win the 1966 World Cup Final?
30 What do the initials HGV stand for?

Answers

Pot-Luck 46 (see Quiz 89)
1 An Officer And A Gentleman. 2 Lira. 3 Gnu. 4 Fox. 5 Tatum. 6 Elizabeth I. 7 Mouth. 8 Adam Faith. 9 John Merrick. 10 1905. 11 Royal Horticultural Society. 12 Zimbabwe and Zambia. 13 Wales. 14 Duke Street. 15 Hairy. 16 Orinoco. 17 12. 18 Louisa M. Alcott. 19 Mississippi. 20 Horatio Nelson. 21 Spain. 22 Nolan. 23 Welwyn. 24 A rose. 25 Fishy. 26 On the moon. 27 James I. 28 Boxing. 29 Amethyst. 30 Bridge.

1 Which drug is Alexander Fleming famous for discovering?
2 Which rays for examining the inside of the body did Röntgen discover?
3 What nationality was philosopher and scientist Aristotle?
4 What was Robert Bunsen famous for?
5 Which Pierre and Marie discovered radium?
6 What was the first name of German scientist Einstein?
7 Fahrenheit is associated with the measurement of what?
8 Which astronomer gave his name to the comet seen every 76 years?
9 What is the first name of physicist Hawking?
10 Which Sir Isaac discovered the law of gravity?
11 What was the nationality of astronomer Galileo?
12 What was Ernest Rutherford the first man to split?
13 Which juice did Jean Nicot extract from tobacco?
14 Which biologist Charles studied the evolution of the species?
15 Which instrument to magnify small objects was invented by Jansen?
16 Which Ernest discovered alpha, beta and gamma rays?
17 What does the scale named after Anders Celsius measure?
18 Which Italian painter drew early ideas for a helicopter?
19 Which American Thomas developed the light bulb?
20 Flymo developed a machine based on the hovercraft for cutting what?
21 Which naturalist Sir David has a film director brother Richard?
22 What did John Dalton define as the smallest particle of substance?
23 What did Lister discover which stopped wounds becoming septic?
24 Which zoologist Desmond broadcast discoveries about man in "The Naked Ape" and "The Human Zoo"?
25 What did Harvey discover is pumped round the body?
26 What was Kay's Flying Shuttle used for in 1733?
27 What is a common vegetable and flower used by Mendel in his theories on genetics?
28 On which continent have the Leakey family made discoveries about man's evolution?
29 What type of engines did George Stephenson develop?
30 What Spinning invention was named after its creator's daughter?

Quiz 93 Pot-Luck 48

Answers - see page 103

1 What name is given to the art of clipping hedges into shapes?
2 How many days in two non-leap years?
3 Which country is a car from if it has the international registration letter P?
4 Who came first as Prime Minister, Macmillan or Chamberlain?
5 Which fruit is used to make the drink kirsch?
6 In darts, what is the highest score from three different trebles?
7 U is the symbol of which chemical element?
8 In "EastEnders" what did Michelle Fowler call her little girl?
9 What kind of creature is a flying fox?
10 How many miles are there in eight kilometres?
11 What type of canoe is spelt the same backwards and forwards?
12 Who recorded the album "So Far So Good"?
13 What is the word for a group of squirrels?
14 Which pop star began legal preceedings against Sony in 1993?
15 Which woodland area of Hampshire is noted for its ponies?
16 What is the name of the BBC's Birmingham studios?
17 Which German philosopher Karl wrote "Das Kapital"?
18 Who was Hare's grave-robbing partner in the 19th century?
19 How many sides in 15 triangles?
20 What is the name of TV cook Berry?
21 What is a male rabbit called?
22 Whom did Zoe Ball replace as presenter of "The Big Breakfast"?
23 What sort of food is Bel Paese?
24 How many athletes are there in an Olympic relay team?
25 What is the opposite of alkali?
26 What traditionally did a fletcher make?
27 What is the first word in the original TV theme song for "Neighbours"?
28 Who rolled down the hill last, Jack or Jill?
29 Who is chat show host Alan Partridge?
30 What part of the human body is treated by a dermatologist?

Answers

Around Ireland (see Quiz 97)
1 Eire. 2 Lake. 3 Irish Sea. 4 Belfast. 5 Emerald Isle. 6 Shamrock. 7 Dublin. 8 Punt. 9 Limerick. 10 Whiskey. 11 Atlantic. 12 Irish and English. 13 Crystal. 14 Galway. 15 Blarney Stone. 16 Kildare. 17 Horse racing. 18 Linen. 19 Patrick. 20 Whiskey and cream. 21 Tweed. 22 East. 23 Ferry ports. 24 Green. 25 Air. 26 Londonderry. 27 Cork. 28 Giant's Causeway. 29 Guinness 30 IRL.

Quiz 94 Painters and Sculptors

Answers - see page 104

1 Which John painted "The Haywain"?
2 What was the surname of outrageous artist Salvador?
3 Which city, famous for its canals, did Canaletto paint?
4 What was the first name of Impressionist painter Cézanne?
5 Which Leonardo painted Mona Lisa?
6 Which parts of the Venus de Milo are missing?
7 Which animals is George Stubbs famous for painting?
8 Which Paul was famous for paintings of the South Seas?
9 Which Vincent lost an ear?
10 What was the first name of pop artist Warhol?
11 How is Francisco de Goya y Lucientes more simply known?
12 Which Greek artist's name means 'The Greek'?
13 Which Spanish painter Pablo was the founder of Cubism?
14 Who was famous for his posters of French dance halls and cabarets?
15 What was the nationality of Rembrandt?
16 Edouard and Claude were Manet and Monet. Which was which?
17 Which items useful on a rainy day did Renoir paint?
18 Which branch of the arts was Barbara Hepworth famous for?
19 What was the nationality of Albrecht Dürer?
20 Which art gallery is in Trafalgar Square?
21 Who painted the ceiling of the Sistine Chapel?
22 In late 1995 the painting of which Royal caused controversy?
23 What is the first name of pop artist Hockney?
24 Which Tudor king is Hans Holbein famous for painting?
25 Which metal is sculptress Elizabeth Frink famous for using?
26 What was the nationality of portrait painter Millais?
27 Which member of the royal family has had his paintings reproduced on a set of stamps?
28 Which London art gallery was founded with the financial support of a sugar merchant?
29 What is the first name of sculptor Moore?
30 Which English artist is famous for his matchstalk men pictures?

Pot-Luck 50 (see Quiz 96)

Answers
1 Paris. 2 Peseta. 3 Yes and no. 4 USA. 5 James Taylor. 6 Charlton, Wimbledon. 7 Piano. 8 Lulu. 9 David Cornwell. 10 Pig. 11 Earth. 12 Dan Dare. 13 A hurricane. 14 New York Herald. 15 Jason Donovan. 16 SIx. 17 Ardiles and Villa. 18 Suicide Is Painless. 19 Potomac. 20 Horse. 21 Vietnam. 22 Cash on delivery. 23 Trumpet. 24 White. 25 Nigel Hawthorne. 26 Granville. 27 Supersonic. 28 Chris Evert. 29 Cologne. 30 Perry Mason.

1 Which cartoon mouse was Pixie's friend?

2 What is the zodiac sign of Aquarius?

3 "An Unearthly Child" was the first episode of which long-running TV series?

4 Who had a No 1 hit with the song "Bridge Over Troubled Water"?

5 What name is given to a person who makes and sells spectacles?

6 In printing and editing what do the letters UC signify?

7 In nursery rhyme, during which season did the Queen of Hearts make the tarts?

8 Which land does Peter Pan come from?

9 What is a young swan called?

10 Errol Brown is lead singer with which group?

11 What life-threatening thing appeared in London for the last time in 1962?

12 Who played Peter Mayle in BBC's "A Year In Provence"?

13 Called cotton candy in America, what's this sweet named in the UK?

14 Which member of the Mitchell family does Gillian Taylforth play in "EastEnders"?

15 Which Christmas decoration is a parasite of the apple tree?

16 What is the name of the disc used in ice hockey?

17 What vehicles race in the Indianapolis 500?

18 In the Nintendo game what is Mario's job?

19 Which Anneka was challenged on TV?

20 What colour did all lupins used to be?

21 In conservation, what do the letters FOE stand for?

22 Who says, "It's the way I tell 'em!"?

23 What was the ninth month of the Roman calendar?

24 On which day of the week does the Queen distribute Maundy Money?

25 Which part of the foot is between the sole and the heel?

26 What is the wife of an Earl called?

27 What was the first name of Admiral Lord Nelson?

28 Which UK soap staged a murder trial in May 1995?

29 What kind of rays cause a suntan?

30 Who is Steve Punt's comic partner?

Quiz 96 Pot-Luck 50

Answers - see page 102

1 In which city is Orly airport?
2 What is the currency of Spain?
3 What two words cannot be said in the opening section of "Take Your Pick"?
4 The Kentucky Derby is a horse race in which country?
5 Who is Sweet Baby James?
6 Which two London teams have been involved with ground share schemes at Crystal Palace's Selhurst Park?
7 In rhyming slang what is a Joanna?
8 How is Marie McDonald McLaughlin Lawrie better known?
9 What is the real name of John Le Carré?
10 What is a Tamworth a type of?
11 What does the prefix geo mean?
12 With which pilot did Jocelyn Peabody explore space?
13 What destroyed millions of British trees in October 1987?
14 Which newspaper sent Stanley to find Livingstone?
15 Who had a No 1 with "Any Dream Will Do"?
16 How many sides has a cuboid?
17 Which two Argentinian footballers were bought by Spurs after the '78 World Cup?
18 What's the theme song of M*A*S*H?
19 Which major river flows through Washington DC?
20 What do you ride on if you take part in three-day eventing?
21 Which country did Ho Chi Minh rule?
22 What do the initials COD mean?
23 What instrument does Kenny Ball play?
24 What colour gloves does a snooker referee wear?
25 In "The Madness of King George" who played King George?
26 Who is Arkwright, the grocer's assistant?
27 Which word means faster than the speed of sound?
28 Who was the first woman to win four consecutive US Open tennis titles?
29 Which word is a German city and a light perfume?
30 Who does Paul Drake do private investigations for?

Answers

Painters and Sculptors (see Quiz 94)
1 Constable. 2 Dalí. 3 Venice. 4 Paul. 5 Da Vinci. 6 Arms. 7 Horses. 8 Gauguin. 9 Van Gogh. 10 Andy. 11 Goya. 12 El Greco. 13 Picasso. 14 Toulouse-Lautrec. 15 Dutch. 16 Edouard Manet, Claude Monet. 17 Umbrellas. 18 Sculpture. 19 German. 20 National Gallery. 21 Michelangelo. 22 Princess of Wales. 23 David. 24 Henry VIII. 25 Bronze. 26 English. 27 Prince Charles. 28 Tate. 29 Henry. 30 L. S. Lowry.

Quiz 97 Around Ireland

Answers - see page 101

Level 1

1 What is another name for the Republic of Ireland?
2 What is Lough the Irish word for?
3 Which Sea is to the east of the Island of Ireland?
4 What is the capital city of Northern Ireland?
5 What sort of jewelled Isle is Ireland often called?
6 Which plant is the Irish emblem?
7 What is the capital of the Republic of Ireland?
8 What is the currency of the Republic of Ireland?
9 Which Irish town gives its name to a saucy rhyme?
10 Spell the Irish version of the drink the Scots call whisky ?
11 Which Ocean is to the west of Ireland?
12 What are Ireland's two official languages?
13 Which type of glass is Waterford famous for?
14 Which Irish flute player James shares his name with a Bay ?
15 Which stone is kissed to receive the gift of smooth talking?
16 Which county shares its name with a fictional TV doctor?
17 Which sport is the Curragh famous for?
18 Which fabric made from flax is Ireland famous for?
19 Who is the patron saint of Ireland?
20 What do you put into Gaelic coffee apart from coffee?
21 Which fabric is Donegal famous for?
22 Is Belfast on the east or the west of the province?
23 What do the towns of Dun Laoghaire and Rosslare have in common?
24 Which colour is associated with Ireland?
25 How would you be travelling if you arrived at Shannon from abroad?
26 Which is further north, Belfast or Londonderry?
27 Which Irish town sounds like something in a wine bottle neck?
28 Which Causeway is said to have been built as a bridge from Ireland to Scotland?
29 Which stout is Dublin world-famous for?
30 What are the international registration letters for Ireland?

Quiz 98 Pot-Luck 51

Answers - see page 108

Level 1

1 In which country was Sid James born?
2 In which TV programme do Arthur Daley and Terry McCann appear?
3 Which John is a snooker player from Liverpool?
4 Who was the last Viceroy of India?
5 On TV, who played Ryder, the narrator in "Brideshead Revisited"?
6 Which colourless, odourless light gas is used to lift airships?
7 Where in London is the Central Criminal Court?
8 In boxing what do the letters TKO stand for?
9 To a year each way, when was "The Generation Game" first shown?
10 Who created "The Flintstones"?
11 In which month is the Spring Bank Holiday?
12 Which Comic charity promoted National Red Nose Day?
13 How is Marian Fitzwalter more usually known?
14 What are the initials of Victorian writer Mr Gilbert?
15 What is the oldest university in the USA?
16 What was the 'profession' of Captain Kidd?
17 Who rode The Pie to victory to win the Grand National?
18 In which game do the players need glass balls?
19 Who wrote "Filthy, Rich and Catflap"?
20 Which three Lloyd brothers have played at Wimbledon?
21 Sid Vicious was a member of which punk band?
22 Which magazine did Hugh Hefner found?
23 Which sport did Bill Beaumont play?
24 What is a young badger called?
25 Which character did Harry Enfield play in the first series of "Men Behaving Badly"?
26 Which type of headgear did Procol Harum sing about?
27 What type of party or social gathering is for women only?
28 What was the nickname of TV cook Graham Kerr?
29 In boxing which weight is between fly and feather?
30 Professor Geoffrey Hoyt operates at which hospital?

Pot-Luck 52 (see Quiz 100)
1 A puppet dog. 2 720. 3 Noel Coward. 4 Edward II. 5 Agony Again. 6 Wireless licence fee. 7 Silver. 8 Daniel. 9 Reginald Perrin. 10 Van Morrison. 11 Cheryl Baker. 12 Bryan Adams. 13 Birds. 14 Pete Best. 15 Neil Diamond. 16 Nancy Sinatra. 17 The Balkan Trilogy. 18 Mowgli. 19 Scaffold. 20 Sophie. 21 Square. 22 The conundrum. 23 Toothpaste. 24 Golf. 25 Ealing comedies. 26 All five of them. 27 All Blacks. 28 Crowther. 29 Six. 30 The Shadows.

Quiz 99   Sounds of the 90s
Level 1
Answers - see page 109

1 Where was Love in the 1994 record breaking hit by Wet Wet Wet?
2 Who had a No1 hit with "Ice Ice Baby"?
3 Who had a hit with the old Osmonds hit "Love Me For a Reason"?
4 Who had a hit in 1992 with "I Will Always Love You", the theme from "The Bodyguard"?
5 Which part of East London sang "Stay Another Day" in 1994 ?
6 Quite simply, what colour is Mick Hucknall's group?
7 Which two squaddies had new hits with old songs?
8 Which pop singer received a knighthood in 1995?
9 Who On The Block were Hangin' Tough in 1990?
10 Who said Any Dream Will Do in his Technicolor Dreamcoat?
11 Whose Sister asked you to Stay in 1992?
12 Who wore Crocodile Shoes in 1994?
13 Who took a Stairway to Heaven before going to Animal Hospital?
14 Who joined George Michael on "Don't Let the Sun Go Down On Me"?
15 "Everything I Do (I Do It For You)" came from a film about which hero?
16 During which conflict was the record "Get Here" a UK Forces favourite?
17 Where were Eternal just a step from in 1994?
18 Which Streets did Bruce Springsteen sing about in 1994?
19 Which 90s band sounds like a fertile spot in the desert?
20 Who is known as The Violin Player?
21 Which Michael sang about Love is a Wonderful Thing?
22 What nationality is Björk?
23 Who had a No 1 with the "Shoop Shoop Song"?
24 Which cartoon group had a No 1 with "Do The Bartman"?
25 Which Ebenezer was in the tile of the song by The Shamen?
26 Which rock star did Elvis Presley's daughter marry?
27 Which band had a top hit with "Country House"?
28 Which night did Whigfield sing about ?
29 Who sang with PJ on the hit "Let's Get Ready to Rhumble"?
30 Who left the role of Hattie in "EastEnders" to take up a pop career?

Quiz 100 Pot-Luck 52

Answers - see page 106

1 On TV who or what was Fred Barker?
2 How many minutes in half a day?
3 Who wrote "Don't Let's be Beastly to the Germans"?
4 Who came first, Edward II or George II?
5 What was the follow up to "Agony" with Maureen Lipman?
6 What was introduced at ten shillings in 1922 and doubled in 1946?
7 Ag is the symbol of which chemical element ?
8 In "Coronation Street" what is Ken and Denise's little boy called?
9 David Nobbs created which character made famous by Leonard Rossiter?
10 Who was lead singer with Them?
11 Who went from Bucks Fizz to "Record Breakers"?
12 Who recorded the album "So far So Good"?
13 Avian relates to which kind of creatures?
14 Who did Ringo Starr replace as drummer with The Beatles?
15 How is Noah Kominsky better known?
16 Who sang with Frank Sinatra on the No 1 "Something Stupid"?
17 Which Trilogy was written by Olivia Manning?
18 What was the name of the boy in Disney's "The Jungle Book"?
19 How were Roger McGough, Mike McGear and John Gorman collectively known?
20 What is the first name of TV cook Grigson?
21 What shape is a boxing ring?
22 What is the final round of "Countdown" called?
23 What was advertised in the first TV 'natural break'?
24 What game is played at St Andrews?
25 "Passport to Pimlico" was the first in the series of which British made films?
26 How many Wimbledon champions retained their 1983 titles in 1984?
27 What is the nickname of the New Zealand rugby team?
28 Which Leslie introduced "The Price Is Right" on UK TV?
29 How many time zones does Canada have?
30 Which group backed Cliff Richard in the 1960s?

Pot-Luck 51 (see Quiz 98)
1 South Africa. 2 Minder. 3 Parrott. 4 Lord Mountbatten. 5 Jeremy Irons.
6 Helium. 7 Old Bailey. 8 Technical Knock Out. 9 1971. 10 Hanna-Barbera.
11 May. 12 Relief. 13 Maid Marian. 14 W.S. 15 Harvard 16 Pirate.
17 Velvet Brown (in the film National Velvet). 18 Marbles. 19 Ben Elton.
20 David, John and Tony. 21 The Sex Pistols. 22 Playboy. 23 Rugby.
24 Cub. 25 Dermot. 26 Homburg. 27 Hen. 28 The Galloping Gourmet.
29 Bantam. 30 Henry Park Hospital (in Medics).

Answers

Quiz 101 Sport - the 90s

Answers - see page 107

Level 1

1 In motor racing, who became the 1992 champion world driver?
2 Which Paul burst into tears after England went out of the 1990 World Cup?
3 Which team were cricket county champions in 1991 and 1992?
4 Which Nick won the British Open in 1990 and 1992?
5 Which tennis player was stabbed while on court?
6 In 1994 which rugby playing Gavin was made an OBE?
7 Which Scottish soccer side monopolized the championship throughout the first half of the 1990s?
8 Which Phil was world darts champion in 1990 and 1992?
9 Which country returned to playing international sport in the 90s?
10 Which England soccer manager became known as a turnip?
11 Which steeplechase did Party Politics win in election year 1992?
12 Which rugby league team won the Challenge Cup every year for the first half of the 1990s?
13 Which Sally won Olympic gold in the 400-metre hurdles?
14 Which manager left Arsenal after taking a 'bung'?
15 Why did no horse win the 1993 Grand National?
16 What is the first name of athlete Akabusi?
17 At which sport did Karen Pickering excel?
18 Which country did Sonia O'Sullivan race for?
19 Which former Villa player David became England's soccer captain?
20 What does Alberto Tomba wear on his feet when he competes?
21 Who does Mary Pierce play tennis for?
22 Which country is snooker star Stephen Hendry from?
23 Which Kenny took Blackburn to the Premiership championship?
24 What is the first name of athlete Regis?
25 Which Miss Martinez beat Martina in a Wimbledon final?
26 Who won the World Drivers' Championship in 1994–95?
27 Which English team won the European Cup Winners' Cup in 1991?
28 In which event was Jonathan Edwards world champion in 1995?
29 What does Steve Backley throw?
30 Which soccer nation were surprise winners of the 1992 European championship?

Answers

Sounds of the 90s (see Quiz 99)
1 All Around. 2 Vanilla Ice. 3 Boyzone. 4 Whitney Houston. 5 East 17. 6 Red. 7 Robson and Jerome. 8 Cliff Richard. 9 New Kids. 10 Jason Donovan. 11 Shakespear's. 12 Jimmy Nail. 13 Rolf Harris. 14 Elton John. 15 Robin Hood. 16 Gulf War. 17 Heaven. 18 Philadelphia. 19 Oasis. 20 Vanessa Mae. 21 Bolton. 22 Icelandic. 23 Cher. 24 The Simpsons. 25 Goode. 26 Michael Jackson. 27 Blur. 28 Saturday. 29 Duncan. 30 Michelle Gayle.

109

Quiz 102 Pot-Luck 53

Level 1

Answers - see page 112

1 What was stored in Fort Knox?
2 What name is shared by TV presenter Cheryl and actor Tom?
3 How much does it cost to buy a station on a British Monopoly board?
4 Who had a No 1 hit with the song "Bohemian Rhapsody"?
5 Who played Aunt Sally on TV in "Worzel Gummidge"?
6 How many strings are there on a Spanish guitar?
7 How did the notorious witchfinder Matthew Hopkins die?
8 In which show was there a feature called "Double or Drop"?
9 Where would you travel to find the Sea of Tranquillity?
10 On which special day in 1964 was "Top of the Pops" first transmitted?
11 In the military sector, what does TA stand for?
12 In which sport does the scoring begin at 15?
13 Called thumbtack in America, what's the name of this in the UK?
14 What game have Spassky, Fischer and Karpov played?
15 What type of hat was worn by Sherlock Holmes?
16 Which sisters had snakes on their heads in place of hair?
17 What was the 'Flying Scotsman'?
18 What are you interested in if you study calligraphy?
19 In sailing, what is a warp?
20 What type of food is a profiterole?
21 In which country was Shergar kidnapped?
22 Who said, "Just like that!"?
23 What was the seventh month of the Roman calendar?
24 Which Russian ruler was known as 'the Terrible'?
25 Which 'copper' tree has reddish brown leaves?
26 What was the surname of landscape gardener Capability?
27 Which musical instrument is played by Larry Adler?
28 Who recorded "Sultans Of Swing"?
29 In mythology what is Neptune the god of?
30 Who is Stephen Fry's comic partner?

Answers

TV - The 90s (see Quiz 104)
1 Jennifer Saunders. 2 Soldier Soldier. 3 Time. 4 Baywatch. 5 The Big Breakfast. 6 Leisure Centre. 7 Lenny Henry. 8 Cracker 9 Of May. 10 Dead Donkey. 11 Spain. 12 Goodnight. 13 Police officer. 14 Cards. 15 Eliott. 16 Hurts. 17 Atkinson. 18 Noel Edmonds. 19 Doctors. 20 Nesbitt. 21 Horses. 22 Twin. 23 Year. 24 Hetty. 25 Yes. 26 Stars. 27 Dibley. 28 Panorama. 29 Jill Dando. 30 Rolf Harris.

Quiz 103　Pot Luck 54

Level 1

Answers - see page 113

1　Which English county did ex Australian captain Allan Border play for?
2　In Parliament what was known as DORA?
3　In sport, who are The Blades?
4　In which musical does the song "Somewhere" appear?
5　Which steam bath originated in Finland?
6　What are protective eyeglasses called?
7　Which comedian created Monsieur Hulot?
8　The Tates and the Campbells appeared in which soap?
9　What is the theme song for "Absolutely Fabulous"?
10　Which dance goes, one-two-three-hop?
11　What is the prompting device used by TV presenters called?
12　What did UXB stand for in "Danger UXB"?
13　Who won the world professional snooker championship for the first time back in 1972?
14　In which House was James Herriot's veterinary practice?
15　Which MP has won two Oscars?
16　Who wrote "The History of Mr Polly"?
17　To five years either way, when was the first LP released commercially in Britain?
18　Which Michael Miles quiz show was revived in the 1990s?
19　Robin Cousins won an Olympic gold medal in which artistic sport?
20　Who created The Muppets?
21　Which piece of furniture is Benjamin Franklin credited with creating?
22　Which sit com shared its name with a food called the staff of life?
23　The Diamond Sculls takes place at which sporting event?
24　What is a group of five performers called?
25　Which sport do the Harlem Globetrotters play?
26　In soccer, which country did Eusebio play for?
27　On TV how is Granny Smith better known?
28　What is the nationality of Tom Conti?
29　Which cookery programme does Fern Britton host?
30　In modern times, how often have the Olympic Games been cancelled due to war?

Answers

Pot Luck 55 (see Quiz 105)
1 Ork. 2 Dave. 3 Two. 4 Gladioli. 5 Mae West. 6 England. 7 John Bunyan.
8 Albatross. 9 South Pacific. 10 Pastry. 11 The Beach Boys. 12 Marie Curie.
13 Panorama. 14 Sheena Easton. 15 Miss Marple. 16 Michael Fish.
17 Boom Bang-a-Bang. 18 Richard Beckinsale. 19 Phil Redmond.
20 Golden Labrador. 21 David Cassidy. 22 Canada. 23 Canada.
24 Baseball. 25 Les Dawson. 26 Dollar. 27 Two. 28 Tobacco smoke.
29 Maria. 30 Eddie Fitzgerald.

1 Who plays Edina in "Absolutely Fabulous"?
2 In which series did Robson and Jerome star?
3 What Goes By in the sit com with Jean and Lionel?
4 What is the series about LA lifeguards called?
5 What is the Channel 4 Breakfast programme called?
6 In "The Brittas Empire" what is Gordon manager of?
7 Who is the comedian husband of Dawn French who stars in "Chef!"?
8 Which series starred Robbie Coltrane as a police psychologist?
9 Which Darling Buds starred David Jason and Pam Ferris?
10 What did you Drop in the series about a newsroom?
11 In which country was "Eldorado" set?
12 What was said to Sweetheart in the series with Nicholas Lyndhurst?
13 What is Nick's job in "Heartbeat"?
14 What was the House made of in the political drama?
15 Which fashion House did Beatrice and Evangeline head?
16 What does Love do in the drama with Adam Faith and Zoë Wanamaker?
17 Which Rowan played the bumbling Mr Bean?
18 Who hosted a crazy Saturday night House Party?
19 What was the profession of Jack and Beth in "Peak Practice"?
20 Which Rab C. was a Glasgow street philosopher?
21 Which animals was the series "Trainer" about?
22 Which Peaks provided a mysterious soap series in 1990–91?
23 How long did Peter Mayle spend in Provence?
24 What was the first name of private detective Mrs Wainthropp?
25 Did summer precede winter in Delia Smith's cookery collections?
26 What did contestants have In Their Eyes in the impersonation show?
27 Dawn French played the vicar of which parish?
28 On which long-running current affairs programme did the Princess of Wales give her first solo interview in 1995?
29 Which Breakfast News presenter took over the Holiday programme?
30 Which Australian presented "Animal Hospital"?

Quiz 105 Pot Luck 55

Answers - see page 111

Level 1

1 Which planet did Mork come from?
2 Who is Cockney Chas's singing partner?
3 How many heads did Dr Doolittle's llama have?
4 What are Dame Edna Everage's favourite flowers?
5 Which blonde sex symbol used the pseudonym Jane Mast?
6 Which is the largest country in Great Britain?
7 Who wrote "Pilgrim's Progress"?
8 Which is the only bird capable of flying all day without flapping its wings?
9 "There is Nothing Like A Dame" comes from which musical?
10 What is something wrapped in if it is served "en croûte"?
11 Which 60s group was formed by the Wilson brothers?
12 Who was the first person known to have died from radiation poisoning?
13 Which word for a wide view is the name of a TV news programme?
14 Which singer was launched into "The Big Time" by Esther Rantzen?
15 Which character has been played by Margaret Rutherford and Joan Hickson?
16 Who assured viewers there were no hurricanes on the way in 1987?
17 Which song did Lulu sing in the Eurovision Song Contest?
18 In "Porridge" who played Ronnie Barker's cell mate?
19 Who created "Brookside"?
20 Which breed of puppy advertises Andrex bathroom tissue?
21 Who shot to fame in the 70s as Keith Partridge?
22 In which country is the Jasper National Park?
23 Which country does snooker star Cliff Thorburn come from?
24 Which sport do the Pittsburgh Pirates play?
25 Which comedian created the character of Cosmo Smallpiece?
26 What is the currency of Australia?
27 How many times did Barry Sheene win the 500cc world motor cycle racing championship?
28 What do you dislike if you are misocapnic?
29 What is Mia short for in Mia Farrow's name?
30 What is the full name of the Coltrane character in "Cracker"?

Pot-Luck 54 (see Quiz 103)
1 Essex. 2 Defence Of the Realm Act. 3 Sheffield United. 4 West Side Story. 5 Sauna. 6 Goggles. 7 Jacques Tati. 8 Soap. 9 Wheel's On Fire. 10 Polka. 11 Autocue. 12 Unexploded Bomb. 13 Alex Higgins. 14 Skeldale House. 15 Glenda Jackson. 16 H.G. Wells. 17 1950. 18 Take Your Pick. 19 Ice skating. 20 Jim Henson. 21 Rocking chair. 22 Bread. 23 Henley Regatta. 24 Quintet. 25 Basketball. 26 Portugal. 27 Supergran. 28 Scottish. 29 Ready Steady Cook. 30 Three - 1916, 1940, 1944.

Answers

1 Which party won a fourth consecutive term of office in the UK in 1992?
2 Which Middle Eastern country was defeated in the Gulf War?
3 Which country was reunified in 1990?
4 Who became Deputy Prime Minister of the UK in 1995?
5 Which Manchester jail was the scene of rioting in 1990?
6 Which envoy of the Archbishop of Canterbury was released from the Lebanon?
7 Which three times winner of the Grand National died?
8 Which rock legend's daughter did Michael Jackson marry?
9 Who succeeded Barbara Bush as the USA's First Lady?
10 Which Dimbleby interviewed the Prince of Wales on TV?
11 Who was the first female presenter of the National Lottery Live?
12 Which member of the royal family divorced and remarried?
13 Which Labour leader resigned after the 1992 General Election?
14 Assassinated Prime Minister Rabin was from which country?
15 Which tax was abandoned in favour of the Council Tax?
16 Which country won the Eurovision Contest in consecutive years in the first half of the decade?
17 Who described 1992 as an annus horribilis?
18 Which heavyweight boxing champion served a prison sentence?
19 Which media magnate drowned in mysterious circumstances?
20 George Carey succeeded Robert Runcie in which post?
21 Jill Morrell conducted a campaign to free which Beirut hostage?
22 Who became president of South Africa in 1994?
23 Which US singer celebrated his 80th birthday in December 1995?
24 Benazir Bhutto returned as prime minister of which Asian country?
25 Which Boris became president of the Russian Federation in 1991?
26 Which meat was at the heart of a scare about BSE?
27 Which link between England and France was opened?
28 Which American football star was acquitted of his wife's murder?
29 The imprisonment of Nick Leeson followed the collapse of which bank?
30 What replaced TV am as ITV's weekly breakfast programme?

Quiz 107 Pot-Luck 56

Answers - see page 117

1 Which Glasgow comedian is married to actress Pamela Stephenson?
2 Who were the parents of Cain, Able and Seth?
3 Which was the first British soccer side to win the European Cup?
4 What is the flavour of Tia Maria?
5 Which Joyce said, "George, don't do that!"
6 In snooker, what is the score from potting the pink?
7 N is the symbol of which chemical element ?
8 In "EastEnders" who is Kathy Mitchell's son by Pete Beale?
9 What is the second month of the year to have exactly 30 days?
10 What name is shared by radio/TV presenter Chris and "Dynasty" actress Linda?
11 In England, where is the National Water Sports Centre?
12 Who recorded the album "A Night At The Opera"?
13 How much was a groat worth?
14 Who hosted "The Last Resort"?
15 What was special about the size of the disc developed by Philips and Sony in the late 1970s?
16 Which two fruits were crossed to produce a nectarine?
17 In which country did judo develop?
18 Who hosts "Blockbusters"?
19 Which pop star was Jeff Banks married to?
20 What is the first name of TV cook Harris?
21 Who is the patron saint of travellers?
22 A caravan is a group of which animals?
23 In the pop song, who wore a "crimson dress that clings so tight"?
24 Who presents a show from Crinkley Bottom?
25 Who picked up the nickname the 'Louisville Lip'?
26 From which film did Duran Duran get their name?
27 Whose summer residence is at Castel Gandolfo?
28 In which city did the charity Oxfam originate?
29 Who asked Wendy Richard to "Come Outside"?
30 Which fashion item was Imelda Marcos famous for collecting?

Pot-Luck 57 (see Quiz 109) **Answers** 1 The Navy Lark. 2 Richard Gordon. 3 USA. 4 Ram. 5 Deputy Dawg. 6 Bobby Robson. 7 Smoked cod's roe. 8 Campion. 9 Gene Roddenberry. 10 One horse power. 11 Greenland. 12 Sari. 13 Eric Cantona. 14 April Fool's Day. 15 Metro Goldwyn Mayer. 16 An anchor. 17 Derbyshire. 18 Smoke. 19 Barbie. 20 Rudolph Valentino. 21 Antiques. 22 Nettle. 23 The Olympic Games. 24 Sahara. 25 F.B.I. 26 Outside. 27 Snap. 28 New Zealand. 29 Newcastle. 30 Plums.

Level 1

1   Which male star shot to fame in "Four Weddings and a Funeral"?
2   In which film shot in Ireland did Australian Mel Gibson play a Scot?
3   Who had to 'Carry On' 500 years after the discovery of America?
4   In which film did Robin Williams dress up as a Scottish nanny?
5   What was the name of the Dustin Hoffman film about Peter Pan?
6   In which film did Whoopi Golberg first get into the habit?
7   Who joined Walter Matthau in the film "Grumpy Old Men"?
8   What did Schindler draw up in the Spielberg film?
9   What is Beethoven in the 1992 film?
10   What is Casper?
11   Who won an Oscar for "Forrest Gump" and "Philadelphia"?
12   Who starred with Demi Moore in "Ghost"?
13   Who was Whitney Houston's Bodyguard?
14   In which film did Anthony Hopkins play the role of Hannibal Lecter?
15   How was Macaulay Culkin left at Home in 1990?
16   What did the cub Simba become in the 1994 Disney film?
17   What kind of Proposal did Robert Redford make concerning Demi Moore?
18   What was Wrong in the Wallace and Gromit Oscar-winning film?
19   Who was the Pretty Woman in the 1990 film?
20   Who did Harry meet in the film with Billy Crystal?
21   Which Park was the Spielberg film about dinosaurs?
22   Where was someone Sleepless in the film with Meg Ryan?
23   Which Disney release told the story of an American Indian heroine?
24   In which series of films would you find Robin and The Joker?
25   Daniel Day-Lewis starred in the Last of what 1992?
26   In which film was Robin Williams the voice of the genie?
27   Who was Nicole Kidman's co star in "Far and Away" whom she later married?
28   Which Judge does Sylvester Stallone play in the comic cult movie?
29   On which street was there A Miracle in the Xmas movie with Richard Attenborough?
30   What colour is the Eye in the 007 film?

Answers

90s Newsround (see Quiz 106)
1 Conservatives. 2 Iraq. 3 Germany. 4 Michael Heseltine. 5 Strangeways. 6 Terry Waite. 7 Red Rum. 8 Elvis. 9 Hillary Clinton. 10 Jonathan. 11 Anthea Turner. 12 Princess Royal. 13 Neil Kinnock. 14 Israel. 15 Poll tax. 16 Ireland. 17 The Queen. 18 Mike Tyson. 19 Robert Maxwell. 20 Archbishop of Canterbury. 21 John McCarthy. 22 Nelson Mandela. 23 Frank Sinatra. 24 Pakistan. 25 Yeltsin. 26 Beef. 27 Channel Tunnel. 28 OJ Simpson. 29 Barings. 30 GMTV.

Quiz 109 Pot-Luck 57

Answers - see page 115

Level 1

1 Which radio programme featured the saying, "Left hand down a bit"?
2 Who wrote the Doctor comic novels?
3 Which country does tennis player Pete Sampras come from?
4 What is a male sheep called?
5 Who exclaims "Dagnabit!"?
6 Who was manager of Ipswich when they first won the F.A. Cup in '78?
7 What is taramasalata made from?
8 Which sleuth drove round East Anglia in a vintage Lagonda?
9 Who created "Star Trek"?
10 What is 1 Cheval-Vapeur equivalent to?
11 From which country's language does anorak come from?
12 What is a traditional Indian dress called?
13 Who scored the only goal in the 1996 FA Cup Final?
14 Boob Day is the Spanish equivalent of what in Britain?
15 In cinema, what does MGM stand for?
16 What is tattooed on Popeye's arm?
17 Which county did England's wicket keeper Bob Taylor play for?
18 If a sign in Germany announced Rauchen Verboten, what could you not do?
19 In the toy world, who is Ken's girlfriend?
20 Which film star's funeral in 1926 was attended by more than 100,000 mourners?
21 What did Lovejoy deal in?
22 Which stinging weed can be used to make a kind of beer?
23 What was held in Britain in 1908 and 1948?
24 In which desert did Mark Thatcher go missing?
25 Which organisation's motto is "Fidelity, Bravery, Integrity"?
26 Would a Scotsman wear a sporran under or outside the kilt?
27 Which card game involves quickly spotting matching pairs?
28 Which country does former Wimbledon finalist Chris Lewis come from?
29 Which city was "The Tube" broadcast from?
30 What is the drink slivovitz made from?

Pot-Luck 56 (see Quiz 107)

Answers

1 Billy Connolly. 2 Adam and Eve. 3 Celtic. 4 Coffee. 5 Grenfell. 6 Six. 7 Nitrogen. 8 Ian. 9 June. 10 Evans. 11 Nottingham. 12 Queen. 13 4d (four old pence). 14 Jonathan Ross. 15 Compact. 16 Peach and plum. 17 Japan. 18 Bob Holness. 19 Sandie Shaw. 20 Valentina. 21 St Christopher. 22 Camels. 23 Pretty Flamingo. 24 Noel Edmonds. 25 Muhammad Ali. 26 Barbarella. 27 The Pope. 28 Oxford. 29 Mike Same. 30 Shoes.

Quiz 110 Hollywood

Level 1

Answers - see page 120

1 Which singer starred in "The Bodyguard"?
2 Which actress Keaton starred in "Father of the Bride II"?
3 Which actor Tom won Oscars in 1993 and again in 1994?
4 Which Holly won an Oscar for a silent role in "The Piano"?
5 Which silent movie star was played by Robert Downey Jr in 1992?
6 Which Welsh actor starred with Jodie Foster in "The Silence of the Lambs"?
7 Which Bob starred in "Mona Lisa" before finding it 'good to talk'?
8 Which Steven directed "Schindler's List"?
9 Which actor Sylvester has the nickname Sly?
10 Who is Donald Sutherland's actor son?
11 What is the first name of "Pulp Fiction" director Tarantino?
12 Which actress Melanie married Don Johnson – twice?
13 Which Nick co starred with Barbra Streisand in "The Prince of Tides"?
14 What is the first name of actress Sarandon ?
15 Which Johnny starred as Edward Scissorhands?
16 Which Scottish actor Sean has an actor son Jason?
17 Which Emilio starred in "Young Guns" I and II?
18 Which Macaulay became one of the highest-paid child stars ever?
19 Which actress Glenn had a "Fatal Attraction"?
20 Which Al starred in "The Godfather" and "Scent of a Woman"?
21 Which actor Mel was born in the US but brought up in Australia?
22 What is the surname of father and daughter Peter and Bridget?
23 Which Robin became Mrs Doubtfire?
24 Which blond Daryl had adventures with the Invisible Man?
25 Who was Alec Baldwin's real and screen wife in "The Getaway"?
26 What is the first name of Joanne Whalley-Kilmer's husband?
27 Liza Minnelli and Lorna Luft are daughters of which Hollywood great?
28 Which actor succeeded Timothy Dalton as James Bond?
29 Which film director's real name is Allen Stewart Konigsberg?
30 Which actor won an Oscar as director of "Dances with Wolves"?

Answers

Pot-Luck 60 (see Quiz 114)
1 Somerset. 2 Jessica Fletcher. 3 Piccadilly. 4 Nancy. 5 Grant. 6 Casino Royale. 7 Bruce Forsyth. 8 Circus. 9 1963. 10 Two. 11 The telephone. 12 Sixpence. 13 Peter Davison. 14 Paul Daniels. 15 George VI. 16 Jack. 17 Manchester. 18 Pauline Collins and John Alderton. 19 Grandfather. 20 Clive Dunn. 21 Bridge. 22 UB40. 23 Roll call. 24 Poet Laureate. 25 California. 26 Wall Street. 27 Eight. 28 Jeremy Isaacs. 29 Wear. 30 ASLEF.

Quiz 111 Pot-Luck 58

Answers - see page 121

Answers - see page 121

Level 1

1 What is the seventh commandment?
2 What sport takes place in a velodrome?
3 In TV comedy, where did Uncle Martin come from?
4 Who sang the theme song for "The Man With The Golden Gun"?
5 Who said, "I shall hear in heaven"?
6 In which card game do you 'peg out'?
7 Which bingo number is clickety click?
8 What was Ivan Lendl's first Wimbledon tournament win?
9 What is another name for Lady's Fingers?
10 Which member of The Monkees appeared in "Coronation Street"?
11 What colour is ebony?
12 What do you have at the bottom of a colander?
13 Who wrote the TV musical drama "Lipstick On Your Collar"?
14 Which magazine called itself the junior TV Times?
15 In which track event do you get wet even when it's not raining?
16 On which track at Pennsylvania Station did the Chattanonnga Choo Choo leave?
17 What colour are French post boxes?
18 What is the nationality of Formula 1 driver Schumacher?
19 Who played Len Fairclough?
20 When during a meal would you have an hors d'oeuvre?
21 Which team did Alf Garnett support?
22 What is the US military academy called?
23 Over what type of food did Edwina Currie resign a ministerial post?
24 Which classical composer did Richard Chamberlain play in "The Music Lovers"?
25 What is the name of the cat which dips its paw in the food tin?
26 Which programme featuring Prunella Scales and Joan Sanderson transferred from radio to TV?
27 What name is given to the style of riding when both the rider's legs are on the same side of the horse?
28 Who tragically died while appearing on Live at Her Majesty's?
29 Where might you find a breeze block?
30 Whose motto is "Nation shall speak unto nation"?

Quiz 112 Geography

Answers - see page 122

Level 1

1 What did Iran used to be called?
2 In which World are underdeveloped countries said to be?
3 Normandy is part of which country?
4 In which Sea is the island of Majorca?
5 Which country does the island of Rhodes belong to?
6 In which US state is Disney World?
7 Which county is abbreviated to Oxon?
8 In which country is the Costa del Sol?
9 Which is further south Yarmouth or Brighton?
10 Is Torremolinos on the coast or inland?
11 Which sea lies between Italy and the former Yugoslavia?
12 On which coast of France are Cannes and St Tropez?
13 If you took a holiday in Gstaad what sport would you practise?
14 In which country is Buenos Aires?
15 In which continent is the holiday destination of Ibiza?
16 Where would you speak English and Maltese?
17 Which island lies at the eastern end of the Mediterranean?
18 Which group of islands does Tenerife belong to?
19 What is the Matterhorn?
20 What is the continent around the South Pole called?
21 Which country does the Loire flow through?
22 What is the world's second highest mountain?
23 In which Ocean is Greenland?
24 On which continent is the Kalahari desert?
25 What is the chief official language of Israel?
26 The Arctic Ocean is not covered mainly by water but by what?
27 Which country has four letters and ends in Q?
28 In which Sea is Cuba?
29 Which Falls are on the border between Zimbabwe and Zambia?
30 On which continent is the Amazon river?

Answers

Hollywood (see Quiz 110)
1 Whitney Houston. 2 Diane. 3 Hanks. 4 Hunter. 5 Charlie Chaplin. 6 Anthony Hopkins. 7 Hoskins. 8 Spielberg. 9 Stallone. 10 Kiefer. 11 Quentin. 12 Griffith. 13 Nolte. 14 Susan. 15 Depp. 16 Connery. 17 Estevez. 18 Culkin. 19 Close. 20 Pacino. 21 Gibson. 22 Fonda. 23 Williams. 24 Hannah. 25 Kim Basinger. 26 Val. 27 Judy Garland. 28 Pierce Brosnan. 29 Woody Allen. 30 Kevin Costner.

Quiz 113 Pot-Luck 59

Level 1

Answers - see page 123

1 What sort of Circle do conjurers join?
2 Which UK coin has a diameter of 3cms?
3 Which football club does Jasper Carrott support?
4 Which musical includes the characters Sky Masterson and Nathan Detroit?
5 What can be the name of a hat and a member of a cricket team?
6 Which sign of the zodiac follows Capricorn?
7 Which game might you be watching if you were at The Belfry?
8 Variola is more commonly called what?
9 Who wrote the play "An Inspector Calls"?
10 What is Diana Prince's other identity?
11 Which Scottish group took their name from a Scritti Politti lyric?
12 Which section do you look for in the newspaper to read what the stars have in store for you?
13 Which musical instrument does Nigel Kennedy play ?
14 Which residence of the Queen's was opened to the public in 1993?
15 In which month is the Le Mans 24 hour race held?
16 Who wrote the theme song to "Harry's Game"?
17 After what is London's Fleet Street named?
18 Which "Knight Rider" travelled to "Baywatch"?
19 Who did Frank Bruno beat to become WBC heavyweight champion in 1995?
20 What is a cassoulet?
21 In which sport would you have an Eskimo roll?
22 What is another name for a Chinese gooseberry?
23 What is a 200th anniversary called?
24 How many players are there in a Rugby League team?
25 In ads, what was BT's bird called?
26 Who is the husband of Queen Noor?
27 What was the name of Hamlet's father?
28 Which puppet appeared with Terry Hall?
29 What is the English name for *Firenze*?
30 To five years either way, when was the Royal Variety show first televised?

Answers

Pot-Luck 58 (see Quiz 111)
1 Thou shalt not commit adultery. 2 Cycling. 3 Mars. 4 Lulu. 5 Beethoven.
6 Cribbage. 7 66. 8 Junior Wimbledon. 9 Okra. 10 Davy Jones. 11 Black.
12 Holes. 13 Dennis Potter. 14 Look-In. 15 Steeplechase. 16 Track 29.
17 Yellow. 18 German. 19 Peter Adamson. 20 Beginning. 21 West Ham.
22 West Point. 23 Eggs. 24 Tchaikovsky. 25 Arthur. 26 After Henry. 27
Side saddle. 28 Tommy Cooper. 29 In a wall. 30 The B.B.C..

Quiz 114 Pot-Luck 60

Answers - see page 118

1. In which English county are Taunton and Wells?
2. Which fictional detective wrote "The Corpse Danced At Midnight"?
3. On the London Underground, on which line is Knightsbridge station?
4. What is the name of Frank Sinatra's daughter?
5. What is the name of Phil's brother in "EastEnders"?
6. In which Ian Fleming novel did James Bond first appear?
7. Who did 1975 Miss World Wilnelia Merced marry in the 1980s?
8. What type of entertainment is the musical "Barnum" about?
9. In which year did "Dr Who" first appear on BBC?
10. Over how many days is an Olympic decathlon held?
11. What did Maureen Lipman, aka Beattie, encourage us to use in the TV advertising campaign?
12. In June 1980, which coin ceased to be legal tender?
13. Who is actress Sandra Dickinson married to?
14. Which magician presents TV's "Wipeout"?
15. Who was the first British monarch to visit America?
16. What is the first name of comedian Dee?
17. 0161 is the dialling code for which city?
18. Which husband and wife team were together in "Upstairs, Downstairs" and "Forever Green"?
19. What is Alec Gilroy's relationship to Vicky in "Coronation Street"?
20. Which member of "Dad's Army" had a chart topping hit?
21. At which game has Omar Sharif represented his country?
22. Which group features the children of 50s and 60s folk singer Ian Campbell?
23. What does Tenko mean in English?
24. C.Day Lewis and John Betjeman have both held which title?
25. In which real state is the fictitious town of Knots Landing?
26. On which Street is the New York Stock Exchange?
27. How many times do you sing "Happy Birthday" if you sing two verses of the song?
28. Who left Channel 4 to become Director of the Royal Opera House?
29. Sunderland lies at the mouth of which river?
30. Of which union was Ray Buckton once a leader?

Geography (see Quiz 112)

1 Persia. 2 Third World. 3 France. 4 Mediterranean. 5 Greece. 6 Florida. 7 Oxfordshire. 8 Spain. 9 Brighton. 10 On the coast. 11 Adriatic. 12 South. 13 Skiing. 14 Argentina. 15 Europe. 16 Malta. 17 Cyprus. 18 Canary Islands. 19 Mountain. 20 Antarctica. 21 France. 22 K2. 23 Arctic. 24 Africa. 25 Hebrew. 26 Ice. 27 Iraq. 28 Caribbean. 29 Victoria. 30 South America.

Answers

Quiz 115 Potluck 61

Answers - see page 119

1 What is the capital city of Hawaii?
2 What is the mint with the hole?
3 What boat is found on the canals of Venice?
4 What is a misanthrope?
5 Where would you find a *kibbutz*?
6 Where are the Quantocks
7 Which England football manager was dubbed a turnip by The Sun?
8 Which London underground station was named after a football club?
9 Who uncrossed their legs to much ado in "Basic Instinct"?
10 Who played the female lead in a sexual harrassment case in the film "Disclosure"?
11 Who founded the Microsoft Corporation?
12 Who wrote the novel "Trainspotting"?
13 Who won the Nobel Prize for Literature in 1995?
14 Where are the Shankly Gates ?
15 In which city did Molly Malone wheel her wheelbarrow?
16 What is the name of the badger's residence?
17 Which office block is located at the junction of Charing Cross Road and Tottenham Court Road?
18 What is the collective noun for Geese?
19 Who is the only cricketer to score 501 in first class cricket?
20 What have Tunbridge Wells, Windsor and Kensington & Chelsea got in common?
21 Who was Admiral Lord Nelson's lover?
22 What was Mozart's middle name?
23 Who won the award for 1996's Satellite TV Personality of the Year?
24 Who was the principal communications officer on the Starship Enterprise?
25 What are the names of the Duchess of York's children?
26 Who got one in the eye at the Battle of Hastings?
27 Who was Don Quixote's sidekick?
28 What is the viral disease of rabbits?
29 Who wrote Winnie The Pooh?
30 Where is the Jorvik centre?

Answers

Pot-Luck 59 (see Quiz 113)
1 Magic. 2 50 pence piece. 3 Birmingham City. 4 Guys and Dolls. 5 Bowler. 6 Aquarius. 7 Golf. 8 Smallpox. 9 J B Priestley. 10 Wonderwoman. 11 Wet Wet Wet. 12 Horoscope. 13 Violin. 14 Buckingham Palace. 15 June. 16 Clannad. 17 The river Fleet. 18 David Hasselhoff. 19 Oliver McCall. 20 A French stew. 21 Canoeing. 22 Kiwi fruit. 23 Bicentenary. 24 13. 25 Buzby. 26 King Hussein of Jordan. 27 Hamlet. 28 Lenny the Lion. 29 Florence. 30 1960.

The Medium Questions

This next selection of questions is getting a little more like it. For an open entry quiz then you should have a high percentage of medium level questions – don't try to break people's spirits with the hard ones just make sure that people play to their ability.

Like all questions this level of question can be classed as either easy or impossible depending on whether you know the answer or not and although common knowledge is used as the basis for these questions there is a sting in the tail of quite a few. Also, if you have a serious drinking squad playing then they can more or less say goodbye to the winner's medals, but that isn't to say they will feel any worse about it.

Specialists are the people to watch out as those with a good knowledge of a particular subject will doubtless do well in these rounds so a liberal sprinkling of pot-luck questions are needed to flummox them.

Quiz 1 Pop: Glam Rock

Answers - see page 127

Level 2

1 What was Slade's first No 1 single? *COZ I LUV YoU*
2 Which group went on a "Teenage Rampage"?
3 Who had a 1970s No 1 with "Oh Boy"? *MUD*
4 Which colour Barry was "(Dancin') On a Saturday Night"?
5 What was Alvin Stardust's name when he charted in the 1960s?
6 Which Gary Glitter song was in Parts 1 and 2?
7 Who penned the T. Rex hits?
8 Who came alive down in "Devilgate Drive"?
9 Who was the leader of Wizzard?
10 Which group had a Noddy as singer?
11 Who was Chapman's song-writing partner?
12 Which Bowie No 1 was a reissue of his that charted in 1969?
13 Which group had a hit with "Angel Face"?
14 Which song has the chorus line "Bang a gong"?
15 Brian Connolly was lead singer with which group?
16 Who played bass guitar in Suzi Quatro's group?
17 How is Paul Gadd better known?
18 Who recorded "Children of the Revolution"?
19 What was Mud's first top ten hit?
20 Which Micky was producer for the Suzi Quatro hits?
21 Who wished that it could be Christmas every day?
22 And who was "Lonely This Christmas"?
23 Who was born Mark Feld?
24 Which Midlands town did Slade come from?
25 Which Alvin Stardust hit was one word repeated three times?
26 In which song intro did the singer talk to each group member before saying "all right fellas, let's go!"?
27 What words appearing in brackets completed the tittle of "I'm The Leader Of the Gang"?
28 What dance was Wizzard's baby doing in the title of a No 1 hit?
29 Which song features the words "Do the fairies keep him sober for a day"?
30 Who was the lead singer with Mud?

Quiz 2 Pot-Luck 1

Answers - see page 128

Level 2

1 How many queens have ruled France?
2 In which country is Baden-Baden?
3 Where in your body is the tibia?
4 What was a doublet?
5 Which English king was nicknamed Rufus?
6 Which county gives its name to a horse known as a Punch?
7 During how many days was Jesus tempted while in the wilderness?
8 Obstetrics is the study of what?
9 Which bird gave Fleetwood Mac a No 1 instrumental?
10 In proverb speech is silver but what is golden?
11 Who became known as "The King of the Wild Frontier"?
12 What is the heavy rain of summer called in Asia ?
13 What is alopecia?
14 Which London station would you arrive at if you travelled from Ipswich?
15 What fruit are you said to be if you are accompanying a courting couple?
16 Frederick the Great was king of which country?
17 Who had a hit with "Positively Fourth Street"?
18 Which city was built on seven hills?
19 What type of creature is a painted lady?
20 What is a lift for food in a restaurant known as?
21 Which Latin phrase means in good faith? *BONA FIDE*
22 What does a misogynist hate?
23 Which American president had a wife known as Ladybird?
24 What name is given to animals that eat grass and plants?
25 What is Delft in Holland famous for? *POTTERY*
26 In the Bible, which king had to decide which of two women was the mother of a child?
27 Fletcher Christian led a mutiny on which ship?
28 Who wrote "Under Milk Wood"? *DYLAN THOMAS*
29 What is the capital of Hawaii?
30 What is the post code known as in America?

Pot-Luck 2 (see Quiz 4)

Answers

1 Iris. 2 Mime. 3 Chicago. 4 Trevor Howard. 5 Bristol. 6 Fungus. 7 Elizabeth. 8 Thomas More. 9 Kennedy. 10 Cuba. 11 Phoenix. 12 Marx Brothers. 13 Piebald. 14 Stoat. 15 Sea sickness. 16 Poland. 17 Thomas à Becket. 18 Animal Farm. 19 Cup and lip. 20 Rhesus. 21 Acute. 22 Isle of Wight. 23 Beethoven. 24 Testator. 25 Violin. 26 Black. 27 I Believe. 28 Chlorophyll. 29 Louisiana. 30 Quicksilver.

Quiz 3 Nature: Animals

Answers - see page 125

1 What is a common name for the asteroidea which have five arms?
2 At what stage of development is the imago stage of an insect?
3 What is the aquatic larva of an amphibian more commonly called?
4 What is a chameleon capable of changing?
5 What does a reptile shed in the process of sloughing?
6 What is another name for snake poison?
7 The aardvark is a native of which continent?
8 Which is the only mammal able to fly?
9 Which type of dark coloured bear is the largest?
10 What do Americans call reindeer? *CARIBOU*
11 Man has seven vertebrae in his neck. How many does a giraffe have?
12 What is the main diet of hedgehogs?
13 Which two colours are wolves?
14 What is the fastest land animal?
15 From which border do Border collies originate?
16 What colour is a chow chow's tongue? *BLUE*
17 What is the mammal *homo sapiens* better known as?
18 Where does an arboreal animal live?
19 What is the smallest breed of dog?
20 Do dolphins have teeth?
21 Which part of the rhino is regarded as an aphrodisiac?
22 Which is the largest of the cats?
23 The ibex is a member of which animal family?
24 Which is generally larger, a wallaby or a kangaroo?
25 How many sets of teeth do most mammals have?
26 What is the black leopard more commonly known as?
27 What do moles mainly feed on?
28 Which country does the breed of dog, shih tzu, come from?
29 What would the Europeans call what the Americans call a moose?
30 What do beavers build?

Quiz 4 Pot-Luck 2

Answers - see page 126

1 What is the coloured part of the eye called?
2 With what type of entertainment is Marcel Marceau associated?
3 Which city was linked with gangster Al Capone in the 1920s?
4 Who starred with Celia Johnson in "Brief Encounter"? *TREVOR HOWARD*
5 In which British city is the station Temple Meads?
6 What is a stinkhorn?
7 What was the name of John the Baptist's mother?
8 Which Tudor figure is the main character in "A Man For All Seasons"?
9 Which American president had the first names John Fitzgerald?
10 In which country is Havana?
11 In legend, which bird rose from its own ashes?
12 Which brothers starred in the film "Duck Soup"? *MARX*
13 What term describes a black and white horse?
14 Which animal does ermine come from?
15 If you have *"mal de mer"* what are you suffering from?
16 The Solidarity movement began in which country?
17 In 1170, which Archbishop of Canterbury was murdered?
18 What kind of farm did George Orwell write about?
19 In proverb, there is "many a slip 'twixt" what and what?
20 Which monkey possess a blood factor that is shared with humans?
21 What type of angle is less than 90 degrees?
22 On which Isle is Osborne House?
23 Who composed the piece of music known as the "Moonlight Sonata"?
24 What name is given in law to a person who makes a will?
25 Stephane Grappelli is famous for playing which instrument?
26 What colour were the shirts of Mussolini's Italian Fascists?
27 Which song was a hit for both The Bachelors and Robson and Jerome?
28 What is the green colouring matter in plants known as?
29 Which American state does cajun music come from?
30 What is another name for mercury?

Quiz 5   TV: Costume Drama

Level 2

Answers - see page 131

1   What were the full first names of the founders of The House of Eliott?
2   Which actress starred in the series "A Woman of Substance"?
3   Which family lived at 165 Eaton Place, London? *BELLAMY*
4   Which actress played wife No 1 in "The Six Wives of Henry VIII" and Mrs Victor Meldrew?
5   Whom did Demelza marry in the drama set in Cornwall?
6   Which 1970s series was based on novels by Anthony Trollope ?
7   Which shipping line did the "Charlotte Rhodes" belong to?
8   Which mistress of Edward VII was played by Francesca Annis?
9   Derek Jacobi played the title role as which Roman emperor?
10   Which saga was about Soames, Irene, Jolyon and their family?
11   In which country was "The Far Pavilions" set?
12   During which war was "By The Sword Divided" set?
13   In "Brideshead Revisited" what was Aloysius?
14   What is the profession of Eleanor Bramwell in the Victorian series?
15   Who played the title role in the series about Elizabeth I?
16   Which compass points formed the title of an American Civil War drama?
17   What was the profession of the Duchess of Duke Street?
18   Which James Bond once played Mr Rochester in a TV version of "Jane Eyre"?
19   Who links "Ab Fab" Saffron and "Pride and Prejudice" Lydia Bennet?
20   In "Upstairs, Downstairs" what was butler Hudson's first name?
21   Which TV drama was about Winston Churchill's mother?
22   In 1995, which husband-seeking American ladies invaded England?
23   Which "Good Lifer" starred on TV as Edward VII's sister?
24   Which romantic hero was played by Colin Firth in 1995?
25   Which series was "Thomas and Sarah" a spin-off from?
26   Which movement was the series "Shoulder to Shoulder" about?
27   Which tyrannical Italian family was the subject of a series in 1981? *BORGIA*
28   Which drama featured Peggy Ashcroft and Geraldine James in wartime India?
29   Who played Churchill in "The Wilderness Years"?
30   Who wrote "Middlemarch", the novel the TV serial was based on?

Answers

Theatre and Musicals (see Quiz 7)
1 Sean Connery. 2 Sarah Brightman. 3 David Essex. 4 Sunset Boulevard.
5 La Cage aux Folles. 6 The Sound of Music. 7 Tony. 8 Nigel Hawthorne.
9 Kiss me Kate. 10 Theatre Royal. 11 Michael Ball. 12 Don Black. 13
Tim Rice. 14 Show Boat. 15 Happy Talk. 16 Siam (now Thailand). 17
West Side Story. 18 Stripper. 19 Stephen Sondheim. 20 Carousel. 21
Michael Crawford. 22 Joyce Grenfell. 23 Wuthering Heights. 24 Mary
Magdalen. 25 Chess. 26 Roger Moore. 27 Petula Clark. 28 Cats. 29
Hair. 30 A Chorus Line.

Quiz 6 Pot-Luck 3

Answers - see page 132

Level 2

1 Which Ancient British priests were associated with mistletoe?
2 What does a theodolite measure?
3 Which poisonous gas is given off from a car exhaust?
4 In Scotland, what are Eigg, Muck and Rhum?
5 What is ornithology?
6 Robert Menzies was prime minister of which country?
7 What is the currency of Poland? ZLOTY
8 Which radio show featured Jimmy Edwards and June Whitfield?
9 In maths, what is meant by three dots in a triangular formation?
10 Traditionally, what does a cooper make?
11 Which motorway goes from east to west across the Pennines?
12 What are workers and drones types of?
13 What is the middle name of Winston S. Churchill? SPENCER
14 On what calendar date is Burns Night?
15 What is the home of a beaver called?
16 How many railway stations are there on a Monopoly board?
17 Which spaceman appeared on the front page of the original "Eagle" comic?
18 What has the body of a lion and the head of a human?
19 Who invented the method by which the blind can read by touch?
20 Who sang the Bond theme "Goldfinger"?
21 What does a costermonger sell? FRUIT & VEG.
22 What did the Italian soldier Garibaldi give his name to?
23 Who wrote "Lorna Doone"?
24 Which sea is north of Turkey?
25 What colour are the flowers of St John's Wort?
26 Segovia is associated with which musical instrument?
27 Cold meat and cold potatoes can produce what dish?
28 Which king is supposed to have hidden in a tree after the Battle of Worcester?
29 Which brothers flew the first manned, powered aeroplane?
30 The Heriot-Watt university is in which city?

Answers

Pot-Luck 4 (see Quiz 8)
1 Yellow. 2 England and France. 3 Sharp. 4 White and yellow. 5 24.
6 Bishop. 7 Animal. 8 Cricket. 9 Van Gogh. 10 Berkshire. 11 Radius.
12 Mont Blanc. 13 Six. 14 H. G. Wells. 15 Runnymede. 16 90 degrees.
17 Bakewell. 18 Yellow. 19 Bad breath. 20 Enid Blyton. 21 Mediterranean. 22 Pontoon. 23 John Denver. 24 Mexico and USA. 25 Hail, Mary. 26 20. 27 Three. 28 Princess Anne. 29 Raymond Chandler.
30 Geology.

Quiz 7 Theatre and Musicals

Level 2

Answers - see page 129

1 Which James Bond was in the chorus in "South Pacific" in London?
2 Which musical star was Andrew Lloyd Webber's second wife?
3 Who played Che in the original stage production of "Evita"?
4 Which was Elaine Paige's first musical on Broadway?
5 Which musical does the song "I Am What I Am" come from?
6 In which musical is Maria von Trapp the heroine?
7 Which theatre award is named after actress Antoinette Perry?
8 Who played C.S. Lewis in "Shadowlands" on stage?
9 Which musical is based on "The Taming of the Shrew"?
10 What is the name of the most famous theatre in London's Drury Lane?
11 Who originally played the role of Alex in "Aspects of Love"?
12 Who wrote the lyrics for "Tell Me on a Sunday" and "Sunset Boulevard"?
13 Who co-produced the revival of "Anything Goes" with Elaine Paige?
14 Which musical is the song "Ol' Man River" from?
15 Which song from "South Pacific" was recorded by Captain Sensible?
16 In which country is "The King and I" set?
17 Which musical are the songs "Tonight" and "Somewhere" from?
18 What was the profession of the heroine in "Gypsy"?
19 Who wrote "Into the Woods" and "A Little Night Music"?
20 In which musical does "You'll Never Walk Alone" appear?
21 Who played the title role in "Barnum" and "Billy"?
22 Which actress was Maureen Lipman's show "Re Joyce" about?
23 Which novel is "Heathcliff" based on?
24 Which character sings "I Don't Know How to Love Him" in "Jesus Christ Superstar"?
25 Which musical is "I Know Him So Well" from?
26 Which former Saint turned down a musical role in "Aspects of Love"?
27 Who replaced Elaine Paige as Norma Desmond in the London production of "Sunset Boulevard"?
28 In which musical do they sing about a "Jellicle Ball"?
29 Which musical hailed the dawning of the age of Aquarius?
30 Which musical is the song "One" from?

TV: Costume Drama (see Quiz 5)
1 Beatrice and Evangeline. 2 Jenny Seagrove. 3 Bellamy family. 4 Annette Crosbie. 5 Ross Poldark. 6 The Pallisers. 7 Onedin Line. 8 Lillie Langtry. 9 Claudius. 10 Forsyte Saga. 11 India. 12 English Civil War. 13 A teddy. 14 Doctor. 15 Glenda Jackson. 16 North and South. 17 Cook. 18 Timothy Dalton. 19 Julia Sawalha. 20 Angus. 21 Jennie. 22 The Buccaneers. 23 Felicity Kendal. 24 Mr Darcy. 25 Upstairs, Downstairs. 26 The suffragettes. 27 The Borgias. 28 The Jewel in the Crown. 29 Robert Hardy. 30 George Eliot.

131

Quiz 8 Pot-Luck 4

Answers - see page 130

1 What colour are gorse flowers?
2 In the 14th century, which two countries fought at Poitiers?
3 In music, a flat sign lowers a note but what sign raises a note?
4 What are the two main colours on the Vatican flag?
5 Chemically pure gold contains how many carats?
6 In chess, which piece always moves diagonally?
7 Are sea-urchins animal, vegetable or mineral?
8 Dexter and May have captained England in which sport?
9 Which artist painted "Sunflowers"?
10 In which county is Windsor Castle?
11 What term is given to the distance from the centre of a circle to the outer edge?
12 Which is the highest mountain in the Alps?
13 How many points are there on a snowflake?
14 Who wrote the story "The Invisible Man"?
15 On which island did King John set his seal to the Magna Carta?
16 How many degrees in a right angle?
17 Which Derbyshire town gives its name to a Tart?
18 Jonquil is a shade of which colour?
19 What is halitosis?
20 Who created the character Kiki the parrot?
21 Which sea does the River Rhone flow into?
22 In which card game can you stick and twist?
23 How is singer/songwriter John Henry Deutschendorf better known?
24 The Rio Grande separates which two countries?
25 In Latin, what does "Ave Marie" mean?
26 How many decades are there in two centuries?
27 How many stripes does a police sergeant have on his arm?
28 Which royal was quoted by the press as saying "Why don't you naff off"?
29 Which writer created Philip Marlowe, the private eye?
30 What is the name for the study of rocks and the earth's crust?

Quiz 9 Football

Level 2

1 What team is known as The Baggies?
2 Which Andy has played for Southampton, Norwich, Chelsea and Aston Villa?
3 What two colours are in Derby's home strip?
4 Who said, "When seagulls follow the trawler it is because they think the sardines will be thrown into the sea"?
5 In which country were the 1990 World Cup finals held?
6 Which city has a team of the same name and a United team?
7 What position did Tommy Lawrence play?
8 Bobby Gould and Phil Neal have both managed which club?
9 Who plays home games at The New Den?
10 Which club is linked with the playing career of Tom Finney?
11 Who managed Liverpool to the 1986 FA Cup and League double?
12 Which country do Brondby come from?   DENMARK
13 Which famous first will always be held by Keith Peacock?
14 Which club did Mark Atkins play for in a Premiership winning season?
15 Which country did Mike England play for?
16 What is the home colour of Crystal Palace?
17 Which country does Anders Limpar come from?
18 Which team had Radford and Kennedy as a strike force?
19 Which club did Peter Beardsley leave when he rejoined Newcastle?
20 Which London striker has played for Arsenal, Crystal Palace, Queen's Park Rangers, Spurs, Chelsea, West Ham and Millwall?
21 Who has managed Everton, Notts County, and Sheffield United?
22 Who used to be a hod carrier before joining Wimbledon?
23 Who was the manager when England won the 1966 World Cup?
24 Which country did Alan Brazil play for?
25 Which soccer side plays at Rugby Park?
26 Which player was involved in Britain's first million pound transfer?
27 Who has scored most goals in FA Cup ties?   TREVOR FRANCIS
28 Which English defender is known as "Rodney"?
29 Which country does Jimmy Quinn play for?
30 Who went to Newcastle from Man Utd in the Andy Cole transfer deal?

Pot-Luck 5 (see Quiz 11)
Answers
1 Alice Cooper. 2 Colditz. 3 Isle Of Man. 4 Decibels. 5 Egypt. 6 Yorkshire. 7 Roxy Music. 8 Golf. 9 Tchaikovsky. 10 60. 11 Sandringham House. 12 Batman. 13 Morocco. 14 Dublin. 15 Elysée Palace. 16 144. 17 Canoeing. 18 June. 19 Boats. 20 When it is about to leave port. 21 Comet. 22 Hansard. 23 Judaism. 24 Australia and New Zealand. 25 Vertical. 26 Five. 27 Four. 28 The eye. 29 Gracie Fields. 30 Mae West.

Quiz 10 Election Fever

Answers - see page 136

1 How long is a Member of Parliament elected for?
2 In which year in the 1970s were there two general elections?
3 How many general elections had the Liberal Democrats contested by 1995?
4 Who has been MP for Old Bexley-Sidcup (Bexley) since 1950?
5 Who became deputy prime minister after the 1995 Tory leadership election?
6 Who was Britain's first black woman MP?
7 Which party leader has the initials J.J.D.?
8 Who became Labour leader after the 1992 election defeat?
9 Which future PM failed to win Dartford for the Tories in 1950 and 1951?
10 Which two Davids headed the Alliance party in 1983?
11 Which prime minister's father was a trapeze artist?
12 The House of Commons consists of how many members?
13 Which Essex seat was won by Tory David Amess against all predictions in 1992?
14 Who gave up the title of Viscount Stansgate to remain an MP?
15 Which MP is the son in law of Alf Garnett's son in law?
16 Which MP takes his dog into the House of Commons?
17 Which MP's father starred in the film classic "The Blue Lamp"?
18 Who wrote the novel "A Parliamentary Affair"?
19 Who resigned as a government minister over the Sara Keays affair?
20 Which party won the general election in 1945?
21 Which former minister has presented "Six O Six" on Radio 5 Live ?
22 Name the 1992 Tory party chairman who lost his Bath seat?
23 Which former deputy Labour leader, whose father was once a Catholic priest, stood down after the 1992 General Election?
24 What was Norman Tebbitt's job before entering Parliament?
25 Which party does Screaming Lord Sutch represent?
26 Who became deputy Labour leader after the 1992 General Election?
27 Who turned from blue to yellow in December 1995?
28 What did the Ecology party change its name to in 1985?
29 What was Dennis Skinner's job before he entered Parliament?
30 Which MP won gold medals at the 1980 and 1984 Olympics?

Answers

Heavy Metal (see Quiz 12)
1 Yardbirds. 2 Black Night. 3 John. 4 Black Sabbath. 5 Iron Maiden. 6 Led Zeppelin III. 7 Meat Loaf. 8 Def Leppard. 9 Birmingham. 10 Deep Purple. 11 AC/DC. 12 Ozzy Ozbourne. 13 Drums. 14 Sandy Denny. 15 Bat out of Hell. 16 David Coverdale's Whitesnake. 17 Machine Head. 18 Dennis Wheatley. 19 Bass Guitar. 20 Ian Gillan. 21 Jimmy Page. 22 Playing guitar solos. 23 An arm. 24 Rick Wakeman. 25 Pyromania. 26 Phil Collins. 27 But I Won't Do That. 28 Rainbow. 29 Iommi. 30 Ted Nugent.

Quiz 11 Pot-Luck 5

Answers - see page 133

1 Which gender-bender name did rock star Vincent Furnier adopt?
2 Which German prison camp did Pat Reid try to escape from?
3 Which island hosts a TT Motor Cycle race in June?
4 What measure is used for sound or noise?
5 Farouk was king of which country?
6 Which county used to be divided into Ridings?
7 Who charted with "Virginia Plain"?
8 Which sport is played at Sunningdale?
9 Who composed the "1812 Overture"?
10 What is the mean of 40, 60 and 80?
11 Which royal residence is in Norfolk?
12 In comics, by what name is Bruce Wayne known?
13 Marrakesh is in which country?
14 In the traditional song, in which city did Molly Malone sell cockles and mussels?
15 What is the official residence of the French president?
16 How many square inches in a square foot?
17 In which sport are there wild water, sprint and slalom events?
18 In which month is the longest day in Britain?
19 Smack and sampan are types of what?
20 When is the Blue Peter flag raised on a ship?
21 What type of heavenly body is named after Edmund Halley?
22 Which book records debates in Parliament?
23 Which religion observes the Passover?
24 Anzac troops come from which two countries?
25 In aviation VTOL stands for what type of take-off and landing?
26 How many lines in a limerick?
27 How many years is the term of office of the American president?
28 In which part of the body is the cornea located?
29 Which singer was born in Rochdale and lived on the Isle of Capri?
30 Which film star gave her name to a life jacket?

Answers

Football (see Quiz 9)
1 West Bromwich Albion. 2 Townsend. 3 Black and white. 4 Eric Cantona. 5 Italy. 6 Dundee. 7 Goal. 8 Coventry. 9 Millwall. 10 Preston. 11 Kenny Dalglish. 12 Denmark. 13 First substitute in a League game. 14 Blackburn. 15 Wales. 16 Red and blue. 17 Sweden. 18 Arsenal. 19 Everton. 20 Clive Allen. 21 Howard Kendall. 22 Vinny Jones. 23 Alf Ramsey. 24 Scotland. 25 Kilmarnock. 26 Trevor Francis. 27 Ian Rush. 28 Tony Adams. 29 Northern Ireland. 30 Keith Gillespie.

Quiz 12 Heavy Metal

Level 2

Answers - see page 134

1 Which group was Jimmy Page in before forming Led Zeppelin?
2 What was Deep Purple's first hit in the singles charts?
3 What is Ozzy Ozbourne's actual first name?
4 Which group were "Paranoid" in the charts?
5 Which group took its name from a medieval instrument of torture?
6 They were known for imaginative cover designs, but what was the title of Led Zeppelin's third album?
7 By what name is Marvin Lee Aday better known?
8 Which group founded the Bludgeon Riffola label?
9 Which city did Black Sabbath come from?
10 Ian Gillan, Graham Bonnet and David Coverdale sang for which group?
11 In which group did Angus Young wear short trousers?
12 Who recorded "Bark at the Moon"?
13 What instrument did Ian Paice play?
14 Which folk singer sang on Led Zep's "The Battle of Evermore"?
15 Which album from 1978 was reissued in 1991 and led to a 1993 sequel?
16 How were Whitesnake credited on their first recordings?
17 "Smoke on the Water" came from which album?
18 Terry Butler changed his group's name to Black Sabbath after reading a novel by which author?
19 What instrument does Iron Maiden founder Steve Harris play?
20 "Naked Thunder" was the first solo album by which singer?
21 Who wrote "Stairway to Heaven"?
22 On stage, Nugent, Kramer and Pinera indulged in what kind of duels?
23 What did Def Leppard drummer Rick Allen lose in a car accident?
24 Which Yes keyboard player was on "Sabbath Bloody Sabbath"?
25 "Rock of Rages" was on which Def Leppard album?
26 Who was guest drummer for Led Zeppelin at the Live Aid concert?
27 What words in brackets end the title "I Would Do Anything For Love?"
28 Which group did Ritchie Blackmore form on leaving Deep Purple?
29 Which guitarist Tony was an original member of Black Sabbath?
30 Which American guitarist had gone partly deaf by the 1980s?

Answers

Election Fever (see Quiz 10)
1 Five years. 2 1974. 3 Two. 4 Edward Heath. 5 Michael Heseltine. 6 Diane Abbott. 7 Paddy Ashdown. 8 John Smith. 9 Margaret Roberts (later Thatcher). 10 Owen and Steel. 11 John Major's. 12 651. 13 Basildon. 14 Tony Benn. 15 Tony Blair. 16 David Blunkett. 17 Jeremy Hanley. 18 Edwina Currie. 19 Cecil Parkinson. 20 Labour. 21 David Mellor. 22 Chris Patten. 23 Roy Hattersley. 24 Airline pilot. 25 Monster Raving Loony party. 26 Margaret Beckett. 27 Emma Nicholson. 28 Green party. 29 Miner. 30 Sebastian Coe.

Quiz 13 Pot-Luck 6

Answers - see page 139

Level 2

1 Who had the first No 1 with "Unchained Melody"?
2 Who were known as Peelers in the 19th century?
3 Duncan Goodhew was famous for which sport?
4 In which country is the Dordogne?
5 What kind of creature is a natterjack?
6 In which radio show did Bluebottle and Eccles appear?
7 Which cricket team plays home county games at Edgbaston?
8 How is the letter S represented in morse code?
9 If something is Cantonese which country does it come from?
10 Who became known as "The Old Groaner"?
11 What is the background colour of motorway signs?
12 In which resort was "Fawlty Towers" set?
13 Orthodontics involves what parts of the body?
14 In China what was the colour of Chairman Mao's "little book"?
15 In which film does Professor Higgins appear?
16 How many ribs does a human have?
17 Zen is a form of what type of religion?
18 What does a pathologist study?
19 In which European country is Malmö?
20 What name is given to a book in which a sea captain charts events on a voyage?
21 What type of pet animal can be Chinchilla or Dutch?
22 What is the longest word that appears in the film "Mary Poppins"?
23 On the road, what does a red circular sign with a white band across it mean?
24 In which city is the Doge's Palace?
25 In the past, what was an Iron Horse?
26 Buff Orpingtons and Plymouth Rocks are types of what?
27 Which city in North Wales has the name of a Welsh saint?
28 In which sport is the Curtis Cup awarded?
29 Which canal takes food through your body?
30 Who wrote the controversial "Satanic Verses"?

Answers

Pot-Luck 7 (see Quiz 15)
1 Buffalo Bill. 2 Valletta. 3 In the neck. 4 A hawk. 5 The Beatles. 6 Spanish. 7 John Milton. 8 Rabbit. 9 Pontius Pilate. 10 Bootlegger. 11 Skye. 12 Benjamin Disraeli. 13 Golf. 14 Mullion. 15 A flower grows. 16 Ball. 17 Black. 18 Sheep. 19 Nepotism. 20 Neville Chamberlain. 21 Aurora Borealis. 22 James I. 23 Hippocratic Oath. 24 Lenska. 25 Champion. 26 Two. 27 Baloo. 28 Blue or violet. 29 Salisbury. 30 Maeve Binchy.

Quiz 14 Food and Drink

Answers - see page 114

1 What country is Pecorino cheese from?
2 What type of pastry are profiteroles made from?
3 Which fruits are usually served "belle hélène"?
4 What is the main flavour of aïoli?
5 Which vegetable can be oyster, chestnut or shitaki?
6 What is wiener schnitzel?
7 How is steak tartare cooked?
8 Which drink is Worcester sauce traditionally added to?
9 Which fish is the main ingredient of Scotch Woodcock?
10 Which area of England are Singing Hinnies from?
11 What is beef fillet cooked in puff pastry called?
12 What gives Windsor Red cheese its colour and flavour?
13 What is a Worcester Pearmain?
14 Which meat is used in Glamorgan sausages?
15 Which vegetables can be Pentland Crown or Maris Bard?
16 What type of food is basmati?
17 What is Roquefort cheese made from?
18 What are the two main ingredients of angels on horseback?
19 Which fruit is a cross between a blackberry and a raspberry?
20 Which type of pasta's name means 'little worms'?
21 What ingredient is included in food in a florentine style?
22 What is pancetta?
23 What is the main ingredient of a black pudding?
24 Which herb is in pesto sauce?
25 In Indian cookery what is naan?
26 What type of food is Cullen Skink?
27 What type of fish is in an Omelette Arnold Bennett?
28 What shape is the pasta called rigatoni?
29 What is couscous made from?
30 What does a Pomfret or Pontefract cake taste of?

Quiz 15 Pot-Luck 7

Answers - see page 137

Level 2

1 How did American showman William E. Cody become known?
2 What is the capital city of Malta?
3 Where in the body is the thyroid gland?
4 In politics what is the opposite of a dove?
5 Which group have had most British No 1 single hits?
6 What is the main language spoken in Mexico?
7 Who wrote "Paradise Lost"?
8 A cony is what sort of animal?
9 When Jesus was crucified, which Roman was governor of Jerusalem?
10 In the United States what name was given to a seller of illegal alcohol?
11 Which Scottish Isle became linked to the mainland by a bridge in 1995?
12 Which British prime minister was known as "Dizzy"?
13 Henry Cotton became famous in which sport?
14 What name is given to a vertical divide in a window?
15 In the song "I Believe", what happens for every drop of rain that falls?
16 Which word of four letters can go after beach and before gown to make new words?
17 What colour is the Northern Line on a London Underground map?
18 Astrakhan comes from which creature?
19 What is the name given to the practice of favouring your own relatives?
20 Which British prime minister spoke of "peace in our time"?
21 What is another name for the Northern Lights?
22 Who was monarch directly after Elizabeth I?
23 What is the name of the medical oath taken by doctors?
24 Which actress Rula married Dennis Waterman?
25 In westerns, what was the name of Gene Autry's horse?
26 How many packs of cards are needed to play bezique?
27 What is the name of the singing bear in Disney's "Jungle Book"?
28 What colour are the flowers of a periwinkle?
29 Which English city was once known as Sarum?
30 Who wrote the novel "The Glass Lake"?

Answers

Pot-Luck 6 (see Quiz 13)
1 Jimmy Young. 2 Policemen. 3 Swimming. 4 France. 5 A toad. 6 The Goon Show. 7 Warwickshire. 8 Dot dot dot. 9 China. 10 Bing Crosby. 11 Blue. 12 Torquay. 13 The teeth. 14 Red. 15 My Fair Lady. 16 24. 17 Buddhism. 18 Diseases. 19 Sweden. 20 Log. 21 Rabbit. 22 Supercalifragilisticexpiali-docius. 23 No entry. 24 Venice. 25 Steam locomotive. 26 Chickens. 27 St Asaph. 28 Golf. 29 Alimentary. 30 Salman Rushdie.

Quiz 16 Sci-Fi Movies

Answers - see page 138

1 Which character was described as "part man, part machine, all cop"?
2 Who played the part of the rebel princess in "Star Wars"?
3 "2001: A Space Odyssey" was based on a short story by whom?
4 What was the first in the five-film series of man and monkey conflict?
5 What planet did long-eared Mr Spock come from?
6 "Judge Dredd" was based on the character from which comic?
7 Which director said, "I'm embarrassed and ashamed that I get paid for doing this"?
8 In which film did Jane Fonda "do her own thing" in the 40th century?
9 What was the Fahrenheit reading in Truffaut's 1960s film?
10 Which hero has been portrayed by Christopher Reeve and Kirk Alyn?
11 Who was the star of "The Terminator" films?
12 Which rock band did the score for the 1970s romp "Flash"?
13 What was Darth Vader's spacecraft in "Star Wars"?
14 In which film did Bruce Willis play a time-travelling criminal?
15 Which creatures mutated in "Them"?
16 In which film did Claude Rains star as someone who was not seen?
17 Which rock star played Newton in "The Man Who Fell To Earth"?
18 In which film does Charlton Heston think he is Earth's last survivor?
19 Which vehicles set out to devour Paris?
20 In which film are people terminated at the age of 30?
21 In titles, which words go before "Stood Still" and "Caught Fire"?
22 Robbie The Robot and Dr Morbius appear in which film?
23 "Alien" posters said that "in space no one can hear you" do what?
24 In the 1953 film how many fathoms did the Beast come from?
25 "How I Learned To Stop Worrying And Love The Bomb" is known by what shorter title?
26 Which veteran actor played Ben (Obi-Wan) Kenobi?
27 In which 1960s film does rocket radiation activate flesh-eating zombies?
28 Which Roddy featured in the "Ape" series?
29 Who is the female companion of Flash Gordon?
30 In "The Incredible Shrinking Man" which creature does the man fight off with a needle?

Answers

Food and Drink (see Quiz 14)
1 Italy. 2 Choux pastry. 3 Pears. 4 Garlic. 5 Mushroom. 6 Veal. 7 It's served raw. 8 Tomato juice. 9 Anchovy. 10 North East. 11 Beef Wellington. 12 Red wine. 13 Apple. 14 None, they are made from cheese. 15 Potatoes and cabbage. 16 Rice. 17 Ewe's milk. 18 Oysters and bacon. 19 Tayberry. 20 Vermicelli. 21 Spinach. 22 Bacon. 23 Blood. 24 Basil. 25 Bread. 26 Soup. 27 Smoked haddock. 28 Tube-shaped. 29 Semolina. 30 Liquorice.

1 Which group backed singer Gary Puckett?
2 If two straight lines are always the same distance apart what are they said to be?
3 Who wrote "The Great Gatsby"?
4 Nat Lofthouse was famous in which sport?
5 In the 14th century what was the bubonic plague called in England?
6 What is another word for a sleepwalker?
7 What do the initials WO stand for as a rank in the army?
8 Which Italian city was painted by Canaletto?
9 Who composed the "Enigma Variations"?
10 In politics, how many readings does a bill have in the House of Commons?
11 Yum Yum and Ko-Ko appear in which opera?
12 In which war was the Victoria Cross first awarded?
13 An ampersand is a sign for which word?
14 In Spanish, which word is used to address a young, or unmarried, lady?
15 The Suez Canal connects the Red Sea with which other Sea?
16 Which country did composer Aaron Copland come from?
17 Where did the Norse gods live?
18 In financial terms, what is the IMF?
19 By what name is musician Raymond O'Sullivan better known?
20 Who composed the music for "West Side Story"?
21 "The City of Dreaming Spires" is which English city?
22 David Ben-Gurion was the first prime minister of which country?
23 What word means to gradually get louder and louder?
24 Troglodytes lived in what particular type of dwelling?
25 The borders of Turkey make up most of the land around which sea?
26 "Somewhere My Love" was the theme tune of which film?
27 How many players are there in a netball team?
28 If you are sinistral, what are you?
29 Who played King Henry VIII in the film "Carry On, Henry"?
30 Mount Parnassus is in which country?

Quiz 18 Around the United States

Answers - see page 144

1 Little Rock is the capital of which US state?
2 On which granite cliff are the faces of four presidents carved?
3 Which language is the first language of 6% of the population?
4 Which natural disaster is the San Andreas Fault prone to?
5 What does DC stand for in Washington DC?
6 Which is the largest US state?
7 In which state is the Grand Canyon?
8 What are a group of six states on the northeast coast known as collectively?
9 How do you spell Mississippi?
10 Which was the first of the original 13 states of the United States?
11 Where is the main space exploration centre in Florida?
12 In which city is almost half of the population of Illinois to be found?
13 How long is the motor race which Indianapolis is famous for?
14 Which town is famous for its jazz music?
15 Which mountainous forest state has a settlement of Crow Indians?
16 What is traditionally easily available in Reno?
17 In which city is La Guardia airport?
18 Which US state has the highest population?
19 Which two New York boroughs begin with B?
20 Key West and Key Largo are off the coast of which state?
21 Which US state used to be called the Sandwich Islands?
22 Which New York street is famous for its fashion stores?
23 The name of which state has four letters, the first and last the same?
24 The discovery of what in 1848 led to the expansion of California?
25 Kansas is the United States' chief producer of which grain?
26 Which Michigan town is famous for the production of motor vehicles?
27 Which New York borough is noted for its skyscraper skyline?
28 Other than White Americans what is the largest racial group on Hawaii?
29 Which US state is the title of a musical by Rodgers and Hammerstein?
30 Which city, the capital of Tennessee, is famous for its music?

Quiz 19 Around England

Answers - see page 141

Level 2

1 Which county did Huntingdonshire become part of in 1974?
2 What is High Wycombe famous for manufacturing?
3 Which atomic energy establishment used to be called Windscale?
4 Which two London boroughs begin with E?
5 Which seaside resort is on the Fylde?
6 What is the low-lying area of East Anglia called?
7 Which city was a Roman fortress called Deva and retains its medieval walls?
8 How many tunnels under the Mersey link Liverpool to the Wirral?
9 In which northern city is the National Railway Museum?
10 The Ribble is the chief river of which county?
11 In which city is the University of East Anglia?
12 Which county is Thomas Hardy associated with?
13 Which part of Oxford is famous for motor car manufacture?
14 Which Devon port has a famous Hoe?
15 Which county is also known as Salop?
16 Which Isle has Needles off its west coast?
17 Where would you find the 18th-century Assembly Rooms and Royal Crescent?
18 Which county does not exist: North, South, East or West Yorkshire?
19 In which town is the shopping complex, the Metro Centre?
20 Where would you find the Backs and the Bridge of Sighs?
21 Alphabetically what is the last county?
22 In which Metropolitan county are Trafford and Tameside?
23 In which National Park is Scafell Pike?
24 On which bank of the Thames is the City of London?
25 Consett is associated with the processing of which two metals?
26 Which city is served by Speke airport?
27 Which county lies between the North Sea and Greater London?
28 What is Lindisfarne also known as?
29 In which county is Hadrian's Wall?
30 From which London station are there trains direct to the continent through the Channel Tunnel?

Answers

Pot-Luck 8 (see Quiz 17)
1 The Union Gap. 2 Parallel. 3 Scott Fitzgerald. 4 Football. 5 The Black Death. 6 Somnambulist. 7 Warrant officer. 8 Venice. 9 Elgar. 10 Three. 11 Mikado. 12 Crimean. 13 And. 14 Señorita. 15 Mediterranean. 16 United States. 17 Valhalla. 18 International Monetary Fund. 19 Gilbert O'Sullivan. 20 Leonard Bernstein. 21 Oxford. 22 Israel. 23 Crescendo. 24 Caves. 25 Marmara. 26 Dr Zhivago. 27 Seven. 28 Left handed. 29 Sid James. 30 Greece.

Quiz 20 Pot-Luck 9

Answers - see page 142

1 In which capital city was Alexander Graham Bell born in 1847?
2 Whose first book was called "Child Whispers"?
3 Which breed of dog is named after a character in a novel by Sir Walter Scott?
4 On which river does Moscow stand?
5 Where do the Greek gods live?
6 Which dancer sang in the rain?
7 What were the names of Wendy Darling's brothers in "Peter Pan"?
8 Which Wilkie Collins' book is said to be the first detective story written in English?
9 Ena Sharples and Elizabeth of Glamis are types of what?
10 Who sits on The Woolsack?
11 Which "ology" is the study of human life?
12 Which planet is nearest to the sun?
13 In which war was The Charge of the Light Brigade?
14 Who was Henry VIII's last wife?
15 Which William led a gang called the Outlaws?
16 If you were awarded an OBE what would you be?
17 Who led the Argonauts in their quest for the Golden Fleece?
18 Who is the Queen's eldest grandchild?
19 What nationality was Richard Wagner?
20 By what name is singer/actor Terrence Nelhams better known?
21 Who wrote the music for "The Nutcracker"?
22 What is the most common breed of guide dog?
23 Which William did Queen Victoria succeed to the throne?
24 Which gas is used in modern airships?
25 What is the capital of Mongolia?
26 In which country were fireworks invented?
27 Who wrote "Agnes Grey"?
28 Where does Miss Marple live?
29 In which tower is Big Ben?
30 Which part of Captain Jenkins was cut off to start a war?

Answers *Around the United States* (see Quiz 18)
1 Arkansas. 2 Mount Rushmore. 3 Spanish. 4 Earthquakes. 5 District of Columbia. 6 Alaska. 7 Arizona. 8 New England. 9 Mississippi. 10 Delaware. 11 Cape Canaveral. 12 Chicago. 13 500 miles. 14 New Orleans. 15 Montana. 16 Divorce. 17 New York. 18 California. 19 Bronx, Brooklyn. 20 Florida. 21 Hawaii. 22 Fifth Avenue. 23 Ohio. 24 Gold. 25 Wheat. 26 Detroit. 27 Manhattan. 28 Japanese. 29 Oklahoma. 30 Nashville.

Quiz 21 The Olympics

Level 2

1 In 1984 which American equalled Jesse Owens' four gold medals?
2 The invasion of which country caused a boycott of the Moscow Olympics in 1980?
3 How many gold medals did Mark Spitz win in Munich in 1972?
4 Which country is 1972 Pentathlon winner Mary Peters from?
5 What colour medal did Sharron Davies win in Moscow?
6 In which two successive Olympics did Daley Thompson win gold?
7 In which team game did Britain's men win gold in Seoul in 1988?
8 Which country has won most summer Olympic medals since 1896?
9 Whose long-jump record in the 1968 Olympics lasted for 24 years?
10 Which boxer won gold for Canada in Seoul in 1988?
11 Which country did athletes with FRG after their names represent?
12 Who won silver at 100 metres in '88 and gold in the same event in '92?
13 What do equestrian medallists Virginia Holgate and Virginia Leng have in common?
14 Which gymnast scored the first perfect ten in Olympic history?
15 Where were the 1964 Olympics held?
16 Who was disqualified after a drugs test in the Men's 100 metres in 1988?
17 Who collided with Zola Budd in the 3000 metres in 1984?
18 Who won Britain's first men's swimming gold for 68 years in 1976?
19 At which sport was Katarina Witt an Olympic champion?
20 In which city were the Winter Olympics held when Torvill and Dean won gold in 1984?
21 What did 1964 Marathon winner Abebe Bikila wear on his feet?
22 Which swimming event was introduced to the Olympics in 1984?
23 Who won gold in the Women's Singles in tennis in 1988?
24 Which British skater won gold in 1980?
25 What are the five colours of the Olympic rings?
26 In 1984 who won gold in the Men's 800 metres and the 1500 metres?
27 In which country were the first modern Olympics held in 1896?
28 Who won the Women's 400-metre hurdles in Barcelona in 1992?
29 How many judges out of nine gave Torvill & Dean full marks for artistic impression in 1984?
30 Who was Britain's first-ever gold medallist in a throwing event in 1984?

1 How many players are there in a British lacrosse team?
2 St Stephen's Day is better known as which day?
3 Who recorded the original of "Love Is All Around"?
4 In which novel does Winston Smith appear?
5 The Duke of Wellington is on the back of which British banknote?
6 Which watch is from 8pm to midnight at sea?
7 Which two countries are divided by the Palk Strait?
8 Which Derbyshire town is noted for a church with a crooked spire?
9 In cartoons, which song does Huckleberry Hound sing?
10 What type of stone is the Koh-i-noor?
11 What is the study of family history called?
12 Which creature sends down share values on the stock exchange?
13 Which sport has its headquarters in St John's Wood, London?
14 Which language was invented for international use?
15 What was climbed "Because it is there"?
16 The Lutine bell is in which London institution?
17 The inspiration for which children's book character died in April 1996?
18 Which drug is obtained from foxglove leaves?
19 In which county is Romney Marsh?
20 Which magazine is the flagship of the Consumers Association?
21 Which four words follow "To be or not to be..."?
22 In France what title was given to the eldest son of the king?
23 What are the colours of the berries of the Mountain Ash?
24 What part of Cyrano de Bergerac's anatomy was particularly large?
25 In Japan what name is given to ritual sacrifice?
26 Whom did Flora Macdonald rescue?
27 Purchase tax was abolished in 1973, but what replaced it?
28 In the song, who regrets she is unable to lunch today?
29 Who was the god of war in Roman mythology?
30 The Gobi Desert is in which continent?

Answers *Pot-Luck 11* (see Quiz 24)
1 Carbon. 2 Branwell. 3 Zeus. 4 The Volga. 5 Sir Isaac Newton. 6 Tesco. 7 The Bilberry. 8 Carmen. 9 Sir Anthony Eden. 10 Surbiton. 11 Fred Astaire. 12 Nagasaki. 13 Normandy. 14 Catch 22. 15 Brown. 16 Twentieth. 17 Light. 18 Black Sea. 19 Mandy Rice-Davis. 20 Simba. 21 Black Rod. 22 Astrologists. 23 Orchestra. 24 Skye Terrier. 25 John Dillinger. 26 Tosca. 27 The North Sea. 28 Butcher. 29 Die Fledermaus. 30 William Murdock.

1 How many times had Wallis Simpson been married before she married Edward VIII?
2 When she married in 1973 who was Princess Anne's bridesmaid?
3 Which prince's last three names are Charles Albert David?
4 What colour was the suit Diana Spencer wore in her engagement photograph in 1981?
5 What is the name of the Princess Royal's second husband?
6 What was Prince Philip's father called?
7 Which Scottish school did Prince Charles go to?
8 What did the Queen agree to pay for the first time in 1992?
9 Who created Princess Elizabeth's wedding dress in 1947?
10 Who interviewed the Princess of Wales when on "Panorama"?
11 Who was the Duchess of York's financial adviser in 1992?
12 In what capacity was Mrs Susan Barrantes invited to the wedding of Prince Andrew and Sarah Ferguson?
13 Whom did Katharine Worsley marry in 1961?
14 Who is the former Serena Stanhope's mother-in-law?
15 Where is the Prince of Wales' home in Gloucestershire?
16 Which organization did Prince Charles set up in 1976?
17 Who is the Queen's second eldest grandchild?
18 Who is Mrs Frances Shand-Kydd?
19 Who is Earl of Chester?
20 Which opera singer sang at the wedding of Charles and Diana?
21 Who designed Diana Spencer's wedding dress?
22 Whose Christian names are Elizabeth Angela Marguerite?
23 Who is the Duke of Kent's sister?
24 Who was known as Uncle Dickie?
25 Which princess's first names are Marie Christine?
26 What is the Princess of Wales' brother's first name?
27 Royal wedding rings are made from gold from which country?
28 Which coloured stone was in Fergie's engagement ring?
29 Who as a child was known to her family as Lilibet?
30 Which branch of the armed forces did Prince Edward briefly join in 1986?

Quiz 24 Pot-Luck 11

Level 2

Answers - see page 146

1 Coal is composed of which element?
2 The Brontë sisters had a brother: what was his name?
3 Who was chief of the Greek gods?
4 What is the longest river in Russia?
5 Who formulated the law of gravity?
6 Sir Leslie Porter is a former chairman of which supermarket group?
7 The blueberry or the whortleberry is also known as what?
8 In which opera does the heroine work in a cigarette factory?
9 Who succeeded Churchill as prime minister in 1955?
10 In which surburban district of London was the "Good Life" set?
11 Who was Ginger Rogers' most famous dancing partner?
12 Two Japanese cities were hit by atomic bombs in World War II. Hiroshima was one: what was the other?
13 William of where won the Battle of Hastings?
14 In which novel does the character Major Major Major Major appear?
15 What is the colour of the live wire in a three-pin plug?
16 In which century did Queen Victoria die?
17 Which word goes after lime and before house to make two new words?
18 What sea lies between Turkey and Russia?
19 Who said, "Well he would say that, wouldn't he?"
20 In Disney's "The Lion King" who is king at the end of the picture?
21 Whom does the monarch send to summon the Commons to her at the State Opening of Parliament?
22 Which 'ologists study the future through the movement of the planets?
23 What musical word is an anagram of cart-horse?
24 What breed of dog was Greyfriars Bobby?
25 Which 1930s US criminal was known as "Public Enemy No 1"?
26 Of which opera is Floria Tosca the heroine?
27 Which sea provides much of Britain's domestic gas?
28 To what trade had highwayman Dick Turpin been apprenticed?
29 Which Viennese opera title when translated is "The Bat"?
30 Who invented gas street lighting?

Answers

Pot-Luck 10 (see Quiz 22)
1 12. 2 Boxing Day. 3 The Troggs. 4 1984. 5 £5. 6 First watch. 7 India and Sri Lanka. 8 Chesterfield. 9 Clementine. 10 Diamond. 11 Genealogy. 12 Bear. 13 Cricket. 14 Esperanto. 15 Mount Everest. 16 Lloyds. 17 Christopher Robin. 18 Digitalis. 19 Kent. 20 Which? 21 That is the question. 22 Dauphin. 23 Red. 24 His nose. 25 Hara-kiri. 26 Bonnie Prince Charlie. 27 VAT – Value Added Tax. 28 Miss Otis. 29 Mars. 30 Asia.

Quiz 25 Nature: Birds

Answers - see page 151

Level 2

1 Which is the commonest bird in Britain?
2 What species of kite breeds in Britain?
3 What is the study of birds' eggs called?
4 An exaltation is a group of which birds?
5 What would you see if there was a Turdus on your window sill?
6 What colour are wild budgerigars?
7 A scapular on a bird is a type of what?
8 Which bird song sounds like chiff-chaff chiff-chaff?
9 Which bird is sacred in Peru?
10 What type of wren is the smallest British bird?
11 What type of birds are ratites?
12 Which birds group to mate and are shot in braces?
13 What name is given to a flock or gathering of crows?
14 What is special about the bones of most birds?
15 Which family of birds does the robin belong to?
16 Golden and argus are varieties of which bird?
17 Which of the senses is poorly developed in most birds?
18 What is special about a palmiped?
19 Which bird lays the largest egg?
20 What is the oldest known fossil bird?
21 What is the main food of the oyster catcher?
22 What is the shaft of a feather called?
23 Which extinct bird was last sighted in Mauritius?
24 What does a syrinx help a bird to do?
25 Which three features distinguish birds from other creatures?
26 What name is given to a castrated cockerel?
27 What is the common name for all small birds of prey?
28 Which bird is the symbol of the RSPB?
29 What name is given to a flock or gathering of starlings?
30 What is the main group in the family Phasianidae?

Answers

Karaoke (see Quiz 27)
1 Is this just fantasy? 2 Unchained Melody. 3 My, my, my Delilah. 4 My Way. 5 Fog. 6 In his kiss. 7 Your head. 8 Chris de Burgh. 9 The curtain. 10 In the wind. 11 She was a showgirl. 12 New York. 13 Eton Rifles. 14 Matchstalk cats and dogs. 15 I feel it in my fingers. 16 Ten. 17 Jolene. 18 All right. 19 Thought control. 20 Midnight. 21 Your lips. 22 This feeling inside. 23 Rosemary and thyme. 24 Guitar George. 25 Tell me more. 26 Good as you. 27 River deep mountain high. 28 Eleanor Rigby. 29 Make me cry. 30 A whiter shade of pale.

149

Quiz 26 Pot-Luck 12

Answers - see page 152

1 Which principality lies between France and Spain in the Pyrenees?
2 Canaan Banana was the first president of which country?
3 What was the name of the Queen of Faeries in "A Midsummer Night's Dream"?
4 Who was divorced from Mark Phillips?
5 What was the name of the girl who visited the Wizard of Oz?
6 Who came directly after Pope John Paul I?
7 Which product was advertised by Supermodel Eva Herzagovia using the slogan "Hello Boys"?
8 Which two stouts are brewed in Cork?
9 Which stretch of water separates Alaska from the Russian mainland?
10 What did Sandie Shaw bare in the Eurovision Song Contest?
11 Who was the last chemist to be prime minister of Britain?
12 In 1979, who sang about "Walking On The Moon"?
13 Which Jane married Gerald Scarfe?
14 How many letters are there in the Greek alphabet?
15 Which elephants have the bigger ears, Indian or African?
16 "If I Were A Rich Man" comes from which stage show?
17 Which word follows "paper" and precedes "gammon" to make two new words?
18 Who was lead singer with The Boomtown Rats?
19 What was the name of Lady Penelope's puppet chauffeur?
20 What was St Luke's profession?
21 Which Michael Caine film was about the battle at Rorke's Drift?
22 In mythology, Minerva was the goddess of what?
23 What is exactly 26 miles and 385 yards long?
24 If you betray your country what crime do you commit?
25 Who was the first presenter of "Stars in their Eyes"?
26 What in France is "Le Figaro"?
27 Who hosted TV's "Every Second Counts"?
28 By what name was Margaret Hookham known on the stage?
29 Who took over as England cricket captain from Graham Gooch?
30 The Lorelei rock is on which river?

Answers

TV: Police Serials (see Quiz 28)
1 Glasgow. 2 Frank. 3 Terry Venables. 4 Dixon of Dock Green. 5 Ruth Rendell. 6 Kojak. 7 Martin Shaw. 8 Jim. 9 John Thaw. 10 Pierce Brosnan. 11 Metropolitan Police. 12 Pepper. 13 Jemima Shore. 14 Tubbs. 15 Juliet Bravo. 16 Dave and Ken. 17 Hawaii Five-O. 18 Morse Code. 19 Magnum. 20 The Avengers. 21 Poetry. 22 Sweeney Todd – Flying Squad. 23 Van de Valk. 24 Basset hound. 25 Cambridge. 26 Los Angeles. 27 Maigret. 28 Z Cars. 29 Radio presenter. 30 Cagney and Lacey.

150

1 What line follows "Is this the real life"?
2 "Time goes by so slowly, And time can do so much," comes from which song?
3 What line comes before "Why, why, why, Delilah?"?
4 "And so I face the final curtain" comes from which song?
5 According to Gazza, what's mine on the Tyne?
6 Finish the line: "If you want to know if he loves you so, It's..."
7 What do you hold up high when you walk through a storm?
8 Who sang "Never seen you looking so gorgeous as you did tonight"?
9 Jason Donovan closed his eyes and drew back what?
10 "The answer, my friend, is blowing..." where?
11 What line comes after "Her name was Lola"?
12 Where are you if you "wake up in a city that never sleeps"?
13 In which song by The Jam is there "a row going on, down in Slough"?
14 What did he paint apart from "Matchstalk Men"?
15 What line comes before "I feel it in my toes"?
16 How many times do you sing "Yeah" in the chorus of "She Loves You"?
17 To whom did Dolly Parton beg "Please don't take my man"?
18 If tonight is the night how is Whitney Houston feeling?
19 According to Pink Floyd, "We don't need no education, We don't need no..." what?
20 What word comes before "Not a sound from the pavement"?
21 Finish the line: "You never close your eyes anymore when I kiss..."
22 Which Elton John line follows "It's a little bit funny"?
23 Which two herbs go with "parsley, sage"?
24 In "Sultans of Swing" who "knows all the chords"?
25 In "Grease", what line comes before "Did she put up a fight?"?
26 Finish the line: "You're not the truth, No-one could look as..."?
27 What four words go after "Do I love you, My oh my"?
28 Who was "wearing a face that she keeps in a jar by the door"?
29 "Do you really want to hurt me? Do you really want to" do what?
30 "Her face at first just ghostly turned" what colour?

Quiz 28 TV: Police serials

Answers - see page 150

1 In which city is "Taggart" set?
2 What is "The Bill"s DI Burnside's first name?
3 Who was co-creator of "Hazell" with Gordon Williams?
4 Which police series had the theme music "An Ordinary Copper"?
5 Who created the character of Chief Inspector Wexford?
6 Which detective called people "Pussycat"?
7 Which actor links "The Chief" and "The Professionals"?
8 What was Bergerac's first name?
9 Which TV cop is married to Sheila Hancock?
10 Who played the title role in "Remington Steele"?
11 Who did Spender work for before being posted back to Newcastle?
12 In "Police Woman" what was Sgt Anderson's nickname?
13 Which series starred Patricia Hodge in the title role?
14 Who was Crockett's partner in "Miami Vice"?
15 In which series did Jean Darblay, then Kate Longton, appear?
16 What were Starsky and Hutch's first names?
17 In which series did Steve Garrett say "Book 'em Danno!"?
18 What sound was the theme music for "Inspector Morse" based on?
19 Which detective shares his name with a chocolate covered ice-cream bar?
20 Which long-running crime series was a spin-off from a programme called "Police Surgeon"?
21 What sort of literature does Commander Adam Dalgliesh write?
22 How did "The Sweeney" get its name?
23 Which series had the chart topping "Eye Level" as its theme tune?
24 What breed of dog was Columbo's companion Fang?
25 In "Dempsey and Makepeace" which university had Lady Harriet graduated from?
26 In which city did "Burke's Law" take place?
27 Which detective has been played by Richard Harris and Michael Gambon?
28 Which series was set in Seaport and Newtown?
29 What was the occupation of Eddie Shoestring?
30 In which series did cops Petrie and Isbecki appear?

Pot-Luck 11 (see Quiz 26)
1 Andorra. 2 Zimbabwe. 3 Titania. 4 Princess Anne. 5 Dorothy. 6 John Paul II. 7 The Wonderbra. 8 Murphy's and Beamish. 9 Bering Strait. 10 Her feet. 11 Margaret Thatcher. 12 The Police. 13 Asher. 14 24. 15 African. 16 Fiddler on the Roof. 17 Back. 18 Bob Geldof. 19 Parker. 20 Doctor. 21 Zulu. 22 Wisdom. 23 The Marathon. 24 Treason. 25 Leslie Crowther. 26 Newspaper. 27 Paul Daniels. 28 Margot Fonteyn. 29 Mike Atherton. 30 Rhine.

Quiz 29 Pot-Luck 13

Level 2

Answers - see page 155

1 Which gas shares its name with Superman's home planet?
2 In politics, to whom does the expression "Father of the House" refer?
3 On which island is Wall Street?
4 What was the name of Welsh hero Prince Llewelyn's dog?
5 What is the study of fluids moving in pipes?
6 What type of person studies the relationship between living organisms and their environment?
7 What was George Washington's wife first name?
8 Which English town is an anagram of ancestral?
9 Where, in Baker Street, did Sherlock Holmes live?
10 What does the word "Bolshoi" mean?
11 In mythology, who was banished by his son Jupiter?
12 Which London borough is the "G" in GMT?
13 Where in London is the Royal Opera House?
14 What is Eric Clapton's middle name?
15 How many dancers feature in a *pas de deux*?
16 Which William wrote a poem about daffodils?
17 What was the name of the World War I ace nicknamed "The Red Baron"?
18 Who is Lady Antonia Fraser's father?
19 Who invented frozen food?
20 What unit is used to measure the gas we use in our homes?
21 What title did Harold Macmillan take?
22 Which monarch founded Eton College?
23 Which Shakespeare play is in three parts?
24 What is a mordant?
25 Which "ology" is the art of ringing bells?
26 How was Achilles killed?
27 Which king was Queen Elizabeth II's grandfather?
28 Which precinct does Ed McBain write about?
29 Who wrote the novel "Dr Zhivago"?
30 Who was prime minister of Britain at the outbreak of World War II?

Answers

Pot-Luck 14 (see Quiz 31)
1 Edward Heath. 2 Alan Sheppard. 3 Crufts. 4 Evil to him who evil thinks it. 5 Psychology. 6 Formic acid. 7 George III. 8 Fred Perry. 9 The Crimea. 10 Meal. 11 Supreme Headquarters Allied Powers in Europe. 12 Terpsichore. 13 Jimi Hendrix. 14 China. 15 Germany. 16 Red. 17 Elizabeth. 18 The Times. 19 Flowers. 20 21. 21 Nitrous oxide. 22 Elizabeth Barrett Browning. 23 Skinner 24 Dermatology. 25 Sulphuric acid. 26 Plastering. 27 Edward Gibbon. 28 Poland. 29 Dorothy L. Sayers. 30 Children.

Quiz 30 Transport

Answers - see page 156

Level 2

1 What is the plate connecting two lengths of railway track called?
2 What, according to tradition, takes four years to paint from end to end?
3 Which letter do post-war tanks all begin with?
4 Outside which London building were traffic lights first installed?
5 In World War II what was a McRobert's Reply?
6 What did LNER stand for?
7 Which famous aircraft carrier was withdrawn from service in 1979?
8 Which was the first true jet to enter passenger service?
9 What is the popular name for the Boeing 747 and the European airbus?
10 What links the Pacific Ocean with the Caribbean?
11 Who introduced the C5 in 1985?
12 Which motorway goes from London to Winchester?
13 Which nickname is given to aircraft such as the Harrier?
14 Who developed the Mini?
15 Which type of transport is Zeppelin associated with?
16 Where is O'Hare International airport?
17 What is the distress word for ships and aircraft?
18 Which four-wheel drive vehicle was launched in 1940?
19 Which word is used to describe the frame, wheels and machinery of a car?
20 The first motor car race was held to Bordeaux and back to where?
21 Which country has the international registration letter M?
22 Which US car manufacturer makes Astra, Corsa and Chevrolet?
23 What is the distance between two rails on a track called?
24 What colour is the District Line on a London Underground map?
25 From which two London stations could you travel to Scotland direct?
26 Which two classes of travel are there on Inter City trains?
27 In terms of tonnes of cargo handled, which is Europe's busiest port?
28 What does 'Volswagen' mean?
29 On which side of the road do the Japanese drive?
30 In which city is Lime St Station?

Answers

Religious Fervour (see Quiz 32)
1 Jesus Christ's. 2 Brazil. 3 Ecumenical Movement. 4 Jehovah's Witnesses. 5 The Salvation Army. 6 Ramadan. 7 Jihad. 8 Buddhism. 9 Japan. 10 Russia. 11 Quakers. 12 Hinduism. 13 Mecca. 14 Hare Krishna. 15 Sikhs. 16 Scientology. 17 Chinese. 18 Mormons. 19 Transcendental Meditation. 20 Rastafarianism. 21 Temple. 22 Islam. 23 Kosher. 24 Eskimos. 25 Unitarians. 26 Church of Christ, Scientist. 27 John and Charles. 28 Immersion. 29 Moonies. 30 Sunday.

Quiz 31 Pot-Luck 14

Level 2

Answers - see page 153

1 Whom did Margaret Thatcher replace as leader of the Tory party?
2 Who hit a golf shot on the moon?
3 Which dog show was first held in Islington in 1891?
4 What does "Honi soit qui mal y pense" mean?
5 In which "ology" were Freud and Jung active?
6 What acid gives nettles their sting?
7 Which king was nicknamed "Farmer George"?
8 Who was the last Briton to win the men's singles at Wimbledon?
9 On which peninsula is the city of Sevastopol situated?
10 Which word goes after piece and before times to make two new words?
11 What was SHAPE?
12 Who was the Greek muse of dance?
13 Which rock guitarist prophetically said, "When you're dead you're made for life"?
14 In which country is Puccini's "Turandot" set?
15 Which country did "Kaiser Bill" rule?
16 What colour of ballet shoes did Hans Christian Andersen write about?
17 What was Mrs Gaskell's first name?
18 Which British newspaper is nicknamed "The Thunderer"?
19 What according to Scott McKenzie did you wear in your hair in San Francisco?
20 After 1928, women over what age were given the vote?
21 What is the correct name for laughing gas?
22 Which poetess had a dog named Flush?
23 In "EastEnders", what is Ethel's last name?
24 Which "ology" is concerned with the human skin?
25 What is H_2SO_4?
26 Finish and browning are used in which building trade?
27 Who wrote the "Decline and Fall of the Roman Empire"?
28 In which country was Catherine the Great born?
29 Who chronicled the cases of Lord Peter Wimsey?
30 Who is UNICEF responsible for?

1 Whose birth shaped the calendar of the Western world?
2 Which country has the largest number of Roman Catholics?
3 Which movement promotes understanding between different branches of the Christian faith?
4 What are members of the Watchtower Movement better known as?
5 Whose newspaper is called "The Warcry"?
6 During which month do Muslims fast from before sunrise to sunset?
7 What term is used in Islam for "Holy War"?
8 Which religion is based on the teaching of Siddhartha Gautama?
9 Shintoism is the native religion of which country?
10 Which country has the largest Orthodox Church?
11 What are members of the Society of Friends called?
12 In which religion are Shiva and Vishnu major gods?
13 Where should Muslims make a pilgrimage to once in their lifetime?
14 How is the International Society for Krishna Consciousness known?
15 Who have uncut hair worn in a turban and uncut beards?
16 Which religion was founded by a science fiction author?
17 What nationality was Confucius?
18 What are members of the Church of Jesus Christ of Latter Day Saints better known as?
19 What does TM stand for in the movement founded by the Maharishi?
20 Dreadlocks in the hair and a musical style are hallmarks of which movement linked with Ethiopia?
21 In Hinduism what is a mandir?
22 Which religion has Sunnis and Shiites?
23 In Judaism treifa foods are forbidden. Which foods are allowed?
24 Shamanism is the dominant religion of which Arctic people?
25 Which Christian group deny the idea of the Trinity?
26 Which Church was founded by Mary Baker Eddy in the USA in 1879?
27 Which two Wesleys founded Methodism?
28 What sort of baptism does the Baptist Church practise?
29 What are members of the Unification Church better known as?
30 In Judaism what is the first day of the week?

Quiz 33 Pot-Luck 15

Level 2

1 Who directed and starred in "A Bronx Tale"?
2 Which of the seven deadly sins begins with G?
3 What was Ghana's former name?
4 The Dutch royal family acquired its name from which French town?
5 Is the corncrake a bird, mammal or reptile?
6 What name is given to animals which do not hunt or eat meat?
7 Over which continent did the ozone hole form?
8 Which tanker suffered a severe oil spill in Alaska in 1989?
9 Where is the pituitary gland?
10 Which structural tissue is found in between the vertebral discs?
11 Which TV series featured a painter and decorator called Jacko?
12 In ads, which sweets are "made to make your mouth water"?
13 In which country would you find polders?
14 In which country are the Angel Falls?
15 What are the twin skyscrapers, 1,361 feet high, in New York called?
16 In which two cities would you find Cleopatra's Needles?
17 In which African country is Timbuktu?
18 Who said, "Marriage is a wonderful invention – but so is the bicycle repair kit"?
19 Which English prime minister was known as "the Great Commoner"?
20 Who was the first person to notice that the Sun had spots?
21 Which metal is the best conductor of electricity?
22 Which actress's real name is Julia Wells?
23 Which secret society refers to God as "the great architect of the Universe"?
24 Which building is used for the election of a pope?
25 With whom did Bing Crosby sing "True Love" in the film "High Society"?
26 Which two colours appear on the UN flag?
27 What is the name of the Welsh Nationalist party?
28 What kind of stone is marble?
29 What name is given to the thousands of small bodies which orbit the Sun?
30 Which island was held by the Knights of St John from 1530 to 1798?

Answers

Soul and Motown (see Quiz 35)
1 Reach Out, I'll Be There. 2 Berry Gordy. 3 Dave. 4 Aretha Franklin. 5 Holland. 6 Otis Redding. 7 The Broken Hearted. 8 Jackie Wilson. 9 The Isley Brothers. 10 James Brown. 11 The Supremes. 12 After the song Tammy by Debbie Reynolds. 13 You Keep me Hangin' On. 14 Wilson Pickett. 15 The Vandellas. 16 Arthur Conley. 17 I'm Still Waiting. 18 Lionel Richie. 19 Gladys Knight. 20 Bobby Brown. 21 Stevie Wonder. 22 The Temptations. 23 Jimmy Mack. 24 William. 25 Midnight. 26 Reflections. 27 Marvin Gaye. 28 Atlantic. 29 Edwin Starr. 30 Junior Walker.

1 In darts, what is the maximum check-out score?
2 Who has won most international soccer caps for England?
3 Which country did boxer Lennox Lewis represent at the Olympics?
4 Which TV sports quiz show is hosted by Nick Hancock?
5 Faldo, Clark and James represented Europe in the 1995 Ryder Cup. Who was the fourth Englishman?
6 What nationality is tennis player Michael Chang?
7 A snooker player makes a break of eight points. Which three colours are potted?
8 In greyhound racing what colour does the first dog wear?
9 For what sport is Ellery Hanley famous?
10 Who won the Superbowl '96?
11 What important role did Oliver McCall play in Frank Bruno's career?
12 At which Grand Prix circuit did Ayrton Senna lose his life?
13 Who was the first man to do the 100-metre breast stroke in under a minute?
14 Which football club has won the English championship the most times?
15 Where was Barry Sheene involved in a 175 mph crash in 1975?
16 Which twisting circuit on the Grand Prix calendar is only 1.95 miles long?
17 Has croquet ever been a sport in the Olympics?
18 Which boxer used to enter the ring to Tina Turner's "Simply The Best"?
19 Name the teams in the Scottish League whose names end in United?
20 In Rugby Union, who is Australia's record try scorer?
21 At which venue was the 1996 B&H Masters snooker tournament played?
22 In speedway racing, how many laps of the track does a race consist of?
23 Apart from England which European country took part in cricket's 1996 World Cup?
24 Which world heavyweight boxing champion died in an air-crash in 1969?
25 Who won a 100-metre breast stroke gold in the 1980 Olympics?
26 In badminton, how many points win a single game?
27 Which trainer is known as the "Queen of Aintree"?
28 Is an own goal allowed for in the rules of hockey?
29 Which two sports take place on a piste?
30 Who only passed his UK motor bike test in February 1996?

Level 2

1 The Four Tops had only one British No 1 What was it?
2 Who was the boss of Tamla Motown?
3 Who sang with Sam on the hit "Soul Man"?
4 Which female soul star has recorded with Elton John, George Michael and George Benson?
5 Who made up the songwriting trio with Holland and Dozier?
6 Who was sitting on the dock of the bay?
7 Who according to Jimmy Ruffin "had love that has now departed"?
8 Which soul singer died in 1984 after lying in a coma for eight years?
9 Rudolph, Ronald and O'Kelley were which singing Brothers?
10 Who is known as "The Godfather Of Soul"?
11 Which group featured Cindy Birdsong?
12 The Motown label was nearly called Tammy. After which Tammy?
13 Which Tamla song starts,"Set me free, why don't you babe"?
14 In the 1960s who was known as "The Wicked Pickett"?
15 Which group backed Martha Reeves?
16 Who recorded the soul classic "Sweet Soul Music"?
17 What was Diana Ross's first solo British No 1?
18 Which singer went solo after performing with the Commodores?
19 Who was backed by The Pips?
20 Which soul singer married Whitney Houston in 1992?
21 Who sang "I Was Made To Love Her"?
22 Eddie Kendricks and David Ruffin were lead singers with which group?
23 Who did Martha Reeves want to "hurry back"?
24 What was Smokey Robinson's real first name?
25 Which hour did Cropper and Pickett write about?
26 Which was the first single in which the Supremes were billed as Diana Ross and The Supremes?
27 Who originally heard it through the grapevine?
28 On which label did Aretha Franklin record in the 1960s?
29 Who had a Tamla hit with "War"?
30 Who fronted the All Stars?

Quiz 36 Pot-Luck 16

Level 2

1 Which instrument did Franz Liszt play?
2 By what name is Betty Jean Persice better known?
3 In which republic of the former USSR is Chernobyl?
4 In which year were East and West Germany unified?
5 Where was the treaty signed that established the EEC?
6 Who won the first Rugby Union World Cup, held in 1987?
7 On which circuit is motor racing's Grand Prix d'Endurance run?
8 Which two South American countries produce the most coffee?
9 What is the capital of Ecuador?
10 Helium belongs to which group of elements?
11 Where in the cell is DNA stored?
12 Who was the author of "Spycatcher" in 1987?
13 Who wrote the play "Waiting For Godot"?
14 Which Australian city is named after William IV's queen?
15 Which Greenpeace ship was sunk in Auckland harbour in 1985?
16 In "Emmerdale" what did Annie Sugden's name change to?
17 What is Del Boy's local?
18 Who was the first director of Britain's National Theatre Company?
19 Which song features the line "I bet you think this song is about you"?
20 Who painted "The Nightwatch?"
21 Which German brothers collected such stories as "Hansel and Gretel"?
22 What nationality was Hans Christian Andersen?
23 Who said, "A Scout smiles and whistles under all circumstances"?
24 Who first urged Beethoven to "roll over" in 1956?
25 What name was given to the practice which tried to turn lead into silver and gold?
26 Who shared a Nobel Prize for physics with his son?
27 What is a chinook?
28 In which country was Rudyard Kipling born?
29 Which poet drowned while sailing off the coast of Italy in 1822?
30 Which British prime minister wrote "Coningsby" and "Sybil"?

Sports Bag (see Quiz 34)

Answers
1 170 – two treble 20s plus bull. 2 Peter Shilton. 3 Canada. 4 They Thinks It's All Over. 5 David Gilford. 6 American. 7 Red, yellow, brown. 8 Red. 9 Rugby League. 10 Dallas. 11 Bruno beat McCall to become the WBC Heavyweight champion. 12 San Marino, Italy. 13 Adrian Moorhouse in 1987. 14 Liverpool. 15 Daytona. 16 Monaco. 17 Yes. 18 Chris Eubank. 19 Ayr and Dundee. 20 David Campese. 21 Wembley Arena. 22 Four. 23 Netherlands. 24 Rocky Marciano. 25 Duncan Goodhew. 26 15 points. 27 Jenny Pitman. 28 Yes. 29 Fencing and skiing. 30 Eddie Kidd.

1 Which film about Arnhem was criticized as "A film too long"?
2 During which war was "Platoon" set?
3 Which Hollywood legend played Kurtz in "Apocalypse Now"?
4 Who played Hawkeye and Trapper John in "M*A*S*H"?
5 How was the film "Patton" known in the UK?
6 For which Robert de Niro film was "Cavatina" the theme music?
7 Who won an Oscar as the Colonel in "The Bridge on the River Kwai"?
8 In "The Colditz Story" what type of building was Colditz?
9 In which English county were the GIs billeted in "Yanks"?
10 What type of soldiers were the four Britons in "The Wild Geese"?
11 Which 1963 film about Allied POWs starred James Garner and Steve McQueen?
12 Hits from which decade were on the soundtrack of "Good Morning, Vietnam"?
13 Which 1981 Mel Gibson film was set in World War I?
14 How were the 12 convicts recruited for a suicide mission known in the 1967 movie?
15 Which novel was "Schindler's List" based on?
16 Which US singer played Von Ryan in "Von Ryan's Express"?
17 Whose café was a meeting place for war refugees in "Casablanca"?
18 Who wrote the novel on which "Where Eagles Dare" was based?
19 Which musical satire on war was directed by Richard Attenborough?
20 Where was it "All Quiet" in the classic film made in 1930?
21 At the time of which World War II event is "From Here to Eternity" set?
22 In "A Town Like Alice" what does "Alice" refer to?
23 Which anti Vietnam war activist starred in "Coming Home"?
24 Who was the subject of the film "The Desert Fox"?
25 Which 1940 film starred Charlie Chaplin as despot Adenoid Hynkel?
26 Who directed "Born on the Fourth of July"?
27 Whose heroes were Clint Eastwood and Telly Savalas in 1970?
28 "The Eagle Has Landed" centres on a plot to kidnap whom?
29 Who won the Oscar for best actress in 1982 for "Sophie's Choice"?
30 In which country is "The Killing Fields" set?

Quiz 38 Pot-Luck 17

Answers - see page 164

Level 2

1 What is Terry Wogan's real first name?
2 What name was given to the 19th-century group who wrecked machines?
3 What is the name of Orson Welles' first film, made when he was 26?
4 Who wrote the television series "The Singing Detective"?
5 Which river runs through the Grand Canyon?
6 Name the geological fault that runs the length of California?
7 Which bandmaster composed "The Stars and Stripes Forever"?
8 Which drug is derived from the willow, *Salix alba*?
9 Where was Captain Cook killed?
10 Where was the Royal Mint until 1810?
11 Which drink did Leonard Rossiter and Joan Collins advertise?
12 What is the full name for DNA?
13 Other than the "Odyssey", which work is Homer famed for?
14 Name the art of making decorative lacework with knotted threads?
15 To which family does the chive belong?
16 Which indoor game was invented by British Army Officers in India in 1875?
17 Which microbe is the basis of the brewing and baking industry?
18 Who wrote the novel "The Van"?
19 In bluegrass music who is Flatt's partner?
20 Philip Glass wrote an opera about which scientist?
21 Who led the crew of the "Argo" in their search for the golden fleece?
22 What planet was home for the aliens in Wells's "The War of the Worlds"?
23 Who is credited with the invention of scat singing?
24 Which group consisted of Les, Eric, Woody, Alan and Derek?
25 Name Mary Quant's shop which revolutionized fashion in the 1960s?
26 Which mountain was first climbed by Edward Whymper in 1865?
27 In fiction, Michael Henchard became mayor of which town?
28 In which TV series did Janet Jackson have a starring role?
29 Who discovered that the universe is expanding?
30 In music, what is meant by *pianissimo*?

Level 2

1 Whose "True Story" did Andrew Morton write about?
2 Which fictional detective is assisted by Captain Hastings?
3 Whose autobiography was called "Past Imperfect"?
4 What was Jeffrey Archer's sequel to "Kane and Abel" called?
5 What is the first name of the novelist A. S. Byatt?
6 In "Alice in Wonderland" what price did the Mad Hatter have on his hat?
7 Who co-wrote "Some Other Rainbow" with Jill Morrell?
8 In which country is the beginning of "The Thorn Birds" set?
9 Which former Beirut hostage wrote "An Evil Cradling"?
10 How is adventure writer David Cornwell better known?
11 Which town is the main setting for the Cadfael novels?
12 Part of whose life story is called "The Path to Power"?
13 Who wrote the biography "Frank Sinatra: An American Legend"?
14 Which alternative comedian wrote "Gridlock"?
15 What was the job of Mellors in "Lady Chatterley's Lover"?
16 Under which pseudonym does Harry Paterson also write?
17 Which comedy actress wrote "When's it Coming Out"?
18 Which Mary Wesley novel transferred to TV with Felicity Kendal and Paul Eddington?
19 Which suspense novelist was the cousin of horror movie actor Christopher Lee?
20 What is the name of Bernard Cornwell's hero, played on TV by Sean Bean?
21 Which politician wrote "A Woman's Place"?
22 Who created the detective Maigret?
23 Whose autobiography is called "Long Walk to Freedom"?
24 Who wrote the tales on which the film "The Jungle Book" was based?
25 In which country was the best seller "Wild Swans" set?
26 Where do Jackie Collins' "Wives, Husbands and Kids" live?
27 What was the name of Lord Peter Wimsey's butler?
28 What were the "Dogs of War" in Frederick Forsyth's novel?
29 Which novel by Victor Hugo became a long-running musical?
30 Whose autobiography is called "Take It Like A Man"?

Quiz 40 Pot-Luck 18

Answers - see page 162

Level 2

1 Who founded the Royal Hospital in Chelsea?
2 What popular drink was known in China as early as 2737 BC?
3 What is the other name for the star Polaris?
4 On how many stone tablets were the Ten Commandments engraved?
5 Who wrote "The Three Sisters"?
6 What was the nickname of Edward Prince of Wales, son of Edward III?
7 Which insects communicate with one another by dancing?
8 Which disease was deliberately introduced in rabbits in the UK?
9 Where are the semicircular canals in the body?
10 What part of a cola tree is used to flavour drinks?
11 Which is the largest Greek island?
12 Whose last two TV series' were aired posthumously on both BBC 1 and Channel 4?
13 Who married Joséphine de Beauharnais and Princess Marie Louise?
14 Lack of iron in the diet may cause which disease?
15 On children's TV, if it's Friday and it's five o'clock what show was on ?
16 Riyadh is the capital of which country?
17 In which Far Eastern country was the Unification Church (Moonies) founded in 1954?
18 Which minister of health inaugurated the National Health Service?
19 Which strait links San Francisco Bay with the Pacific?
20 Which famous gardener helped landscape Blenheim and Stowe?
21 Which insect sometimes eats its male mate during copulation?
22 What was the first national park established in the United States in 1872?
23 What is the scientific name for the windpipe?
24 Which bean is the richest natural vegetable food?
25 In which city would you find the Blue Mosque?
26 What is the currency of Algeria?
27 In which port did Sir Francis Drake "singe the King of Spain's beard"?
28 Where was Mohammed born?
29 What is the commonest element in the Earth's crust?
30 Which George Orwell novel showed the dangers of excessive state control?

Quiz 41 Food and Drink: Wine

Answers - see page 167

1 Claret wine is produced in the region surrounding which French city?
2 What would be the term to describe a dry champagne?
3 In which country is the wine-growing Barossa Valley?
4 Which white wine grape variety is most widely planted in California?
5 In which country is the Marlborough wine region?
6 Retsina is native to which country?
7 Which wine has the varieties Malmsey and Sercial?
8 What is the normal capacity for a bottle of wine?
9 In which country is Rioja produced?
10 Along which river is most of France's Sauvignon Blanc cultivated?
11 What colour are most English wines?
12 Which scientist discovered that yeast causes fermentation?
13 What is a crate of twelve bottles of wine called?
14 Which country does Sukhindol wine come from?
15 In which part of the United States is the Zinfandel grape chiefly cultivated?
16 What is the first name of wine writer Ms Robinson?
17 In which country is the wine-making area of Stellenbosch?
18 How many normal size wine bottles would you have in a Methuselah?
19 How are fizzy wines, other than champagnes, described?
20 In which area of Italy is Chianti Classico produced?
21 Would a French wine described as "*doux*" be medium sweet or medium dry?
22 What are the three styles of port?
23 What colour are most of the wines from France's Anjou region?
24 In which South American country is Casablanca Valley?
25 Which red wine is drunk when young and is called "*nouveau*"?
26 In which country was a vine variety called "vegetable dragon pearls"?
27 Which wine can be "*fino*" or "*oloroso*"?
28 What is Moët et Chandon?
29 Who is the female wine expert on the BBC's "Food and Drink" programme?
30 Along which river and its tributaries do the German vineyards lie?

Rugby (see Quiz 43) 1 Gloucester. 2 Brad Fittler. 3 Warrington. 4 Jonah Lomu. 5 Leicester. 6 Swinton. 7 Paul Ringer. 8 Brian Bevan. 9 Twickenham. 10 Nick Farr-Jones. 11 Scott Quinnell. 12 Jamie Salmon. 13 Widnes. 14 Dennis Betts. 15 Rob Howley. 16 Halifax. 17 Joel Stransky. 18 London Crusaders. 19 Harlequins. 20 Rugby League Cup Final Man of The Match. 21 1995. 22 William Webb Ellis. 23 Hull Kingston Rovers and Barrow. 24 Gareth Edwards. 25 The British Lions. 26 France. 27 Brian Robinson. 28 Wakefield Trinity, Warrington, Widnes, Workington Town. 29 Eddie Waring Memorial Trophy. 30 John Player Trophy.

Answers

Quiz 42 Pot-Luck 19

Level 2

Answers - see page 168

1 What became Glenn Miller's signature tune?
2 Picardy is in the northeast of which country?
3 NUPE was the National Union of what?
4 Which cathedral has the highest spire in Britain?
5 Who sang "Hey, babe, take a walk on the wild side"?
6 The Brenner Pass links which two countries?
7 Which two fruits are anagrams of each other?
8 What is the chief member of a lifeboat crew called?
9 In geography, which term means the joining of two rivers?
10 Which musical note follows fah?
11 How many phases of the moon are there in a lunar month?
12 Which river flows through Cambridge?
13 In geometry what type of line bisects a circle?
14 Which university is based at Milton Keynes?
15 What on your body would a trichologist be concerned with?
16 Which instrument did Jack Benny play?
17 What was Gilbert White's field of work?
18 In the board game Cluedo what is the name of the Reverend?
19 Brussels, Honiton and Nottingham are all renowned for which product?
20 Which radio serial is "an everyday story of country folk"?
21 What are Giles, Low and Trog known for?
22 Who wrote that "The workers have nothing to lose but their chains"?
23 What have you done if you have committed patricide?
24 Which donkey is Winnie the Pooh's friend?
25 In which district are Hawes and Ullswater?
26 Who was Webster Booth's singing partner?
27 In the Bible, where was the traveller going to in the parable of the Good Samaritan?
28 To what kind of meeting was Mahatma Gandhi going when he was assassinated?
29 What colour are Aylesbury ducks?
30 How is singer Elaine Bookbinder better known?

Answers

Nature: Fish (see Quiz 44)
1 The tail. 2 Red/orange. 3 Tuna. 4 Herring. 5 Roe. 6 Tench. 7 Salmon.
8 Whale shark. 9 Sardine. 10 Blue/black. 11 Liver. 12 Carp. 13 Fish
rearing. 14 Silver bream. 15 Whelk. 16 Small shark. 17 Rock salmon.
18 Hermit crab. 19 On its back. 20 Trout. 21 Ten. 22 Izaak Walton. 23
Flatfish. 24 Sprats. 25 Round its mouth. 26 A grain of sand. 27 Pike.
28 Red mullet. 29 Dover sole. 30 Clam.

Quiz 43 Rugby

Answers - see page 165

1 Which county play at Kingsholm?
2 Who captained Australia in the 1995 World Cup Final?
3 Which League club is nicknamed "The Wires"?
4 Whom did Will Carling describe as a "freak"?
5 Who plays at home at Welford Road?
6 Which League side play at Bury FC's ground, Gig Lane?
7 Who was the first Welshman to be sent off playing for his country at Twickenham?
8 Who played League between 1946 and 1964 and created a record for most tries in a career?
9 Where are you if you are at "Billy Williams' cabbage patch"?
10 Who captained Australia in their World Cup win in 1991?
11 Which nephew of Barry John became a Wigan player?
12 Who played for both England and New Zealand in the 1980s?
13 Which League club is nicknamed "The Chemics"?
14 Who captained England in the 1995 World Cup Final?
15 Who scored on his debut for Wales against England in 1996?
16 Who play at Thrum Hall?
17 Who kicked the winning goal in extra time in the 1995 World Cup Final for South Africa?
18 What was the previous name of London Broncos?
19 Who plays at the Stoop Memorial Ground?
20 To whom is the Lance B. Todd Memorial Trophy awarded?
21 In what year did Scotland first win at Parc des Princes?
22 Who in 1883 picked the ball up and ran with it to "discover" rugby?
23 Which two clubs play at home at Craven Park?
24 Who played for Wales in 53 consecutive games from 1967 to 1978?
25 In Union, which international team name was first used in 1924?
26 Who can win the Five Nations but not the Triple Crown?
27 Who scored most tries for Ireland in the 1991 World Cup?
28 Apart from Wigan name four teams beginning with a W who have been League champions?
29 In League, what is awarded for the BBC TV try of the season?
30 What was the Regal Trophy previously called?

Quiz 44 Nature: Fish

Answers - see page 166

1 Where is a fish's caudal fin?
2 What colour are the spots on a plaice?
3 What sort of fish is a skipjack?
4 Which family does the anchovy belong to?
5 Caviare is which part of the sturgeon?
6 Tinca tinca is the Latin name of which fish?
7 Alevin and parr are stages in the development of which fish?
8 What is the world's largest fish?
9 What is a young pilchard called?
10 What colour is a live lobster?
11 From which part of the cod is a beneficial oil produced?
12 The minnow is the smallest member of which family?
13 What is pisciculture?
14 Which fish has been nicknamed "tin plate"?
15 What is a buckie another name for?
16 What sort of fish is a dogfish?
17 What is a dogfish called when it is bought for food?
18 Which type of crab lives in hollow objects such as snail shells?
19 Where is a fish's dorsal fin?
20 Which fish has the varieties brown, sea or rainbow?
21 How many arms does a squid have?
22 Who wrote "The Compleat Angler"?
23 Flounder is a common name for which type of fish?
24 What are brisling also called?
25 Where would you find barbels on a fish?
26 What starts an oyster developing a pearl in its shell?
27 Which fish has the same name as an early infantry weapon?
28 Which fish is also called goatfish or surmullet?
29 What is another name for the common European sole?
30 What is a geoduck?

Quiz 45 Pot-Luck 20

Answers - see page 171

1 What have these in common: Job, Judges and Habakkuk?
2 Which device is used on a guitar fretboard to raise the pitch of the strings?
3 Which king was reigning in Britain at the start of the First World War?
4 In imperial measurement, how many yards are in a chain?
5 What kind of tree is an osier?
6 On TV, "who was feared by the bad, loved by the good"?
7 With what do you play a vibraphone?
8 On a ship what are the scuppers?
9 With which sport is Peter Alliss associated?
10 Who became ruler of Spain after the Spanish Civil War?
11 In literature, how many Arabian Nights were there?
12 Which singer said, "You're not drunk if you can lie on the floor without holding on"?
13 Black, Italian and Lombardy are all types of which tree?
14 In which war was the Battle of Jutland?
15 What is the square root of 169?
16 Which actress's real name is Camille Javal?
17 What is the name given to the lowest layer of the atmosphere?
18 What was added to rum to make the drink grog?
19 In London where is Poet's Corner?
20 In ads, who is "your flexible friend"?
21 For which of these games would you use dice: ludo, whist, hopscotch, snakes-and-ladders?
22 What instrument would you use to measure the diameter of a cylinder?
23 In which month is Michaelmas Day?
24 In which English county would you find the coastal resort of California?
25 In which game does the term "cannon" occur?
26 For what is Elizabeth Fry chiefly remembered?
27 What fruit do we get from a rose?
28 What was Cleo Laine's job before she was a singer?
29 Which ocean is crossed to sail from San Francisco to Sydney?
30 Who was the British member of The Monkees?

Answers

Pot-Luck 21 (see Quiz 47)
1 Yew. 2 Greece. 3 February. 4 Portugal. 5 Everton. 6 It had no toes.
7 Computer languages. 8 Five and a half. 9 Brass In Pocket. 10 Model T
Ford. 11 Max Wall. 12 Watt. 13 Straws. 14 A spy or informer. 15 Order
or command. 16 Stitches. 17 The Merchant of Venice. 18 Bob Dylan. 19
Adam Ant. 20 By rubbing it legs against its wings or together. 21
Massachusetts. 22 Stephen. 23 Tennis. 24 Wore them. They are very wide
trousers. 25 Paris. 26 Charles Edward Stuart. 27 The Rolling Stones. 28
Georgia. 29 Whatever Happened to the Likely Lads. 30 Thomas.

Quiz 46 Pop: Dance and Disco

Level 2

Answers - see page 172

1 Who was "Dancin' On The Ceiling" in 1986?
2 Which Village People chart hit was made up of initial letters?
3 Which boy's name took Sister Sledge to No 1 in 1985?
4 Cheryl Jones and Sandra Denton spiced up their names to what?
5 Which group's name features three of the natural elements?
6 Which Doors song was given the disco treatment by Amii Stewart?
7 In which song does the line "Too Ra Loo Ra Loo Rye Aye" appear?
8 Which girl group backed Disco Tex?
9 Who was too sexy in 1991?
10 Whose name comes before The Mastermixers?
11 Which Richie Valens 1950s hit charted for Los Lobos in 1987?
12 Who was "Never Gonna Give You Up" in 1987?
13 Who did Madonna tell "don't preach" in the 1986 No 1?
14 Which country do Black Box come from?
15 Who recorded "Funky Stuff" and "Jungle Boogie"?
16 Which group found success in the 1970s with "Night Fever"?
17 Who teamed up with Take That in "Relight My Fire"?
18 Who recorded "Wham Rap"?
19 Who else was on "Keep On Pumpin' It" along with The Visionmasters and Tony Knight?
20 What was on the B side of Boney M's "Rivers Of Babylon"?
21 Which disco hit singer thought that "Love's Unkind"?
22 What was a No 1 for The Simpsons?
23 Who had "A Night To Remember" in 1982?
24 While Tina Charles loved to love, what did her baby love to do?
25 In his baggy trousers, what name is rapper Stanley Burrell known as?
26 Who had "Heartache" in 1987?
27 Caron Wheeler, Kym Mazelle featured with who?
28 Who recorded the 1970s disco song "You're My First My Last My Everything"?
29 Who sang "Dance, Dance, Dance"?
30 How is Robert Bell better known?

Answers

Around Europe (see Quiz 48)
1 Albania. 2 Oberammergau. 3 Yugoslavia. 4 Malta. 5 Austria's. 6 Spain and Portugal. 7 The Hague. 8 Strait, Turkey. 9 Munich. 10 Greece. 11 Italy. 12 Liechtenstein. 13 Baltic. 14 France, Italy, Switzerland and Austria. 15 Russia. 16 Cologne. 17 Iceland. 18 Denmark and Norway. 19 Moldova. 20 The Netherlands. 21 Belgium. 22 Lorraine and Nancy. 23 Denmark. 24 Mont Blanc. 25 Germany's. 26 Bulgaria. 27 Finnish and Swedish. 28 Red Cross. 29 The Algarve. 30 Ukraine.

Quiz 47 Pot-Luck 21

Level 2

1 From which wood were longbows made?
2 In which country is the Corinth Canal?
3 Which month is "fill-dike"?
4 Of which European country are Madeira and the Azores a part?
5 Which club did Gary Lineker play for immediately before going to Barcelona?
6 In a poem by Edward Lear, what was peculiar about the "Pobble"?
7 Pascal, Cobol and Basic are all types of what?
8 In yards, how long was a rod, pole, or perch?
9 What was the first No 1 single of the 80s?
10 What is or was a tin lizzie?
11 Which comedian's catch phrase was, "Now there's a funny thing"?
12 What name is given to the unit of electrical power?
13 According to the proverb what do drowning men clutch?
14 What is a copper's nark?
15 What is the modern equivalent for the word behest?
16 Back, blanket and buttonhole are all types of what?
17 In which Shakespeare play is Shylock introduced?
18 Which folk singer wrote the song "The Times They are A-Changin'"?
19 In pop, who was King of the wild frontier?
20 How does a grasshopper produce its distinctive sound?
21 Of which US state is Boston the capital?
22 Who came to the throne of England on the death of Henry I?
23 With which sport do you associate Rosemary Casals?
24 What did people do with Oxford bags?
25 In which city is Sacré Coeur?
26 Who assumed the guise of Betty Burke?
27 Brian Jones was in which pop group?
28 Which is the home state of former president Jimmy Carter?
29 In which TV series sequel did Bob marry Thelma?
30 What is Sean Connery's real first name?

Quiz 48 Around Europe

Level 2

1 Which country's capital is Tirana?
2 Where is a passion play staged every ten years?
3 Which state was Macedonia part of from 1945 to 1991?
4 Which island holds the George Cross?
5 Which country's highest mountain is the Grossglockner?
6 Which countries are on the Iberian Peninsula?
7 Where is The Netherlands' seat of government and administration?
8 What are the Dardanelles and where are they?
9 Which southern German city is famous for its October beer festival?
10 Which country is called Elleniki Dimokratia or Hellenic Republic?
11 Which country's chief river is the Po?
12 Which country, whose capital is Vaduz, has no armed forces?
13 Which sea lies to the north of Poland?
14 In which four countries are the Alps?
15 Which country covers 10% of the globe's land surface?
16 By what English name is Köln known?
17 Which country's landscape is made up of volcanoes and geysers?
18 Between which countries does the Skagerrak lie?
19 What are Bessarabia, Moldavia and a former part of the USSR now known as?
20 Which country has had a prime minister called Wim Kok?
21 Albert II became king of which country in 1993?
22 A region of eastern France has a girl's name with another girl's name as its capital. What are they?
23 Which country do Greenland and the Faeroe Islands belong to?
24 What is France's highest point?
25 Whose upper house of Parliament is called the Bundesrat?
26 Which country's currency is the lev?
27 What are the two official languages of Finland?
28 Which aid organization's emblem is the Swiss flag with its colours reversed?
29 Which Portuguese province borders Spain and the Atlantic Ocean?
30 Which is Europe's largest country after Russia?

Quiz 49 TV: Children's TV

Answers - see page 175

Level 2

1 What is the longest running children's TV programme?
2 What did the letters in "TISWAS" stand for?
3 Who was the "Saturday Girl" on "Multi-Coloured Swap Shop"?
4 Which series was a children's predecessor of "Monty Python"?
5 Which village's postmistress is called Mrs Goggins?
6 What was "Fingermouse" made from?
7 Who fought against Bulk and Texas Pete?
8 Who presented his own "Cartoon Time" and "Cartoon Club"?
9 Which three singers from "Rainbow" were given their own series?
10 Which show ended ruefully with "Bye bye, everybody, bye bye"?
11 Which show was first presented by Emma Forbes and Andi Peters?
12 Which 1970s ecologists had their own TV series?
13 Which family had a daily help called Mrs Scrubbitt?
14 Which magazine programme had a mascot called Murgatroyd?
15 What sort of animal was Parsley in "The Herbs"?
16 Who had magical adventures and lived at 52 Festive Road?
17 Which pre-school programme was the first programme on BBC2?
18 Which former "Blue Peter" presenter's mother is Gloria Hunniford?
19 Who were Andy Pandy's two best friends?
20 In which 1980s/1990s series did Robin of Islington and Little Ron appear?
21 In which show for the under fives did The Muppets first appear?
22 In "Rag, Tag and Bobtail" which was the hedgehog?
23 What was the registration number of Lady Penelope's pink Rolls?
24 Who is associated with the catchphrase "Get Down Shep"?
25 Which show is TV's answer to The Guinness Book of Records?
26 Who replaced Moony and Sunshine in "Rainbow"?
27 Who took over from Phillip Schofield as presenter of Children's BBC?
28 In which county was Camberwick Green?
29 Who gave his name to the early bulletins of "Newsround"?
30 What is the logo on a Blue Peter badge?

Another Ireland (see Quiz 51)
1 Two. 2 Stone. 3 Oak or blackthorn. 4 Belfast. 5 Shannon. 6 Lough Neagh. 7 Lead-zinc. 8 Lava. 9 Enniskillen. 10 Mountains of Mourne. 11 Cork. 12 Abbey Theatre. 13 Macgillicuddy's Reeks. 14 Golden Vale. 15 Antrim, Armagh. 16 Queen's. 17 Mountain peaks. 18 St Brigit. 19 TV listings. 20 Pence. 21 Waterford. 22 The Twelve Bens. 23 Hills. 24 Queen's County. 25 Leinster. 26 Bells. 27 Kerry, Kildare, Kilkenny. 28 Political parties. 29 University of Ulster. 30 Armagh, Belfast, Derry/Londonderry.

Answers

173

Quiz 50 Pot-Luck 22

Level 2

1 Which Verdi opera is set in Berkshire in England?
2 Who created a garden at Sissinghurst in Kent?
3 Who sang the James Bond theme "From Russia With Love"?
4 What is Prince William's second name?
5 What chicken dish is named after a battle of the Napoleonic Wars?
6 Who wrote the 1988 novel "Prime Time"?
7 During which war were concentration camps first introduced?
8 Which famous writer was married to archaeologist Sir Max Mallowan?
9 Who invented the Flying Shuttle in 1733?
10 What kind of gas was used in the trenches during World War I?
11 Who sang "Islands In The Stream"?
12 Which Sondheim musical tells the story of a murdering barber?
13 What breed of retriever takes its name from a North American bay?
14 What does a Geiger Counter measure?
15 In which "ology", founded in the early 1950s, is self awareness paramount?
16 When does Britain's lease on Hong Kong officially expire?
17 Who defeated Richard III at Bosworth in 1485?
18 Which Hollywood actress's real name was Lucille Le Sueur?
19 Beaumaris, Conway and Harlech are famous for what type of building?
20 Whom did the religious assassins known as Thugs worship?
21 If you were an LLD what profession would you be involved in?
22 Which famous brothers made a movie called "A Night at the Opera"?
23 What is a tine?
24 Who was the first regular female presenter of "Points of View"?
25 Which William featured in the title of a Benjamin Britten opera?
26 Which country was invaded during Operation Barbarossa?
27 Which famous children's author and artist lived and worked in the Lake District for much of her life?
28 How many of Henry VIII's wives were called Anne?
29 What did miners use to find out if there was gas in a pit?
30 Of which party were Bill Rodgers and Roy Jenkins founder members?

Quiz 51 Around Ireland

Level 2

1 How many wheels does a jaunting car have?
2 On what would you see Ogham writing?
3 Which of two kinds of wood can a shillelagh be made from?
4 In which city is the Maze Prison?
5 Which is Ireland's chief river?
6 Which lake is the British Isles' largest?
7 What is the mine at Navan famous for?
8 What are the columns of the Giant's Causeway made from?
9 What is the county town of Fermanagh?
10 Which mountains stretch from Carlingford Lough to Dundrum Bay?
11 Which county's Irish name is Corcaigh?
12 What is Dublin's most famous theatre called?
13 What are the highest uplands in Ireland?
14 What is the name of the fertile vale in Limerick?
15 Which two of the counties of Northern Ireland begin with A?
16 What is Belfast's university called?
17 What are Slieve Donard and Slieve Commedagh?
18 Whose Saint's day is celebrated on 2nd February?
19 If you bought the RTE Guide what information would you receive?
20 What is the Irish punt divided into?
21 Which is further north Waterford or Cork?
22 What are the quartzite mountains in Connemara called?
23 What are drumlins?
24 What did Laoighis used to be called?
25 Which province of southeast Ireland includes the counties of Wexford and Wicklow?
26 What is St Ann's Shaldon Church famous for?
27 Which three counties of the Republic of Ireland begin with K?
28 What are Fianna Fail and Fine Gael?
29 Which university is at Coleraine?
30 Which three places in Northern Ireland may officially use the title "city"?

Quiz 52 Pot-Luck 23

Answers - see page 174

Level 2

1 Which English boxer had Muhammad Ali (Cassius Clay) on the floor?
2 Who bought Queen Elizabeth II her first corgi?
3 Which highly insoluble substance is opaque to X-rays?
4 What is the study and functioning of human societies called?
5 "Lay your head upon my pillow" appears in which Perry Como song?
6 Which king and queen ruled Britain jointly from 1689 to 1694?
7 What nationality was detective writer Ngaio Marsh?
8 What branch of Christianity still flourishes in Russia?
9 Whom did Zeus seduce when he assumed the guise of a swan?
10 What does "SWALK" stand for?
11 On TV, who played George Smiley in "Smiley's People"?
12 What is the male reproductive organ of a plant called?
13 In the song, "I danced with a man, who danced with a girl who danced with..." whom?
14 Which William was concerned with abolishing slavery?
15 Who commanded the Prussian troops at the Battle of Waterloo?
16 Who took her pen name from Ibsen's "Rosmersholm"?
17 Whose real name is Bernard Schwarz?
18 Krypton, neon, radon, xenon and helium are what kind of gases?
19 Who was the last prime minister to be created an earl?
20 In the Bible, which book comes after Saint John?
21 Which breed was described by Aristotle as "a cross between a dog and a tiger"?
22 Who is papa's daughter in the Renault ad?
23 The functioning of living organisms is the concern of which "ologists"?
24 What is fear of rain called?
25 What is Dolly Parton's theme park in Tennessee called?
26 Who created Monsieur Pamplemousse?
27 Who wrote the "Female Eunuch"?
28 Who was Thor's father?
29 What did the "D" stand for in Franklin D. Roosevelt?
30 Which American told Madam Butterfly that he loved her?

Answers *Pot-Luck 22* (see Quiz 50)
1 Falstaff. 2 Vita Sackville-West. 3 Matt Monro. 4 Arthur. 5 Chicken Marengo. 6 Joan Collins. 7 The Boer War. 8 Agatha Christie. 9 John Kay. 10 Mustard gas. 11 Kenny Rogers and Dolly Parton. 12 Sweeney Todd. 13 Chesapeake Bay Retriever. 14 Radioactivity. 15 Scientology. 16 1997. 17 Henry VII. 18 Joan Crawford. 19 Castles. 20 The goddess Kali. 21 The legal profession (Doctor of Law). 22 The Marx Brothers. 23 The prong of a fork. 24 Anne Robinson. 25 Billy Budd. 26 USSR. 27 Beatrix Potter. 28 Two. 29 Caged birds. 30 The Social Democratic party.

Quiz 53 Sport: Tennis

Answers - see page 179

Level 2

1. Who was the first unseeded man to win Wimbledon?
2. Which tennis star married Tatum O'Neal?
3. How many times did Martina Navratilova win the Wimbledon singles?
4. What was Evonne Goolagong's married name?
5. Which Australian pair dominated the men's doubles in the late 1960s?
6. Who is the only black American to have won the men's singles at Wimbledon?
7. Who is Czech Cyril Suk's famous sister?
8. In which year did Ivan Lendl win Wimbledon?
9. Which British pair won the Wimbledon mixed doubles in 1987?
10. Who sobbed on the Duchess of Kent's shoulder when she lost her Wimbledon final to Steffi Graf?
11. Which woman French player won the Australian Open in 1995?
12. Which duo released "Rock 'n' Roll" with the Full Metal Rackets?
13. Which cup for women was contested between the US and Britain?
14. Where is the final of the US Open played?
15. Which US champion was married to British player John Lloyd?
16. Who was the first male tennis player to win 100 tournaments?
17. Which two women competed in the all-British Wimbledon final in 1961?
18. What is the international team competition for men called?
19. What are the colours of the All England Lawn Tennis Club?
20. Who was the then youngest-ever woman to receive a Women's International Tennis Association ranking in 1982?
21. What did line judge Dorothy Brown do in a 1964 Wimbledon match?
22. Whom did Virginia Wade beat in the final to win Wimbledon in 1977?
23. Which German won the Wimbledon men's singles in 1991?
24. Who won his first US Open title in 1990?
25. Between 1980 and 1995 only one French men's open winner has won Wimbledon. Who?
26. What is the surface of the courts at Roland Garros in Paris?
27. Why did Catherine McTavish make Wimbledon history in 1979?
28. Who was stabbed on court by a fan of her chief rival?
29. What is the score in tennis when the tie break is introduced?
30. Who was once described as Garbo with ground strokes?

Pop: Duos (see Quiz 55)
1 Chas and Dave. 2 Wake Up Little Suzie. 3 Husband. 4 Wham! 5 Sweet dreams (are made of this). 6 Donkey. 7 Simon and Garfunkel. 8 Lionel Richie. 9 Opportunity Knocks. 10 Kiki Dee. 11 Esther and Abi. 12 L. S. Lowry. 13 Gimme Dat Ding. 14 Love you. 15 Marvin Gaye. 16 Everly Brothers. 17 Mel and Kim. 18 One. 19 Charles and Eddie. 20 Soft Cell. 21 Phil Spector. 22 John Travolta and Olivia Newton-John. 23 The World. 24 Roger Whittaker, Des O'Connor. 25 Erasure. 26 Teddy Johnson. 27 Nomad. 28 One. 29 Homeward Bound. 30 Pet Shop Boys.

Answers

Quiz 54 Pot-Luck 24

Answers - see page 180

1 What kind of dancer was Mr Bojangles?
2 Which William featured as a team captain in "A Question of Sport"?
3 Where did William III defeat a French and Irish army in 1690?
4 Which famous novelist's middle name was Sydenstricker?
5 What was American inventor Thomas Edison's middle name?
6 What does hydrogen combine with to form water?
7 Where in the House of Lords do peers with no party loyalties sit?
8 What is the northernmost point of the British mainland?
9 Which cartoon cat is the creation of Jim Davis?
10 What is the process by which plants use light to make food?
11 Which branch of medical science is concerned with muscle?
12 Which actor's real name was Reginald Carey?
13 Prince George of Denmark was the husband of which English queen?
14 What was the true vocation of the detective in the stories by G. K. Chesterton?
15 In darts, who won the World Masters five times between 1977 and 1984?
16 Whom did Orpheus attempt to rescue from the underworld?
17 In the song, how many little girls were in the back seat a-kissin' and a-huggin' with Fred?
18 What does ENO stand for?
19 A plant produced by crossing different species is known as what?
20 What was the Birmingham Royal Ballet previously known as?
21 Which cartoon character has a tattoo of an anchor on his arm?
22 On what day in 1939 did Britain declare war on Germany?
23 Which French writer lived with the composer Chopin?
24 Which programme has Judith Harn and Carol Vorderman presented?
25 What is the most abundant gas in the atmosphere?
26 Who was the first woman elected to the British Parliament?
27 Where on the human body is the skin the thinnest?
28 What breed originated in the 1850s when a greyhound was mated with an Irish wolfhound?
29 Which advertiser says, "We care because you do"?
30 Which "ology" is concerned with the study and treatment of crime?

Answers

Pot-Luck 25 (see Quiz 56)
1 Pythagoras. 2 Taxi driver. 3 Michael Foot. 4 She was her half-sister. 5 Surbiton. 6 The Arctic Ocean. 7 Scandinavian. 8 Nothing at all. 9 USA. 10 Pampas grass. 11 Swan Lake. 12 Ewart. 13 Robert Baden-Powell. 14 Colleen McCullough. 15 The 1920s. 16 Hydrogen. 17 Zanussi. 18 Red. 19 Borzoi. 20 212 degrees. 21 Palaeontology. 22 Michael Buerk. 23 James VI of Scotland, who was James I of England. 24 Call for the Dead. 25 Finland. 26 Diana. 27 M. 28 Mimi's (in La Bohème). 29 Lancelot. 30 Andrew Lloyd Webber.

Quiz 55 Pop: Duos

Answers - see page 177

Level 2

1 How are Messrs Hodges and Peacock better known?
2 "It's four o'clock and we're in trouble deep" comes from which Everly Brothers song?
3 What relation was Sonny to Cher in their single-making days?
4 Pepsi and Shirlie provided backing vocals for which superstar group?
5 What was the first Eurythmics top ten single back in 1983?
6 What little animal did Nina and Frederick sing about?
7 Which duo were made up of Paul and Art?
8 Whom did Diano Ross duo with on "Endless Love"?
9 Which TV show gave Peters and Lee their first break?
10 Who did Elton John sing with on his first British No 1?
11 What were the first names of the Ofarims?
12 Which artist did Brian and Michael sing about?
13 What was The Pipkins' only hit?
14 According to Peter and Gordon, to know you is to do what?
15 "It Takes Two" featured Tammi Terrell and who else?
16 Which duo has spent most weeks in the UK single charts?
17 Who were respectable in 1987?
18 How many of duo Miki and Griff were female?
19 Which duo had a No 1 with "Would I Lie To You"?
20 Which duo comprised Marc Almond and David Ball?
21 Who produced Ike and Tina Turner's "River Deep Mountain High"?
22 Which male/female singing duo had 16 weeks at No 1 in 1978?
23 According to "Tears for Fears", what did everyone want to rule?
24 Which duo charted with the "The Skye Boat Song"?
25 Which duo appeared in drag in an Abba tribute?
26 Who partnered Pearl Carr in the 1959 Eurovision Song Contest?
27 Who charted with "(I Wanna Give You) Devotion"?
28 How many girls in the duo Everything But the Girl?
29 Which Simon and Garfunkel song starts "I'm sitting in a railway station"?
30 How are Christopher Lowe and Neil Tennant better known?

Answers

Tennis (see Quiz 53)
1 Boris Becker. 2 John McEnroe. 3 Nine. 4 Cawley. 5 Newcombe and Roche. 6 Arthur Ashe. 7 Helena Sukova. 8 He never won it. 9 Jeremy Bates & Jo Durie. 10 Jana Novotna. 11 Mary Pierce. 12 John McEnroe and Pat Cash. 13 Wightman Cup. 14 Flushing Meadow. 15 Chris Evert. 16 Jimmy Connors. 17 Christine Truman and Angela Mortimer. 18 Davis Cup. 19 Green and Purple. 20 Steffi Graf. 21 Fell asleep. 22 Betty Stove. 23 Michael Stich. 24 Pete Sampras. 25 Bjorn Borg. 26 Clay. 27 Its first woman umpire. 28 Monica Seles. 29 Six games all. 30 Gabriela Sabatini.

Quiz 56 Pot-Luck 25

Answers - see page 178

1 Whose famous theorem is concerned with the sums of the squares of the sides of right-angled triangles?

2 What was "Mastermind" winner Fred Housego's job?

3 Whom did Neil Kinnock succeed as leader of the Labour party?

4 What relation was Mary I to Elizabeth I?

5 In which suburb was "The Good Life" set?

6 Which ocean lies to the north of Russia?

7 In which mythology does Yggdrasil feature?

8 What did the "S" stand for in Harry S. Truman?

9 Which country is Afrika Bambaataa from?

10 What is *Cortaderia selloana* better known as?

11 Of which ballet is Prince Siegfried hero?

12 What was William Gladstone's middle name?

13 Who led the British forces during the Siege of Mafeking?

14 Who wrote "The Thorn Birds"?

15 In which decade did John Logie Baird invent television?

16 What gas is given off by pouring dilute sulphuric acid on to granulated zinc?

17 Who produces "the appliance of science"?

18 What colour is the "This Is Your Life" book

19 What is another name for the Russian wolfhound?

20 What is the boiling point of water on the Fahrenheit Scale?

21 Which "ology" is concerned with fossils?

22 Which reporter fronted the film footage that sparked off Band Aid?

23 Whose nickname was "the Wisest Fool in Christendom"?

24 In which book did John le Carré's George Smiley first appear?

25 Which European country has the longest border with Russia?

26 A temple to whom was sited at Ephesus?

27 Who was 007's boss?

28 In opera, whose tiny hand was frozen?

29 What was landscape gardener Capability Brown's real first name?

30 Which composer had a Broadway hit with "Song and Dance"?

---

1 In which month in 1914 did the First World War begin?
2 What were people told to "keep burning" in the hit song of 1914?
3 What was the occupation of Edith Cavell who was shot by the Germans on a spying charge?
4 Who became prime minister of Britain in 1916?
5 What did George V ban in his household to encourage others to do the same, and help the war effort?
6 In the 1915 song where did you "Pack Up Your Troubles"?
7 How did Lord Kitchener die?
8 At which battle in 1916 were there said to be a million fatalities?
9 Which new weapon was introduced in battle in 1916?
10 What was the 1914–18 war known as until 1939?
11 What was the nationality of dancer Mata Hari, shot as a spy?
12 In which year did the United States enter the First World War?
13 Why were British soldiers called Tommies (short for Tommy Atkins)?
14 Which new British military force was established in 1918?
15 The German attack on which country caused Britain to enter the Second World War?
16 Which German word meaning "lightning war" entered the English language?
17 According to the World War II poster what did "Careless Talk" do?
18 What was the nickname of anti-British broadcaster, William Joyce?
19 According to Churchill he had nothing to offer in 1940 but what?
20 Which great evacuation of 1940 was called Operation Dynamo?
21 What was the German air force called?
22 What were the Local Defence Volunteers renamed?
23 Which fruit was no longer imported after 1940?
24 Which US bandleader went missing over the Channel in 1944?
25 Where did the Bevin Boys work?
26 What was the popular name for pilotless aircraft, V-1s?
27 What was snoek?
28 Who commanded the Allied forces which invaded Europe on D-Day?
29 Which scantily clad female had a daily strip in the "Daily Mirror"?
30 In which French city did Germany surrender in World War II?

Level 2

1 Which country is Kiri Te Kanawa from?
2 What are the Christian names of the three tenors?
3 Which German composer's only opera was "Fidelio"?
4 Which Gilbert and Sullivan opera is set in the Tower of London?
5 Which composer from East Anglia wrote the opera "Peter Grimes"?
6 What was the nationality of ballet composer Aaron Copland?
7 What was the name of Gounod's opera based on Doctor Faustus?
8 How did Lehár describe the Widow in his operetta?
9 Who wrote "Madame Butterfly" and "La Bohème"?
10 Which opera does "Nessun Dorma" come from?
11 Which work did The Who call a rock opera?
12 Where was the Barber from in the title of Rossini's opera?
13 How is Kurt Weill's "Die Dreigroschenoper" better known?
14 What does an operetta have which an opera usually doesn't?
15 Which Russian dancer gave his name to a famous racehorse?
16 Who wrote the ballets "Swan Lake" and "The Nutcracker"?
17 Which surname is shared by composers Johann and Richard?
18 What was the profession of Frederick Ashton?
19 Which controversial dancer died when her scarf caught in the wheels of her sports car?
20 What is the religious equivalent of opera without costumes and scenery?
21 Which Russian ballerina gave her name to a meringue dessert?
22 Who was Margot Fonteyn's most famous dancing partner?
23 Which classical and show dancer danced on stage with The Princess of Wales?
24 What is the nationality of Alicia Markova?
25 For which sporting event was "Nessun Dorma" a TV theme tune?
26 What is Lesley Garrett's home county?
27 Which Italian composer's English name would be Joseph Green?
28 Which Russian-born composer wrote "The Rite of Spring"?
29 In ballet what is a jeté?
30 Which ballet has the same name as a love story by Shakespeare?

Quiz 59 Pot-Luck 26

Answers - see page 181

Level 2

1 Who or what is Sweet William?
2 How did Princess Grace of Monaco die?
3 Which horror movie actor's real name is William Pratt?
4 Who "discovered" whom at Ujiji in 1871?
5 Which gas has the chemical symbol H?
6 Which character says, "He is the very pineapple of politeness"?
7 Which breed of setter is named after a British duke?
8 Who wrote "Paradise Postponed"?
9 In which fictional county do The Archers live?
10 Which George did the Prince Regent become?
11 What is Hyacinth Bucket's absentee son called?
12 Who claimed to be the Listening Bank?
13 Which "ologists" study bumps on the human head?
14 Who wrote the book "William the Detective"?
15 Which Russian city used to be called Leningrad?
16 How many faces did the Romans believe Janus to have?
17 kHz is an abbreviation for what?
18 What is Radio 4's morning news programme called?
19 *Hedera helix* is better known as what?
20 What kind of dances are Hamilton House and Petronella?
21 Which duo wrote and first recorded "Mud Mud, Glorious Mud"?
22 Which group of men who took part in the American War of
    Independence have given their name to an American rocket?
23 Who wrote the novel "The Bell"?
24 Which planet did Herschel discover in 1781?
25 How many atoms of oxygen are there in one molecule of water?
26 What is philosophy the study of?
27 Who is Emma Forbes's mother?
28 The USSR annexed three Baltic states in 1940. Latvia and Lithuania were
    two: what was the third?
29 Who was Helen of Troy's husband?
30 What does the "C" in TUC stand for?

World Wars (see Quiz 57)
1 August. 2 Home fires. 3 Nurse. 4 Lloyd George. 5 Alcohol. 6 In your
old kit bag. 7 Lost at sea. 8 Somme. 9 Tank. 10 The Great War. 11 Dutch.
12 1917. 13 Sample name on recruitment form. 14 RAF. 15 Poland. 16
Blitzkrieg. 17 Costs Lives. 18 Lord Haw Haw. 19 Blood, toil, tears and
sweat. 20 Dunkirk. 21 Luftwaffe. 22 Home Guard. 23 Bananas. 24
Glenn Miller. 25 Coalmines. 26 Doodle-bug or buzz bomb. 27 Fish. 28
Eisenhower. 29 Jane. 30 Reims.

Answers

Quiz 60 Movies: Comedies

Answers - see page 182

Level 2

1 What breed of dog was Beethoven in the film of the same name?
2 Where is Macaulay Culkin separated from his parents in "Home Alone 2"?
3 Which trio took the Road to Rio, Bali, Morocco and Utopia, etc?
4 Who was the baby's voice in "Look Who's Talking"?
5 Which tough guy was the star of "Kindergarten Cop"?
6 What was the subtitle of "Police Academy 6"?
7 Which film was about the activities of unemployed parapsychologists in New York?
8 Who won an Oscar for "Tootsie"?
9 Who was Richard Gere's co-star in "Pretty Woman"?
10 Which actors played the two revenging con men in "The Sting"?
11 In which area of New York is "Crocodile Dundee" set?
12 Which country singer starred in "Nine To Five"?
13 Which studios produced "Honey I Shrunk the Kids"
14 Which movie with Warren Beatty was based on a strip cartoon?
15 Which English actor starred in "The Muppet Christmas Carol"?
16 Who played the title roles in "When Harry Met Sally"?
17 What was the profession of the Patrick Swayze character in "Ghost"?
18 Which was the first "Carry On" film?
19 Who is the police inspector in "The Pink Panther" films?
20 Which late superstar's wife stars in "The Naked Gun" films?
21 What was the sequel to "Three Men and a Baby"?
22 Which film included the song "Raindrops Keep Fallin' on My Head"?
23 What was the nationality of Mrs Doubtfire in the film of the same name?
24 Who played the role of Wendy in "Hook"?
25 In the film "Babe" who or what is "Babe"?
26 Who is Whoopi Goldberg hiding from in "Sister Act"?
27 In which film is Tom Hanks a small boy in a grown man's body?
28 Which historic event triggers the plot in "Some Like It Hot"?
29 Who directed "Annie Hall" and "What's New Pussycat"?
30 Who were Chico, Gummo and Zeppo's two brothers?

Answers

Opera and Ballet (see Quiz 58)
1 New Zealand. 2 Placido (Domingo), José (Carreras) and Luciano (Pavarotti). 3 Beethoven. 4 The Yeomen of the Guard. 5 Benjamin Britten. 6 American. 7 Faust. 8 Merry. 9 Puccini. 10 Turandot. 11 Tommy. 12 Seville. 13 The Threepenny Opera. 14 Spoken dialogue. 15 Nijinsky. 16 Tchaikovsky. 17 Strauss. 18 Choreographer. 19 Isadora Duncan. 20 Oratorio. 21 Pavlova. 22 Rudolf Nureyev. 23 Wayne Sleep. 24 English. 25 1990 World Cup. 26 Yorkshire. 27 Giuseppe Verdi. 28 Stravinsky. 29 Jump. 30 Romeo and Juliet.

184

Quiz 61 Pot-Luck 27

Answers - see page 187

Level 2

1 Who wrote the music for the "The Threepenny Opera"?
2 Which botanist gave his name to fuchsias?
3 What nationality was ballet star Rudolf Nureyev?
4 Who is known as "The Big Yin"?
5 Which two countries fought for supremacy in the Punic Wars?
6 Who left an unfinished novel called "Sanditon"?
7 Which former newsreader has advertised Vaseline hand cream?
8 Who was LB in "Dynasty"?
9 Who carried the spirits of dead warriors to Valhalla?
10 The Soviet secret police are known by their initials: what are they?
11 Who took over the ITV franchise from TVS in 1991?
12 Which ballet company is "resident" at London's Royal Opera House?
13 Which William was married to Mary II?
14 Who said, "To err is human but it feels divine"?
15 What does Magnus Magnusson say he will do if he's started?
16 Which fruit is dried to make prunes?
17 If an elderly couple are happily married who are they likened to?
18 Who's real name is Sofia Scicolone?
19 Which sport is played at Rosslyn Park?
20 What do we call a period of play in polo?
21 Which country's name means The Saviour?
22 How many cents are there in a US nickel?
23 With which country do you associate the drink pernod?
24 Which TV newsreader presented "Treasure Hunt"?
25 What do we call what the Spaniards call an *autopista*?
26 Of which country is Tripoli the capital?
27 If you had an escutcheon, what would be shown on it?
28 Which city has given its name to a wheelchair and to a bun?
29 Which animal is associated with Paddy McGinty?
30 How much in old money was a tanner?

Answers

Pot-Luck 28 (see Quiz 63)
1 Donald Campbell. 2 Hannibal. 3 Wilbur Smith. 4 Hyde Park. 5 Canada. 6 William Golding. 7 Cowboy. 8 White or red. 9 Edgar Rice Burroughs. 10 Suffolk. 11 Caretaker. 12 Buzz Aldrin. 13 Spinning. 14 Chalk. 15 Tights. 16 One. 17 Farming, agriculture. 18 Ice. 19 Democrat and Republican. 20 Calder Hill, Cumbria. 21 Jack and Annie Walker. 22 Louis XVI. 23 Made to measure. 24 Retract them. 25 The pot. 26 Busman's holiday. 27 Walter Matthau. 28 A wig. 29 Arthur Askey. 30 An error in a program.

Quiz 62 Golf

Level 2

Answers - see page 188

1 Who was involved with John Daley in the 1995 British Open play-off?
2 Which Northern Ireland golfer secured victory for Europe on the final day of the 1995 Ryder Cup?
3 Who is nicknamed "The Great White Shark"?
4 Which actress did Sam Torrance marry?
5 What is the women's equivalent of the Ryder Cup?
6 Which European Open gave Seve Ballesteros his first-ever European win back in 1976?
7 Where does Ernie Els hail from?
8 What does the D stand for in Arnold D. Palmer?
9 What is a bunker known as in the United States?
10 What is the maximum number of clubs permitted in a golf bag?
11 Which English player scored a hole in one on the final day of the 1995 Ryder Cup?
12 Who was the first German to win the German Open?
13 Where is the "home of golf"?
14 Name the veteran golfer who won the 1995 US Masters tournament?
15 Which country will host the 1997 Ryder Cup?
16 In stroke play, what is the penalty for playing the wrong ball?
17 What do the initials PGA stand for?
18 What is the amateur's equivalent of the Ryder Cup?
19 At which "appetizing" course did Sandy Lyle win the 1985 British Open?
20 Who is "The Golden Bear"?
21 Which is the oldest golf club in England?
22 At what age can a player join the Seniors' Tour?
23 Name Europe's 1997 Ryder Cup captain?
24 Which Henry won his first British Open in 1934?
25 What nationality is golfer Vijay Singh?
26 Which British golfer won the British Open in 1969?
27 Which famous American played his last British Open in 1995?
28 In which tournament does a player win a green jacket?
29 Which golfer was non-playing captain of the 1985 Ryder Cup team?
30 Which showbiz golfer says, "I'm in charge"?

1 Who was the last person to hold both water and land speed records?
2 Which general of ancient Carthage is associated with proboscidean mammals?
3 Who wrote the novel "The Seventh Scroll"?
4 In which park is the Serpentine?
5 Of which country is Baffin Island a part?
6 Who wrote the novel "Lord of the Flies"?
7 In South America, what is a gaucho?
8 What colour are the flowers of the hawthorn?
9 Which US writer created Tarzan?
10 Ipswich is the administrative headquarters of which English county?
11 What job is done by a concierge?
12 Which astronaut was the second man to set foot on the moon?
13 With what industry is the inventor Richard Arkwright associated?
14 What is the common name for calcium carbonate?
15 What do we call what the Germans call "Strumpfhose"?
16 In chess, how many squares can the king move at a time?
17 With which industry is the Royal Smithfield Show concerned?
18 On what type of surface is the sport of curling played?
19 What are the main two political parties in the United States?
20 Where in England was the first commercial nuclear power station built?
21 Who were the first landlords of the Rovers' Return?
22 Which French king was husband to Marie Antoinette?
23 What are bespoke clothes?
24 What can cats do with their claws that dogs cannot do?
25 According to the proverb, what shouldn't call the kettle black?
26 What sort of a holiday is it if you do the same thing as in your job?
27 Which actor's real name is Walter Matasschansayasky?
28 What is a peruke?
29 Whose catchphrase was "Hello, playmates"?
30 In the world of computing what is a bug?

Quiz 64 Jazz and Blues

Level 2

Answers - see page 186

1 What was Louis Armstrong's nickname?
2 Which 1960s band featured Eric Clapton and Jimmy Page?
3 Which singer recorded the "When Harry Met Sally" soundtrack?
4 In which city were Kenny Ball and his jazzmen at midnight?
5 Which 1920s blues singer recorded "Down Hearted Blues"?
6 What was Chris Barber's only hit single?
7 Whose quartet famously decided to "Take Five"?
8 Who recorded the album "The Blues, The Whole Blues and Nothing But The Blues"?
9 What was John Mayall's group known as?
10 What instrument did Earl Hines play?
11 Which jazz-funk saxophonist had a hit in 1987 with "Songbird"?
12 Which jazz musician opened a London club in 1959?
13 Who played Billie Holliday in the film "Lady Sings The Blues"?
14 Which clarinettist lived from 1909 to 1986 and had his "Story" told in a 1955 film?
15 Which veteran blues performer recorded "The Healer"?
16 How is singer Clementina Dinah Campbell better known?
17 Which trumpeter talks of Mornington Crescent in a radio panel game?
18 Under what name did Marion Walter Jacobs record?
19 What instrument is associated with Courtney Pyne?
20 Who sang "He's A Tramp" in Disney's "Lady And The Tramp"?
21 Who recorded "Hoochie Coochie Man" and "Got My Mojo Working"?
22 Which virtuoso jazz drummer started out in a vaudeville act as Baby Trapps the Drum Wonder?
23 In which country was Alexis Korner born?
24 Which bluesman had a No 1 with "Let The Heartaches Begin"?
25 What was the name of Mr Acker Bilk's Jazz Band?
26 What name was Michael Bolton born with?
27 What instrument is associated with Monty Sunshine?
28 Which guitarist released the album "Ballads and Blues"?
29 Who turned "Three Blind Mice" into "Experiments With Mice"?
30 Which group were formed by Bruce, Baker and Clapton?

Answers

Golf (see Quiz 62)
1 Constantino Rocca. 2 Philip Watson. 3 Greg Norman. 4 Suzanne Danielle. 5 Curtis Cup. 6 Dutch Open. 7 South Africa. 8 Daniel. 9 Trap. 10 14. 11 Howard Clark. 12 Bernhard Langer. 13 St Andrews. 14 Ben Crenshaw. 15 Spain. 16 Two strokes. 17 Professional Golfers' Association. 18 Walker Cup. 19 Sandwich. 20 Jack Nicklaus. 21 Royal Blackheath, Kent, founded 1608. 22 50 years. 23 Seve Ballesteros. 24 Cotton. 25 Fijian. 26 Tony Jacklin. 27 Arnold Palmer. 28 US Masters. 29 Tony Jacklin. 30 Bruce Forsyth.

188

1 What is the term for a herd of whales?
2 To an Australian what is a wool-grower?
3 By what name is Formosa now known?
4 What have Thistle, Brent and Ninian in common?
5 Who became queen of The Netherlands in 1980?
6 Who wrote the poem that begins, "Shall I compare thee to a summer's day"?
7 What name goes after Bobby to name a footballer and before Heston to name an actor?
8 What is Al Pacino's full first name?
9 Provence and Brittany are both parts of which country?
10 Who played the scarecrow, Worzel Gummidge, on television?
11 Nowadays, who might wear a wimple?
12 Which country lies immediately south of Estonia?
13 In geography, what is a cataract?
14 Which English soccer team plays at home at Molyneux?
15 In America what is Airforce One?
16 With which sport do you associate Karen Pickering?
17 Who was the lead singer of the group, The Who?
18 What does the reference book, Crockfords, list?
19 For which county does Dominic Cork play cricket?
20 Where in the body is the humerus?
21 In which country is the city of Jakarta?
22 As what did Grimaldi achieve fame?
23 In which US city is Grand Central Station?
24 Of which ancient empire was Nebuchadnezzar king?
25 In which art did Sir Henry Irving become famous?
26 When the sun is at its zenith, where is it?
27 The tears of which creatures are said to be a sign of insincere grief?
28 In which sport does the Harlequin Club compete?
29 For what achievement is Valentina Tereshkova famous?
30 Where does the M5 go to and from?

1 Whom did Naomi Campbell replace in a yogurt ad because she was younger?

2 Which former model is married to actor Leigh Lawson?

3 Who became engaged to Bon Jovi musician, Tico Torres, in 1995?

4 Which model has been married to rock star Bill Wyman and footballer Pat Van Den Hauwe?

5 What is the first name of model Auermann?

6 Who was Michael Hutchence's girlfriend before Paula Yates?

7 What is the profession of Claudia Schiffer's fiancé?

8 Which cosmetic house did Liz Hurley become the face of in 1995?

9 Which famous photographer was Marie Helvin married to?

10 Which model was famous for the ad in which she returned all her man's gifts but kept the car keys?

11 Which designer is well known for her pink hair?

12 Which fruit gave its name to ex-model Debbie Moore's dance studio?

13 Which former model did Ringo Starr marry?

14 Who is the designer daughter of food critic Egon Ronay?

15 In what area of fashion is Barbara Daly famous?

16 Which famous hairdresser married Lulu?

17 Which garment is Jean-Paul Gaultier famous for wearing?

18 Which supermodel's name has been linked with that of actor Johnny Depp?

19 Who said, "A woman is as young as her knees"?

20 Who designed Liz Hurley's famous "safety pin" dress?

21 Who was crowned Supermodel of the Year in 1995?

22 What is the first name of designer St Laurent?

23 Which cosmetic house did Charles Revson found?

24 Which is the home country of Mrs Rod Stewart, model Rachel Hunter?

25 Which pop singer was designer/TV presenter Jeff Banks married to?

26 What is the surname of Designer of the Year, John?

27 Which London street was famous for its 1960s boutiques?

28 Which hairdresser pioneered the geometric haircut in the 1960s?

29 Which Italian city is at the heart of the fashion industry?

30 Which Vivienne is famous for her outrageous designs?

1   The names of which three African countries begin with the letter Z?
2   What covers 85% of Algeria?
3   Famine in which country triggered the Band Aid Charity?
4   What do the initials OAU stand for?
5   Of which country is Ouagadougou the capital?
6   What is the Harmattan?
7   Which is further west, Uganda or Kenya?
8   Which country used to be called South West Africa?
9   Which substance, used to make a drink, is Ghana's main export?
10 Which lake lies between Kenya, Tanzania and Uganda?
11 What is Africa's highest mountain?
12 Which European language is an official language of Angola?
13 In which African country is El Alamein, scene of a World War II battle?
14 Which country is the main economic power in West Africa?
15 Which country is further north Rwanda or Burundi?
16 Which language is Afrikaans derived from?
17 Near which major landmark is the Boiling Pot?
18 What is the area of savanna in West Africa called?
19 South Africa is the world's leading exporter of what?
20 Which Moroccan city is the name of a famous film?
21 The Kalahari Desert lies chiefly in which country?
22 What is the largest country in Africa?
23 What is the Okavango Swamp famous for?
24 In which country are the political parties ANC and Inkatha?
25 Which African country is the tiger native to?
26 Which man-made structures would you see at Aswan and Kariba?
27 Does most of Africa lie to the north or to the south of the Equator?
28 Which country occupies the Horn of Africa?
29 Which sound is unique to many African languages including Xhosa?
30 What is the administrative capital of South Africa?

Quiz 68 Pot-Luck 30

Answers - see page 190

1 According to the proverb, what is better than no bread?
2 What kind of animal is a Persian Blue?
3 Who composed the opera "Carmen"?
4 On a ship or boat what is a painter?
5 What kind of food is gazpacho?
6 Where in London is the statue of Peter Pan?
7 Who had a hit with "This Little Bird"?
8 In geometry, what is meant by concentric?
9 Which wooden puppet was first written about by Carlo Collodi?
10 In which of Dickens's novels does Sam Weller appear?
11 Which food, not rationed during World War II, was rationed after it?
12 In which year did Sir Winston Churchill die?
13 What is the name of the marmalade cat created by Kathleen Hale?
14 For what is the Médoc area of France famous?
15 What are Cheshire, Gouda and Gorgonzola?
16 How is Cherilyn La Pier better known?
17 As what did Beau Brummel achieve fame?
18 Which country used to have a coin called a bawbee?
19 Who was the first presenter of "Family Fortunes"?
20 What do we call what the Italians call *pesce*?
21 In London, the Cambridge, the Lyric and the Adelphi are all what?
22 Of which country was Field-Marshall Smuts prime minister?
23 Which religious writer was born in Elstow, near Bedford?
24 What word can go after salad and before gown?
25 In which year was the Gunpowder Plot?
26 Who wrote the novels "Sons and Lovers" and "The Rainbow"?
27 What does a chandler make?
28 Which metal do we make from bauxite?
29 Black, Whooper, and Bewick are all types of which bird?
30 What is a golden hello?

Quiz 69 Nature: Trees

Level 2

1 What do conifers have in their cones?
2 Which tree's leaves are the symbol of The National Trust?
3 Which three coniferous trees are native to Britain?
4 Which garden tree with yellow flowers has poisonous seeds?
5 What colour are the flowers of the horse chestnut tree?
6 In which country did the bonsai technique develop?
7 Which tree do we get turpentine from?
8 In which continent did the monkey-puzzle tree originate?
9 Which tree produces cobs and filberts?
10 Aspen is from which family of trees?
11 Is the wood of a coniferous tree hard or soft?
12 What is the more common name for the great maple?
13 What sort of environment do alder trees grow in?
14 Which tree is cork obtained from?
15 In which county is England's largest forest?
16 Which tree is sago obtained from?
17 Which beech tree has purplish leaves?
18 What is the Spanish chestnut also called?
19 Which tree can be English, American or Eurasian?
20 To which family does the umbrella tree belong?
21 The teak is native to which continent?
22 Which wood is used for piano keys?
23 Which maple's sap is used to make maple syrup?
24 To which family does the osier belong?
25 Which is thought to be the tallest tree in the world and one of the longest-lived?
26 Which tree produces "keys"?
27 What colour flowers does a jacaranda tree have?
28 Which tree produces the seeds from which cocoa is made?
29 To which group of trees do blue gum and red gum belong ?
30 What is the linden tree also called?

Quiz 70 Pot Luck 31

Level 2

Answers - see page 196

1 In which country did the poets Keats and Shelley both die?
2 How many tusks does a warthog have?
3 What is the nearest star to the solar system?
4 Who wrote "Porgy and Bess"?
5 Who was king of France at the time of the French Revolution?
6 Which card game has two forms, called auction and contract?
7 In which country does the Amazon rise?
8 Graphite is composed of which element?
9 In ads, which sign meant "happy motoring"?
10 What can be seen from Earth only once every 76 years?
11 Who was prime minister of Australia from 1983 to 1991?
12 Where was the Mount Pinatubo eruption?
13 Who burned his guitar at the Monterey Pop Festival in 1967?
14 What is brighter than a hundred million suns?
15 Who became potter to King George III in 1806?
16 What does "m" stand for in Einstein's equation $E=mc^2$?
17 Which sign of the zodiac is represented as a man pouring water from a jug?
18 Who preferred "50,000 rifles to 50,000 votes"?
19 Who devised the modern system for naming and classifying plants and animals?
20 Whose fan did Oscar Wilde write about?
21 What name is given to the set of fans at the front of a jet engine?
22 Who won the '96 Oscar for Best Director?
23 On the shores of which lake does Toronto stand?
24 What is the scientific name for the lemon tree?
25 On which day in 1066 was William the Conqueror crowned king of England?
26 What is the currency of the British colony of Bermuda?
27 Sir Christopher Wren was a professor in which scientific field?
28 What is the name of the national airline of Spain?
29 Who was Pinocchio's father?
30 Where are the Tivoli Gardens?

Pot-Luck 32 (see Quiz 72)
1 XY. 2 Plato. 3 Atmospheric pressure. 4 Barbara Woodhouse. 5 Gamma.
6 Orange. 7 Indonesia's. 8 Thirty. 9 Literature and Science. 10 Miles
Davis's. 11 James Chadwick. 12 Emporio. 13 Opera. 14 Lyle Lovett.
15 Edward Heath. 16 Solomon Grundy. 17 Dr No. 18 Pink Floyd. 19
The binary system. 20 Saturday. 21 Tuna fishing. 22 Pancreas. 23 17th
century. 24 Victoria. 25 Crystal Palace. 26 Atlas Mountains. 27
American Civil War. 28 Della Street. 29 Periodic table. 30 Osiris.

Answers

Quiz 71 Cricket

1 What does the first C stand for in TCCB?
2 Which county did David Gower play for apart from Leicestershire?
3 Which West Indies star with bat and ball scored over 8,000 Test runs?
4 Which teams played in the final of cricket's World Cup in 1992?
5 Who did Ray Illingworth replace as England's chairman of selectors?
6 Which county won the Championship in 1990 and 1991?
7 What was remarkable about the 16 overs that South Africa's Hugh Tayfield bowled against England at Durban in 1957?
8 Who was England's youngest and later oldest postwar Test player?
9 Which player broke a leg in a Test series against New Zealand in 1992?
10 In 1995, Jack Russell took how many catches in a Test to create a new world record?
11 Which three counties did Ian Botham play for?
12 Which county have won the championship most times?
13 Where is Kent's cricket ground headquarters?
14 Edmonds and Emburey were the spinning duo for which county?
15 Which all-rounder took 100 wickets and scored 1000 runs in 16 seasons between 1903 and 1926?
16 What are the Christian names of Australia's Waugh brothers?
17 Where do Middlesex play home matches?
18 On which West Indian island is Sabina Park?
19 What was the result of the 1995-96 Test series between South Africa and England?
20 Which English county has Brian Lara played for?
21 Who was the "bodyline" bowler?
22 Gloucestershire cricketers of the 1870s W. G. and E. M. had what surname?
23 Who are the only father and son to captain England?
24 Which Englishman took 19 wickets in a 1956 Test against Australia?
25 Who was bowling for Glamorgan when Sobers hit six sixes in an over?
26 How many test centuries did Geoff Boycott score for England?
27 What is the umpire's signal for a no-ball?
28 Who was selected for all World Cups from 1975 to 1995?
29 Which was the first new county to join the championship in the 1990s?
30 Who was West Indian captain before Richie Richardson?

Quiz 72 Pot-Luck 32

Level 2

1 Which sex chromosomes are possessed by a human male?
2 Whose political philosophy is expounded in "The Republic" and "The Laws"?
3 What does a barometer measure?
4 Who on TV issued the comand to "sit"?
5 What is the third letter of the Greek alphabet?
6 What is the flavour of Grand Marnier?
7 Whose national airline is called Garuda?
8 How many counters are on a backgammon board at start of play?
9 What was the title of the last book written by Aldous Huxley?
10 In the 1950s whose quintet did John Coltrane play with?
11 Who discovered the neutron?
12 Under what label does Giorgio Armani design clothes?
13 What word can go after soap and before house?
14 Which country singer married Julia Roberts in 1993?
15 Which prime minister brought in a 10.30pm TV curfew in 1973?
16 In the nursery rhyme who was married on a Wednesday?
17 Which Bond movie featured the partially dressed Ursula Andress?
18 Which British rock band had Syd Barrett among its founders?
19 Which number code system is based on the digits 1 and 0?
20 On which night of the week was the show "Wogan" first broadcast?
21 What type of driftnet fishing caused the deaths of hundreds of dolphins in the 1980s?
22 Which organ of the body secretes insulin?
23 In which century was tea first brought to Europe?
24 Of which Australian state is Melbourne the capital?
25 What was built in Hyde Park for the Great Exhibition of 1851?
26 Mount Toubkal is the highest peak of which mountain range?
27 Which war started with the bombardment of Fort Sumter?
28 Who was Perry Mason's secretary?
29 What name is given to the most used table of the elements?
30 Who was the Egyptian god of the underworld?

Answers — **Pot-Luck 31** (see Quiz 70)
1 Italy. 2 Four. 3 Alpha Centauri. 4 George Gershwin. 5 Louis XVI. 6 Bridge. 7 Peru. 8 Carbon. 9 Esso. 10 Halley's Comet. 11 Bob Hawke. 12 The Philippines. 13 Jimi Hendrix. 14 A supernova. 15 Josiah Spode. 16 Mass. 17 Aquarius. 18 Benito Mussolini. 19 Linnaeus. 20 Lady Windermere's. 21 Compressor. 22 Mel Gibson. 23 Lake Ontario. 24 Citrus limon. 25 Christmas Day. 26 Bermuda dollar. 27 Astronomy. 28 Iberia. 29 Geppetto. 30 Copenhagen.

Quiz 73 Hi Tech: Inventions

Level 2

1 Which method of fast writing did Isaac Pitman develop?
2 Which two major electronics companies developed the compact disc in 1979?
3 What was invented by US students using aluminium flan cases?
4 In which country was the first modern motorway created?
5 Who registered the first patents for the railway sleeping car?
6 Which Swiss company developed the first widely used instant coffee?
7 Which rubber-based product was patented in the United States in 1869?
8 Why was the invention of the electric iron useless in America in 1882?
9 What was American Mr Bissel's dust-collecting invention?
10 What was the surname of King Camp who invented the safety razor?
11 What was the occupation of Dom Pierre Perignon who developed the champagne process?
12 What type of pens did Pentel invent?
13 Which building toy was designed by a Dane, Ole Kirk Christiansen?
14 What is unusual about Mark Button's invention, the Koosh ball?
15 Which Kimberley Clark Co invention was first called Celluwipes?
16 Which form of precautionary medicine was discovered by Edward Jenner?
17 What was the nationality of saxophone inventor Adolphe Sax?
18 Which type of transport did John Outram invent in 1775?
19 Which sauce did Henry Heinz invent in 1876?
20 JVC launched VHS format in 1976, but what does VHS stand for?
21 Which drink was created when Indian army officers added quinine to soda water to help fight malaria?
22 In which country were cultured pearls first obtained?
23 What was Alka-Seltzer first marketed as?
24 The Penny Black was the first adhesive stamp, how was the Penny Red a first?
25 In which country were banknotes first used?
26 Which weapon did Samuel Colt develop and popularize?
27 Which musical instrument did American Rickenbacher create?
28 What was based on the Victorian game called Magic Square?
29 What did the owner of the Humpty Dumpty store in Oklahoma invent?
30 Which type of fastening was first used on snow boots?

Quiz 74 Pot-Luck 33

Answers - see page 200

1 What is the Aurora Australis also called?
2 Which three South American countries does the Equator cross?
3 What was the first X-rated film to win an Oscar?
4 What is the name of the national airline of Israel?
5 Which singer's real name is Declan McManus?
6 What did Tic-Tac throw in the Bond movies?
7 What did Little Polly Flinders spoil?
8 Who wrote "Anna Karenina"?
9 What metallic element is mixed with tin to form the alloy bronze?
10 Who was the founder of the Christian Science movement?
11 Whose insurance company "won't make a drama out of a crisis"?
12 In which city did Karl Marx write "Das Kapital"?
13 How is the Caribbean island of St Christopher more familiarly known?
14 Which planet has a pink appearance?
15 Who was world professional billiards champion from 1968 to 1980?
16 Which is the most northerly capital city in Europe?
17 Name the New York baseball player who married Marilyn Monroe?
18 Which country is the world's leading producer of copper?
19 Which acid builds up in the muscles during severe exercise?
20 Who circumnavigated the world solo in "Gipsy Moth IV" in 1966–67?
21 Which Australian city stands near the mouth of the Yarra river?
22 What common mineral is formed by the fossilization of vegetation?
23 Which game show hears Tony Green shouting the scores?
24 Which comic playwright wrote the trilogy "The Norman Conquests"?
25 Who discovered that the universe is expanding?
26 Who is George Logan better known as?
27 What form of energy is produced by an electric motor?
28 Which beautiful youth did the Greek goddess Aphrodite love?
29 Who said "When you are as great as I am, it's hard to be humble"?
30 Which country's flag shows a green star on a red background?

Quiz 75 Pop: Solo Stars

Answers - see page 197

Level 2

1 Did John Lennon have a solo single No 1 in his lifetime?
2 Which Cliff Richard hit starts "Imagine a still summer's day"?
3 Colonel Tom Parker launched which star?
4 Which was Madonna's first UK top ten hit?
5 Which singer recorded "Every Picture Tells A Story"?
6 Who had a hit with the original version of "Sealed With A Kiss"?
7 Which former barber charted from 1953 to 1973?
8 Which lady was "Lost In France"?
9 What was a hit for both Frankie Vaughan and Shakin' Stevens?
10 How is Brenda Mae Tarpley better known?
11 Geographically, what links Gracie Fields and Lisa Stansfield?
12 Which Jason Donovan single is made up of initials?
13 Tom Jones sang for which Bond film?
14 Which solo star had his first No 1 in a duo with Marc Almond in 1989?
15 Apart from Michael Jackson, which female singer charted with "Ben"?
16 What was Adam Faith's first single?
17 Which Rod Stewart hit starts "Wake up, Maggie..."?
18 Can you remember who sang "I Remember You"?
19 What was George Michael's first solo No 1?
20 Whose "Wonderful World" was a bigger hit as a reissue 26 years after the original?
21 Which Roy Orbison hit begins, "A candy coloured clown they call the sandman"?
22 Mariah Carey was named after which song in "Paint Your Wagon"?
23 Which singer was "Crazy" with his first single success?
24 Which superstar has been chairman of Watford football club?
25 Which female singer recorded "Heaven is a Place on Earth"?
26 Which label did Michael Jackson first record on?
27 According to Tina Turner, what was the speed limit in Nutbush?
28 Who was born in the United States of Irish-Italian parents and with the middle names Frederick Joseph ?
29 Who sang that she was "born in the wagon of a travelling show"?
30 Which Percy Sledge classic charted in the mid-1960s and mid-1980s?

Answers

Hi Tech: Inventions (see Quiz 73)
1 Shorthand. 2 Sony and Philips. 3 Frisbee. 4 Italy. 5 Pullman. 6 Nestlé.
7 Chewing gum. 8 Homes did not have electricity. 9 Carpet sweeper. 10
Gillette. 11 Monk. 12 Felt tips. 13 Lego. 14 It doesn't bounce. 15 Paper
handkerchiefs. 16 Vaccination. 17 Belgian. 18 Tram. 19 Tomato ketchup.
20 Video Home System. 21 Tonic water. 22 Japan. 23 Cold cure. 24
Perforated. 25 Sweden. 26 Revolver. 27 Electric guitar. 28 Crossword
puzzles. 29 Supermarket trolley. 30 Zip.

1 Who painted "The Blue Boy" and "Mr and Mrs Andrews"?
2 Which Pierre-Auguste painted "Umbrellas" and "The Bathers"?
3 What is Leonardo da Vinci's "La Gioconda" also known as?
4 Which English cricketer is a keen amateur watercolour artist?
5 Whose Progress did William Hogarth paint?
6 What is arguably the most famous painting by Dutchman Frans Hals?
7 Which Egyptian sculpture is more than 73 metres long?
8 Which 1960s art vogue was based on optical illusion?
9 What is paint applied to in a fresco?
10 Which sculpture did Auguste Bartholdi give to the United States?
11 What is notable about the woman in Ingres' "Valpinçon Bather"?
12 What type of work is Albrecht Dürer famous for?
13 Where in the United States would you find Washington's head 18 metres high?
14 What art form is a Japanese netsuke?
15 Who painted "Bubbles", which has been used in a soap ad?
16 Which English sculptor produced rounded forms such as "Reclining Figure"?
17 Which Spaniard is known for his hallucinatory paintings?
18 Which Dutch painter is well known for his self-portraits?
19 Who painted Campbell soup tins and Marilyn Monroe?
20 What type of paintings is Joshua Reynolds famous for?
21 A statue in Afghanistan of which religious teacher is 53 metres high?
22 Whose "Irises" and "Sunflowers" were two of the world's most expensive paintings at auction?
23 What is the binding medium in gouache technique?
24 Which Spaniard founded the Cubist movement?
25 Of which school of painting was Claude Monet a leading exponent?
26 For which art style is David Hockney famous?
27 Which performers were a favourite subject for painter/sculptor Degas?
28 In which country was the French painter Marc Chagall born?
29 In which county is "Constable country", named after its famous son?
30 What was the first name of sculptor Epstein?

Quiz 77 Pot-Luck 34

Level 2

1 Which captain of Darwin's ship HMS "Beagle" became governor of New Zealand?
2 What was W. H. Auden's first name?
3 Who had the word "Skytrain" printed on one side of his aircraft?
4 What source of light is used in producing a hologram?
5 Which Bond movie was a hit for Sheena Easton?
6 Who classified the elements into the periodic table?
7 Where in Canada is the world's second-largest French-speaking city?
8 Which character did Clark Gable play in "Gone With the Wind"?
9 Which tsar conquered Kazan and Siberia in the 16th century?
10 What name is given to a plant which dies down at the end of the growing season?
11 In which year did Britain abandon the gold standard?
12 Which Italian artist included Halley's comet in a fresco of the Nativity?
13 Which object took almost seven hours to rise from the Solent in 1982?
14 Which "Dad's Army" actor was married to Hattie Jacques?
15 What name is given to the genetic make-up of an individual?
16 Where did chess originate in the second century AD?
17 What happened to the main character in Kafka's "Metamorphosis"?
18 What style of music was pioneered by jazzmen Charlie Parker and Dizzy Gillespie?
19 Which 18th-century priest discovered that plants absorb air?
20 Cecil Beaton won Oscars for his designs for which two films?
21 In the rhyme, what is Friday's child?
22 What is the name given to the chief religious leader of a synagogue?
23 Which two countries fly supersonic passenger aircraft?
24 What did Mahatma Gandhi train to become?
25 Where would you find an avenue of sphinxes?
26 Which instrument did Lionel Hampton introduce to jazz?
27 Who played the Riddler in "Batman Forever"?
28 Who was the last prisoner to be held at Spandau?
29 Which rock star, known as "Slowhand", received an OBE in 1995?
30 Which theme from a film did the BBC use for the 1984 Olympics?

Pot-Luck 35 (see Quiz 79)
1 Spanish. 2 Hamlet. 3 Hindu. 4 Henry V. 5 Squirrel. 6 Zimbabwe. 7 The Medway. 8 Queen Alexandra. 9 Cricket. 10 Keith Richard. 11 Isaac. 12 James II. 13 Canary. 14 Manitoba. 15 Italy. 16 Battle of Bosworth. 17 Noel Coward. 18 Bench. 19 Canada. 20 Eyes. 21 Tea. 22 Anne Boleyn. 23 Etna. 24 The Seagull. 25 Salome. 26 Magyar. 27 On its tail. 28 Gerald Ford. 29 Coal or coal tar. 30 Suez Canal.

Answers

Quiz 78 TV: Sci Fi

Level 2

Answers - see page 204

1 In "Doctor Who" what does TARDIS stand for?
2 Which programme began with the control voice saying "There is nothing wrong with your television set"?
3 In which series did scientist Dr Sam Beckett appear?
4 What was the Six Million Dollar Man's previous occupation?
5 In which sci-fi series did Joanna Lumley and David McCallum star?
6 What was unusual about Dr Peter Brady and Dr Daniel Westin?
7 Which time traveller came by flying saucer to 1980s London?
8 Which Edwardian adventurer, trapped in ice, thawed out in 1966?
9 What was Steve Zodiac's spacecraft?
10 Where were the Robinson family lost in the 1960s series?
11 What is Doctor Who always called in the series?
12 Which series has had Eartha Kitt in the role of Catwoman?
13 Who played Jamie in "Doctor Who" and Joe Sugden in "Emmerdale"?
14 What were Captain Kirk's two Christian names?
15 How was Diana Prince better known?
16 What did "A" stand for in the name of the 1960s series?
17 What was special about the Man from Atlantis, Mark Harris?
18 Which 11th-century wizard became trapped in the 20th century?
19 In "Doomwatch" what was Doomwatch?
20 Who travelled in "The Liberator" fighting The Federation?
21 What was the surname of Professor Bernard whose name has become synonymous with early TV sci-fi?
22 What was the title of the Star Trek series which resumed in 1990?
23 Which series preceded "Galactica 80"?
24 In "Doctor Who" what was the Daleks' most famous command?
25 In "Star Trek" what colour was Mr Spock's blood?
26 Which children's series featured Spectrum and Colonel White?
27 Which series is remembered for Diana seeming to swallow a mouse?
28 What was the surname of global rescuers Jeff, Scott and Virgil?
29 In which 1970s series had 95% of the world's population been wiped out by a killer virus?
30 What sort of vehicle was Stingray?

Answers

Beer (see Quiz 80)
1 Hops. 2 Campaign for Real Ale. 3 Dutch. 4 Trouble shooter, John Harvey-Jones. 5 Tetley's. 6 Guinness. 7 Boddingtons. 8 Adnams. 9 Bitter. 10 Stella Artois. 11 Cider is non-alcoholic, hard cider is alcoholic. 12 Carlsberg. 13 Fuller's. 14 Brown/black. 15 Heineken. 16 Belgium. 17 Yeast. 18 Greene King. 19 Cider. 20 February (Valentine's Day). 21 Ale. 22 Ruddles. 23 Bass. 24 Horse-drawn drays. 25 Samuel Smith's. 26 Scottish and Newcastle. 27 Australian. 28 Wells (Charles Wells). 29 Beer sausages. 30 Shepherd Neame.

Quiz 79   Pot-Luck 35

Answers - see page 201

1 What is the main language spoken in Chile?
2 In which Shakespeare play do we meet two grave diggers?
3 Which Eastern religion includes the caste system?
4 Who was king of England from 1413 to 1422?
5 What animal lives in a drey?
6 In which African country is the city of Bulawayo?
7 On which river do Rochester, Chatham and Gillingham stand?
8 Which queen started a nursing service for soldiers?
9 In which sport was Sir Donald Bradman famous?
10 Who said, "I never had any problems with drugs, only with policemen"?
11 In the Bible, name the son who Abraham was asked to sacrifice?
12 Who was the last Roman Catholic king of England?
13 What sort of bird is a Cinnamon Norwich?
14 Winnipeg is the capital of which Canadian province?
15 Of which country was Aldo Moro prime minister?
16 At which battle was Richard III killed?
17 Who wrote the operetta "Bitter Sweet" and the play "Private Lives"?
18 What do we call a group of bishops?
19 Which country does a car come from if it shows CDN as the international registration letters?
20 What part of the body would be affected if you suffered from myopia?
21 What cargo did the ship "Cutty Sark" carry?
22 Who was the mother of the first Queen Elizabeth?
23 What is the name of the famous active volcano on the island of Sicily?
24 Which bird is also the name of a play by Chekhov?
25 Who asked for the head of John the Baptist?
26 Which is the main language spoken in Hungary?
27 Whereabouts on a whale are its flukes?
28 Who succeeded Richard Nixon as president of the United States in 1974?
29 From what do we get saccharine?
30 Which important ship canal was built by Ferdinand de Lesseps?

Quiz 80 Beer

Answers - see page 202

Level 2

1 What does beer contain which ale traditionally did not?
2 What does CAMRA stand for?
3 What nationality is the lager giant Grolsch?
4 Who did Tolly Cobbold name their Tollyshooter after?
5 Which brewers sponsored the England Test cricket team in 1995?
6 Which beer was said to be "good for you"?
7 Which Manchester brewery was acquired by Whitbread in 1989?
8 Which beer is made in Southwold in Suffolk?
9 Which has more hops, bitter or mild?
10 Which company has sponsored a pre-Wimbledon tennis tournament?
11 In the United States what is the difference between cider and hard cider?
12 What is advertised as "probably the best lager in the world"?
13 On which brewer's site in Chiswick has there been a brewery for more than 300 years?
14 What colour is porter?
15 Which lager "reached the parts other beers couldn't reach"?
16 Where are lambic and faro beers made?
17 What expected ingredient is missing from lambic and faro beers?
18 Which brewery makes Abbot Ale?
19 Which West Country drink can be sweet, dry or rough?
20 In which month do the Arundel Brewery make "Romeo's Rouser"?
21 What was originally stronger, ale or beer?
22 For which beer is Rutland famous?
23 Which brewer has Stones and Worthington Best Bitter?
24 What do Thwaites, Wadworth and Young's have in common regarding deliveries?
25 Which brewer operates from the oldest brewery in Yorkshire?
26 Which company produces McEwan's and Theakston's?
27 What is the nationality of Foster's?
28 Which brewer's logo is an eagle and produces Eagle IPA?
29 What beer product does the Leather Britches brewery also produce?
30 Which Kent brewer is believed to be the oldest continuous brewer in the country?

Answers

TV: Sci Fi (see Quiz 78)
1 Time And Relative Dimensions In Space. 2 The Outer Limits. 3 Quantum Leap. 4 Astronaut. 5 Sapphire and Steel. 6 Invisible. 7 Dominick Hide. 8 Adam Adamant. 9 Fireball XL5. 10 Space. 11 The Doctor. 12 Batman. 13 Frazer Hines. 14 James Tiberius. 15 Wonder Woman. 16 Andromeda. 17 Half man, half fish. 18 Catweazle. 19 Government department. 20 Blake's Seven. 21 Quatermass. 22 The Next Generation. 23 Battlestar Galactica. 24 Exterminate. 25 Green. 26 Captain Scarlet and the Mysterons. 27 V. 28 Tracy. 29 Survivors. 30 Submarine.

1 When a cow stands up, which legs does it get up on first?
2 Who sang the "On the good ship Lollipop"?
3 According to the proverb, what is the better part of valour?
4 When driving a car in Britain what is the hand signal for turning left?
5 In ads, what were you using if your fingers did the walking?
6 From which London railway station do you normally travel to Bristol?
7 In which film is the Harry Lime theme?
8 Which American city is named after a British prime minister?
9 Where would you find a dead man's handle?
10 How is Concetta Franconeri better known?
11 On which river does swan-upping take place?
12 Which country lies immediately east of Iraq?
13 Which London building is nicknamed 'Ally Pally'?
14 Who claimed that "History is Bunk"?
15 In which English city is the cathedral known as "Paddy's Wigwam"?
16 From which port was the bulk of the British Expeditionary Force in France evacuated in 1940?
17 Which architect designed New York's Guggenheim Museum?
18 Who wrote" Gulliver's Travels"?
19 In which city was General Gordon put to death?
20 What kind of animal is a pipistrelle?
21 According to the proverb which fruit tastes sweetest?
22 What was the name for the ancient Egyptian good luck charm in the shape of a beetle?
23 Who was depected in "Spitting Image" as a slug?
24 Who said "Father, I cannot tell a lie"?
25 By what name do we often call nitrous oxide?
26 In German fable who sold his soul to Mephistopheles?
27 What do Bluebell, the Watercress,and the Severn Valley all have in common?
28 What is Freddie Starr's real name?
29 Which sport did David Duckham play?
30 What is the unit of currency in Iran?

Answers

Pot-Luck 37 (see Quiz 83)
1 Slander. 2 Russ Conway. 3 Jet. 4 The Crusades. 5 1961. 6 Newfoundland. 7 Aardvark. 8 Dr Crippen. 9 Tom & Jerry. 10 Can-can. 11 Joan Sims. 12 All work and no play. 13 Daisy. 14 House of Lords. 15 Bulgaria. 16 Sikh. 17 Mushrooms or toadstools. 18 Canada. 19 Equipment. 20 Marchioness. 21 Tunisia. 22 The Salvation Army. 23 Joshua. 24 John Williams. 25 Tasman Sea. 26 Limited. 27 Grapefruit. 28 Scampo. 29 Ernest. 30 The Dam Busters.

Quiz 82 World Football

Answers - see page 208

1 Which Rio-based club is named after a Portuguese navigator?
2 Which Japanese city is home to Grampus Eight?
3 For which national team does Abedi Pele play?
4 On which day of the week do the Spanish usually play football?
5 Which shirt number do Italian clubs reserve for their star player?
6 Which Dutch side play their games in the Philips Stadium?
7 Which Spanish team did Gary Lineker play for?
8 What country was in three of the first four European finals?
9 Which city is home to Racing Club and River Plate?
10 At which ground do the Republic of Ireland play home games?
11 Which former goalie coached both Juventus and Lazio?
12 In which European country are the headquarters of UEFA?
13 Which French side did Trevor Steven play for?
14 Where did Aston Villa win the European Cup in 1982?
15 Where in France is the ground known as Le Stadium?
16 Which Serie A club is based on the islands of Sardinia?
17 In which stadium was the Final of the 1992 Olympic tournament held?
18 In what year was the first ever European Cup match played?
19 Argentina's Diego Maradona played for which club side during 1992–93?
20 Independiente are a leading club in which country?
21 Which side beat Arsenal in the 1995 European Cup Winners' Cup with a goal in the last minute of extra time?
22 In which country was the 1992 European Championship staged?
23 Name the the beaten finalists in the 1994 World Cup final?
24 The quickest goal in a World Cup tournament was scored by Bryan Robson against which country in 1982?
25 Which country became the first to win the World Cup three times?
26 Which Spanish side did Howard Kendall once manage?
27 Which was the first British team to lift the European Cup after a penalty shoot-out?
28 Alfredo di Stefano played international football for three countries – Argentina, Spain and which other country?
29 Which item of kit was made compulsory by FIFA in 1990?
30 Who is the only player to score a hat-trick in a World Cup final?

Quiz 83 Pot-Luck 37

Answers - see page 205

1 If libel is a written defamation, what is oral defamation?
2 Which pianist had hits with "Side Saddle" and "Roulette"?
3 Which word can go after jumbo and before black?
4 What name was given to the mediaeval warlike expeditions to the Holy Land?
5 In which year was the first manned space flight?
6 In Canada, of which province is St John's the capital?
7 Which animal's name literally means "earth pig"?
8 Who was the first major criminal to be arrested as a result of the use of radio?
9 Who made their screen debut in "Puss In Boots"?
10 Which dance is usually performed to "Orpheus in the Underworld"?
11 Who played the part of Mrs Wembley in "On The Up"?
12 According to the proverb what makes Jack a dull boy?
13 Of which flower is ox-eye a type?
14 In Britain which is the ultimate court of appeal?
15 What country did tennis-playing sisters Katerina and Manuela Maleeva come from?
16 Amritsar is a holy city for the followers of which religion?
17 What are ink-caps, death caps and puffballs all types of?
18 Which country was once called New France?
19 What does the second E in the acronym ERNIE stand for?
20 What is the wife of a marquis called?
21 In which country is the ruined city of Carthage?
22 Which religious body publishes a magazine called "The War Cry"?
23 In the Bible, who led the Israelites to the Battle of Jericho?
24 Whom did Julian Bream partner in the album "Together"?
25 Which sea lies between New Zealand and Australia?
26 The initials plc stand for what type of public company?
27 What is the common name for the fruit citrus grandis?
28 What is the singular of scampi?
29 What was Sergeant Bilko's first name?
30 What daring raid was led by Guy Gibson?

Answers

Pot-Luck 36 (see Quiz 81)

1 Back. 2 Shirley Temple. 3 Discretion. 4 Turning your right arm in a circle. 5 Yellow Pages. 6 Paddington. 7 The Third Man. 8 Pittsburgh. 9 In an electric train, tube train. 10 Connie Francis. 11 The Thames. 12 Iran. 13 Alexandra Palace. 14 Henry Ford. 15 Liverpool. 16 Dunkirk. 17 Frank Lloyd Wright. 18 Jonathan Swift. 19 Khartoum. 20 A bat. 21 Forbidden Fruit. 22 The scarab. 23 Kenneth Baker. 24 George Washington. 25 Laughing gas. 26 Faust. 27 Railways. 28 Freddie Starr. 29 Rugby Union. 30 The rial.

Quiz 84 Modern History: Trouble Spots Level 2

Answers - see page 206

1 Who fled his "Peacock Throne" into exile in 1979?
2 Where did the mujahideen resist Soviet attack?
3 Which country was the scene of the Mau Mau rebellion in the 1950s?
4 How long did the Arab-Israeli War of 1967 last?
5 Which English World War II veteran was a Beirut kidnap victim?
6 Which Argentinean cruiser was sunk outside an exclusion zone during the Falklands War?
7 Where did Russian troops crush an anti-Soviet uprising in 1956?
8 Where did the Sandinistas overthrow the government in 1979?
9 Who was president of Egypt during the Suez Crisis in 1956?
10 In which Bay was there a failed attempt by exiled Cubans to invade Cuba?
11 Where in North Africa did a war for independence take place between 1954 and 1962?
12 In 1996, where in London was an IRA bomb planted to end a ceasefire?
13 In the Middle East conflict what does PLO stand for?
14 Where did ZANU and ZAPU fight for independence?
15 Who ousted Ferdinand Marcos as president of the Philippines?
16 In which war was Operation Desert Storm?
17 Where did Greeks and Turks clash in major unrest in 1964?
18 Who fought against Iran in the 1980–88 conflict?
19 Which war was fought along the 38th parallel?
20 Which two public figures were assassinated in the United States in 1968?
21 Where in the 1960s was there a Cultural Revolution?
22 In which country did the My Lai massacre take place?
23 Who was the Argentinean president during the Falklands conflict?
24 Biafra was a breakaway state from which African country?
25 In which country did Steve Biko die in detention ?
26 Which city's "Spring" was ended by a Soviet invasion in 1968?
27 Whom did Vietnam gain independence from in 1954?
28 Where in Uganda was a hijacked Air France plane stormed in 1976?
29 Which country disintegrated following the outbreak of civil war in 1992?
30 In which Peking square were pro-democracy demos violently suppressed?

Quiz 85 Pot-Luck 38

Answers - see page 211

1 Which novel is about a boy called Billy Casper who trains a hawk?
2 Martina Navratilova won most doubles trophies with which partner?
3 With what is Threadneedle Street associated?
4 In which art has Beryl Grey achieved fame?
5 Who lives in a kraal?
6 Whose real name was Ronald Wycherly?
7 What colour is angelica?
8 With which country is the famous soldier Robert Clive associated?
9 What happens in a vortex?
10 To which section of the orchestra does the tuba belong?
11 In the song, who stuck a feather in his hat called macaroni?
12 What's the first Ealing Comdey?
13 What is the county town of Shropshire?
14 In which sporting event does the winning team move backwards?
15 What is a fandango?
16 Eau-de-nil is a shade of what colour?
17 Which revolution began in 1917?
18 Who is said to have introduced the habit of smoking into this country?
19 After seven which is the next highest prime number?
20 In boxing at what weight do you fight if you weigh over 12 stone 7 pounds?
21 Who wrote the novel "Jane Eyre"?
22 Until the country's recent division, what was the capital of Yugoslavia?
23 Which drink is known as eau-de-vie?
24 In which country were turkeys first found?
25 What is a carillon?
26 How many moves are there in a chess game in which White opens and wins with Fool's Mate?
27 In which month each year is Battle of Britain week?
28 In a bullfight who kills the bull?
29 What size of bottle is a magnum?
30 What is David Frost's middle name?

Answers

Pot-Luck 39 (see Quiz 87)
1 Genesis. 2 A space. 3 Crab. 4 Richard Burtong. 5 Belgium. 6 The Importance of Being Ernest. 7 In your foot. 8 Paperback Writer. 9 Places of the same height. 10 The parson. 11 Beauty. 12 Laurel and Hardy. 13 Swan. 14 B. 15 Joe Louis. 16 China. 17 British admirals. 18 Long-distance running. 19 Charles. 20 The Merchant of Venice. 21 At the base of the neck. 22 Spain. 23 Sahara. 24 Izaak Walton. 25 To smell. 26 Cardiff City. 27 72 (accept 65–79). 28 Mummy Woodentop. 29 Texas. 30 New Year's Eve.

Quiz 86 Folk and Country

Level 2

Answers - see page 212

1 Who was known as "Gentleman Jim"?
2 Which country anthem starts. "Sometimes it's hard to be a woman"?
3 Which John Denver song did Peter, Paul and Mary take in the charts?
4 Which Dolly Parton song was a chart hit for Whitney Houston?
5 Who sang with the Clancy Brothers throughout the 1960s?
6 Which country star had a hit with "Kiss An Angel Good Morning"?
7 Which singer/songwriter penned "The Last Thing On My Mind"?
8 Which country star has had five husbands, including George Jones, and been kidnapped?
9 Which group was fronted by singer/songwriter Dave Cousins?
10 Which folk singer was called "Judas" for going electric?
11 Which city in eastern England has been the venue for a long-standing folk festival?
12 Who wrote "Your Cheatin' Heart"?
13 Which Rochdale Cowboy was a 1970s folk club favourite?
14 Who recorded the album "No Fences"?
15 Who is the long time lead singer with Steeleye Span?
16 Who declared "Thank God I'm A Country Boy"?
17 In what language was Fairport Convention's only English hit sung?
18 Which guitarist teamed up with Mark Knopfler on "Neck and Neck"?
19 Who wrote US dust-bowl songs and "This Land Is Your Land"?
20 How did Patsy Cline die?
21 Who took "There But For Fortune" into the UK single charts?
22 Under what name did Brenda Gail Webb become famous?
23 Who wrote the folk club classic "Streets Of London"?
24 Who wrote "Where Have All The Flowers Gone"?
25 How is Alexandra Denny better known?
26 Who recorded the album "Shotgun Willie"?
27 How are the trio of Yarrow, Stookey and Travers better known?
28 Who was on "Honky Tonk Angels" with Dolly Parton and Tammy Wynette?
29 Which Latin carol gave Steeleye Span a chart hit?
30 Which boy with a girl's name did Johnny Cash sing about?

Answers

Action movies (see Quiz 88)
1 Long Island. 2 Sean Connery. 3 Bruce Willis. 4 The Godfather. 5 Superman.
6 John Woo. 7 The architect. 8 Dr No. 9 Detroit. 10 Lee Van Cleef. 11
Raiders of the Lost Ark. 12 William Wallace. 13 Chicago. 14 Stallone. 15 Live
and Let Die. 16 Daniel Day-Lewis. 17 David Lean. 18 Patriot Games. 19
Directing. 20 On Her Majesty's Secret Service. 21 De Niro. 22 Unforgiven.
23 Faye Dunaway. 24 Kathleen Turner. 25 Car chase. 26 The Spy Who Loved
Me. 27 True Grit. 28 Dirty Harry. 29 Liam Neeson. 30 Lois Maxwell.

Quiz 87 Pot-Luck 39

Level 2

Answers - see page 209

1 Which book of the Bible tell us about the creation of the world?
2 What is a lacuna?
3 Edible, blue and hermit are all types of which creature?
4 Who played Thomas A Becket to Peter O'Toole's Henry II?
5 In which country is Waterloo, site of the Napoleonic battlefield?
6 In which play does Miss Prism appear?
7 Where is the metatarsal arch?
8 Which Beatles song was the theme for "Read All About It"?
9 On a map, which places are joined by a contour?
10 In the song, which official is waiting "for me and my gal"?
11 What is pulchritude?
12 Which film comedians are associated with the phrase, "That's another fine mess you got me in"?
13 Which creature's song refers to a final speech or performance?
14 Which letter of the alphabet is used to describe a soft lead pencil?
15 Who was nicknamed the Brown Bomber?
16 In which country were there originally mandarins?
17 Who or what are Effingham, Grenville, Benbow and Collingwood?
18 For which sport is Gordon Pirie remembered?
19 What was Buddy Holly's real first name?
20 Which of Shakespeare's plays involves a pound of flesh?
21 Where are your clavicles?
22 A lady would wear a mantilla in which country?
23 In area, which is the world's largest desert?
24 Who wrote "The Compleat Angler"?
25 What do your olfactory organs help you do ?
26 Which soccer team plays at Ninian Park?
27 To within a margin of seven more or less, what is a grown man's normal pulse rate in beats per minute?
28 Who had a daily help called Mrs. Scrubbit?
29 Which DIY store claims that it is "the big one"?
30 Which festival is called Saint Sylvestre or San Silvestro in certain countries?

Answers

Pot-Luck 38 (see Quiz 85)
1 Kestrel for a Knave, by Barry Hines (Kes). 2 Pam Shriver. 3 Bank of England. 4 Ballet (dance). 5 A Zulu. 6 Billy Fury. 7 Green. 8 India. 9 Everything swirls around. 10 Brass. 11 Yankee Doodle. 12 Passport to Pimlico. 13 Shrewsbury. 14 Tug of war. 15 Dance. 16 Green/blue-green. 17 Russian Revolution. 18 Sir Walter Raleigh. 19 Eleven. 20 Heavyweight. 21 Charlotte Bronte. 22 Belgrade. 23 Brandy. 24 North America. 25 Set of bells. 26 7. 27 September. 28 Matador. 29 Holds two ordinary bottles. 30 Paradine.

1 Off which island is "Jaws" set?
2 Who played Harrison Ford's father in "Indiana Jones and the Last Crusade"?
3 Who is the cop battling with terrorists in "Die Hard"?
4 Which films are about the Corleone family?
5 What is Christopher Reeve's most famous role?
6 Who directed "Broken Arrow"?
7 In "Towering Inferno" Steve McQueen was the fireman: what was Paul Newman?
8 Which was the first Bond movie?
9 Where was the Beverly Hills Cop based?
10 Who was Bad in Spaghetti Westerns?
11 Which was the first of the "Indiana Jones" films to be released?
12 Which hero did Mel Gibson play in "Braveheart"?
13 In which city is "The Untouchables" set?
14 Who was involved in the writing of the "Rocky" and "Rambo" films?
15 Which was the first Bond film with Roger Moore?
16 Who played the starring role in "Last of the Mohicans"?
17 Who directed "Lawrence of Arabia"?
18 Which film starred Harrison Ford as an ex-CIA man?
19 For what did Kevin Costner win an Oscar in "Dances with Wolves"?
20 Which was George Lazenby's only Bond film?
21 Who starred as Jake La Motta in "Raging Bull"?
22 Which Clint Eastwood film won an Oscar for Gene Hackman as the sheriff of Big Whiskey?
23 Who played Bonnie to Warren Beatty's Clyde?
24 Who co-starred with Michael Douglas in "Romancing the Stone"?
25 What was the memorable, and at that time innovative, scene in "Bullitt"?
26 Which Bond film had the song "Nobody Does It Better"?
27 In which film did John Wayne win his only Oscar?
28 Which movie preceded "Magnum Force" and "The Enforcer"?
29 Who plays the title role in "Rob Roy"?
30 Who plays Miss Moneypenny in the early Bond films?

Level 2

1 Which country has been officially called Myanmar since 1989?
2 Which country is made up of over 800 islands including Viti Levu?
3 Which desert covers part of China and Mongolia?
4 What title does the head of state of Nepal have?
5 Which 7000-island country lies in the Pacific, northeast of the South China Sea?
6 How is the Republic of China better known?
7 To which country does East Timor belong?
8 Which neighbouring countries' currency is the won?
9 What was the name of Bangladesh between 1947 and 1972?
10 In which country are the Cameron Highlands?
11 What are the majority of the islands of Micronesia composed of?
12 Which country is bordered by Laos, Vietnam and Thailand?
13 Which sea lies to the north of Iran?
14 What is Japan's highest mountain?
15 How many vowels are there in Kyrgyzstan?
16 Which country's official name in Hindi is Bharat?
17 What are China's famous "warriors" made from?
18 Which country's capital is Ulan Bator?
19 In which two countries is the Thar desert?
20 Which social system is divided into brahmins, ksatriyas vaisyas and sundras?
21 Where were Gurkhas originally from?
22 Which area of Russia has had the lowest temperatures in the world recorded there?
23 When "The Sound of Music" was shown in Korea what was missing?
24 What are the Seychelles' three official languages?
25 What is the capital of Singapore?
26 Which country's flag is a red circle on a green background?
27 Which Pacific islands share their name with a wise man in the Bible?
28 What did Ho Chi Minh City used to be called?
29 Which country has designated Chachoengsao as its new capital?
30 How many rivers does Tonga have?

Answers

Round Britain - Scotland (see Quiz 91)
1 Distillery. 2 Sir Walter Scott. 3 Southwest. 4 Extinct volcano. 5 Bird sanctuary. 6 St Giles Cathedral. 7 Bute. 8 Holyrood House. 9 Aberdeen. 10 Nuclear Power. 11 Two. 12 Princes Street. 13 Glamis Castle. 14 Silicon Glen. 15 Caledonian Canal. 16 Iona. 17 Meadowbank. 18 Tay Bridge. 19 Bell's. 20 Blair Castle. 21 Fingal's Cave. 22 Scone Palace. 23 Loch Ness. 24 Perth. 25 Culloden. 26 Dee. 27 Abbeys. 28 Stone Age. 29 Loch Lomond. 30 Tomatin.

Quiz 90 Pot-Luck 40

Level 2

Answers - see page 216

1 Of which country is Freetown the capital?
2 What is the term for a group of partridges?
3 What was the occupation of the legendary "Casey Jones"?
4 According to the proverb what is the mother of invention?
5 What is an area of water separated from the open sea by a coral reef?
6 In cricket how many balls are there in an over?
7 In the London theatre what is the longest-running play ever?
8 Which toilet roll ad features a Labrador puppy?
9 In astronomy what are falling stars properly called?
10 What are Hickling, Barton, and Breydon Water?
11 In 1989, which electronic giant bought Columbia Pictures?
12 What is meant by the Italian phrase "che sara sara"?
13 What does an American mean when he talks of a check in a restaurant?
14 Whom might you expect to see working in a dig?
15 If a ship runs up a yellow flag what does it mean?
16 Which is the smallest bird in the world?
17 Which Saint's day fall on 30 November?
18 In fiction who lived in the stables at Birtwick Hall?
19 Who was Oberon?
20 Can you name a hydrocarbon fuel?
21 In cookery, what is meant by coddling?
22 Which trade is especially likely to use an awl?
23 What was pioneered by the Austrian physician Dr Mesmer?
24 In World War II on what were we "going to hang out the washing"?
25 In which city was there formerly a parliament building called the Reichstag?
26 In which London building is the Whispering Gallery?
27 Which duo have produced songs for Tottenham Hotspur?
28 With which ceremony do we associate orange blossom?
29 What name was given to an airship that could be steered?
30 According to the ad, what couldn't Ian Botham eat three of?

Answers

Pot-Luck 41 (see Quiz 92)
1 35p. 2 Powys. 3 George Michael. 4 On a staircase. 5 Naturalist, entomologist. 6 Archbishop of Canterbury. 7 St Bruno. 8 Loudspeakers. 9 Lynne Perrie (Ivy Brennan). 10 In a low voice. 11 Atlantic. 12 Wagons, carts. 13 Rosary. 14 Leonardo. 15 Postage stamps. 16 It turns blue. 17 Margaret Mitchell. 18 Gerald Durrell. 19 Anatomy. 20 Seizure of power. 21 Clown (mime). 22 Revelation. 23 Anna Ford. 24 At right angles. 25 Venezuela. 26 Birmingham. 27 Rupert Murdoch. 28 Channel Islands. 29 212. 30 Skiving.

1 Edradour is the smallest what in Scotland?
2 Which famous Scottish writer lived at Abbotsford by the Tweed?
3 In which direction from Edinburgh do the Pentland Hills lie?
4 What is Berwick Law?
5 What is the Bass Rock famous as?
6 Which cathedral is also known as the High Kirk of Edinburgh?
7 Rothesay is the chief town of which island?
8 What is at the foot of the Royal Mile in Edinburgh?
9 Which city is at the mouth of the rivers Don and Dee?
10 What is produced at Torness?
11 How many bridges are there over the Firth of Forth?
12 What lies between Charlotte Square and St Andrew's Square?
13 Where was the childhood home of the Queen Mother?
14 What is the industrial area in and around Livingston nicknamed?
15 Which canal links the lochs of the Great Glen?
16 Which historic island is off the southwest tip of the Isle of Mull?
17 What is the name of Edinburgh's stadium where the Commonwealth Games have been held?
18 Which rail bridge is the longest in Europe?
19 Which famous whisky is made at Blair Athol?
20 Which baronial castle is the seat of the only British subject allowed to maintain his own private army?
21 What is the most famous cave on Staffa?
22 Which palace was once the site of a famous coronation stone?
23 Which loch contains the largest volume of fresh water in the British Isles?
24 Which city is often called The Fair City?
25 Leanach farmhouse can be seen on which moorland field of battle?
26 On which river does Balmoral stand?
27 Remains of what type of building are at Kelso and Jedburgh?
28 What type of village can be seen at Skara Brae?
29 Which loch is the largest stretch of inland water in Britain?
30 Where is Scotland's largest malt whisky distillery?

Quiz 92 Pot-Luck 41

Answers - see page 214

1 If VAT is 17.5% what is the VAT on an item costing £2?
2 In which county are the Brecon Beacons?
3 Whose real name is Georgius Panayiotou?
4 Where would you find treads and risers close together?
5 As what did Henri Fabre achieve fame?
6 Whose official residence is Lambeth Palace?
7 Who was advertised as the patron saint of pipe smokers?
8 What are woofers and tweeters?
9 Which former "Coronation Street" star is comedian Duggie Brown's sister?
10 What is meant by "sotto voce"?
11 In which ocean is the Sargasso Sea?
12 What are made by wainwrights?
13 What do Catholics call the string of beads they use when praying?
14 Who painted the most famous version of "The Last Supper"?
15 What is the subject matter covered by a Gibbons's catalogue?
16 What happens when red litmus paper is put in an alkaline solution?
17 Who wrote the novel "Gone with the Wind"?
18 Which naturalist is the author of " My Family and Other Animals"?
19 What word is used for the science dealing with the body structure?
20 What is a coup d'état?
21 As what kind of entertainer did Grock achieve fame?
22 Which is the last book of the Bible?
23 Which TV newsreader was married to cartoonist Mark Boxer?
24 How do bevel gears engage with one another?
25 Of which country is Caracas the capital?
26 Which soccer side plays at St Andrews?
27 In which capital is the statue of a small boy, the Mannekin Pis?
28 Where, today, would you find a bailliwick?
29 In 1985, which media tycoon bought 20th Century Fox?
30 What are you doing if you are swinging the lead?

Quiz 93 Flowers

Level 2

1 What is the common name for the antirrhinum?
2 Which hanging basket favourite is also called pelargonium?
3 What qualities do the flowers helichrysum and acroclinium have?
4 By what name is Solidago known?
5 What type of bell is a campanula?
6 Which yellow, pink-flushed rose was bred by Meilland in 1945?
7 Which wild flower as also known as the knapweed?
8 What flower has rung-like leaflets?
9 What would you find in an anther on a stamen?
10 What is the common name for the plant Impatiens?
11 Which flowers are said to symbolize the Crucifixion?
12 Which flower, also called chalk plant or baby's breath, is a favourite with flower arrangers ?
13 Bachelor's buttons are a variety of which yellow wild flower?
14 Which flower's seeds are pickled to make capers?
15 Which animals love nepeta ,giving it its common name?
16 What sort of hyacinth is a muscari?
17 Which flower – Lychnis – shares its name with a fictional detective?
18 Which two flowers would you find in an orchestra?
19 Which flower gets its name from a Persian or Turkish word for turban?
20 Which plant is grown not for its flowers but for its silvery seed pods?
21 Which family do azaleas belong to?
22 Jonquils are members of which family?
23 Which plant is also called the torch lily?
24 Which climbing plant has the variety Nelly Moser?
25 Which flower's foundation varieties are alba, gallica and damascena?
26 Which plant was named after the Greek goddess of the rainbow?
27 What sort of purplish-blue daisies are types of aster?
28 Which bloom's name means golden flower, although it can be many different colours?
29 What colour is the rose silverjubilee?
30 Which country sent the first dahlia seeds to Europe?

Answers

Pot-Luck 43 (see Quiz 97)
1 Eros. 2 Green. 3 Friday. 4 Sailing/yachting. 5 Flyweight. 6 Sheep. 7 David Lloyd George. 8 Christine Keeler. 9 Julie Covington. 10 Yellow. 11 Prime minister. 12 Eldorado. 13 Bank manager. 14 Dark Blue. 15 La Paz. 16 Sculpture. 17 Oxo. 18 Hymn book. 19 Raven. 20 Astro. 21 Netherlands. 22 Colorado river. 23 Archery. 24 Femur. 25 Atlantic. 26 Kookaburra. 27 Greyfriars. 28 Calvary or Golgotha. 29 David McCallum. 30 Polo.

Quiz 94 Pot-Luck 42

Answers - see page 220

1 ICBM stands for Inter-Continental what?
2 What was a matchlock?
3 In which TV show did creatures cry "Exterminate!"?
4 What is the male equivalent of a ranee?
5 In chemistry, what is a substance which cannot be split into simpler substances?
6 According to the Germans, who were the 'Ladies from Hell'?
7 Who created "Till Death Us Do Part"?
8 In "Two Little Boys", what did each boy have that was wooden?
9 Which American rodent builds dams and fells trees?
10 In which river was Jesus Christ baptized?
11 In which Shakespeare play does a forest apparently move?
12 What do Americans call a pack of cards?
13 Which soccer team is nicknamed "The Pensioners"?
14 What was the name of the first nuclear-powered submarine?
15 Which country produces most wine in the world?
16 Which word can go after funny and before china?
17 If you were driving at 50 miles per hour, at how many kilometres per hour would you be going (approximately)?
18 Which English king died at the age of 15?
19 In which sport are stones and a broom used?
20 Which drink was promoted by, "I'd Like To Teach The World To Sing"?
21 Of which country was John George Diefenbaker prime minister?
22 In which language did Aristophanes write his plays?
23 Of which country was Archbishop Makarios prime minister?
24 Which member of U2 has the real name of Paul Hewson?
25 Of which US state is Little Rock the capital?
26 Which part of the body is described by the word labial?
27 In which West Country city is the railway station St David's?
28 For which country did Dennis Law play soccer?
29 Which British king reigned from 1830 to 1837?
30 First held in 1983, how many years elapsed befor the second Athletics World Championships?

Answers - see page 221

1 Which is the oldest British flat classic race?
2 How many winners did Gordon Richards ride in the 1947 season?
3 Which jockey riding Shergar in 1981 won in his first Derby ride?
4 Which jockey won the Prix de l'Arc de Triomphe from 1985 to 1987 on three different horses?
5 Where did Britain's first evening meeting take place?
6 Who rode Henbit, Nashwan and Erhaab to Derby victories?
7 Which horse, in 1977, became the first to win the Mackeson and Hennessy in the same season?
8 Which course celebrated 100 years of racing in July 1987?
9 Who was the first woman to ride a winner over fences in Britain?
10 In 1925 at Windsor, bookmakers went on strike. Against what?
11 Where was the Derby held during the two World Wars?
12 On which course in Australia is the Melbourne Cup run?
13 Which jockey had most Classic wins before Lester Piggott?
14 Which was the first racecourse equipped with a photo-finish camera?
15 On which horse did Princess Anne win her first flat race?
16 Diomed was the first winner of which great race?
17 Which race came first, the 1000 Guineas or 2000 Guineas?
18 What is Dick Hern's real first name?
19 Which gossip columnist was owner of My Purple Prose?
20 Where is the Happy Valley racecourse?
21 What is the first name of Peter Scudamore's father?
22 In betting, how much is a monkey?
23 In which Surrey town is Sandown racecourse?
24 Lester Piggott shares his birthday with which annual event?
25 In which country did Steve Donoghue ride his first winner?
26 What is the real first name of Richard Dunwoody?
27 Son of a famous father, who had his first winner at Kempton in 1978?
28 In his 1990 comeback which horse gave Lester Piggott his first winner?
29 How many individual bets make up a Yankee?
30 How many Grand Nationals did Desert Orchid win?

Answers

Flowers (see Quiz 93)
1 Snapdragon. 2 Geranium. 3 Everlasting. 4 Golden Rod. 5 Canterbury bell.
6 Peace. 7 Cornflower. 8 Jacob's ladder. 9 Pollen. 10 Busy Lizzie. 11
Passion flower. 12 Gypsophila. 13 Buttercups. 14 Nasturtium. 15 Cats
(Catmint). 16 Grape hyacinth. 17 Campion. 18 Viola, Bugle. 19 Tulip
(tuliban). 20 Honesty. 21 Rhododendron. 22 Narcissus. 23 Red hot poker.
24 Clematis. 25 Rose. 26 Iris. 27 Michaelmas daisy. 28 Chrysanthemum.
29 Pink. 30 Mexico.

Quiz 96 Pop music: Worldwide

Level 2

Answers - see page 218

1 Who did Celine Dion represent in the 1988 Eurovision Song Contest?
2 What is Demis Roussos' home country?
3 Which country does James Last come from?
4 U Got 2 Know where Cappella are from, do you?
5 Their first No 1 was "The Sun Always Shines on TV": where were they from?
6 Members of Los Bravos were from Spain and from where else?
7 Which opera singer had a hit with "Amigos Para Siempre" (Friends for Life) in 1992?
8 Which Minogue sister had a hit with "Love and Kisses"?
9 Who duetted with Freddie Mercury on "Barcelona"?
10 Where does Whigfield hail from?
11 Which Australian had three consecutive no 1s between December 1988 and June 1989?
12 Which country won the Eurovision Song Contest in 1992, 1993 and 1994?
13 Which country are Bob and Ziggy Marley associated with?
14 Where is 70s chart topper Charles Aznavour from?
15 Which Rolf Harris record went to No 1 in 1969?
16 Who said "I Don't Wanna Dance" in 1982?
17 Which film theme gave Vangelis a hit in 1981?
18 Who was "Missing You" in 1988?
19 Who had a hit with "Guaglione"nearly 40 years after his first No 1?
20 Which Irish group sang "Love Me For a Reason" in 1994?
21 Which song and show started as a Eurovision interval filler?
22 Which famous widow was "Walking on Thin Ice" in 1981?
23 From which island group did Boney M hail?
24 In 1977 Baccara said "Yes, Sir, I Can..." what?
25 Who sang "Perhaps Love" with John Denver?
26 Who did Abba win Eurovision for in 1974?
27 What are the first names of father and son musicians Jarre?
28 Whose first No 1 was "Nothing Compares 2 U"?
29 What was Jane Birkin and Serge Gainsbourg's famous recording?
30 Swedish Sylvia sang "Y Viva" where?

Answers

Pot-Luck 42 (see Quiz 94)
1 Ballistic missile. 2 Gun. 3 Dr Who. 4 Rajah. 5 Element. 6 Scottish Highland soldiers in kilts. 7 Johnny Speight. 8 Horse. 9 Beaver. 10 The Jordan. 11 Macbeth. 12 A deck. 13 Chelsea. 14 Nautilus (in 1955). 15 France. 16 Bone. 17 80 kilometres per hour. 18 Edward VI. 19 Curling. 20 Coca Cola. 21 Canada. 22 Greek. 23 Cyprus. 24 Bono. 25 Arkansas. 26 The lips. 27 Exeter. 28 Scotland. 29 William IV. 30 Four.

1 In Greek mythology, who is the god of love?
2 At night what colour light is shown on the starboard side of a ship?
3 Which day of the week is the Muslim holy day?
4 If you were using a spinnaker, what would you be doing?
5 What is the lightest weight in boxing?
6 What kind of animal is a merino?
7 Who was the first prime minister to make use of Chequers?
8 In political scandal, who said, "Discretion is a polite word for hypocrisy"?
9 Who went from the "Rock Follies" to "Evita"?
10 What colour jersey is worn by the leader in the Tour de France?
11 What other title is held by whoever is the First Lord of the Treasury?
12 What was the name of the mythical South American city of gold?
13 In "Dad's Army" what was Captain Mainwaring's day job?
14 On a London Underground map, what colour is the Piccadilly line?
15 What is the capital of Bolivia?
16 In which art has Barbara Hepworth become famous?
17 In the ads, what does Lynda Bellingham use to make gravy?
18 What sort of book was compiled by Moody and Sankey?
19 Which bird did Noah first send out of the ark?
20 How is Terence Williams of UB40 better known?
21 Of which country is Ajax a famous football team?
22 Which river flows through the Grand Canyon in the United States?
23 What sport would you practise if you were a toxophilite?
24 What is the name of the bone in your thigh?
25 In which ocean are the Azores?
26 Which Australian bird is famous for laughing?
27 Which school did Billy Bunter go to?
28 What is the name of the hill where Jesus Christ was crucified?
29 Which Man from U.N.C.L.E. was married to Jill Ireland?
30 Which royal sport would you see at Cowdray Park and Hurlingham?

1   Who are the parents of Fifi Trixiebelle, Peaches and Pixie?
2   What is the profession of Princess Stephanie of Monaco's husband?
3   Who is Tiggy Legge-Bourke nanny to?
4   What is the name of Earl Spencer's former model wife?
5   What is the first name of the crown prince of Spain?
6   Before their resignations in 1996 who did Patrick Jephson and Steve Davies work for ?
7   Who is heir to the throne of Monaco?
8   Which "Baywatch" star married Tommy Lee?
9   What were the two married names of the late Jacqueline Bouvier?
10   On which Caribbean island did Princess Diana spend her first Christmas after the Queen announced she should divorce Prince Charles ?
11   Which actress/model gave birth to twins at the age of 44 on November 30th, 1995?
12   What nickname was given to the group of artists which included Dean Martin, Frank Sinatra and Peter Lawford ?
13   Which superstar and former playboy is Annette Bening married to?
14   Which one-time Hollywood pair have a daughter called Dakota ?
15   Maria Maples is the wife of which famous property tycoon?
16   Which actress is the wife of Simon MacCorkindale?
17   What is the name of the daughter of former "Catwoman"Eartha Kitt?
18   Which Man United football star's name was linked with Dani Behr?
19   Who was Athina Roussel's multi-millionairess mother?
20   What is the first name of Michael Caine's wife?
21   From which US state does model Jerry Hall come?
22   Who was Mrs Larry Fortensky until early 1996?
23   Who is Lady Helen Taylor's mother?
24   Who was widowed in 1990 when her husband's boat went out of control?
25   What colour is jet setter Ivana Trump known for wearing?
26   Which southern French resort holds a yearly film festival?
27   Which film star is Mrs Carlo Ponti?
28   Which actress won a legal battle against Random House in 1996 ?
29   Which actress/model advertises Revlon Flex hair products?
30   Which crown did actress/model Mary Stavin receive in the 1970s?

Answers

Popular Classics (see Quiz 100)
1 Handel. 2 Enigma Variations. 3 Beethoven. 4 Finlandia. 5 The Pearl Fishers. 6 Iolanthe. 7 Washington Post. 8 Air on a G String. 9 Pachelbel. 10 From the New World. 11 The Four Seasons. 12 Frederick Delius. 13 Guitar. 14 Elijah. 15 Eine Kleine Nachtmusik (A Little Night Music). 16 Ravel. 17 Animals. 18 Purcell. 19 The Thieving Magpie. 20 The Planets. 21 Choral Symphony. 22 Violin. 23 Peter and the Wolf. 24 Ballet. 25 The Ring. 26 Computer. 27 Land of Hope and Glory. 28 Danube. 29 Britannia rules the waves. 30 France.

Quiz 99   Pot-Luck 44

Level 2

Answers - see page 225

1   The River Ganges is a holy place for the followers of which religion?
2   What is the name for the home of an eagle?
3   Where was Robbie Burns born in Ayrshire?
4   Which Shakespearian play takes place in Illyria?
5   Which two leaders had a meeting in the Brenner Pass in World War II?
6   Tom Thumb, Tennis Ball and Winter Density are all types of what?
7   Which flower is particularly associated with Mary, the Madonna?
8   On which Yorkshire moor was a battle fought on July 2nd, 1644?
9   Which music hall comedian was known as the "Cheeky Chappie"?
10 In which industry was Lord Nuffield a pioneer?
11 Which word describes architecture dating from the time of James I?
12 What word describes the minimum number of members on a committee in attendance for it to reach valid decisions?
13 Who composed the "Thunder and Lightning" Polka?
14 Which war was fought in the Far East from 1950 to 1953?
15 What type of animal is a Kerry Blue?
16 In which year was the evacuation of Dunkirk?
17 Which German pianist took a walk in the Black Forest in the 1960s?
18 What does an ancmometer measure?
19 What is a filbert?
20 Which strait links the Black Sea and the Sea of Marmara?
21 What does a lexicographer write or make?
22 What was the name of the prison in "Porridge"?
23 Who or what live in a holt?
24 Which city was once known as Eboracum?
25 In 1915, which British liner was sunk by a German submarine?
26 "Match of the Day" has been used as a TV title for soccer and which other sport?
27 By what name is mid-Lent Sunday popularly known?
28 In ads, what is Homepride's head chef called?
29 Of the Seven Wonders of the World, where was the Colossus?
30 Which gorge is crossed by the Clifton suspension bridge?

Answers

Pot-Luck 45   (see Quiz 101)
1 Ways of ringing church bells. 2 Goat. 3 Nigeria. 4 Eye. 5 Its passion play (held every ten years). 6 Carlisle. 7 Ginger Rogers. 8 Forehead. 9 Palm Sunday. 10 Take My Breath Away. 11 Ivor Novello. 12 A watch. 13 Jerusalem. 14 Lemmings. 15 Tax collector. 16 Ring road. 17 Dr Samuel Johnson. 18 Hamlet. 19 Evening. 20 Sheep. 21 Journalists, the press. 22 Edinburgh. 23 A wreath. 24 Sparking plug. 25 Norwegian. 26 Anthea Redfern. 27 Composer. 28 Bernard Montgomery. 29 Noelle Gordon. 30 Roy Walker.

1 Who wrote "The Hallelujah Chorus"?

2 From which work does the piece "Nimrod" come from?

3 Who wrote the concerto called "The Emperor"?

4 Which work by Sibelius represented the defiance of the Finns?

5 Which Bizet opera features the duet "Au Fond du Temple Saint"?

6 In which Gilbert and Sullivan opera do fairies take over Parliament?

7 Which US newspaper shares its name with a march by Sousa?

8 Which work by Bach became famous in a cigar advertisement?

9 Who wrote Pachelbel's Kanon?

10 What is Dvorak's 9th Symphony, written in the US, often called?

11 Which Vivaldi composition did Nigel Kennedy popularize?

12 Who wrote "On Hearing the First Cuckoo in Spring"?

13 For which instrument is Joaquín Rodrigo most famous?

14 Which Old Testament prophet was the subject of an oratorio by Mendelssohn?

15 Which title of a composition by Mozart was translated by Stephen Sondheim into the name of a musical?

16 Who wrote the Bolero Torvill and Dean danced to?

17 What was in the Carnival in the Saint-Saëns composition?

18 Which English composer's 300th anniversary took place in 1995?

19 What is the English title of "La gazza ladra" by Rossini?

20 Which suite is Gustav Holst's most famous composition ?

21 What is Beethoven's 9th Symphony known as?

22 For which instrument did Paganini chiefly compose?

23 Which famous piece by Prokofiev is for orchestra and narrator ?

24 What type of performance was "The Rite of Spring" written for ?

25 What is the Wagner opera cycle which includes "Siegfried" and "Die Walküre"?

26 What are pieces by Iannis Xenakis written with the aid of?

27 How is the "Pomp and Circumstance March" better known?

28 Which river is celebrated in Johann Strauss's most famous waltz?

29 Which line follows "Rule Britannia" in the chorus of the song?

30 Who is Russia's opponent in the campaign commemorated in the "1812 Overture"?

Quiz 101 Pot-Luck 45

Answers - see page 223

1 What are Steadman triples, Plain Bob Caters and Gransire triples?
2 What kind of animal is a chamois?
3 In which African country is the city of Ibadan?
4 Which part of the body would be affected by astigmatism?
5 For what is Oberammergau famous?
6 Which city is the administrative headquarters of Cumbria?
7 Which actress/dancer's real name was Virginia McMath?
8 Where in your body is the frontal bone?
9 On which day does the Church celebrate Jesus entering Jerusalem?
10 Which Berlin hit advertised a car?
11 Who wrote "The Dancing Years" and "King's Rhapsody"?
12 What is the collective noun to describe a number of nightingales?
13 With which holy city is the name Zion associated?
14 Which Scandinavian animals are famous for running over cliff tops?
15 Before he became a disciple of Jesus, what was Matthew's job?
16 What does road sign with a white capital letter R on a green background indicate?
17 Boswell wrote the biography of which famous writer?
18 Ophelia appears in which Shakespeare play?
19 To what does the adjective crepuscular refer?
20 In Australia, what animal is a jumbuck?
21 Who or what is meant the Fourth Estate?
22 Which city has or had the nickname Auld Reekie?
23 What was awarded to winners in the original Olympic Games?
24 In a car what is the device called that secures electrical ignition?
25 What nationality was the playwright Ibsen?
26 Who was Bruce Forsyth's second wife?
27 As what did Bela Bartok achieve fame?
28 Who commanded the Allied ground forces in the Normandy invasion of 1944?
29 Which "Crossroads" star had been used by John Logie Baird in TV experiments?
30 Whose catchphrase is, "It's good but it's not right"?

Quiz 102 Shock Rock

Level 2

Answers - see page 228

1 Nancy Spungeon was the girlfriend of which punk performer?
2 Which grunge purveyor blew his brains out in 1994?
3 Which glam rocker proclaimed himself the "Godfather of Punk"?
4 Who was murdered by his father on his birthday in 1984?
5 Who had No1 albums in 1982 with "Number of the Beast" and "Seventh Son of a Seventh Son" in 1988?
6 Which interviewer who challenged The Sex Pistols to swear on TV?
7 Which 1960s hit singer was famous for his trousers splitting on stage?
8 Which group made the top ten in 1991 after 20 minor hits over 15 years?
9 Which rock superstar did Mark Chapman gun down?
10 "Aquarius" came from which show that shocked 1960s audiences?
11 Who started life as John Lydon?
12 Who recorded "Grimly Fiendish" with the record number GRIM 1?
13 Who recorded – and set himself on – "Fire"?
14 Which group recorded the album "Nevermind"?
15 In 1993 what was Snoop Doggy Dogg arrested for?
16 Which Frankie Goes To Hollywood hit was banned by the BBC?
17 Which group was formed by Jello Biafra in the late 1970s?
18 Who was manager of The Sex Pistols?
19 The film "The Rose" was loosely based on whose life?
20 Which actress should have partnered Serge Gainsbourg on "Je t'aime" but withdrew from the project?
21 Which Sinatra song did Sid Vicious record?
22 Who were the "Hersham Boys"?
23 What is Boy George's real name?
24 Whose stage act included simulated "killings" of a doll and a chicken?
25 Reg Presley was said to be "too suggestive" with which group?
26 Which cult hero did Val Kilmer play in a 1991 Oliver Stone movie?
27 Who in 1966 spoke of being "more popular than Jesus'"?
28 Who released the solo album "Blaze of Glory" which included tracks from "Young Guns II"?
29 Which Australasian rock band includes singer Michael Hutchence?
30 Who released the then extremely controversial "Let's Spend the Night Together" in 1967?

Answers

Around Australia (see Quiz 104)
1 Sydney. 2 Great Barrier Reef. 3 Ayers Rock or Uluru. 4 Canberra. 5 Pacific and Indian. 6 Bondi Beach. 7 The Northern Territory. 8 Botany Bay. 9 Brisbane river. 10 Queensland. 11 Western Australia. 12 The Blue Mountains. 13 Alice Springs. 14 Melbourne. 15 Wave Rock. 16 The Gold Coast. 17 Kakadu National Park. 18 Kuranda, Queensland. 19 Fraser Island. 20 Cairns. 21 Great Dividing Range. 22 Surfers' Paradise. 23 Cape Tribulation. 24 Perth. 25 The Bungle Bungle Range. 26 The Twelve Apostles. 27 Mount Bartle Frere. 28 Adelaide. 29 The Pinnacles. 30 Cape York.

Quiz 103 Pot-Luck 46

Answers - see page 229

1 Who said, "Anyone who hates children and dogs can't be all bad"?
2 In our solar system which planet takes the least time to orbit the sun?
3 What is the name of René's wife in "Allo Allo"?
4 Whose cave inspired Mendelssohn to compose his Hebrides overture?
5 Who wrote the Waverley novels?
6 Which word can go after blue and before neck?
7 What tragedy occurred in Skopje in 1963?
8 Is an okapi animal or vegetable or mineral?
9 What sort of commercials did ITV ban in 1965?
10 On which country's stamps would you find the words Magyar Posta?
11 Whom did Joe Bugner defeat in his comeback fight in Sydney, in 1986?
12 Where was Marat when Charlotte Corday murdered him?
13 Nickelodeon was a name given to a juke box. What was it originally?
14 At what did Antonio Stradivari achieve fame?
15 To one place of decimals, how many centimetres equal one inch?
16 By what English name is the mountain Yr Wyddfa known?
17 Is the suburb of Southgate in the north, south, east or west of London?
18 Which famous British film company is associated with the symbol of a man striking a gong?
19 In Greek tragedy, which king married his own mother?
20 Which star sign is shared by Pat Cash and Steffi Graf?
21 Whose real name is Steveland Judkins?
22 In geometry, how many degrees are there in a complete circle?
23 In which kind of building is there a transept?
24 In London, which road runs from Charing Cross to Fleet Street?
25 Which alloy of tin and lead is used for making tankards and mugs?
26 What Egyptian obelisk stands on the Thames Embankment?
27 If someone is an Old Wykehamist to which school did he go?
28 What is the surname of underwater film makers Hans and Lotte?
29 What does a Frenchman mean when he says "Quel dommage"?
30 In which book does Emma Harte first appear?

Answers

American Sport (see Quiz 105)
1 National Football League. 2 Ice hockey. 3 Pittsburgh Steelers. 4 Baseball. 5 No-one. It was cancelled because of a strike by players. 6 Ice hockey. 7 Houston. 8 Washington. 9 Georgman Herman Ruth. 10 USSR and Yugoslavia. 11 Roy Wegerle. 12 London Ravens. 13 American football. 14 Los Angeles Rams. 15 1970. 16 Six. 17 Basketball. 18 Yogi. 19 New York. 20 Basketball. 21 The visiting team. 22 1994. 23 American football. 24 Canada. 25 Scott Hamilton and Brian Boitano. 26 The Pro Bowl. 27 Nancy Kerrigan and Tonya Harding. 28 Green Bay Packers. 29 Baseball. 30 Nine.

1 Which city with 3 million inhabitants is Australia's largest?
2 What is the name of the world's longest reef?
3 Which sacred rock is the world's largest monolith?
4 What is the capital of Australia?
5 Which two oceans are to the east and west of Australia?
6 What is the name of the surfing beach on the outskirts of Sydney?
7 Darwin is the capital of which state?
8 At which famous east coast bay did James Cook arrive in April 1770?
9 Which meandering river is Brisbane built around?
10 Which state is commonly called the Sunshine State?
11 Perth is the capital of which Australian state?
12 Which mountain range to the west of Sydney was partly destroyed by bush fires in December 1993?
13 Which is the nearest major town to the southwest of Ayers Rock?
14 What is the capital of the state of Victoria?
15 Which granite formation, formed by the wind, is to the east of Perth?
16 What is the coastline to the south of Brisbane called?
17 Which national park, known for its Aboriginal rock paintings and wildlife, lies to the east of Darwin?
18 Which "village in the rainforest" at the highest end of the Barron Gorge is the home to the only permanent Aboriginal theatre in Australia?
19 What is the world's largest sand island northeast of Brisbane?
20 What is Queensland's most northerly city?
21 Which mountain range runs parallel to the east coast for 4000 kilometres?
22 Which famous surfing beach is to the south of Brisbane?
23 Where does the rainforest meet the sea in northern Queensland?
24 Which state capital lies on the Swan River?
25 Which range of domed mountains lies in Purnululu National Park?
26 Along the Great Ocean Road in Victoria what 12 off-coast formations would you discover?
27 Which mountain, at 1611 metres, is the highest in Queensland?
28 Which Australian city hosted its final Formula 1 race in 1995?
29 Which fossilized remains of an ancient forest are found in the Nambung
30 Which cape is at the northernmost tip of Australia in Queensland?

Quiz 105 American Sport

Level 2

Answers - see page 227

1 In American football was does NFL stand for?
2 Which sport do the Buffalo Sabres play?
3 Which club was the first to win the Super Bowl two years in succession on two occasions?
4 Which sport has a Hall of Fame at Cooperstown, New York?
5 Who won the Baseball World Series in 1994?
6 In which sport is the Stanley Cup awarded?
7 Where are the Astros baseball team from?
8 Which city do the Redskins American football team come from?
9 What were "Babe" Ruth's real first names?
10 Which two countries other than the United States have won Olympic gold medals at basketball?
11 Which US soccer player was with Blackburn and Coventry?
12 The first Budweiser Bowl in the UK in 1986 was won by which team?
13 The Princetown College rules drawn up in 1867 affect which sport?
14 Which US soccer team plays at Anaheim Stadium?
15 In American football in which year did the AFL and the NFL merge?
16 How many people are there in an ice hockey team?
17 What game is played by the Detroit Pistons?
18 What was the nickname of baseball's Lawrence Peter Berra?
19 Giants and Jets have triumphed in the Super Bowl for which city?
20 The invention of which sport is credited to Dr J. A. Naismith?
21 In baseball, which team bats first?
22 Which year were American professionals first allowed to enter the World Basketball Championships?
23 Which sport do the Miami Dolphins play?
24 In which country were the rules for modern ice hockey formulated?
25 Which two American men won ice skating Olympic gold in the 1980s?
26 Which trophy do teams from AFC and NFC players contest?
27 Which two US women skaters had a battle on and off the rink in 1994?
28 Which team won the first Super Bowl?
29 Which sport do the Atlanta Braves play?
30 How many players are there in a baseball team?

Answers

Pot-Luck 46 (see Quiz 103)
1 W. C. Fields. 2 Mercury. 3 Edith. 4 Fingal's. 5 Sir Walter Scott. 6 Bottle. 7 Earthquake. 8 Animal. 9 Cigarettes. 10 Hungary's. 11 James Tillis. 12 In his bath. 13 US cinema (admission was a nickel). 14 Violin maker. 15 2.5. 16 Snowdon. 17 North. 18 The Rank Organization. 19 Oedipus. 20 Gemini. 21 Stevie Wonder. 22 360. 23 Church (or cathedral). 24 The Strand. 25 Pewter. 26 Cleopatra's Needle. 27 Winchester College. 28 Hass. 29 "What a pity". 30 A Woman of Substance.

Quiz 106 Pot-Luck 47

Level 2

1 Who composed the opera "The Tales of Hoffman"?
2 Why were Bob Hope and Bing Crosby "Like Webster's Dictionary"?
3 For what is Frank Lloyd Wright famous?
4 Who wrote a novel about Kenilworth in Warkwickshire?
5 What are the Howard League concerned with?
6 Mount Ararat is the traditional resting place of which ship or boat?
7 In "Treasure Island", which sailor dreamed of toasted cheese?
8 In South America what kind of building is a hacienda?
9 Which country won the Battle of Flodden?
10 In a fairy story a queen had to guess the name of a little man or lose her baby. What was his name?
11 In which book would you find Mrs Do-as-you-would-be-done-by?
12 What did the M stand for in the name of writer Louisa M. Alcott?
13 Which pop singer's real name is Mary O'Brien?
14 What term is given to the making of patterns by inlaying different coloured pieces of wood?
15 In which art did John and Ethel Barrymore achieve fame?
16 What new denomination of coin was isssued in the UK in 1983?
17 In the United States what item of clothing do they call suspenders?
18 Which city does Willie Thorne come from?
19 Which is these is not a freshwater fish: cod, pike, carp, roach?
20 Which choc bar was supposed to help you work, rest and play?
21 Who wrote the Inspector Morse novels?
22 What is a mazuka?
23 In which Libyan seaport did Australian forces endure a long siege in World War II?
24 What is the common name for solidified carbon dioxide?
25 Nowadays, which is the largest British bird?
26 With which composer is the German town of Bayreuth associated?
27 Which university is situated at Uxbridge in Middlesex?
28 Which is the highest female voice?
29 What kind of material is cheesecloth?
30 Under Hitler, who was Nazi minister of propaganda?

1 In which film does Robert De Niro ask "are you talkin' to me?"?
2 Who wrote the book on which "The Russia House" was based?
3 Whom was the Jackal trying to assassinate in " The Day of the Jackal"?
4 Which president is being referred to in "All the President's Men"?
5 Who won an Oscar for "The Accused"?
6 Where does the action of "Predator" take place?
7 What is Hitchcock said to have used for the blood in "Psycho"?
8 Which three actors have each played Richard Hannay in "The 39 Steps"?
9 Who played the role of South African Donald Woods in "Cry Freedom"?
10 What sort of establishment is the setting for "The China Syndrome"?
11 For which film did the reviewer write "Enough to make you kick the next pigeon you come across"?
12 What relation is Carter to Cain in "Raising Cain"?
13 On whose novel is the Sissy Spacek film "Carrie" based?
14 Who play the getaways in the remake of "The Getaway"?
15 What is the relationship between Tippi Hedren of Hitchcock's "Marnie" and Melanie Griffith of "A Stranger Among Us"?
16 What does Bridget Fonda advertise for and get Jennifer Jason Leigh?
17 In which classic film do Mrs Danvers and Maxim de Winter appear?
18 Whose "Fatal Attraction" to Glenn Close cost him dear?
19 For which film did Steven Spielberg win his first Oscar as Director?
20 Who were the first performers to win the Best Actor and Actress Oscars in the same film after Henry Fonda and Katharine Hepburn in 1981?
21 Who starred in Hitchcock's "Dial M For Murder" and "Rear Window"?
22 Where was Jack Lemmon's son "Missing"?
23 In which classic film is "Rosebud..."a piece in the jigsaw puzzle?
24 In Hitchcock's "Frenzy" what are the victims strangled with?
25 Who costarred with Oscar-winner Jane Fonda in "Klute"?
26 In "The Crying Game" to which organization does the gunman belong?
27 Which film based on an Anthony Shaffer play starred Michael Caine and Laurence Olivier?
28 Which Apollo mission was the subject of a film with Tom Hanks?
29 What was described as "Five criminals. One line up. No coincidence"?
30 Who causes terror in "The Hand That Rocks the Cradle"?

Answers *Hi Tech: Scientists* (see Quiz 109)
1 Hertz. 2 Becquerel. 3 Copernicus. 4 Stephen Hawking. 5 Nuclear fission.
6 Trigonometry. 7 Kelvin. 8 Atomic particles. 9 Bessemer. 10 Radar.
11 DNA. 12 Ampère. 13 Descartes. 14 Davy 15 HIV 16 Chadwick.
17 Hydrogen bomb. 18 Cathode ray tube. 19 Boyle. 20 Faraday. 21 First woman. First person to receive it twice. 22 Andrei Sakharov. 23 Werner von Braun. 24 Logarithms. 25 Polonium, radium 26 Multiply 27 Taxonomy. 28 Metric. 29 Galapagos. 30 Explosion of the atomic bomb..

Quiz 108 Pot-Luck 48

Answers - see page 230

Level 2

1 Which woman climber perished on K2 in 1995?
2 What name links Hastings, New Romney, Hythe, Dover and Sandwich?
3 In ads, which toothpaste gave you a ring of confidence?
4 According to Napoleon, what does an army march on?
5 In April 1967, what famous first did Shirley Preston achieve in London?
6 Which city is a holy one for three religions?
7 In Scotland what style of cloth was illegal from 1745 to 1782?
8 In land area which is the world's largest continent?
9 Of which country is Jutland a part?
10 In what kind of theatre did Vesta Tilley become famous?
11 Who in 1984 scored the first nine-dart 501 finish in a major event?
12 In the Wild West, for what was Annie Oakley famous?
13 Which word is used for a group of quails?
14 Which actor used to play Alec Gilroy in "Coronation Street"?
15 What would be the state of a person in "Carey Street"?
16 From which London station would you leave if travelling to Carlisle?
17 In a Shakespeare play who kills Desdemona?
18 Who wrote "The Decline and Fall of the Roman Empire"?
19 What do Roman Catholics call the state or place where souls are purified after death?
20 What was the title of Dick Francis's first horse-racing thriller?
21 Which empire was ruled by Titus?
22 Which song contains the words, "Johnny is a joker, he's a bird"?
23 What kind of plant is maidenhair?
24 On TV, whose boss was Dr Gillespie?
25 Which was the last year which looked the same when the figures were looked at upside down?
26 Which Old Testament book is about the sufferings of one man?
27 Who has presented both "Newsnight" and "University Challenge"?
28 Which planet is also known as the Red Planet?
29 How is Louis Winogradsky better known?
30 In mythology who were the Amazons?

Answers

Pot-Luck 106 (see Quiz 47)
1 Offenbach. 2 They were Morocco bound. 3 Architecture. 4 Sir Walter Scott.
5 Prison reform. 6 Noah's Ark. 7 Ben Gunn. 8 (Large) estate/farmhouse.
9 England. 10 Rumpelstiltskin. 11 The Water Babies (by Charles Kingsley).
12 May. 13 Dusty Springfield. 14 Marquetry. 15 Acting. 16 £1. 17 Braces
18 Leicester. 19 Cod. 20 Mars. 21 Colin Dexter. 22 A dance. 23 Tobruk.
24 Dry ice. 25 Mute swan. 26 Wagner. 27 Brunel University. 28 Soprano.
29 Muslin. 30 Goebbels.

Quiz 109 Hi tech: Scientists

Answers - see page 231

1 Who discovered radio waves?
2 Who gave his name to a unit of radioactivity?
3 Which 16th-century scientist proposed that the Earth orbited the Sun?
4 Who is best known for his theory of black holes?
5 On what did Otto Hahn, Lise Meitner and Fritz Strassman work?
6 In which branch of mathematics was Hipparchus a pioneer?
7 Which Baron of Largs gave his name to the degrees on the absolute scale?
8 What does Hans Geiger's Geiger counter detect?
9 Whose process decarbonized iron?
10 Which tracking device did Sir Robert Watson-Watt develop?
11 What did Crick, Watson and Wilkins determine the structure of?
12 Who formulated a law of electromagnetism and pioneered techniques in measuring electricity?
13 Which French philosopher created analytical geometry?
14 Which English chemist discovered the most elements?
15 Which virus was Robert Gallo one of the first to identify?
16 Which English physicist discovered the neutron?
17 What type of bomb did Edward Teller develop?
18 What sort of tube did William Crookes invent?
19 Who gave his name to the law that states that the pressure of gas is proportional to its volume?
20 Which physicist and chemist gave his name to the law of induction?
21 In terms of Nobel prizes how did Marie Curie achieve two "firsts"?
22 Which physicist who contributed to the development of Soviet nuclear weapons was also a civil rights campaigner?
23 Which German-born rocket engineer worked on the space programme?
24 Which aids to calculation did John Napier devise?
25 Which two elements did the Curies discover?
26 Leibnitz's calculating machine was the first to perform which function?
27 Which word was Candolle the first to use in the classification of plants?
28 For which measuring system did Joseph Louis Lagrange lay the foundations?
29 Which Islands inspired Darwin write "The Origin of Species"?
30 For which Soviet development was Igor Kurchatov team leader?

Quiz 110 Pot-Luck 49

Answers - see page 236

Level 2

1 When it is made in Europe, what are the three main ingredients of a kedgeree?
2 If a violinist is playing pizzicato, what is he doing?
3 For what kind of building is Rievaulx in North Yorkshire famous?
4 Which alcoholic drink is flavoured with juniper?
5 What is the legal term for telling lies under oath?
6 In which town in 1914 was an archduke assassinated?
7 What was a Sopwith Camel?
8 In which London park would you find Birdcage Walk?
9 What was the trade of the famous Russian Faberge?
10 Who composed "Finlandia"?
11 In adverts, which drink could be taken "Anytime, any place anywhere"?
12 What is a dactylogram?
13 Which group of islands are you going to if you are sailing to Skye?
14 Whom did Edward VII marry?
15 Who said, "Juantorena opens his legs and shows his class"?
16 From the fibres of which plant is linen made?
17 In a book, what is a frontispiece?
18 Which king was responsible for building the Tower of London?
19 What instrument is Larry Adler famed for?
20 How many equal angles are there in an isosceles triangle?
21 What marine mammals include belugas, blues and sperms?
22 In which city is Sauchiehall Street?
23 On an American Monopoly board, what are B & O, Reading, Short Line and Pennsylvania?
24 For what are the letters OM an abbreviation?
25 What is shepherd's purse?
26 Which day of the week is the Jewish sabbath?
27 Whose official residence is the Mansion House in London?
28 Over which country did the Ptolemies once rule?
29 In mythology, of what were the pipes of Pan made?
30 How is Thomas Hicks better known?

Answers

Pop Groups (see Quiz 114)
1 Paul Weller. 2 Dozy. 3 None of them. 4 Luvvers. 5 Pink Floyd. 6 Monday.
7 Pray. 8 U2. 9 Keith Moon. 10 UB40. 11 The Osmonds. 12 Supertramp.
13 Waterloo Sunset. 14 Thin Lizzy. 15 Manfred Mann. 16 The Moody Blues.
17 Status Quo. 18 Scotland. 19 Electric Light Orchestra. 20 Jackson Five.
21 Jam. 22 The Move. 23 Stars. 24 T. Rex. 25 The Eagles. 26 The Troggs.
27 10cc. 28 Spandau Ballet. 29 Culture Club. 30 Seven Seas of Rye.

1 What was the first series starring Smith and Jones called?
2 Which comedy show had Shirley Bassey singing in a hobnail boot?
3 Which show had the Enid Blyton spoof "Five Go Mad in Dorset"?
4 Who were the first two regular team captains in "Have I Got News For You?"?
5 Who created Algernon the Rasta and the Reverend Nat West?
6 Which writer hosts the ITV predecessor of "Auntie's Bloomers"?
7 Who was the female in the 1980s "Three of a Kind"?
8 What was Peter Cook and Dudley Moore's revue show called?
9 Which comedian had a St Bernard called Schnorbitz?
10 Who was the resident vocalist on "That Was The Week That Was"?
11 Who was famous for the Angela Rippon impersonations in "Not The Nine O'Clock News"?
12 Who closed his show with the phrase "May your god go with you"?
13 Who came to fame in "The Comedians" before heading for Walford?
14 Which comedian had a hit with "Funky Moped"?
15 On which club show was the music provided by Shep's Banjo Boys?
16 Who joined French and Saunders in the writing of "Girls on Top"?
17 In "The Frost Report" John Cleese was upper class and Ronnie Barker middle class: who was working class?
18 In which show would you find "The Argument Clinic" and the game show "Blackmail"?
19 Which 90s show featured "Jessie's Diets"?
20 Who was the first chairman of TV's "Whose Line Is It Anyway?"?
21 Who wrote for his own show under the pseudonym Gerald Wiley?
22 Who was Captain Fantastic in "Do Not Adjust Your Set"?
23 Who created the "Spitting Image" puppets?
24 Who is sports commentator Alan Partridge's true alter ego?
25 Who beat Victoria Wood to win "New Faces"?
26 Who has his own series "...Who Else"?
27 Who created Stavros, the kebab shop owner?
28 Who was the dumb, giggly blonde on "Rowan and Martin's Laugh In"?
29 Who is Jennifer Saunders' "alternative" comedian husband?
30 Which Scottish show featured Helen Lederer and Gregor Fisher?

Quiz 112 Boom and bust

Answers - see page 238

Level 2

1 What does GATT stand for?
2 Where would you see the Dow Jones index?
3 What is a group of producers acting together to fix prices called?
4 Why is Yemen unique in terms of currencies?
5 Which body assesses whether a takeover is in the public interest?
6 The Channel Islands, Gibraltar and the Isle of Man use British currency but, economically, what else do they have in common?
7 What is the chancellor of the exchequer's official London address?
8 Other than in Denmark where is the Danish krone used?
9 What name is given to economic activities which are unrecorded?
10 In which continent is the CFA franc a widespread currency?
11 In which country is the multinational Samsung based?
12 What is a country's GNP?
13 In which country was OPEC founded?
14 Which common market area does CARICOM deal with?
15 The European Union came into being in 1993 after which treaty?
16 In which country is the multinational Nestlé based?
17 Which area of the economy is the CAP concerned with?
18 What is the Japanese share index called?
19 What does ERM stand for?
20 Which states are referred to as the Visegrad Group or CEFTA states?
21 Who were the first two countries to withdraw from the ERM?
22 Which country is the world's largest coffee exporter?
23 Where is the headquarters of the International Monetary Fund ?
24 What name is given to the leading Western economic powers?
25 APEC encourages trade between countries bordering which ocean?
26 Where would you see the FT-SE share index?
27 What position did John Major hold immediately before becoming prime minister in 1990?
28 What does ECU stand for in terms of European Monetary Union?
29 What is the OFT?
30 Where is the headquarters of the Organization for Economic Cooperation and Development?

Answers

Pot-Luck 49 (see Quiz 110)
1 Fish/eggs/rice. 2 Plucking the strings. 3 Its abbey. 4 Gin. 5 Perjury. 6 Sarajevo. 7 Aeroplane. 8 St James's Park. 9 Goldsmith. 10 Sibelius. 11 Martini. 12 A fingerprint. 13 Inner Hebrides. 14 Princess Alexandra of Denmark. 15 David Coleman. 16 Flax. 17 A photograph or illustration. 18 William the Conqueror. 19 Harmonica. 20 Two. 21 Whales. 22 Glasgow. 23 Stations. 24 Order of Merit. 25 A wild flower. 26 Saturday. 27 Lord Mayor of London. 28 Egypt. 29 Reeds. 30 Tommy Steele.

1 Under what name did Dino Crocetti achieve fame?
2 Tsar Kolokol is the biggest what in the world?
3 In which fictitious Hampshire town does Chief Inspector Wexford work?
4 Which politician's memoirs appeared in the book "Upwardly Mobile"?
5 In the Victorian age what did Mary Ann Cotton gain notoriety as?
6 What instrument did Nat King Cole play?
7 Cleopatra supposedly bathed in the milk of which animal?
8 Who was the first Eliza Doolittle in the stage version of "My Fair Lady"?
9 What was tested at Bikini Atoll in 1954?
10 The Boat Race course is situated between Putney and where?
11 Charles II gives his name to which type of animal?
12 Who played the monster in the 1931 movie "Frankenstein"?
13 Who sang about Mr Woo?
14 Who had a flagship called "Victory"?
15 What toy is named after US president Theodore Roosevelt?
16 How is Michael Barrett better known in the pop world?
17 Which famous person did John Wilkes Booth shoot?
18 What is the pigment inside red blood cells?
19 Legendary footballer Billy Wright married one of which singing sisters?
20 Who is the patron saint of mountaineers?
21 Who played Ma Larkin to David Jason's Pa?
22 Which ocean is the world's deepest?
23 Who was the author of the bestselling "Country Diary of an Edwardian Lady"?
24 Which bandleader shared his name with a British prime minister?
25 In advertising, what were the "too good to hurry mints"?
26 In geography what is a shoal?
27 What is a ban on international trade with a country called?
28 In broadcasting what does CNN stand for?
29 What is the upper age limit for contestants in "The Crystal Maze"?
30 What is Rumpole's first name in the character created by John Mortimer?

Answers

TV: Comedy (see Quiz 111)
1 Alas Smith and Jones. 2 Morecambe and Wise. 3 The Comic Strip Presents. 4 Paul Merton, Ian Hislop. 5 L. Henry. 6 Denis Norden. 7 Tracey Ullman. 8 Not Only... But Also. 9 Bernie Winters. 10 Millicent Martin. 11 Pamela Stephenson. 12 Dave Allen. 13 Mike Reid. 14 Jasper Carrott. 15 The Comedians. 16 Ruby Wax. 17 Ronnie Corbett. 18 Monty Python's Flying Circus. 19 The Fast Show. 20 Clive Anderson. 21 Ronnie Barker. 22 David Jason. 23 Fluck and Law. 24 Steve Coogan. 25 Marti Caine. 26 Rory Bremner. 27 Harry Enfield. 28 Goldie Hawn. 29 Adrian Edmondson. 30 Naked Video.

Quiz 114 Pop Groups

Answers - see page 234

Level 2

1 Who was lead singer with Style Council?
2 Who sang with Dave Dee, Beaky, Mick and Tich?
3 How many of The Walker Brothers were related to each other as brothers?
4 Which group backed Lulu on the original "Shout"?
5 Which group featured Dave Gilmour and Roger Waters?
6 Which day did The Boomtown Rats not like?
7 What was Take That's first No 1?
8 Which Irish supergroup started life known as Feedback?
9 Who was the Who's original drummer?
10 Which group formed their own label Dep International?
11 Merrill, Jay, Wayne, Jimmy and Donny made up which group?
12 Which group made the album "Crisis? What Crisis"?
13 Which Kinks hit starts, "Dirty old river, must you keep rolling..."?
14 Which group was led by Phil Lynott?
15 Paul Jones and Mike D'Abo both sang lead with which group?
16 Justin Hayward and Denny Laine were members of which group?
17 Which group opened the Wembley Stadium section of Live Aid?
18 Wet, Wet, Wet come from which country?
19 Which group sang about Horace Wimp?
20 How were The Jacksons credited on their early hits?
21 Whose first top ten single was "The Eton Rifles" in 1979?
22 Which group used the main theme from the 1812 Overture in their first single hit?
23 Which Simply Red album contained "For Your Babies"?
24 Which glam group asked "Metal guru, is it you?"?
25 Which group wanted to "Take It To The Limit"?
26 Which group had the original hit with "Love Is All Around"?
27 Who thought that "Life Is A Minestrone"?
28 Gary and Martin Kemp were members of which group?
29 Which group had seven consecutive top four hits until the release of "The Medal Song"?
30 What was Queen's first hit?

1 Who brews London Pride?
2 Name the three Musketeers?
3 Which cartoonist draws the Doonesbury strip?
4 Which premier was Huddersfield's most famous son?
5 Which Dutch river is also the name of a beer?
6 Who executed a one-man stage invasion to disrupt Michael Jackson's appearance at the 1996 Brit Awards?
7 What is the postal code for Kilburn?
8 Which item of lingerie is also the language of the inhabitants of the Western Pyrenees?
9 What was the county town of Rutland?
10 Who was the girl on the motorcycle?
11 What is the currency of South Africa?
12 What is the largest bay in the world?
13 Which mill town produced, at one time, 99% of the world's cotton?
14 What was Glenn Miller's signature tune?
15 Which famous poet lived in Dove Cottage?
16 Which is the most distant planet in the universe?
17 Who was the leader of the wolfpack in "The Jungle Book"?
18 Which Formula One rookie came second in the 1996 Australian GP?
19 Who wrote the poem "The Lady of Shallot"?
20 Who wrote the "Just William" stories?
21 Which Underground line is Marble Arch station on?
22 What was the name of the oil tanker that ran aground in Wales in February 1996?
23 Where did Edward VIII spend most of WWII?
24 Who retired as undefeated heavyweight boxing champion of the world?
25 What is the name of the heroine of Jane Austen's novel "Pride and Prejudice"?
26 Which Irish mountains sweep down to the sea?
27 Which satellite TV station began broadcasting topless darts in 1996?
28 Who was the sixth TV Doctor Who?
29 Which 1969 film featured cockney ram-raiders in Turin?
30 Which member of the Grateful Dead died in 1995?

Answers

Pot-Luck 50 (see Quiz 113)
1 Dean Martin. 2 Bell. 3 Kingsmarkham 4 Norman Tebbit. 5 A mass murderer. 6 Piano. 7 Ass. 8 Julie Andrews. 9 Hydrogen bomb. 10 Mortlake. 11 Dog. King Charles Spaniel. 12 Boris Karloff. 13 George Formby. 14 Lord Nelson. 15 Teddy bear. 16 Shakin' Stevens. 17 Abraham Lincoln. 18 Haemoglobin. 19 The Beverley Sisters. 20 Saint Bernard. 21 Pam Ferris. 22 Pacific. 23 Edith Holden. 24 Ted Heath. 25 Murray Mints. 26 An area of sandbanks. 27 Embargo. 28 Cable News Network. 29 40. 30 Horace.

The Hard Questions

If you thought that this section of this book would prove to be little or no problem, or that the majority of the questions could be answered and a scant few would test you then you are sorely mistaken. These questions are the *hardest* questions *ever*! So difficult are they that any attempt to answer them all in one sitting will addle your mind and mess with your senses. You'll end up leaving the pub via the window while ordering a pint from the horse brasses on the wall. Don't do it! For a kick off there are 3,000 of them, so at 20 seconds a question it will take you over 16 hours and that's just the time it takes to read them. What you should do instead is set them for others – addle your friends' minds.

Note the dangerous nature of these questions though. These are you secret weapons use them accordingly unless, of course, someone or some team is getting your back up. In which case you should hit them hard and only let up when you have them cowering under the bench whimpering "Uncle".

These questions work best against league teams, they are genuinely tough and should be used against those people who take their pub quizzes seriously. NEVER use these questions against your inlaws.

Quiz 1 Pop: One-Hit Wonders

Level 3

Answers - see page 243

1 Which school had a No 1 with "There's No One Quite Like Grandma"?
2 Which American answer to Band Aid sang "We Are the World"?
3 Which musical did Lee Marvin's sole hit, "Wandrin' Star", come from?
4 According to 1950s star Kitty Kalen what do "Little Things Mean"?
5 Which pop festival gave Matthews Southern Comfort a hit?
6 Which member of the cast of "Dad's Army" sang "Grandad"?
7 Who recorded "Let It Be" in 1987 for a disaster fund?
8 Where had Charlene never been to in 1982?
9 Who said "Move Closer" in 1985?
10 What is Marie Osmond's only solo hit?
11 Which Beatles song did The Overlanders take to No 1?
12 With the theme song for which sporting event did Kiri Te Kanawa have her only chart hit in 1991?
13 What was the nickname of Michael Wilson who had "Another Sleepless Night" in 1990?
14 Which footballer was "Head Over Heels in Love" in 1979?
15 Who was all The Commentators on "N-N-Nineteen Not Out"?
16 Who were the first two one-hit wonders to reach the top with the same song? BAND AID 84   BAND AID II (89)
17 Two members of which group sang on both of them?
18 Which Twins sang "When" in 1958?
19 Whom did Ricky Valance tell he loved her in 1960?
20 Which airways featured on Typically Tropical's only No 1?
21 What is John Denver's only solo UK single hit?
22 Who joined New Order on England New Order's "World in Motion"?
23 Which travel terminal provided a hit for Cats UK?
24 With which TV theme did Geoffrey Burgon have his only hit in 1981?
25 What was the Johnny Mann Singers' only hit?
26 Who got to No 3 in 1968 with "Judy in Disguise (With Glasses)"?
27 What did The Pipkins say "Gimme" in 1970?
28 Which qualification sang "I won't let you down" in 1982?
29 Which TV character gave Ken Barrie his only chart hit?
30 Which "Coronation Street" star sang "Where Will You Be?" in 1968?

Answers

Performance Arts (see Quiz 3)
1 Vocal with no instrumental accompaniment. 2 The man. 3 Not in English.
4 Break dancing. 5 Piccolo. 6 Berlin. 7 Diaghilev. 8 Trombones and tubas.
9 Pogo. 10 Singspiel. 11 Rock 'n' roll. 12 Saturday Night Fever.
13 Keyboard. 14 Cakes given as competition prizes. 15 Festival Ballet.
16 Boston, Charleston. 17 Three. 18 Paul Jones. 19 Samba. 20 Egypt.
21 Kazoo. 22 Lyre. 23 Festivities associated with the building of a new barn. 24 World War II. 25 Balanchine. 26 Ukelele. 27 Bullfighter's cloak.
28 Cannes. 29 Not touching partner. 30 Morris dancing.

1 Who shot the Archduke Franz Ferdinand?
2 In fiction, what were Milly Molly Mandy's proper names?
3 Which monarchs sat on the Peacock Throne?
4 Of what is a lux a unit?
5 In the early 19th century what did George Shillibeer bring to London?
6 Who first claimed that the world was not flat but a sphere?
7 Who was the first woman to fly the Atlantic single-handed?
8 Which animals communicate by touch, smell and dance?
9 Around which French town is the champagne industry centred?
10 Which northerly castle is owned by the Queen Mother?
11 At what speed in mph does a wind become a hurricane?
12 Who officially opened the 1936 Olympiad?
13 What was the name of the first talking cartoon?
14 Which competition was organized by Mecca Ltd to coincide with the 1951 Festival of Britain?
15 Who invented the coordinate system to compare relationships on a graph?
16 What colour is the ribbon of the Victoria Cross?
17 Who or what lived in Honalee?
18 Which profession would use the terms occlusion, isohyet and adiabatic?
19 What name is used to describe a baby salmon?
20 What is the real name of 'Mr Motivator'?
21 Who was Steve McGarrett's great enemy in "Hawaii Five-O"?
22 Who anonymously entered a contest in Monaco to find his lookalike and came third?
23 Where in Spain was Pablo Picasso born?
24 Who was Edward VI's mother?
25 Which sea has no coast?
26 Who was the first Briton to organize a continental holiday tour?
27 Where is the highest traffic density in the world?
28 Who discovered oxygen in 1774?
29 Which bird can fly the fastest?
30 Which is the largest human organ?

Answers

Pot-Luck 2 (see Quiz 4)
1 Dublin. 2 Prostitute. 3 Pope John Paul II. 4 The Tories. 5 The Scottish red deer. 6 Frank Richards. 7 Number 13. 8 Yellow. 9 Scotland's largest cave. 10 The sixpence. 11 Chewing gum. 12 St Cecilia. 13 As a swan. 14 Sunny Afternoon. 15 Solomon. 16 Tom Cruise. 17 The White Tower. 18 Tetley. 19 The Huguenots. 20 The Anglican Church. 21 Greenland. 22 Per Lindstrand. 23 Betty Boo. 24 Scunthorpe United. 25 Baronet. 26 Aluminium. 27 China. 28 A palindrome. 29 John Adams. 30 Triangle.

Quiz 3 Performance Arts

Answers - see page 241

1 How is *a cappella* music performed?
2 Which dancer performs a variation in a *pas de deux*?
3 What did the BAFTA-winning films, "Carmen", "Babette's Feast" and "Farewell My Concubine" have in common?
4 Which dancing from the 1980s has dancers performing acrobatic feats?
5 Which instrument is also called the octave flute?
6 At which film festival is the Golden Bear awarded for best film?
7 Which impresario founded the Ballets Russes?
8 In a standard modern symphony orchestra which two brass instruments would be on the back row?
9 Which punk dance became popular in the mid-1970s?
10 What is a play with alternating musical pieces called?
11 Which dance is part jive, part improvisation?
12 Which 1970s film is seen as greatly popularizing disco dancing?
13 What type of instrument is a celestea?
14 Why is a cakewalk so called?
15 What did the English National Ballet used to be called?
16 Which two dances take their names from US towns?
17 What is the minimum number of voices for performing a glee?
18 Which singer/radio DJ's name is also the name of a 19th-century dance?
19 Which dance is the *bossa nova* a type of?
20 Where are castanets thought to originate?
21 What is a mirliton another name for?
22 Which instrument are violins and violas descended from?
23 Why were barn-dances so called?
24 During which period did the jitterbug gain popularity?
25 Who founded the New York City Ballet?
26 Which instrument's name is the Hawaiian word for jumping flea?
27 In the *paso doble* what is the female dancer supposed to be? *BULLFIGHTER CLOAK*
28 At which film festival is the Palme d'Or awarded for best film?
29 What sort of dancing trend did the twist set?
30 Which dancing has fertility through death and rebirth as a common theme?

Quiz 4 Pot-Luck 2

Answers - see page 242

1 Which city is known in its own language as Baile Atha Cliath?
2 Kitty Fisher was 18th-century London's most highly paid what?
3 Which pope was shot by Mehmet Ali Agca on May 13th, 1981?
4 Which political party takes its name from a band of Irish outlaws? *TORIES*
5 Which is the largest wild animal in the British Isles?
6 Who created Billy Bunter?
7 People who are terdekaphobic are afraid of what?
8 What colour is worn for funerals in Egypt?
9 What is the Great Smoo?
10 Which British coin ceased to be legal tender on June 30th, 1980?
11 What is manufactured from the sapodilla tree?
12 Who is the patron saint of music?
13 In mythology, in what form did Zeus visit Leda?
14 Which song starts, "The taxman's taken all my dough..."?
15 Who was David's son in the Bible?
16 Whose first box office film was called "Risky Business"?
17 Which is the oldest part of the Tower of London?
18 Which company first introduced tea bags in Great Britain in 1952?
19 What were the French Protestants led by Henry of Navarre known as?
20 Which Church's doctrine is set out in the Thirty-Nine Articles?
21 Which country left the EC in 1985?
22 Who joined Richard Branson in his transatlantic hot-air balloon flight?
23 Who is Alison Clarkson better known as?
24 Which soccer team did Ian Botham play for?
25 What does the abbreviation Bt signify after a name?
26 In the Earth's crust which metal is the most abundant?
27 In which country are women excluded from any graveside rituals?
28 What type of word reads the same forwards and backwards?
29 Who was the second president of the United States? *John ADAMS*
30 Which musical instrument can be formed from the word "altering"?

1 Nanninga was the first sub to score in a World Cup Final... for who?
2 Which team are known as the Cherries?
3 What was strange about the tackle that ended the career of keeper Chic Brodie of Brentford back in 1970?
4 Which German player asked, "Is there a diving school in London?"?
5 Who was the first manager to win the Premier League?
6 Which country won the first World Cup held in 1930?
7 Which German club did Kevin Keegan play for?
8 Mike Walker and Martin O'Neill walked out on which chairman?
9 Who was the first uncapped player sold for over £1,000,000 in Britain?
10 What name is shared by Scunthorpe, Southend and Rotherham?
11 At which Meadow do Shrewsbury play?
12 Which club does snooker promoter Barry Hearn support?
13 Which country did Emlyn Hughes play for?
14 Which manager's autobiography is entitled "Against the Odds"?
15 Which 4th Division team reached the first League Cup Final in 1962?
16 Who played in the first FA Cup Final ever to end 3–3?
17 Which team paid a record £1,000 for Alf Common in 1905?
18 Newcastle play at St James' Park but who plays at St James Park?
19 Who captained the Man Utd team that won the 1968 European Cup?
20 Who scored Scotland's only goal in the 1986 World Cup Finals in Mexico?
21 Where in England do you go to shout "Come on, you greens"?
22 Who scored England's only goal in the final stages of the 1992 European Championship?
23 Stokoe (Sunderland) and Revie (Leeds) were rival managers in the 1973 FA Cup Final. For which teams were they rivals as Cup Final players?
24 If you are at Turf Moor who is playing at home?
25 Which major club trophy did Bob Paisley *not* win for Liverpool?
26 Which club has been managed by Brian Clough and Jimmy Armfield?
27 Which club has played in the Premier League with a strip of yellow shirts?
28 Which team is known as "The Bairns"?
29 Man Utd were the first team to score 9 in a Premier game. against whom?
30 At which Lane did Wimbledon play when they entered the League?

Quiz 6 Pot-Luck 3

Answers - see page 248

Level 3

1 Which organ in the body is affected by otitis?
2 Which was the first country, in 1824, to legalize trade unions?
3 In Britain in which season does the Earth move faster round the Sun?
4 Which is the smallest state of Australia?
5 In which castle was Edward II murdered?
6 In which year was North Sea oil discovered?
7 Californian and Stellar's are types of what?
8 What is a group of cats called?
9 Which African tribe is known for being the tallest people in the world?
10 What is measured by an interferometer?
11 Which famous cliffs in Acapulco are used by daring divers?
12 Who broke Muhammad Ali's jaw in 1973?
13 How was Natasha Gurdin better known?
14 Which airline's identification code is VS?
15 Which country decided by referendum against joining the European Union in 1994?
16 Who was the only English pope?
17 The kingdom of Navarre was divided between which two countries?
18 Which river does the water in real Irish Guinness come from? *THE LIFFE*
19 In which Gilbert and Sullivan opera is eating a sausage roll a secret sign?
20 On which river is the Kariba Dam? *ZAMBESI*
21 What is studied in the science of somatology?
22 Which football club was the first to use artificial turf?
23 Who is the patron saint of metal workers?
24 From which district in France do the majority of fine clarets come?
25 Who set up the first printing press in England in 1476?
26 In the film "Carry On Columbus" who played the title role?
27 If the image in the mirror shows the time as five past two, what time is it?
28 In heraldry what is meant by "couchant"?
29 Who was the leader of the first black band to play at Carnegie Hall?
30 Who was the Greek goddess of retribution?

Quiz 7 Great Buildings

Answers - see page 245

Level 3

1 Which is Britain oldest cathedral?
2 Jørn Utzon designed the Sydney Opera House as a result of what?
3 What is the Taj Mahal made from?
4 In which Parisian square is the Arc de Triomphe?
5 What is the cathedral of the diocese of London?
6 What was the highest building in the world until 1930?
7 Who ordered the building of St Basil's Cathedral in Moscow?
8 Which library in Venice was described as "the richest and most ornate building since antiquity"?
9 Who had Hampton Court Palace built?
10 Which dukes does Chatsworth House in Derbyshire belong to?
11 Which stately home was used in the film "Brideshead Revisited"?
12 Why is the Washington Memorial smaller now than when it was built?
13 The twin towers of the World Trade Center are not the same height but what is the difference in storeys?
14 Other than in Egypt, where were pyramids built? VERSAILLES
15 Which French château has a Hall of Mirrors?
16 In which US city is the Sears Tower?
17 Where was Europe's largest Gothic cathedral rebuilt after World War II?
18 Which chain store proprietor commissioned the then tallest inhabitable building in the world in 1913?
19 Which famous statue, brought back as war loot by Napoleon, is still housed in the Louvre?
20 When was Blackpool Tower built?
21 Which plan did Prince Charles describe as "a monstrous carbuncle"?
22 Where would you find Britain's tallest blocks of flats?
23 In which area of Paris is the Basilica of Sacré Coeur?
24 Where is the largest church in the world?
25 Who designed it?
26 Where is the Shwa Dagon Pagoda?
27 In which city is Rastrelli's Winter Palace?
28 Which cathedral, opened in 1962, contains the ruins of the old cathedral?
29 Where in India is the Golden Temple, centre of the Sikh religion? AMRITSAR
30 Why is the White House white?

Quiz 8 Pot-Luck 4

Answers - see page 246

Level 3

1 How many old pennies were there in a guinea?
2 What is a fly agaric?
3 Which is the most densely populated Welsh county?
4 How is Russ Roberts better known?
5 What was Margaret Mitchell's only book?   *GONE WITH THE WIND*
6 What is a Mexican "black howler"?
7 Who was elected president of the Philippines in 1986?
8 Which is the world's longest insect?
9 Who invented the first motion picture camera?
10 What was the speed limit in Britain fixed by the Motor Car Act of 1903?
11 In which town was the first test tube baby born in 1978?
12 Which naval tradition ceased in 1970?
13 Which English king had to pawn his crown to raise money?
14 Who invented the Polaroid camera in 1947?
15 Which TV programme began broadcasting daily on July 29th, 1949?
16 Whose funeral was upset by flooding in Maidenhead in 1852?
17 What was Ali Baba's female slave called?
18 What does an Arab horse have less of than any other?
19 Which satellite sent the first live TV transmission between America and Europe?
20 By what other name is the angel shark known?
21 What does "cap-a-pie" mean?
22 Which Roman emperor ordered St Peter to be crucified?
23 The British Military Academy is at Sandhurst; where is the American?
24 In which country did the study of geometry originate?
25 What is OPEC an acronym of?
26 What was Mickey Mouse's original name?
27 Which amateur jockey's first winner was Gulfland at Redcar in 1986?
28 Where in Norway were the 1994 Winter Olympic games held?
29 In which novel does the character Quebec Bagnet appear?
30 What is an ungulate?

Answers

Pot-Luck 3 (see Quiz 6)
1 The ear. 2 Britain. 3 Summer. 4 Tasmania. 5 Berkeley Castle. 6 1966.
7 Sea-lions. 8 A clowder. 9 The Sudanese Dunka tribe. 10 The wavelength of light. 11 La Quebrada. 12 Ken Norton. 13 Natalie Wood.
14 Virgin Atlantic. 15 Norway. 16 Nicolas Breakspear. 17 France and Spain. 18 The Liffey. 19 The Grand Duke. 20 Zambezi. 21 The body.
22 Queen's Park Rangers. 23 St Eligius. 24 Médoc. 25 William Caxton.
26 Jim Dale. 27 9.55 – five to ten. 28 Lying down. 29 Count Basie.
30 Nemesis.

248

Quiz 9 Royals

Level 3

Answers - see page 251

1 Who was the first royal bride to include her family's motto on her marital coat of arms?
2 Who said "We live above the shop"?
3 Which club was Prince Charles not allowed to join at Cambridge?
4 Princess Anne was the only female competitor at the Montreal Olympics not to be given which test?
5 On which occasion did Elizabeth II make her last curtsey?
6 Where did Princess Diana's mother have a farm at the time of the royal engagement?
7 Who designed Princess Margaret's engagement ring?
8 Whose autobiography was called "The Heart Has Its Reasons"?
9 Who said "She's more royal than the rest of us" about whom?
10 In which year this century were there three kings of Britain?
11 What are the first names of Princess Diana's sisters and brother?
12 What was tied in a Windsor knot and who introduced the fashion?
13 What did George V refer to as "a mixed grill"?
14 What was Princess Margaret's luxury on "Desert Island Discs"?
15 Where are Charles and Diana said to have met?
16 How is the heir to the throne known in Scotland?
17 What name links Earl Spencer and the Duchess of Windsor's first husband?
18 What was Prince Charles' nickname for Mark Phillips?
19 Whom did the royal family refer to as Uncle Dickie?
20 What are Prince Edward's first names?
21 In "Private Eye", who are Brenda and Yvonne?
22 Which close relative does Prince Charles share his birthday with?
23 Why is Prince Michael's middle name Franklin?
24 Who is the father of the Earl of St Andrews?
25 Who or what were Susan, Sugar, Honey, Whisky and Sherry?
26 Of the Queen's children who was the heaviest at birth?
27 This century, how many second sons have succeeded to the throne?
28 Which radio programme did the Queen Mother never miss as she said it gave her knowledge of middle-class life?
29 Who is taller, the Queen or Princess Margaret?
30 Which monarch this century was left-handed?

Answers

Pot-Luck 5 (see Quiz 11)
1 Arsenal. 2 Bending the knee. 3 Harry S. Truman. 4 Chromosomes. 5 An exaltation. 6 Jupiter. 7 Joni Mitchell. 8 Salmon. 9 Hungary. 10 Longleat. 11 1947. 12 A lucifer. 13 Neptune. 14 Whooping cough. 15 IBM. 16 Gerald Ford. 17 1965. 18 Fish. 19 The Royal College of Physicians. 20 Lord Protector. 21 Myanmar. 22 John Constable. 23 Mark Twain. 24 1973. 25 Charles Lindbergh. 26 The leaves. 27 The Birdman of Alcatraz. 28 300. 29 Etymology. 30 Lake Titicaca.

Quiz 10 Margaret Thatcher

1 What was Margaret Thatcher's maiden name?
2 As a barrister what did she specialize in?
3 How did Macmillan describe Margaret Thatcher's privatization policy?
4 What is the date of Margaret Thatcher's birthday?
5 Which Oxford college did she attend?
6 In which department was her first shadow ministerial job?
7 The scrapping of which benefit brought controversy in June 1971?
8 Who was second to Thatcher in the Tory leadership battle in 1975?
9 Which Thatcher aide was killed by a bomb in the House of Commons car park in March 1979?
10 Whom did Thatcher quote on the steps of No 10 on becoming prime minister?
11 Whom did she describe as "A man we can do business with"?
12 About what did she say, "Failure? The possibility does not exist"?
13 At which Brighton hotel did she survive a bomb in October 1984?
14 Who signed the Anglo-Irish Agreement with Thatcher in 1985?
15 Which project did she give the go-ahead to in January 1986?
16 Which two members of her cabinet resigned over the Westland affair?
17 Which three Labour leaders did Thatcher beat in general elections?
18 What did Sir Alan Walters advise Thatcher on?
19 Who was her most famous press secretary?
20 Why could Mrs Thatcher have been called Lady Thatcher from 1990?
21 In an interview before the 1990 Brit Awards Thatcher named two of her favourite tunes. "Telstar" was one; what was the other?
22 Where was Thatcher described as a circus buffoon in September 1990?
23 What was Geoffrey Howe's cabinet position when he resigned in 1990?
24 Where was Margaret Thatcher when news came that she had failed to win the first leadership ballot?
25 During which rally was Mark Thatcher lost in 1982?
26 What was the first volume of her autobiography called?
27 Whom did Geoffrey Howe back in the Heseltine/Hurd/Major contest?
28 Which title did Mrs Thatcher take for her life peerage?
29 Who described Thatcher as "nice and cuddly" when he met her?
30 For which seat was she a candidate before winning Finchley?

Answers

The Beatles (see Quiz 12) 1 Please Please Me. 2 Winston. 3 Pete Best. 4 Day Tripper. 5 Lucy in the Sky with Diamonds. 6 A record store. 7 Julian and Sean. 8 The White Album. 9 Thank Your Lucky Stars. 10 The Quarrymen. 11 Helen Shapiro. 12 Penny Lane/Strawberry Fields Forever. 13 Rattle their jewellery. 14 Stuart Sutcliffe. 15 Harmonica. 16 All four. 17 My Sweet Lord. 18 The Ed Sullivan Show. 19 Fred Lennon (John's long-absent father). 20 Parlophone. 21 Not Only...But Also. 22 Evening Standard. 23 Yellow Submarine. 24 In His Own Write. 25 White bag. 26 San Francisco (1966). 27 Silver Beetles. 28 Yesterday. 29 How Do You Sleep? 30 MBE.

Quiz 11 Pot-Luck 5

Level 3

Answers - see page 249

1 Which soccer team did England cricketer Denis Compton play for?
2 What are you doing if you are genuflecting?
3 Who was president of the United States at the end of World War II?
4 What are there 46 of in a normal human body cell?
5 What do we call a group of larks?
6 Which planet has at least 13 moons?
7 How is Roberta Joan Anderson better known?
8 Parr, smolt and grilse are all stages in the growth of what?
9 Where does "Bull's Blood" originate?
10 What is the Marquis of Bath's Wiltshire home called?
11 In which year did India gain independence from Britain?
12 In the war song "Pack Up Your Troubles" what do you need to light a fag?
13 Which planet was discovered by Johann Galle in 1846?
14 What is pertussis more commonly known as?
15 Which company introduced its first commercial computer in 1953?
16 Which US president achieved the highest grade in the boy scouts?
17 When was hanging abolished in Britain?
18 What do ichthyologists study?
19 Which body founded the anti-smoking organization, ASH, in 1971?
20 What title was Oliver Cromwell given in 1653?
21 To what did Burma change its name in 1989?
22 Which painter was born at East Bergholt?
23 Which American writer was christened Samuel Langhorne Clemens?
24 In which year did Ireland join the EC?
25 Who was the first solo aviator to fly the Atlantic non-stop?
26 Which part of a rhubarb plant is poisonous?
27 Convict Robert Stroud was better known as who?
28 What is the maximum score possible in a game of ten-pin bowling?
29 What name is given to the study of the origins of words?
30 What is the highest large lake in the world?

Quiz 12 The Beatles

Answers - see page 250

Level 3

1 What was The Beatles' first Top Ten hit single?
2 What was John Lennon's middle name?
3 Which original Beatle did Ringo Starr replace?
4 What was on the other side of the single "We Can Work It Out"?
5 Which Beatles song was banned by the BBC because its initials were said to be drug-related?
6 What did Brian Epstein manage before The Beatles?
7 What are John Lennon's two sons called?
8 How was the double album, "The Beatles", better known?
9 On which show did they make their first national TV appearance?
10 Which group did John Lennon form and name after his school in 1956?
11 Whom did The Beatles support on their first nationwide tour?
12 Which double-sided hit titles were Liverpool placenames?
13 On the Royal Variety Show John Lennon invited those in the cheaper seats to clap. What did he tell those in the more expensive seats to do?
14 Which Beatle died in Hamburg in 1962?
15 Which solo instrument did John Lennon play on "Love Me Do"?
16 How many Beatles appeared on one "Juke Box Jury" in 1963?
17 What was George Harrison's first solo hit?
18 On which show were The Beatles watched by 73 million in the US?
19 Who made a record called "That's My Life" in 1965?
20 What was the first label The Beatles recorded on with George Martin?
21 On which TV show did John Lennon read his own poetry?
22 In which paper was John Lennon's remark that The Beatles were more popular than Jesus?
23 Which cartoon film did The Beatles make in 1969?
24 What was John Lennon's book published in 1964 called?
25 What did John and Yoko appear on stage in at the Albert Hall in 1968?
26 Where was the last live Beatles' performance?
27 What were the group known as immediately before being known as The Beatles?
28 Which Beatles song is the most recorded song of all time?
29 Which song was a jibe by John Lennon at Paul McCartney?
30 What were The Beatles awarded by the Queen in 1965?

Answers

Margaret Thatcher (see Quiz 10) **1** Roberts. **2** Taxation law. **3** Selling the family silver. **4** October 13th. **5** Somerville. **6** Transport. **7** Free school milk. **8** William Whitelaw **9** Airey Neave. **10** St Francis of Assisi. **11** Gorbachev. **12** Falklands invasion. **13** Grand Hotel. **14** Dr Garret FitzGerald. **15** Channel Tunnel. **16** Michael Heseltine and Leon Brittan. **17** Callaghan, Foot and Kinnock. **18** Economic affairs. **19** Bernard Ingham. **20** Denis Thatcher was knighted. **21** How Much is That Doggie in the Window? **22** Iraqi press. **23** Deputy prime minister. **24** Paris. **25** Paris–Dakar. **26** The Downing Street Years. **27** Heseltine. **28** Baroness Thatcher of Kesteven. **29** Paul Gascoigne. **30** Dartford.

Quiz 13 Pot-Luck 6

Answers - see page 255

Level 3

1 Australia's Barossa Valley is noted for which industry?
2 Which actress was jailed in 1982 for tax evasion?
3 Which French building did architects Nervi, Breuer and Zehrfuss create?
4 Who recorded the LP "Electric Ladyland"?
5 Who wrote the famous nursery rhyme "Mary had a little lamb"?
6 After which mythological Greek character was the drug morphine named?
7 In which year did Britain go decimal?
8 What is the world's fastest-moving insect?
9 What was the capital of the Roman province of Britain before Londinium (London)?
10 Who is the author of the 1994 book "The Swan"?
11 At what height does a pony become a horse?
12 Which bird was selected in 1961 as the British national bird?
13 Who invented neon lights in 1911?
14 Which country was the first to insist upon car registration plates?
15 What was the original name of the flagship the "Golden Hind"?
16 Who was the first sovereign to be addressed as "Your Majesty"?
17 Which painting was stolen and kept for two years by V. Peruggio?
18 When did the first televised debate of the House of Lords take place?
19 What is the Capital of Western Samoa?
20 In which country did the first Christmas stamp appear in 1898?
21 Which volcano erupted to give the greatest explosion in recorded history?
22 For what did the Swede Jenny Lind achieve fame?
23 How many legs has a lobster?
24 Which MP called for Buckingham Palace and Windsor Castle to be sold?
25 Which is the largest of the anthropoid apes?
26 Who is the magical spirit of the air in Shakespeare's "The Tempest"?
27 Who wrote the lyrics to "A Whiter Shade Of Pale"?
28 How many Oscars for best director did Alfred Hitchcock win?
29 Which paper was first published as the "Daily Universal Register"?
30 Which grain is used to make malt whisky?

Answers

Pot-Luck 7 (see Quiz 15)
1 Two Little Boys. 2 The Iceni. 3 The Babylonians. 4 Washington. 5 Whoopi Goldberg. 6 Thierry Vigneron. 7 Edward II. 8 The Po. 9 Venus. 10 Leprosy. 11 Lydia in Asia Minor. 12 Tallahassee. 13 10,080. 14 Bangladesh. 15 Andrei Sakharov. 16 Eric Morecambe. 17 Goalkeeper. 18 Julie Andrews. 19 Patricia. 20 Grapes. 21 Knock. 22 1910. 23 Manchester United. 24 Margaret Thatcher. 25 Boeing 707. 26 Robbie Coltrane. 27 Dick Turpin. 28 The meaning of words. 29 Saigon. 30 Lady Jane Grey.

Quiz 14 Food and Drink

Level 3

1 What do you add to béchamel to make an aurore sauce?
2 What three main ingredients are added to mayonnaise to make a Waldorf salad?
3 What is a *Kugelhupf*?
4 In which country do red onions originate?
5 What is added to cheddar cheese to make Ilchester cheese?
6 What is laver?
7 What type of fish are Arbroath smokies?
8 What size eggs are between 60 and 65 grams?
9 What type of milk was mozzarella cheese originally made from?
10 What sort of meat is used in a guard of honour?
11 What is something cooked in if cooked "*en papillote*"?
12 What do you add to vegetables to make a salmagundi?
13 What are Pershore eggs and Marjorie's seedlings?
14 What are the two main ingredients of a Hollandaise sauce?
15 What colour top do bottles of unpasteurized milk have?
16 What is the chief ingredient of boxty bread?
17 In which English county is Brie made?
18 What is the main meat ingredient of faggots?
19 Which has most fat: double cream, crème fraîche or whipping cream?
20 What is Cornish yarg cheese coated with?
21 Which country does *skordalia* come from?
22 What shape is the pasta called *farfalle*?
23 What is the main ingredient of *dal*?
24 In Indian cuisine what is *ghee*?
25 Where does *coulibiac* originate and what is it?
26 Which term in Italian cooking means "soft but firm"?
27 What is a carbonade cooked in?
28 How is steak cooked if cooked blue?
29 How does *paella* get its name?
30 What is the main vegetable ingredient of moussaka?

Quiz 15 Pot-Luck 7

Level 3

Answers - see page 253

1 Which song contains the line, "Each had a wooden horse"?
2 Which tribe rose in revolt against the Romans and was led by Boadicea?
3 Who were the first people to measure the year?
4 Where is the headquarters of the International Monetary Fund?
5 Who was the voice of the female hyena in "The Lion King"?
6 Who was the first pole-vaulter to clear 19 feet?
7 Who was the first Prince of Wales?
8 Which is the longest river in Italy?
9 Which is the brightest planet visible to the naked eye?
10 What is Hansen's Disease more commonly called?
11 Which country was the first in the world to introduce coinage?
12 What is the state capital of Florida?
13 How many minutes are there in a week?
14 What is the most densely populated country in the world?
15 Which scientist was known as the "father of the Soviet H-bomb"?
16 Which comedian died of a heart attack in May 1984 at the age of 58?
17 Which position did Pope John Paul II play in the Polish amateur soccer team?
18 Who is Julie Elizabeth Edwards better known as?
19 Alfred Hitchcock's daughter appeared in "Psycho". What is her name?
20 What does a viticulturist cultivate?
21 Which Irish village is famous for its shrine to the Virgin Mary?
22 In which year this century did a seven-year revolution begin in Mexico?
23 Which football team was formerly known as Newton Heath?
24 Who signed the Single Act Treaty for Britain in 1986?
25 Which Boeing plane entered commercial service in 1958?
26 How is Anthony McMillan better known?
27 Who, in 1948, was the first black boxer to win a British title?
28 Of what is semantics the study?
29 What was Ho Chi Minh City called before 1975?
30 Who was the shortest-reigning British monarch?

Quiz 16 Marilyn Monroe

Answers - see page 254

1 Which surname other than Baker did Norma Jean use?
2 Which 1952 film gave Monroe her first big role?
3 Which actress co-starred with Monroe in "Gentlemen Prefer Blondes"?
4 To which city do the girls go to look for rich husbands?
5 Who was Monroe's second husband?
6 What type of sportsman was he?
7 How long had they been married before Monroe filed for divorce?
8 Which film had the title "The Wrong Kind of Girl" on TV?
9 Which 1950 film with Monroe in a minor role is famous for the line, "Fasten your seatbelts – it's going to be a bumpy night."?
10 Who were Monroe's two flatmates in "How to Marry a Millionaire"?
11 In "The Seven Year Itch" where does Monroe keep her underwear?
12 Whom did Monroe marry in June 1956?
13 Who directed Monroe in "The Seven Year Itch" and "Some Like It Hot"?
14 Who played the Prince to Monroe's Showgirl in the film?
15 Who died shortly after making "The Misfits" with Monroe?
16 Where did Monroe appear from when she sang "Happy Birthday" to President Kennedy?
17 What career did Marilyn Monroe embark on in 1946?
18 At which Actors' Studio did she study?
19 In which city was "The Prince and the Showgirl" made?
20 How old was Norma Jean when she first married?
21 How many times does Monroe sing "you" in one chorus of "I Wanna Be Loved By You"?
22 Who played Monroe's friends Daphne and Geraldine in "Some Like It Hot"?
23 What was the name of the Monroe character?
24 Why was she fired from "Something's Got to Give" ?
25 Monroe said "I have been on a calendar but never ..." what?
26 What did Monroe pose on, on that notorious calendar?
27 Which English singer appeared with Monroe in "Let's Make Love"?
28 In which city did Monroe die?
29 What was the official cause of death?
30 In which film did she co-star with Cary Grant and Ginger Rogers?

Answers

Food and Drink (see Quiz 14)
1 Tomato purée. 2 Apple, celery and walnuts. 3 Cake. 4 Italy. 5 Beer and garlic. 6 Seaweed. 7 Haddock. 8 Three. 9 Buffalo. 10 Neck of lamb. 11 Paper. 12 Duck and chicken. 13 Plums. 14 Egg yolks and butter. 15 Green. 16 Potatoes. 17 Somerset. 18 Liver. 19 Double cream. 20 Nettle leaves. 21 Greece. 22 Bows or butterflies. 23 Lentils. 24 Clarified butter. 25 Russia, fish pie. 26 Al dente. 27 Beer. 28 Very rare. 29 From the pan it's cooked in. 30 Aubergines.

Quiz 17 Pot-Luck 8

Answers - see page 259

1 Which sweets vanished in 1984, but were reintroduced in 1994?
2 Which was the first British daily paper to sell a million copies a day?
3 What happened on screen for the first time in India in 1977?
4 In 1993 which film star bought himself a £12 million Gulfstream G-3 jet?
5 Swiss architect Charles-Edouard Jeanneret is better known as who?
6 What are also known as "The Decalogue"?
7 Who composed the tune to "Twinkle, Twinkle, Little Star"?
8 Which pop singer played in goal for Real Madrid?
9 In Arthurian legend, what is the Holy Grail?
10 Why was income tax first levied in Britain?
11 Which herb is called milfoil?
12 How is the settlement the Town of Our Lady, the Queen of the Angels, by the Little-Portion River known today?
13 Which leading Nazi was born in Egypt?
14 What is psychometry?
15 In which novel does the land of Glubbdubdrib appear?
16 Which poet sold his home, Newstead Abbey, to pay his debts?
17 Who is the dictatorial father figure in Dickens' "Hard Times"?
18 What type of animal is a vmi-vmi?
19 Which animal was once called a foul marten?
20 In which year did women gain the vote in Switzerland?
21 Which English county has the longest coastline?
22 Where is Charles Darwin buried?
23 Where in the world can the largest cannon be seen?
24 Which bird is said to eat live sheep?
25 Who invented the sextant?
26 Which British car was the first to sell over a million models?
27 In which city was the first underground railway?
28 What are the pointed pieces called on a ship's anchor?
29 Which detective lived in Cabot Cove, Maine?
30 What is a polyptych?

Quiz 18 Elvis Presley

Answers - see page 260

Level 3

1 What was Elvis Presley's middle name?
2 Which song did he sing to win a talent contest at the age of ten?
3 Which country guitarist produced Elvis's early RCA records?
4 What was his wife Priscilla's maiden name?
5 Which white gospel group provided vocal backings on Elvis's recordings in the 1950s and 1960s?
6 Which label signed Presley before selling his contract to RCA a year later?
7 What were Elvis's parents called?
8 What was Elvis's first film?
9 Where was he posted when he joined the army in 1958?
10 Which was his first ever recording, made at Sam Phillips' studio?
11 What was his first US No 1?
12 Who were the remainder of the so-called Million Dollar Quartet, who recorded at Sun and whose recordings were released in 1990?
13 Who took charge of Presley's career when he moved to RCA?
14 What was the fourth of four consecutive No 1s between November 1960 and May 1961?
15 What was Elvis Presley's music publishing company called?
16 Which Elvis hit owes a debt to the Italian song "O Sole Mio"?
17 Which was Presley's only million seller between 1962 and 1969?
18 What was his first UK No 1?
19 Which city was the focus of Presley's work in the 1970s?
20 Which record went to No 1 after his death in 1977?
21 Which dancer co-starred with Presley in "GI Blues"?
22 Which is the only part of Britain Presley set foot on?
23 Which Elvis film was a western?
24 Because his movements were so controversial, only which part of Elvis was it suggested should be shown on TV?
25 Which operation did James Peterson carry out on Presley in March 1958?
26 What did the US Post Office issue in 1993?
27 What was the name of Elvis's famous mansion and where was it?
28 Which double-sided single was the top seller of the 1950s in the US?
29 Which Elvis hit was a No 1 for Dusty Springfield?
30 What was Elvis's last No 1 record in the UK in his lifetime?

Answers

Pot-Luck 9 (see Quiz 20)
1 Oscar Wilde. 2 The Case of the Terrified Typist. 3 Hercules. 4 France. 5 George Cowley. 6 Poppaea. 7 Ambulance driver. 8 Nano. 9 King Faisal. 10 Pinocchio. 11 Wembley Stadium, London. 12 The wettest place in Great Britain. 13 1922. 14 Scatterbrook. 15 Inchworm. 16 Teflon. 17 A flight. 18 Phobos. They are moons of Mars. 19 Ben Jonson. 20 A chaffinch. 21 In autumn. Name for a colchinium. 22 Noel Coward. 23 Riche Havens. 24 A couple. 25 66,250 mph. 26 Smell. 27 Lou Reed. 28 The help the American Indians gave to the first white settlers. 29 Harry Allen. 30 An expert on China.

Quiz 19 Charles Dickens

Level 3 ▮▮▮

Answers - see page 257

1 In "A Tale of Two Cities" what is the occupation of Sydney Carton?
2 In "Nicholas Nickleby" who is Ralph Nickleby's clerk?
3 Which of his novels did Dickens say he liked the best?
4 In Oliver Twist's burgling expedition with Bill Sikes what sort of injury does Oliver receive?
5 Which historical events are the background to "Barnaby Rudge"?
6 Who are David Copperfield's two vastly different schoolfriends?
7 Which court case is at the heart of "Bleak House"?
8 In "Hard Times" who is Mr Bounderby's housekeeper?
9 In "Little Dorrit" who are Amy's brother and sister?
10 In "Great Expectations" what is Pip's full name?
11 In "Our Mutual Friend" whom does Eugene Wrayburn marry?
12 In "A Tale of Two Cities" what is the name of the grave robber?
13 In "Oliver Twist" what is Rose's relation to Oliver discovered to be?
14 In "David Copperfield" who does David's aunt Betsey Trotwood live with?
15 In "The Old Curiosity Shop" what is Little Nell's surname?
16 In "Edwin Drood" at whose school at Cloisterham was Rosa brought up?
17 Which two Suffolk towns are the background for scenes in "Pickwick Papers"?
18 In "David Copperfield" how did Ham die?
19 In "Great Expectations" what is the profession of Joe Gargery?
20 What are Nip and Bullseye?
21 In "Oliver Twist" how does Bill Sikes perish?
22 In "Bleak House" who is Lady Dedlock's daughter, at first assumed dead?
23 In "Hard Times" who tries to seduce Louisa Bounderby, née Gradgrind?
24 What offence had inhabitants of the Marshalsea prison committed?
25 In "Nicholas Nickleby" what is the final fate of Squeers?
26 In "David Copperfield" who was "willin'"?
27 In "Pickwick Papers" who is Mr Pickwick's landlady?
28 In "Oliver Twist" who adopts Oliver?
29 In "The Old Curiosity Shop" who is Samson Brass's sister?
30 In "Great Expectations" whom did Estella first marry?

Level 3

1 Who said, "Philosophy teaches us to bear with equanimity the misfortunes of others"?

2 Which was the only case that Perry Mason ever lost in court?

3 Name the horse that pulled Steptoe and Son's rag-and-bone cart?

4 Which country has the most world championship wins for angling?

5 Whom did Gordon Jackson play in "The Professionals"?

6 What was the name of Nero's second wife?

7 What type of work did Ernest Hemingway do during World War I?

8 Which prefix denotes a one thousand millionth part?

9 Which Saudi Arabian king was assassinated in 1975?

10 In 1940 which classic Disney cartoon was made?

11 Where was the main arena for the 1948 Olympic Games?

12 Achnashellach is usually credited with what unfortunate title?

13 In which year did Mussolini seize power in Italy?

14 Where did Worzel Gummidge live?

15 What is a looper caterpillar called in the United States?

16 Polytetrafluoroethylene is usually known as what?

17 What name is given to swallows in the air?

18 What is the partner of Deimos?

19 Who was the first poet laureate?

20 What would you have seen if there is a *Fringilla coelebs* outside?

21 When would you see a naked lady in the garden?

22 Who wrote a song called the "The Stately Homes of England"?

23 Who opened the original Woodstock rock festival?

24 In "I Belong To Glasgow", how many drinks do I get on a Saturday?

25 To a thousand either way, what is the speed of the Earth in mph in its orbit round the Sun?

26 If a person is anosmic, they have no sense of what?

27 How is Louis Firbank better known?

28 The Americans celebrate Thanksgiving in remembrance of what?

29 Who was Britain's last chief hangman?

30 What is a Sinologist?

Quiz 21 Sports Bag

Answers - see page 263

1 In Australian Football where is the AFL Grand Final played?
2 What is another name for windsurfing?
3 What two differences are there between the position and paddle of someone in a canoe and someone in a kayak?
4 In which two countries is curling most popular?
5 What is the longest-lasting, non-motorized sporting event in the world?
6 What is the biathlon a combination of?
7 What is Brian Gamlin of Bury credited with devising?
8 Which electrical appliance joined the London Monarchs?
9 What two types of bowling green are there?
10 In which part of London was the first equestrian jumping competition?
11 What are the three types of sword used in fencing?
12 Billiards probably gets its name from the French word "billiard". What is a billiard?
13 Who was first world champion at darts and which country did he represent?
14 What does karate mean, describing this kind of fighting?
15 What did the sport, baggataway, become?
16 In what year did boxing become a legal sport?
17 Which sport does the Fédération Internationale des Quilleurs control?
18 In which sport do you use a chistera?
19 Which sport is played on the largest pitch of any game?
20 Where is the world's oldest tobogganing club?
21 In which three Olympic sports do men and women compete together?
22 Which sport developed from a game called gossima?
23 Which sport has three lifts, squat, bench press and dead lift?
24 What is the object of sumo wrestling?
25 In judo which dan is the highest in the grading of black belts?
26 How does a hurl differ from a hockey stick?
27 How do you luge?
28 Aside from asymmetric bars, what are the three events for women gymnasts in the Olympics?
29 In which country was greyhound racing's first regular track?
30 How many players are there in a Gaelic football team?

Quiz 22 Pot-Luck 10

Answers - see page 264

1 What is a solecism?
2 What is collateral kin?
3 What gas propels the cork from a champagne bottle?
4 What British public service ceased on June 12th, 1921?
5 When did Celtic first have numbers on the back of their shirts?
6 What colour cap is worn by an English cricketer capped for his country?
7 Who won the 1994 US Open tennis title?
8 By what name was the outlaw Harry Longbaugh better known?
9 What was Richard Burton's original name?
10 What is the name of the RAF free-fall parachute team?
11 In what year did Spain and Portugal join the EC?
12 Which Country and Western singer joined Bob Dylan on the latter's album, "Nashville Skyline"?
13 Which is the only Christian country in Asia?
14 Which fruit contains the most calories?
15 What is the minimum age for a three-star cognac?
16 What publication was launched in 1920 by American bank clerk DeWitt Wallace?
17 What was Hayley Mills' first film?
18 Who played David Vincent in "The Invaders"?
19 Which king converted Leeds Castle, in Kent, into a royal palace?
20 Who in the Old Testament is eaten by dogs?
21 What tune is Liechtenstein's national anthem sung to?
22 Who wrote the words of the hymn "Jerusalem"?
23 Who was Priapus in Greek mythology?
24 Which charge card was launched in Britain in September 1963?
25 What is the name of the world's largest flower?
26 What opened in 1894 and closed in London's Strand in 1988?
27 Where did Indian ink originally come from?
28 Who said, "Make love in the afternoon ... It's the only time for it"?
29 Which romantic poet wrote "The Bride of Abydos"?
30 How is Thomas Derbyshire better known?

Answers

Pot-Luck 11 (see Quiz 24)
1 Adolf Hitler. 2 Eltham, London. 3 Pickles. 4 Fishing. 5 Wren. 6 Benjamin Franklin in September 1752. 7 Traffic islands. 8 1852 in London. 9 Case for a ship's compass. 10 William the Conqueror. 11 One. 12 Sicily and parts of mainland Italy. 13 Saccharine. It's an anagram. 14 Jimmy Nail. 15 Colin Baker. 16 Beryl Reid. 17 Halibut. 18 Ascribing human feelings to objects. 19 Juno. 20 Admiral of the Fleet. 21 In India. 22 1945. 23 J. J. Thomson. 24 Long jump, high jump, triple jump and pole vault. 25 Sting. 26 Mega City 1. 27 168. 28 The Globe theatre. 29 A host. 30 Saltpetre, carbon and sulphur.

Quiz 23 TV Gold

Answers - see page 261

Level 3

1 Which Alan Bleasdale offering won the BAFTA Drama award in 1982?
2 Which comedy series starred Dave King and Joe Marcell as tramps?
3 Which 1960s TV personality always ended his show in a white E-type Jaguar?
4 Which Alan Plater TV adaptation starred Kenneth Branagh as Guy Pringle?
5 Where did Ken Barlow's father get the money that enabled him to move out of Coronation Street?
6 Who played Josephine opposite Ernie Wise's Napoleon?
7 Who is the richest person to have accepted a bit-part on "Bread"?
8 Which Eastender thought his father was Pete Beale when it was Kenny?
9 What was Robin Tripp studying when he lived upstairs from the Ropers?
10 Who was Sid's next-door neighbour in "Bless This House"?
11 Which quiz and chat show host devised "Whose Baby"?
12 Which department at Crossroads Motel was run by Vera Downend?
13 Which actress fluttered into the role of "Laura and Disorder"?
14 Which "Good Life" star played the lodger in "Goodbye Mr Kent"?
15 Which series about two girls and a guy was called "Three's Company" in the United States?
16 Which "Blue Peter" presenter was in "Space 1999" and "Fallen Hero"?
17 Which comedy featured characters called Terry Collier and Bob Ferris?
18 Which member of The Grateful Dead was known as 'Captain Trips'?
19 Which 1960s soap cast Haverhill in Suffolk as Angleton new town?
20 Which TV series starred Leslie Phillips and Donald Sinden as vicars?
21 Which comedy series married David Jason to Gwen Taylor?
22 Which quiz show was originally part of "Wednesday Night Out"?
23 Which Hywel Bennett series had the same title as a drama about a poet?
24 Who ran away to stay with Susan Barlow?
25 Where does Polly Sherman work?
26 Which two female TV stars are team captains on "Give Us A Clue"?
27 Who is Frank Muir's most regular writing partner?
28 Who died in 1988 when he fell off a horse while filming in Spain?
29 Who was always trying to borrow food in "Sykes"?
30 Which series linked Polly James and "District Nurse" Nerys Hughes?

1 Who once said: "What good fortune for those in power that people do not think"?

2 Where was Bob Hope born?

3 Which dog found the World Cup when it went missing in 1966?

4 Which British sport has the most participants?

5 What is the commonest bird in the British Isles?

6 Who designed the first lightning-conductor?

7 What road safety measure was introduced in the streets of Liverpool in 1860?

8 When and where was the first public lavatory opened in Britain?

9 What is a binnacle?

10 Which king built Windsor Castle?

11 How many lungs do snakes have?

12 Where can you find porcupines in Europe?

13 How can cane chairs be rearranged to produce something sweet?

14 How is James Bradford better known?

15 Who played the sixth Dr Who?

16 Who won a BAFTA award for her cameo role in "Smiley's People"?

17 What is the common name for the fish *Hippoglossus hippoglossus*?

18 What is pathetic fallacy?

19 Who was the Roman goddess of marriage?

20 What is the top rank in the Royal Navy?

21 Where was the decimal system developed?

22 When was the International Monetary Fund established?

23 Who discovered the electron?

24 In athletics, what are the four jumping events?

25 Who recorded the album "The Dream of the Blue Turtles"?

26 In which city does Judge Dredd work?

27 How many spots are there on a full set of 28 dominoes?

28 Which London landmark theatre was burnt down in 1613?

29 What is a group or flock of sparrows called?

30 What was the first gunpowder made of?

Answers — **Pot-Luck 10** (see Quiz 22) 1 A violation of grammar or syntax. 2 Relatives belonging to a person's own generation. 3 Carbon dioxide. 4 Sunday postal services. 5 1994. 6 Blue. 7 André Agassi. 8 The Sundance Kid. 9 Richard Jenkins. 10 The Falcons. 11 1986. 12 Johnny Cash. 13 The Philippines. 14 The avocado pear. 15 Five years. 16 Reader's Digest. 17 Tiger Bay. 18 Roy Thinnes. 19 Henry VIII. 20 Jezebel. 21 God Save the Queen. 22 William Blake. 23 A fertility god. 24 American Express. 25 Rafflesia, which grows up to one metre across. 26 Lyons teashops. 27 China. 28 Arnold Wesker. 29 Lord Byron. 30 Tommy Cannon.

Quiz 25 Capital Punishment

Answers - see page 267

1 What was the capital of Russia before Moscow?
2 What is the capital of Andorra?
3 What lies to the north of Algiers?
4 Which country has the last capital alphabetically?
5 What was Harare's former name?
6 Which Asian capital is at the head of the Mekong Delta?
7 Which capital is known as Leukosia or Lefkosa by its inhabitants?
8 What is the capital of Hong Kong?
9 Which capital is on the slopes of the volcano Pichincha?
10 Which is further north, Pakistan's new capital, Islamabad, or the former one, Karachi?
11 St John's is the capital of Antigua and Barbuda but on which island does it stand?
12 Which capital's former name was Christiania?
13 In Berlin which avenue runs east from the Brandenburg Gate?
14 Which capital is the largest city in Africa?
15 Where was Botswana's seat of government prior to 1965, after which it moved to Gaborone?
16 What was the capital of Italian East Africa between 1936 and 1941?
17 Which capital lies on the river Helmand?
18 In Paris what links the Arc de Triomphe and the Place de la Concorde?
19 Which new capital's main architect was Oscar Niemeyer?
20 Which capital's main industrial area is Piraeus?
21 In which capital is the Teatro Colón opera house?
22 What is the full name of the capital of Colombia?
23 Which capital's heating comes from natural hot springs?
24 What did New Delhi replace as the capital of British India in 1912?
25 On which sea is the Azerbaijani capital Baku?
26 Which capital is known as the Eternal City?
27 What is the capital of Bahrain?
28 Which capital began as the village of Edo?
29 Which capital in the West Indies is to be found on New Providence Island?
30 Which capital houses the Great Mosque and the Gate of God?

Pop: MOR (see Quiz 27)
1 Bing Crosby, White Christmas. 2 Burt Bacharach and Hal David. 3 Barbra Streisand. 4 None. 5 Andy Williams. 6 Sonny and Cher. 7 Des O'Connor. 8 Jambalaya. 9 Roger Whittaker. 10 Herb Alpert. 11 James Last. 12 Mantovani. 13 Peter Skellern. 14 Mary Hopkin. 15 Jack Jones. 16 Charles Aznavour. 17 Barber. 18 Harry Connick Jnr. 19 Johnny Mathis. 20 Shirley Bassey. 21 Leo Sayer. 22 Bert Kaempfert. 23 Henry Mancini. 24 Syd Lawrence. 25 Stranger in Paradise. 26 Al Martino. 27 Nat King Cole. 28 Helen Reddy. 29 Mike Flowers' Pops. 30 Gerry Goffin.

1 Whom did Paris select as the most beautiful goddess?
2 Who sails "The Black Pig"?
3 In which year did Hitler come to power in Germany?
4 Who formulated the periodic table of elements commonly used today?
5 Which domestic animals gather in clowders?
6 Who discovered the three basic laws of planetary motion?
7 Who was the first secretary-general of the United Nations?
8 Which living fish was thought to have been extinct for 60 million years?
9 Which country's wine may be labelled DOCG?
10 Who designed Blenheim Palace?
11 Who is the only British prime minister to have been assassinated?
12 Who gave Henry II the right to invade and conquer Ireland?
13 What is the name of the nearest star, other than the Sun, to Earth?
14 When was the first appendix operation performed?
15 For what line of business was model manufacturer Airfix originally known?
16 Which gift did the Americans receive from the French in 1886?
17 What is the penalty for drug trafficking in Saudi Arabia?
18 What is a crapulous person full of?
19 What is sophistry?
20 How is Camille Javal better known?
21 Which subatomic particle is named after the Greek word for "first"?
22 What was the name of the first feature-length animated film?
23 Henry Cooper became the British and Empire Heavyweight champion on January 12th, 1959. Who was his defeated opponent?
24 What is the colour of the bull on an archery target?
25 In which sport are Doggetts Coat and Badge awarded?
26 Who founded the first public library in the City of London?
27 By what name was Asa Yoelson better known?
28 The RAF motto is "Per Ardua Ad Astra". What does it mean?
29 Which EC country has the highest level of carbon monoxide?
30 Which of the Seven Wonders of the Ancient World survives today?

Answers

Cricket (see Quiz 28)
1 Phil Caddick. 2 The Oval. 3 Shane Warne (in 1994). 4 Durham. 5 He was a Man Utd fan and wanted to watch the FA Cup Final. 6 Bob Woolmer. 7 Philip Eric. 8 Essex. 9 Kepler Wessels. 10 West Germany. 11 Bob Willis. 12 Darren Gough. 13 Lancashire. 14 Mark Burgess. 15 355. 16 Yorkshire and Leicestershire. 17 Brian McMillan. 18 Wally Hammond. 19 New Zealand. 20 Richardson. 21 Somerset. 22 Hubert. 23 Phil Neale. 24 Surrey. 25 Colin Cowdrey. 26 "Jimmy" Binks. 27 Derbyshire. 28 Malcolm Nash (Sobers batting, in 1968). 29 Viv Richards. 30 Richard Ellison.

Quiz 27 Pop: MOR

Answers - see page 265

1 What is the top-selling single of all time and who sang it?
2 Which partnership wrote "Walk On By" for Dionne Warwick?
3 Who has recorded with Neil Diamond, Barry Gibb and Don Johnson?
4 How many No 1 singles has Neil Diamond had?
5 Who recorded film themes "Moon River" and "Love Story"?
6 Cherilyn and Salvator are the first names of what popular 60s duo?
7 Who had a Top Twenty hit in 1969 with "Dick-A-Dum-Dum"?
8 Which Carpenters hit was the name of a food dish?
9 Whose hits mention Durham, Skye and the New World?
10 Which trumpeter was a co-founder of A & M Records?
11 Who in 1993 became second only to Elvis Presley with his number of album chart entries?
12 Which hugely successful orchestra leader was born Annunzio Paolo?
13 Who has recorded with northern brass bands and sung the songs of Fred Astaire and Hoagy Carmichael?
14 Who won "Opportunity Knocks" and was signed by the Apple label?
15 Which MOR singer's father was famous for his "Donkey Serenade"?
16 Which French singer's autobiography was called "Yesterday When I Was Young"?
17 What was Perry Como's job before becoming a singer?
18 Whose music was on the soundtrack of "When Harry Met Sally"?
19 Who has recorded with Deniece Williams and Gladys Knight?
20 Who was known as 'The Tigress of Tiger Bay'?
21 Who had a transatlantic hit with "When I Need Love"?
22 Which German bandleader was the first to record The Beatles?
23 Who wrote film themes "Days of Wine and Roses" and the Pink Panther?
24 Which British orchestra emulated the sound of Glenn Miller?
25 What was Tony Bennett's first chart entry and only UK No 1?
26 Who was chosen for the role of Johnny Fontane (reputedly based on Frank Sinatra) in "The Godfather"?
27 Whose many hits included "When I Fall in Love" and "Too Young"?
28 Whose first US No 1 was the self-penned "I Am a Woman"?
29 Who took easy listening into the top ten at Christmas 1995?
30 Who was Carole King's songwriting partner in the 1960s?

Quiz 28 Cricket

Answers - see page 266

1 Which bowler ended Brian Lara's record-breaking Test innings of 375?
2 At which ground did Malcolm take nine wickets in a 1994 Test innings?
3 After Hugh Trumble's Ashes hat-trick in 1904, who was the next Australian to repeat the feat?
4 With which county did Ian Botham end his playing career?
5 Why was New Zealand's Ken Rutherford happy for the one-day Test on May 21st, 1994 to be washed out by rain?
6 Who left Warwickshire in 1994 to become coach to South Africa?
7 What are Alan Knott's two middle names?
8 The Benson & Hedges Cup in 1979 was the first trophy for which county?
9 Who was skipper of South Africa in their 1994 return to England?
10 In which country was England batsman Paul Terry born ?
11 Aside from Botham, which English bowler achieved the 300 Test wickets?
12 In 1994 who gave his son the middle names David and Michael after the Australian batsman whom he dismissed the day after the baby's birth?
13 Who won the Gillette Cup in 1970, 1971 and 1972?
14 Who led New Zealand to their first-ever victory against England in 1978?
15 To ten either way, how many Test wickets did Dennis Lillee take?
16 Which two counties did Dickie Bird play for?
17 Who topped the South African batting and bowling averages in the 1994 Test series against England?
18 Which England captain was the first Test outfielder to take 100 catches?
19 For which country did Peter Petherick take a Test hat-trick in 1976?
20 What was the surname of 1950s England players Derek and Peter?
21 Which English county did New Zealander Martin Crowe play for?
22 What is Clive Lloyd's middle name?
23 Who skippered both Lincoln at football and Worcester at cricket in 1993?
24 Which county did Jack Hobbs play for?
25 Who drove down a one-way street going to see his son captain England?
26 Which Yorkshire wicket-keeper had the first names James Graham?
27 Which English county did Michael Holding play for?
28 Which bowler was the first to be hit for six sixes in an over?
29 Which West Indian player turned out for Antigua in the 1978 World Cup?
30 Which Kent bowler took 17 wickets in two of the 1985 Australian series?

Quiz 29 Pot-Luck 13

Level 3

Answers - see page 271

1   In which decade was flogging abolished in Britain?
2   What sort of word is made up from initial letters of other words?
3   What is a necropolis?
4   Where did the Vikings originally come from?
5   What is the coldest substance?
6   Who wrote the book "Chitty Chitty Bang Bang"?
7   In which sport is there a york round?
8   Who wrote the song "If"?
9   In cricket how many runs is a Nelson?
10 Which British prime minister once said, "Is a man an ape or an angel? Now I am on the side of the angels"?
11 By what name is Jim Moir better known?
12 When was the first free vertical flight of a twin-rotor helicopter?
13 What does an aphyllous plant not have?
14 For how long did Alexander the Great rule?
15 What is the central administrative body of the Catholic Church?
16 Which decade saw the introduction of instant coffee?
17 Which country produces the most potatoes?
18 Who launched the "Daily Mail"?
19 Who was stripped of the title Miss Hungary in 1936 when it was found out she was not yet 16?
20 Which film did newspaper magnate William Randolph Hearst inspire?
21 Which city is built on the site of the Aztec capital Tenochtitlan?
22 To which king in the Bible was Jezebel married?
23 Which famous American singer was described in "Life" magazine in 1974 as having a "half-melted vanilla face"?
24 What do you do in music when you play a piece "con brio"?
25 What punishment did the Vestal Virgins of Rome suffer if they betrayed their vows of chastity?
26 Where is Britain's Royal Mint situated?
27 Which is the largest seed in the world?
28 To 20 years each way, when was Hyde Park opened to the public?
29 Why is the Queen Hotel, Pontefract, called a calendar hotel?
30 If you suffer from cherophobia what are you afraid of?

Answers

Pot-Luck 14 (see Quiz 31)
1 The Spectator. 2 His cousin, Celeste. 3 George II (Dettingen, 1743).
4 Hydrogen. 5 A barren. 6 The Milky Way. 7 1963. 8 Chelonia.
9 Germany. 10 Blenheim. 11 The Third World. 12 Poppies. 13 About eight minutes. 14 Carl Koller. 15 Saudi Arabia. 16 The Chisholm Trail.
17 Jack the Ripper. 18 An instrument for enlarging or reducing drawings.
19 Jerry Lewis. 20 Shanghai. 21 Electric current. 22 Long sight. 23 106.
24 Lord Palmerston. 25 Goodbye, Mr Chips. 26 Milk. 27 Paul Neal.
28 The 1920s. 29 The Netherlands. 30 The Picts.

Quiz 30 Transport

Answers - see page 272

Level 3

1 What was the name of the first commercial atomic-powered ship?
2 Who devised the prototype for the "Beetle"?
3 What was the first car to be powered by a gas turbine?
4 Who first patented the seat belt in 1903?
5 Which rail line, opened in 1830, was the world's first inter-city service?
6 Who introduced the TL tractor with four directional wheels in 1926?
7 In 1775 who invented the tram drawn by two horses?
8 What was the first hot-air balloon, called the Montgolfier, made of?
9 In air flight, what is the characteristic of aerodynes?
10 Where did the Wright brothers fly their first glider in 1900?
11 What was the first airliner, which was put into service in 1933?
12 Who invented the preselector gearbox for battle tanks in 1917?
13 Who founded the Great Western Railway using a seven-foot wide track?
14 Which famous ocean liner made its maiden voyage in May 1936?
15 Who invented the "air bag" anti-shock air cushion?
16 Who made the first airship flight in 1852 in a hydrogen-filled craft powered by a steam engine?
17 What does the "U" in U-Boat stand for?
18 What did French engineer Georges Messier invent in 1924?
19 Who in 1878 invented the electric staff which prevents trains on single-track lines colliding?
20 Who built the first submarine which was tested in the River Thames?
21 Who invented laminated windscreens in 1909?
22 What was the name of the first successful flying boat built in 1912?
23 Which brothers built the first American petrol-driven motor cars in 1892?
24 On which railway was the first buffet car created in 1899?
25 Which airline company first made a commercial flight in a Boeing 747 from New York to London?
26 Which German company created the electronically variable shock-absorber in 1987?
27 What first left Gare de l'Est in Paris on October 4th, 1883?
28 Who built the Calcutta flying boats used by British Imperial Airways?
29 Which British doctor invented the disc brake in 1902?
30 Where was the first take-off by a manned helicopter in 1907?

Answers

European Community (see Quiz 32) **1** Six. **2** European Coal and Steel Community. **3** Euratom. **4** Ireland, Denmark. **5** Foreign secretaries. **6** Transport. **7** 20. **8** Their national governments. **9** Brussels. **10** European Council. **11** Three times a year. **12** Luxembourg. **13** Conservatives. **14** Six months. **15** EU citizenship. **16** Pillars. **17** Subsidiarity. **18** Germany (99). **19** European Investment Bank. **20** Jacques Delors. **21** Butter. **22** De Gaulle. **23** Treaty of Brussels. **24** Roy Jenkins. **25** VAT payments. **26** Greenland. **27** Corporal punishment of children if parents disapproved. **28** EFTA. **29** Deputy foreign secretary. **30** Five years.

Quiz 31   Pot-Luck 14

Level 3

Answers - see page 269

1   Which journal did Addison and Steele found?
2   Whom did Babar the Elephant marry?
3   Who was the last British king to lead an army into battle?
4   Of which element is tritium an isotope?
5   What is the collective noun for a group of mules?
6   In which galaxy is the Earth?
7   In what year did Valentina Tereshkova become the first woman in space?
8   To which order of reptiles do turtles and tortoises belong?
9   Trockenbeerenauslese come from which country?
10   In which palace was Winston Churchill born?
11   Which expression was coined by Alfred Sauvy in the early 1950s to describe countries with underdeveloped economic structures?
12   In "Penny Lane" what is a nurse selling from a tray?
13   How long does the light of the Sun take to reach the Earth?
14   Who discovered the pain-killing properties of cocaine?
15   Which country is the world's largest oil producer?
16   What was the name of the cattle route from Texas through Oklahoma to the Red Hills at Abilene, Kansas?
17   Who murdered Catherine Eddowes on September 30th, 1888?
18   What is an eidograph?
19   Joseph Levitch is better known as who?
20   Which city has the largest population in the world?
21   What is controlled by a rheostat?
22   What would you have if you were hypermetropic?
23   How many times was Bobby Charlton capped for England?
24   Whose last words were, "Die, my dear doctor! That's the last thing I shall do!"?
25   Which James Hilton novel was turned into a film classic about school life?
26   What does a galactophagist like to drink?
27   What is the real name of Red Adair, the American fire-fighter?
28   In which decade did the "*par avion*" airmail stickers appear in Britain?
29   Which EU member state has the highest population density?
30   Kenneth I ruled which people in the 9th century?

Answers

Pot-Luck 13   (see Quiz 29)   **1** 1940s. **2**   Acronym. **3**   Cemetery.
4 Gotland. **5** Solid helium. **6** Ian Fleming. **7** Archery. **8** David Gates.
9 111. **10** Benjamin Disraeli. **11** Vic Reeves. **12** 1907, by Paul Cornu.
13 Leaves. **14** 12 years. **15** The Curia. **16** 1938, Nescafé. **17** The USSR.
18 Alfred Harmsworth, Viscount Northcliffe, in 1896. **19** Zsa Zsa Gabor.
20 Citizen Kane. **21** Mexico City. **22** Ahab. **23** Elvis Presley. **24** Play
vigorously. **25** Live burial. **26** Llantrisant, Wales. **27** Double coconut.
28 1637. **29** It has 365 windows (days), 12 original bedrooms (months), four
floors (seasons) and seven entrances (days of the week). **30** Gaiety.

271

Quiz 32 European Community

Answers - see page 270

1 How many countries were in the EEC at its beginning in 1957?
2 What did the Treaty of Paris set up in 1951?
3 What was the European Atomic Energy Commission known as?
4 Who joined the EC in 1973 with Britain?
5 Who are the members of the Council of Ministers?
6 For which area is Commissioner Neil Kinnock responsible?
7 How many commissioners are there?
8 Who appoints them?
9 Where is the Commission's headquarters?
10 What are the meetings of the heads of government called?
11 How many times do they meet?
12 Where is the secretariat of the European Parliament based?
13 Which British political party is included in the European People's Party group in the European Parliament?
14 How long does a European Council presidency last?
15 What qualification do you need to stand for the European Parliament?
16 What did the Maastricht Treaty call each of the three areas of the EU?
17 Which principle in the Maastricht Treaty says the Community will act on policies which member states would find difficult to deal with alone?
18 Which country has the most MEPs?
19 What is the EU bank called?
20 Who preceded Jacques Santer as Commission president?
21 In 1987 what did the EC sell to the USSR for 6p per pound?
22 Which statesman vetoed Britain's entry into the EEC in the 1960s?
23 Which treaty allowed Britain's entry into the EC?
24 Who was the first British president of the EC Commission?
25 What did Margaret Thatcher threaten to withhold if the EC did not cut Britain's budget contribution in 1980?
26 Who voted to withdraw from the EC in February 1982?
27 What did the European Court outlaw in the same month?
28 Of which trading association was Britain a member prior to joining the EEC?
29 Which post did Ted Heath hold when Britain first tried to join the EEC?
30 How long is an MEP elected for?

Answers

Transport (see Quiz 30) **1** The Savannah. **2** Ferdinand Porsche. **3** Rover. **4** Gustave Desiré Liebau. **5** Liverpool to Manchester. **6** Georges Latil. **7** John Outram. **8** Pack-cloth covered with paper. **9** They are heavier than air. **10** Kitty Hawk. **11** Boeing 247. **12** Major Wilson. **13** I. K. Brunel. **14** The Queen Mary. **15** Daimler-Benz. **16** Henri Giffard. **17** Unterseeboot. **18** First hydraulic suspension system. **19** Edward Tyer. **20** Cornelius Drebbel. **21** E. Benedictus. **22** The Flying Fish. **23** Charles and Frank Duryea. **24** Great Central Railway. **25** Pan Am. **26** Boge. **27** The Orient Express. **28** Short Brothers. **29** Dr Lanchester. **30** Lisieux, France.

Level 3

1 When was Prohibition introduced in the United States?
2 Which metal melts at 30 degrees centigrade?
3 Which animals congregate in musters?
4 How many "sisters" make up the Pleiades?
5 Which group of ships was known as the 'The First Fleet'?
6 What is the influence of gravity on plants called?
7 What colour is the wine Tokay?
8 Floors Castle is the Scottish home of which duke?
9 In which decade did the Falkland Islands first become a British colony?
10 In which war did the Battle of Isandhlwana take place?
11 In miles, how far from the Earth do meteors usually burn out?
12 In which century was the last outbreak of the Black Death in England?
13 When did Green Shield stamps come into use in Britain?
14 In 1803 what did the United States double?
15 Which prison closed on March 21st, 1963?
16 What is an eponym?
17 How is Marie Gresholtz better known today?
18 What is special about the words rose, oven, send, ends?
19 What is the heaviest element in the world?
20 Who founded Eton?
21 How many players were on the field at the end of the 1990 World Cup Final?
22 Which sport was banned in England in 1849?
23 Who scripted, directed and appeared in "The Plank"?
24 Ronald Wycherley is better known as who?
25 What is nostology?
26 To five years either way, in which year did London's first airport open?
27 Who is the patron saint of Germany?
28 When were the first British passports in the new red European format issued?
29 On which country did the United States declare war in 1898?
30 Which British university was the first to offer a degree in brewing?

Quiz 34 Speed Kings

Level 3

1 Who is the youngest-ever Formula 1 double world champion?
2 Which British driver had five British Grand Prix wins during the 1960s?
3 Who did Barry Sheene ride for when he won his world championships?
4 Which 1957 motor racing champion was the oldest of all time?
5 Who was the only Australian motor racing world champion in the 1960s?
6 Which motor cyclist won 122 world championships?
7 Which driver was runner-up in the world championship in '63, '64 and '65?
8 Which Brazilian was world champion driver in 1972 and 1974?
9 What was the nationality of Mario Andretti?
10 Which driver won the world championship posthumously in 1970?
11 Which New Zealander won the motor racing championship in 1967?
12 What is the nationality of Nelson Piquet?
13 How many times did Graham Hill win the Monaco Grand Prix?
14 Which Belgian won Le Mans six times between 1969 and 1982?
15 Who was driving for Ferrari when they became the first manufacturer to have 100 Grand Prix wins?
16 Who was the British driver with most Grand Prix wins before Nigel Mansell?
17 How many times was Ayrton Senna world champion?
18 At which sport did Ivan Maugher win six world titles?
19 Which British motorcyclist won 14 Isle of Man Tourist Trophy titles?
20 Which Briton broke the world land speed record in the US in 1983?
21 What is the nationality of Keke Rosberg?
22 Who was world championship driver in 1964 and motorcycling champion seven times?
23 Who was the first Briton to win the world motor racing championship?
24 Who had 16 Grand Prix wins between 1955 and 1961?
25 Which Briton was world champion in 1976 and retired three years later?
26 Which two Britons had six Grand Prix wins in a season and still failed to win the world championships?
27 Who drove the McLaren to its first Grand Prix win in 1968?
28 What is Gilles Villeneuve's home country?
29 Which driver apart from Senna lost his life in the 1994 Formula 1 season?
30 Which Grand Prix did Damon Hill win for the first time in 1994?

Pot-Luck 16 (see Quiz 36)
1 Frances. 2 Charlie Drake. 3 Noel Coward. 4 Six. 5 Gary Gilmore before his execution. 6 The sea horse. 7 The Phoenician. 8 Ten. 9 The Battle of Culloden in 1746. 10 Nine. 11 The International Red Cross. 12 Grumpy, Sleepy, Happy, Bashful, Sneezy, Dopey, Doc. 13 India. 14 Giant hailstones. 15 Baton Rouge. 16 A kiss. It is mistletoe 17 British Airways. 18 Charlie's Angels. 19 A paddling. 20 Orion. 21 Queen Victoria. 22 Beetles. 23 New Zealand. 24 Eaton Hall. 25 In 1812, during the Napoleonic Wars. 26 Silver. 27 Earth. 28 See in the dark. 29 Barbed wire. 30 Francis Scott Key.

Answers

Quiz 35 Pop: Novelty Songs

Level 3

1 What did Dora Bryan want for Christmas in 1963?
2 Who took his "Ding-a-ling" to No 1?
3 Which two versions of "Itsy Bitsy Teeny Weeny Yellow Polka Dot Bikini" have hit the charts 30 years apart?
4 On which of Rolf Harris's chart hits did we first hear a didgeridoo?
5 Which vocalist called himself The Joan Collins Fan Club?
6 Which TV series did the vocalists on "Whispering Grass" come from?
7 Which DJs were Laurie Lingo and the Dipsticks?
8 Which "EastEnders" star had a hit with "The Ugly Duckling"?
9 Who sang "Red Machine in Full Effect"?
10 Who was Mr Bean's backing group?
11 What are the only words on Lieutenant Pigeon's first No 1?
12 Who sang "They're Coming to Take Me Away Ha-Haaa" in 1966?
13 How was the Belgian Soeur Sourire known in Britain?
14 Which Jasper Carrott single was once banned by the BBC?
15 What was the title of Paul Gascoigne's Gazza Rap?
16 Who was "Walking Backwards for Christmas" in the 1950s?
17 Who got to No 1 in 1958 with "Hoots Mon"?
18 Who argued about "Bangers and Mash" in 1961?
19 What was the first thing Scaffold said "Thank U Very Much" for?
20 Who recorded with The Red Nosed Burglars and the D Cups?
21 Which Superstar recorded "Love Me Tender" nearly 30 years after Elvis Presley?
22 How long did it take Mr Blobby to reach No 1 in December 1993?
23 Who helped The Stonkers get a hit with "The Stonk"?
24 Which duo had a minor hit with "Reet Petite" in 1993?
25 What was the full title of Harry Enfield's 1988 hit?
26 'Two Pints of Lager and a Packet of Crisps Please' was a hit for which band?
27 Which "Dad's Army" character had a No 1 hit?
28 Who accompanied Chas and Dave on "Snooker Loopy"?
29 What was on the other side of Spitting Image's "Santa Claus is on the Dole"?
30 Which song did The Wurzels base their "Combine Harvester" on?

Answers

Pot-Luck 15 (see Quiz 33) **1** 1920. **2** Gallium. **3** Peacocks. **4** Seven. **5** Ships transporting the first convicts to Australia in 1788. **6** Geotropism. **7** White. **8** The Duke of Roxburgh. **9** 1830s. **10** The Zulu War of 1879. **11** About 50 miles. **12** 20th century – in 1914 in Liverpool. **13** 1958. **14** Its size. **15** Alcatraz. **16** A word formed from a name. **17** Mme Tussaud. **18** They form a word square so the words read the same across and down. **19** Osmium. **20** Henry VI. **21** Argentina had two players sent off. **22** Cockfighting. **23** Eric Sykes. **24** Billy Fury. **25** Study of senility. **26** 1919. **27** St Boniface. **28** 1988. **29** Spain. **30** Heriot-Watt.

Quiz 36 Pot-Luck 16

Level 3

Answers - see page 274

1 What is the Princess of Wales' middle name?
2 How is Charles Springall better known?
3 Which playwright told besuited actress Edna Furber that she looked like a man, and was given the reply "So do you."?
4 What was Patrick McGoohan's identity number in "The Prisoner"?
5 Whose last words were, "Let's do it"?
6 Which is the only fish able to hold objects in its tail?
7 From which alphabet did all the Western alphabets originate?
8 How many months were there in the old Roman year?
9 What is generally regarded as the last major battle on British soil?
10 How many sides has a nonagon?
11 Which medical body was set up at the Geneva Convention in 1864?
12 What are the names of all of Snow White's Seven Dwarfs?
13 In which country was "Release Me" singer Englebert Humperdinck born?
14 In July 1923 what freak weather conditions killed 23 people in Rostov, USSR?
15 What is the state capital of Louisiana?
16 *Viscum album* provides an excuse for stealing what?
17 What did BOAC and BEA form on their merger?
18 What was the collective name of Sabrina, Jill and Kelly?
19 What is the term for a group of ducks?
20 In which constellation are the stars Bellatrix and Betelgeuse?
21 Who was the first British monarch to live in Buckingham Palace?
22 Which order in the classification of animals has most members?
23 Which country has a wine-producing area centred on Gisborne?
24 What is the Cheshire seat of the Duke of Westminster?
25 When did Britain last go to war against the United States?
26 With which metal is the Iron Cross edged?
27 Which planet lies between Venus and Mars?
28 What does scotopic vision allow you to do?
29 What did Lucien B. Smith first patent in 1867?
30 Who wrote the words of "The Star Spangled Banner"?

Quiz 37 The Movies: Charlie Chaplin (Level 3) ▮▮▮

Answers - see page 279

1 In which part of London did Chaplin spend his early life?
2 What was his elder brother and fellow performer called?
3 What did the troupe, The Eight Lancashire Lads, do?
4 With which company did Chaplin travel to the United States in 1910?
5 For which company did Chaplin make his first films?
6 Who played the title role in "The Kid" in 1921?
7 Which film appeared in 1925 and had sound added in 1942?
8 Which wife of Chaplin co-starred in "Modern Times"?
9 How many times did Chaplin marry altogether?
10 Which was Chaplin's first sound film?
11 Whom did he choose to play the young ballerina in "Limelight"?
12 Which type of sound was heard in "City Lights" in 1931?
13 From which film, for which Chaplin wrote the music, did Petula Clark have a No 1 with "This Is My Song"?
14 Which former silent movie star joined Chaplin in "Limelight"?
15 What is odd about Chaplin's comments on his ex-wife, Lita Grey, in his autobiography?
16 Who was Chaplin's last father-in-law?
17 What was his last wife called?
18 Which film distributing company did Chaplin found with D.W. Griffith, Douglas Fairbanks and Mary Pickford?
19 Who bought the company out in 1940?
20 Which of Chaplin's sons starred with him in "A King in New York"?
21 Which was the last film Chaplin made in the United States?
22 In which split-reel film did The Tramp first appear?
23 Which daughter of Chaplin starred in Doctor Zhivago?
24 How did Emil Jannings score over Chaplin in 1929?
25 Where did Chaplin live after being banned from the US in 1953?
26 Which award did Chaplin receive in 1975?
27 What did Chaplin win his Oscar for in "Limelight"?
28 On which day of the year did Chaplin die?
29 What happened on March 2nd the following year?
30 Who played the roles of Chaplin's parents in a 1989 TV series "The Young Chaplin"?

Answers

Classic Women Writers (see Quiz 39)
1 Clergyman. 2 Pride and Prejudice. 3 Harriet Smith. 4 Sense and Sensibility. 5 Jennifer Ehle 6 Elizabeth, Anne, Mary. 7 Fanny Price. 8 Northanger Abbey. 9 Emma Thompson. 10 Charlotte. 11 Currer, Ellis and Acton Bell. 12 The Tenant of Wildfell Hall, Agnes Grey. 13 Brussels. 14 Their brother, Patrick Branwell. 15 Nicholls. 16 St John Rivers. 17 Lowood. 18 Villette. 19 Emily. 20 Mrs Gaskell. 21 Liverpool. 22 Isabella. 23 Edgar Linton. 24 George Eliot. 25 Eppie. 26 Middlemarch. 27 Dorlcote. 28 Carpenter. 29 Frankenstein. 30 Elizabeth Barrett Browning.

Quiz 38 Pot-Luck 17

Answers - see page 280

1 What is an encyclical?
2 Which famous TV cook died in 1994 at the age of 83?
3 What is the Latin name for the apple or fruit in general?
4 For which Sunday newspaper was Clement Freud a football correspondent?
5 Which Hollywood film studio was founded in 1915 by Carl Laemmle?
6 Whom did the Walrus and the Carpenter invite to walk with them?
7 Where did the old London Bridge move to from the Thames?
8 In which language was the New Testament originally written?
9 Which famous dancer's legs were insured for $650,000?
10 Which Glen Miller tune did Peter Sellers request for his own funeral?
11 In Roman mythology, who was the husband of Juno?
12 Where does the name Fray Bentos come from in connection with corned beef?
13 Who were the first group to have four consecutive double-sided hits?
14 How is Joyce Frankenberg better known?
15 Which Russian ruler imposed a beard tax?
16 What is blennophobia?
17 Which comic actor and writer co-wrote the book "Life and How to Survive It"?
18 Who wrote "The Napoleon of Notting Hill"?
19 Where is the Devil's Tower?
20 What is the smallest breed of dog?
21 For how many months each year does a dormouse hibernate?
22 What were Franklin D. Roosevelt's four freedoms of democracy?
23 How was Alexander the Great's body preserved?
24 On the Chinese calendar which animal represents the year 2000?
25 How many "Monty Python" series were made?
26 The black swan is native to which country?
27 Who invented the game roulette?
28 Where was the wheel clamp first used in Europe?
29 What were the first false teeth made of?
30 What was the name of the captain of the "Titanic"?

1 What was the occupation of Jane Austen's father?
2 Which Austen novel was originally called "First Impressions"?
3 Whom does Emma take under her wing in the novel of the same name?
4 Which Austen novel was first called "Elinor and Marianne"?
5 Who played Elizabeth Bennet in TV's "Pride and Prejudice" in 1995?
6 Who are Sir Walter Elliot's three daughters in "Persuasion"?
7 In "Mansfield Park" what is the name of the heroine?
8 In which Austen novel do we meet Catherine Morland?
9 Who wrote the screenplay for "Sense and Sensibility"?
10 Of the Brontë sisters that survived to adulthood who was the eldest?
11 Which pseudonyms did the Brontë sisters use when they published a collection of poems in 1846?
12 Which two novels did Anne Brontë write?
13 Where did Charlotte and Emily go to study languages in 1842?
14 Which member of the Brontë family died in the same year as Emily?
15 What was Charlotte's married name?
16 In "Jane Eyre" who cares for Jane after she flees Thornfield Hall?
17 In "Jane Eyre" what is the name of the asylum based on Cowan Bridge where Charlotte Brontë's sisters contracted the consumption from which they died?
18 Which novel by Charlotte reflects her life as a governess abroad?
19 Who is the character of Shirley Keeldar based on in "Shirley"?
20 Which author of "Cranford" wrote the "Life of Charlotte Brontë" in 1857?
21 In which city does Mr Earnshaw first find Heathcliff?
22 Whom does Heathcliff marry?
23 Whom has Catherine Earnshaw married when Heathcliff returns from his three-year absence?
24 How is Mary Ann Cross better known?
25 Whom does Silas Marner adopt?
26 Which George Eliot novel is subtitled "A Study of Provincial Life"?
27 What is the name of the mill in "Mill on the Floss"?
28 What is the occupation of Adam Bede?
29 What is the title of Mary Wollstonecraft Shelley's "tale of terror"?
30 How is Elizabeth Moulton better known?

Quiz 40 Pot-Luck 18

Level 3

Answers - see page 278

1 Who won the Booker prize for fiction in 1993?

2 In which decade did India go metric?

3 How is Leslie Heseltine better known?

4 The okapi is a relative of which animal?

5 What type of animal is the tucotucco?

6 Complete Lord Acton's phrase "Power tends to corrupt... "?

7 What was Bing Crosby's real first name?

8 Which famous scientist started out as a bookbinder's apprentice?

9 What is the fastest living creature regularly raced for sport?

10 In which trade did a Butcher, a Cooper and a Mariner work together?

11 What did Leo Baekeland invent in 1909?

12 Which animals in London are connected with Edwin Landseer?

13 What did 19th-century French physician René Laënnec develop?

14 Who said, "All the art in the world isn't worth a good potato pie"?

15 Who was the longest-reigning European monarch?

16 What does the DIN number denote in photographic film?

17 In polite society, what does a man do on two legs, a woman sitting down and a dog on three legs?

18 What famous first was achieved by William Tayton?

19 Name the TV host who was expelled from Orpington secondary modern school?

20 Which fish "shoots" its food?

21 What language did Jesus speak?

22 Which Roman emperor died at York in AD 211?

23 To ten years either way, until when were mules part of the British army?

24 In which American novel is there a character called Little Eva?

25 In which county is the Seikan tunnel?

26 Which comic-strip detective was created by Chester Gould?

27 Which athlete set six world records in less than an hour in 1935?

28 What is the name of the violent northwesterly wind that blows over the Adriatic?

29 Which land was first sighted by Vasco da Gama on a Christmas Day?

30 "Spend, spend spend" was the cry of which winner of the football pools?

Answers

Pot-Luck 17   (see Quiz 38) 1 A letter sent by the pope to all Catholic archbishops. 2 Fanny Cradock. 3 Malum. 4 The Observer. 5 Universal. 6 The oysters. 7 Lake Havasu City, Arizona, United States. 8 Greek. 9 Fred Astaire's. 10 In the Mood. 11 Jupiter. 12 A port on the River Uruguay. 13 UB40. 14 Jane Seymour. 15 Peter the Great. 16 Fear of slime. 17 John Cleese. 18 G. K. Chesterton. 19 Wyoming. 20 The chihuahua. 21 Six. 22 Of speech, of worship, from want, from fear. 23 It was kept in a large jar of honey. 24 The Dragon. 25 Four. 26 Australia. 27 Blaise Pascal. 28 Paris. 29 Ivory. 30 Edward J. Smith.

Quiz 41 Spirits and Cocktails

Level 3

Answers - see page 283

1 Which cocktail would you find in a toolbox?
2 What is the best-known type of Hollands called?
3 What is the Russian drink *kvass* made from?
4 What is Drambuie made from?
5 What spice is used in a whisky sling?
6 What turns gin into a pink gin?
7 What are the traditional ingredients in a daiquiri?
8 What is added to brandy to make a sidecar?
9 What is the principal spirit in a Harvey Wallbanger?
10 What is a cocktail of rye whisky, vermouth and angostura called?
11 What is the brandy Birngeist made from?
12 Which drink was Prince Charles caught ordering while at Gordonstoun?
13 If a cocktail is served "in a mist", how is it served?
14 What is a dry Manhattan called?
15 What is the fruit in an old-fashioned?
16 What makes a whisky a whisky sour?
17 What are the two main ingredients of a *cuba libre*?
18 Which former prime minister do you get if you mix cinzano, apricot brandy and angostura bitters?
19 What savoury ingredient do you include in a Sputnik?
20 What does an Alexandra taste of?
21 Which card game is a mix of cinzano bianco, gin and maraschino?
22 What do you add to champagne to make a champagne flip?
23 What type of plant is tequila made from?
24 Which distillery was the first to conform to the licensing laws which made other stills illegal in 1823?
25 With which US state is bourbon most associated?
26 Which state does Jack Daniels come from?
27 Where is the original home of bacardi?
28 What is *slivovitz* made from?
29 What sort of drink is Barbancourt?
30 Where is the Talisker whisky distillery?

Answers

Rugby (see Quiz 43) 1 Seddon drowned in Australia. 2 J. P .R. Williams. 3 Gus Risman. 4 Zimbabwe. 5 Abdel Benazzi. 6 New Zealander. 7 Cardiff. 8 Simon Geoghegan. 9 New Zealand. 10 England. 11 Leicester. 12 Gavin Hastings. 13 M. J. K. Smith. 14 Kevin O'Flanaghan (Irish RFC and Arsenal). 15 Bill Beaumont. 16 Currie Cup. 17 Peter Phillips (Princess Anne's son). 18 Australia. 19 Brian Lochore. 20 Auckland Warriors. 21 Bath. 22 Argentina. 23 Gareth Edwards. 24 Michael Dods. 25 Ranfurly Shield. 26 Lumberjack. 27 Nigel Walker. 28 Army doctor. 29 1995 World Cup semi-final v England. 30 Small volcanic island.

281

Quiz 42 Pot-Luck 19

Answers - see page 284

Level 3

1 What is the Duke of Argyll's stately home called?
2 In which month is Beaujolais Nouveau released for consumption?
3 Which spice comes from the crocus?
4 Who was the first person to sail single-handed non-stop around the world?
5 Which star is situated almost exactly above the North Pole?
6 What sort of creature is a tarantula hawk?
7 From which flower is digitalis obtained?
8 Whom did Harry Secombe play in the musical film "Oliver"?
9 Peter and Edmund were the boys, but which girls visited Narnia?
10 Which soccer club did Boris Becker have trials with?
11 What was the first British film to exceed the 20-million box office total?
12 Where was the world's first lighthouse, built of white marble?
13 Which Radio 4 show does Antony Clare host?
14 In music what key is a piece written in if it has five flats?
15 Which tree has English, white and slippery varieties?
16 Which English county is known as the "county of sunsets"?
17 Which psychiatrist wrote "Bird of Paradise"?
18 Who was the special guest on the 1,000th edition of "Wogan"?
19 Which politician had a dog called Pushinka?
20 Who in 1982 went topless at the England v Australia rugby game?
21 Which church leader had 27 wives?
22 Which is the brightest star?
23 Who invented the first safety match?
24 What is the function of scuppers on ships?
25 Which English queen banned mirrors as she grew old?
26 Which was the first stately home to open to the public?
27 When were driving tests first introduced in Britain?
28 Who was created by Mary Tourtel?
29 In Greek mythology which gift was given to Cassandra by Apollo?
30 Where would you find the *vox humana* and *vox angelica* together?

Answers

Modern History: Dictators (see Quiz 44)
1 Austria. 2 Art school. 3 Trying to overthrow the Bavarian government.
4 Night of the Long Knives. 5 Colonel Stauffenberg. 6 Axis. 7 Italian resistance. 8 Tonton Macoute. 9 First Consul. 10 Elba. 11 Generalissimo.
12 Man of steel. 13 National Movement. 14 1939. 15 Ferdinand Marcos.
16 Benigno Aquino. 17 Leopoldo Galtieri. 18 Very Mighty Ruler. 19 13.
20 Mao Tse Tung. 21 1979. 22 Born the same year. 23 General Zia.
24 Ceausescu. 25 Nicholas II. 26 Ho Chi Minh. 27 Pol Pot. 28 Tito.
29 Gaddafi. 30 Suharto.

282

Quiz 43 Rugby

Level 3

1 Why did A. E. Stoddart take over from R. L. Seddon as captain on the Lions' first tour of Australia and New Zealand?
2 Which rugby international won junior Wimbledon in 1966?
3 Whose Rugby League career lasted from 1929 to 1954?
4 Which African side was invited to the Rugby Union World Cup in 1987?
5 Which Moroccan was sent off in his first international for France in 1990?
6 What nationality is Murray Kidd?
7 For which club did fly half turned broadcaster Cliff Morgan play?
8 Which Irish winger was described by Bill McLaren as "an electric eel"?
9 Where was the first Rugby Union World Cup held?
10 Who did Russian Prince Obolensky play for in 1936?
11 Which was the first Union club to win the John Player Cup three years in a row?
12 Who kicked six penalty goals for Scotland on his debut in 1986?
13 Which England cricket captain was capped for England at rugby?
14 Which Irish doctor was capped at Rugby Union and soccer?
15 Who preceded Steve Sale as England captain?
16 What is South Africa's inter-provincial tournament called?
17 Which member of the royal family played in a rugby international?
18 In which country do Randwick play?
19 Who captained the 1967 touring All Blacks?
20 Which team did Andy Platt and Dean Bell join after leaving Wigan?
21 Which Union side won the League for the 4th consecutive season in 1994?
22 Which country did Hugo Porta play for?
23 Who won 53 caps without missing a single game?
24 Who scored all his team's points for Scotland in the 19-14 win against France in 1996?
25 What is New Zealand's inter-provincial championship called?
26 What was France's Olivier Merle's former profession?
27 Which Welsh player was a champion hurdler?
28 What is the occupation of Scotland's Rob Wainwright?
29 Which match was Jonathan Davies' last game of league for Wales?
30 What did New Zealanders suggest should be named after Jonah Lomu following the Rugby World Cup?

1 In which country was Hitler born?
2 What type of school did he attend in Munich?
3 Why was Hitler imprisoned in 1923?
4 What name was given to the occasion in 1934 when Hitler had members of his own party murdered by the SS?
5 Who tried to assassinate Hitler in 1944?
6 What name was given to the link between Hitler's Germany and Mussolini's Italy?
7 Which organization executed Mussolini?
8 Which civilian militia was established under Papa Doc Duvalier?
9 Which title did Napoleon take in 1799, instituting a military dictatorship?
10 What was Napoleon given sovereignty over after his abdication in 1814?
11 What title did Stalin assume when he became war leader?
12 What does the word "Stalin" mean?
13 What was Spain's only legal party after the Civil War?
14 When did Franco become absolute leader of Spain?
15 Who declared martial law in 1972 in the Philippines?
16 Which opposition leader in the Philippines was murdered in 1983?
17 Who was the leader of Argentina at the beginning of the Falklands War?
18 What does the name Genghis Khan mean?
19 How old was Ghenghis Khan when he succeeded his father?
20 Which leader launched his "Great Leap Forward" in 1958?
21 When did Saddam Hussein become president of Iraq?
22 Chaplin played a Hitler-like figure in "The Great Dictator" but what else did they have in common?
23 Which leader sanctioned the execution of President Bhutto in 1979?
24 Which Romanian leader was shot with his wife at Christmas 1989?
25 Who was the last tsar of Russia?
26 Which Vietnamese leader had a city named after him?
27 Who was the leader of the Khmer Rouge?
28 Which Communist leader's real name was Josip Broz?
29 Who overthrew King Idris to gain power in 1971?
30 Which Indonesian president was responsible for the invasion of East Timor in 1975?

Quiz 45 Pot-Luck 20

Level 3

Answers - see page 287

1 In which cathedral were the first Anglican women in Britain ordained?
2 What is the name of Jewish New Year?
3 Which confectionery product changed the colour of one of its sweets from light-brown to blue in 1989?
4 Who was Canada's first prime minister?
5 What were the first words spoken on a film soundtrack?
6 Which film won more Oscars than any other movie?
7 Who provided the voice for Woody Woodpecker?
8 W. C. T. Dobson is credited in the 1840s with sending the first what?
9 Who, in 1962, had a hit with "Speedy Gonzales"?
10 Which conductor said, "The English may not like music but they absolutely love the noise it makes"?
11 Which creature lost its tail in the doors of Noah's ark?
12 "In Utmost Good Faith" is the motto of which organization?
13 What is the devil's coach horse?
14 In which city is the British National Lifeboat Museum?
15 What was it that the American writer H. L. Mencken defined as "the worship of jackals by jackasses"?
16 Who were the two hosts of "Family Fortunes" before Les Dennis?
17 Which Beautiful South song begins, "He was just a social drinker..."
18 What was the first book printed from movable type in 1456?
19 What is the Pentateuch?
20 How many teeth does a mature male horse have?
21 By what name is the marsupial *Sarcophilus harrisi* better known?
22 What was produced by Henry D. Perky of Denver, Colorado, in 1893?
23 What is the colour of lobsters' blood?
24 The Greek for a "circle of animals" gave its name to what?
25 What is the largest and heaviest satellite in the solar system?
26 Which No 1 single included the bracketed words "In Perfect Harmony"?
27 Who invented the first replaceable razor blade?
28 What kind of lights were first used in 1868 near Parliament Square?
29 Where was the world's first cast-iron bridge built?
30 Horatio Nelson lost his right eye in 1794 at Calvi during the French Revolutionary War. When and where did he lose his right arm?

Answers

Pot-Luck 21 (see Quiz 47)
1 Anne Boleyn. 2 Scout. 3 Albert Einstein. 4 £12. 5 Frankie Valli. 6 A ray. 7 1964. 8 York. 9 1856. 10 Winston Churchill (about Stafford Cripps). 11 24. 12 Elias. 13 All anagrams of animals. 14 The chinook. 15 New Kids On The Block. 16 The Outlaws (in Richmal Crompton's books). 17 1965. 18 Tribophysics. 19 A labour. 20 Helium. 21 Francis II of France. 22 A reticulated python. 23 Gunner Parkin. 24 The Duke of Beaufort. 25 In 1842, after the First Opium War. 26 John Arbuthnot. 27 The Dog Star. 28 Dental caries. 29 A person who obtains income from investments. 30 Tom Morris.

Quiz 46 Pop: Instrumentals

Answers - see page 288

Level 3

1 The Shadows first record went to No 1 – what was it?
2 Who left The Shadows and recorded "Diamonds" on their own?
3 Whose first hit was "Lonely Bull" and then went on to be one of the most successful instrumentalists of all time?
4 What was Perez Prado's 1994/5 hit?
5 Which new record label was "Tubular Bells" recorded on?
6 Whose album was "Oxygène"?
7 Who won an Oscar for the music from "Chariots of Fire"?
8 Where and at what time was Kenny Ball chartwise in 1961?
9 Which film theme was a chart No 1 for the Hugo Montenegro Orchestra?
10 In 1994 which group had a No 1 with a record with the same name as themselves ?
11 Which military band had a hit with "Amazing Grace"?
12 Which clarinettist had an early 1960s hit with the theme for a TV serial?
13 Who recorded "Walk-Don't Run"?
14 Which instrument does Sandy Nelson play?
15 Which guitarist's real name is Brian Robson Rankin?
16 Which pianist's reply to criticism was "I cried all the way to the bank."?
17 Who recorded "Let's Have A Party" and "Let's Have Another Party"?
18 The theme from which TV serial gave Juan Martin a Top Ten hit?
19 Who was the leader of Manuel and his Music of the Mountains?
20 Who had a hit with "The Hustle"?
21 Which Vivaldi concertos were popularized by Nigel Kennedy?
22 Who had No 1s with "Side Saddle" and "Roulette"?
23 What was the title of the pieces on a theme by Paganini recorded by Julian Lloyd Webber?
24 Which instrument is Horst Jankowski playing in his "Walk in the Black Forest"?
25 Which group included Tristan Fry, Herbie Flowers and Kevin Peek?
26 Whose "March" took Joe Loss into the charts in 1964?
27 Which 1950s star was known as Mr Piano?
28 Who joined James Last on the recording "Together at Last"?
29 From which TV series did Jan Hammer's "Crockett's Theme" come?
30 Which guitarist had a hit with the theme from "The Deer Hunter"?

Geography: The Weather (see Quiz 48)
1 Egypt. 2 Relating to phenomena of the atmosphere. 3 Solstice. 4 Cumbria. 5 Cold front. 6 Fastnet. 7 Rockies. 8 Softly melted hail. 9 Cirrus. 10 Mirage, Strait of Messina, Italy. 11 Doldrums. 12 Dry, warm, blowing down a mountain. 13 Alaska (wind). 14 Grey. 15 Russian wind. 16 Occluded front. 17 Typhoon. 18 Spain. 19 German Bight. 20 South Africa. 21 12. 22 Iran and Afghanistan. 23 Sirocco. 24 Rhône. 25 Australia. 26 Isobars. 27 Eye of the storm. 28 Sandstorm. 29 Excessive dust, e.g. after a volcanic eruption. 30 Andes.

Answers

1 Which queen of England had 11 fingers?
2 In "The Lone Ranger" what was the name of Tonto's horse?
3 Which world-famous scientist said that any man who likes marching had been given a brain for nothing: just the spinal column would have done?
4 To £5 either way, how much did a colour TV licence cost in 1974?
5 How is Francis Castellucio beter known?
6 What type of fish is a torpedo fish?
7 In which year was Nelson Mandela sentenced to life imprisonment?
8 What is the British city of Eboracum called today?
9 To ten years either way, when was the Victoria Cross instituted?
10 Who said, "There but for the Grace of God, goes God"?
11 Into how many international time zones is the world divided?
12 What was Walt Disney's middle name?
13 What is the link between the words act, flow, loin and shore?
14 In the Rocky Mountains what is the dry wind that is warm in winter and cool in summer?
15 How did the group Nynuk become known in order to find chart success?
16 Which group were made up of Douglas, Ginger, Henry and William?
17 When did Rhodesia declare UDI?
18 What is the physics of friction properly called?
19 What is the collective noun for several moles?
20 What does hydrogen fuse into in the Sun's core?
21 Who was Mary Queen of Scots' first husband?
22 What is the longest snake in the world?
23 Which character was writing home to give the name to the series "It Ain't Half Hot Mum"?
24 Which duke owns Badminton, setting for the well-known horse trials?
25 To ten years either way, when did Hong Kong become a British crown colony?
26 Who invented the caricature John Bull?
27 How else is the star Sirius known?
28 What is the most common disease in the world?
29 What is a rentier?
30 Who won the first British Open Golf championship?

Quiz 48 Geography: The Weather (Level 3)

Answers - see page 286

1 Which country has the driest inhabited area in the world?
2 What does "meteorological" mean?
3 What name is given to an occasion when the equator is furthest from the Sun?
4 Which county is England's wettest?
5 Which usually travels faster, a cold front or a warm front?
6 Which sea area is immediately to the south of Ireland?
7 Over which mountains does the chinook blow?
8 What is graupel?
9 The name of which type of cloud is Latin for a lock of hair?
10 What is Fata Morgana and where would you see it?
11 What is the belt of light variable winds near the equator called?
12 What sort of wind is föhn wind?
13 Where would you experience a williwaw?
14 What colour are altostratus clouds?
15 What is the buran?
16 What is the name of a front where a cold front has overtaken a warm front?
17 What is a hurricane called in the Pacific?
18 Where is the tramontana?
19 Which sea area lies due east of Dogger and Humber?
20 Where does the berg wind blow?
21 What number does the Beaufort scale go up to in international use?
22 In which two countries does the Seistan sand wind blow?
23 What is the hot, dry North African wind which blows from the Sahara called?
24 Down which valley does the mistral blow?
25 Where would you experience a southerly buster?
26 What are lines joining places of equal atmospheric pressure called?
27 What is the centre of a hurricane called?
28 What does a haboob create?
29 What causes a blue moon?
30 Over which mountains does the pampero blow?

Quiz 49 Pot-Luck 22

Level 3

Answers - see page 291

1 Who confessed to opium eating?
2 Under what name did William White find fame on TV?
3 Difford and Tilbrook were songwriters for which group?
4 Who was Mussolini's mistress, who was executed with him?
5 What are the four groups that make up the ape family?
6 According to Lord Birkenhead, who devoted the best years of his life to preparing impromptu speeches?
7 Which creature is involved in the French equivalent of an April Fool?
8 Who was the first musician to be made a life peer?
9 What is the deepest lake in the world?
10 What is a male swan called?
11 Who said, "Genius is 1 per cent inspiration and 99 per cent perspiration"?
12 Which was the first country to make seat belts compulsory?
13 Who created and provided the voice of Basil Brush?
14 To ten years either way, when did Britain launch its first submarine?
15 In which country was Princess Margaret born?
16 In which decade did Pablo Picasso die?
17 Who said, "For years politicians have promised the moon. I am the first one to be able to deliver it."?
18 Which prison did Mike Hammer actor, Stacy Keach, spend time in?
19 In a 1980 tragedy who or what was Alexander Keilland?
20 What does the whale shark feed on?
21 Who left a fortune in his will to develop a new phonetic alphabet?
22 What is the only working distillery in Northern Ireland?
23 Who was the first king to award medals to his troops for bravery?
24 Who wrote "Bambi"?
25 Where in China is the Forbidden City?
26 Who drew the cartoon comic-strip character Andy Capp?
27 Although first to finish, why was Fred Lorz disqualified in the 1904 Olympic marathon?
28 Who said of his troops, "I don't know what effect these men will have upon the enemy but, by God, they terrify me"?
29 What is nephology?
30 Henry III put three barleycorns in a line to make which measurement?

Answers

Pot-Luck 23 (see Quiz 51) **1** The trapdoor failed to open. **2** Trinity College, Dublin. **3** Hattie Jacques. **4** Peru. **5** Edinburgh Festival. **6** Paul Merton. **7** Jensen and Vilfort. **8** Frankie Laine. **9** Because of the sacking of Viv Richards and Joel Garner. **10** Robert Ford. **11** The Duke of Wellington. **12** L.A. Law. **13** They both begin with the word 'midnight' **14** 18. **15** 18. **16** Putrid pot. **17** Orange. **18** Lord Northcliffe **19** Captain Blood. **20** Ruth Ellis. **21** 1950s. **22** Attempting to swim the rapids at Niagara Falls. **23** Reginald Perrin. **24** Teddy bear. **25** Peace. **26** The Humblebums. **27** July 29th, 1981. **28** Jim Fixed It For Me. **29** 81 per cent. **30** Netherlands.

Quiz 50 Pop: Euro Rockers

Answers - see page 292

Level 3 ▮▮▮

1 Which country won the first Eurovision song contest in 1956?
2 Which Austrian sang "Rock Me Amadeus" in 1986?
3 Who sang the song called "Volver a Empezar" in his own language?
4 Who was runner-up to Ireland's Linda Martin in the 1992 Eurovision?
5 From which countries were Enigma, who had a No 1 with "Sadness"?
6 "Raindrops Keep Falling on my Head" is Sacha Distel's only chart entry, but how many times did it do so?
7 Who was the first person to win Eurovision for Britain?
8 Whose first UK chart hit was "Joe Le Taxi"?
9 Which two songs has Cliff Richard sung in Eurovision?
10 Who had a hit with "Lambada" in 1989?
11 Which band had a hit with "Ça plane pour moi"?
12 "Young Parisians" was a hit for which UK band?
13 Which country won Eurovision with "A-Ba-Ni-Bi" and "Hallelujah"?
14 Who were the only UK Eurovision winners in the 1980s?
15 What was Nicole's "Ein bisschen Frieden" in English?
16 What is A-Ha's home country?
17 When Abba won Eurovision with "Waterloo" who represented Britain?
18 Who had a No 1 in 1981 with "Computer Love"?
19 In which year were there four Eurovision winners tying for first place?
20 What was Gigliola Cinquetti's 1974 hit whose second line was "Before you break my heart"?
21 Where do Clubhouse hail from, who had hits with "Do It Again – Billie Jean" and "Light My Fire"?
22 Which artist was the first to win Eurovision twice?
23 What was The New Seekers' 1972 Eurovision entry?
24 Which "Opportunity Knocks" winner represented Britain on Eurovision?
25 What nationality were Nina and Frederick who had a 1960 hit with "Little Donkey"?
26 Who was the first person to win Eurovision for Ireland?
27 Which Swiss band had a Top Ten hit with "The Race" in 1988?
28 For which event did Helmut Zacharias have a Melody hit in 1964?
29 Who won Eurovision for Britain in 1976?
30 What was unusual about the 1995 Eurovision song contest winner?

Answers

Tennis (see Quiz 52) **1** Olga Morozova. **2** The Queen. **3** Pancho Gonzales and Charlie Pasarell. **4** Eight games all. **5** Jean Borotra. **6** Helena Sukova. **7** Peter Fleming. **8** Roger Taylor. **9** Angela Mortimer, Christine Truman. **10** Australian. **11** Lori McNeil. **12** Kevin Curren. **13** Emilio, Javier. **14** Andrea Jaeger. **15** Lacoste. **16** It was televised. **17** Donald Budge. **18** Rod Laver. **19** Jaroslav Drobny. **20** Steffi Graf. **21** 1968. **22** Margaret Court, Maureen Connolly. **23** Wear white flannels instead of shorts. **24** Boris Becker. **25** George VI (1926). **26** Kathy Rinaldi. **27** John and Tracy Austin. **28** MCC. **29** Manuel Santana. **30** Chuck McKinley.

Quiz 51 Pot-Luck 23

Answers - see page 289

1 In 1885, after being sentenced to death by hanging, how did John Lee survive three attempts by the hangman?
2 Where is the Book of Kells?
3 Who was John Le Mesurier's second wife?
4 Which country did Paddington bear come from?
5 Which festival was founded in 1947 and run by Rudolf Bing?
6 Which entertainer started life as Paul Martin?
7 Who scored the goals in the 1992 European Championship final?
8 Who was the first performer to have British No 1 hits?
9 Why did Ian Botham resign from Somerset Cricket Club?
10 Who shot Jesse James?
11 Who was Arthur Wellesley better known as?
12 Which series featured the firm McKenzie, Brackman, Chaney and Kusak?
13 What is the lyrical link between "Memory" and "Green Door"?
14 How many French kings were named Louis?
15 In 1858 how many apparitions of the Virgin Mary did Bernadette Soubirous see at Lourdes?
16 What is the exact translation of "potpourri"?
17 What flavour does the liqueur curaçao have?
18 Which legendary pressman said, "News is something that someone somewhere doesn't want to see printed"?
19 Which film first established Errol Flynn's fame as a swashbuckling actor?
20 Who was the last woman to be hanged in Britain?
21 In which decade did Disneyland open in California?
22 How did English Channel swimmer Matthew Webb die?
23 Joan Greengross was secretary to which fictional salesman?
24 Which toy is named after US president Theodore Roosevelt?
25 In Greek mythology, what was Irene the goddess of?
26 Billy Connolly was a member of which group?
27 On what date was Prince Charles married to Lady Diana Spencer?
28 What words appear on a "Jim'll Fix It" medal?
29 To 5 per cent either way, what percentage of the adult male population in Britain smoked in 1947?
30 In which country did the sport of speed skating originate?

Answers

Pot-Luck 22 (see Quiz 49) **1** Thomas de Quincy. **2** Larry Grayson.
3 Squeeze. **4** Claretta Petacci. **5** Chimpanzees, gorillas, gibbons and orang-utans. **6** Winston Churchill. **7** Fish. **8** Benjamin Britten. **9** Lake Baikal.
10 A cob. **11** Thomas Edison. **12** Czechoslovakia. **13** Ivan Owen.
14 1901. **15** Scotland. **16** 1973. **17** Richard Nixon. **18** Reading Jail.
19 A floating hotel for North Sea rig workers. **20** Plankton. **21** George
Bernard Shaw. **22** Bushmills. **23** Charles I, in 1643. **24** Felix Salten.
25 Beijing. **26** Reg Smythe. **27** He journeyed part of the way by car.
28 The Duke of Wellington. **29** Meteorological study of clouds. **30** Inch.

Quiz 52 Tennis

Answers - see page 291

1 Whom did Chris Evert beat to win her first Wimbledon Singles title?
2 Who presented Virginia Wade with her Wimbledon trophy in 1977?
3 Who contested Wimbledon's longest-ever match?
4 At what score was the tie break used when it was first introduced at Wimbledon in 1971?
5 Which player was known as the "Bounding Basque"?
6 Which woman tennis player's mother was a Wimbledon finalist in 1962?
7 With which doubles partner did John McEnroe have most success?
8 Which British man got to three Wimbledon semi-finals in the 60s and 70s?
9 How are Mrs Barrett and Mrs Janes better known?
10 What nationality did Hana Mandlikova take after leaving Czechoslovakia?
11 Who knocked Steffi Graf out of Wimbledon in the first round in 1994?
12 Whom did Becker beat to become the youngest Wimbledon champion?
13 What are Aranxia Sánchez-Vicario's tennis-playing brothers' names?
14 Who was the first player Martina Navratilova beat to win Wimbledon after her first three victories over Chris Evert ?
15 Which French tennis player gave his name to a range of sportswear?
16 What "first" happened at Wimbledon in 1937?
17 Who was the first player to win the Grand Slam?
18 Who was tennis's first millionaire?
19 Which exiled Czech beat Ken Rosewall at Wimbledon in 1954?
20 Who played her first professional match against Tracy Austin in 1982?
21 In which year did Wimbledon go open?
22 Who were the only two women to win Grand Slams before Steffi Graf?
23 What is Yvon Petra famous for being the last man to do?
24 Who said on losing his title in the second round at Wimbledon, "I lost a tennis match, not a war. Nobody got killed."?
25 Which future king played a doubles match at Wimbledon?
26 Who was the first player to win all four US Girls Under 12 titles in 1979?
27 Who were the first siblings to win the Wimbledon Mixed Doubles?
28 Who did the LTA take over from in the management of tennis?
29 Who won the Men's Singles at Wimbledon in 1966 and lost in the first round the following year?
30 Who was the only American to win the Men's Singles at Wimbledon in the 60s?

Quiz 53 Pot-Luck 24

Level 3

Answers - see page 295

1 Whom did Peeping Tom see naked?
2 Who played the incidental music for the BBC's acclaimed drama "Edge Of Darkness"?
3 Who directed "The Seven Samurai"?
4 Where is the US National Radio Astronomy Observatory?
5 In Ancient Egypt what kind of bird is represented by Horus?
6 Which common water pollutant is believed to be harmful to babies?
7 What is the function of the Islets of Langerhans?
8 Which is the largest species of flatfish?
9 Where on the Pacific coast does the Trans-Siberian railway terminate?
10 Who designed the city of New Delhi?
11 Which new policy in 1958 was an attempt to achieve "true communism" in China?
12 Which element is the most toxic substance known?
13 Which philosopher invented "the Superman"?
14 Which Indian poet and philosopher was the first Asian to win the Nobel Prize for Literature?
15 How did the suffragette Emily Davison meet her death in 1913?
16 What was the codename of the US development of the atom bomb?
17 Which planet has the Great Red Spot?
18 Lully was composer at the court of which king?
19 What do the French call the English Channel?
20 The classic text about which sport was written by Izaak Walton in 1653?
21 Brazilian Oscar Niemeyer followed which profession?
22 What is the link between saying "Madam, I'm Adam" and "Ma, I am"?
23 What did Thomas Blood try to steal in London in 1671?
24 What is the name of the southern lights?
25 What element gives amethyst its violet colour?
26 How is Bob van Winkle better known?
27 What is the name given to the study of the origins of the cosmos?
28 Which technique developed by the painter Seurat uses small dabs of colour laid side by side?
29 Who was the first chairman of "The Good Old Days"?
30 Which month is named after a two-faced god?

Answers

Pot-Luck 25 (see Quiz 55)
1 Marco Polo. 2 Thomas Huxley. 3 Ralph Vaughan Williams. 4 Robert Frost.
5 Foudrinier. 6 Auguste and Louis Lumière. 7 The Birth of a Nation.
8 Anther. 9 Four. 10 Simon Dee. 11 Telemetry. 12 Minoan. 13 1986.
14 IMF – The International Monetary Fund. 15 In a flying accident. 16 American Civil War. 17 Académie Française. 18 Jingles. 19 Jean Baptiste de Lamarck. 20 Exxon Corporation. 21 Peter Dawson. 22 The end of the watch. 23 Order of the Purple Heart. 24 Whitby. 25 None. 26 Unchained Melody. 27 Vienna. 28 Boulder Dam. 29 Karen Blixen. 30 Hendrik Verwoerd.

Quiz 54 Pop: Frank Sinatra

Level 3

Answers - see page 296

1 What is Sinatra's middle name?
2 What are his children called?
3 What was Sinatra's own record label, founded in 1961, called?
4 Who was Sinatra's most frequent arranger in the 1940s?
5 For which film did Sinatra win an Oscar in 1953?
6 Which character in "The Godfather" is said to be based on Sinatra?
7 Which famous Sinatra song was the first to become a hit after being featured in a TV show?
8 Where was Sinatra born on 12 December 1915?
9 Which Sinatra hit was also a hit in Britain for Matt Monro?
10 What was Sinatra's big 1966 hit – a No 1 in 13 countries?
11 Who was Sinatra's second wife?
12 What was Sinatra's first No 1 in Britain?
13 What was the English version of "Comme d'Habitude"?
14 Which album did he release three years after announcing his retirement?
15 Which song did Sinatra sing in "Robin and the Seven Hoods"?
16 In which musical did he co-star with Gene Kelly?
17 From which musical does "The Lady is a Tramp" come and who did Sinatra sing it to in the film?
18 With which French singer did Sinatra duet in "Duets" in 1993?
19 Who was his male co-star in "Guys and Dolls"?
20 In which film did Sinatra co-star with Laurence Harvey, Janet Leigh and Angela Lansbury ?
21 Who sang with Sinatra on "Me and My Shadow"?
22 Which No 1 did Sinatra have with his elder daughter?
23 Which song won Sinatra a Grammy in 1965?
24 Who was Sinatra's third wife?
25 Which US cities feature in two of Sinatra's hit singles titles?
26 In which film did Sinatra sing the song with the lines "Have you heard, it's in the stars, next July we collide with Mars"?
27 Who was Sinatra's fourth wife, Barbara, previously married to?
28 What did the Sinatras call their 96-foot yacht?
29 In which year did "My Way" first hit the UK charts?
30 Which hit single did Sinatra record with Count Basie?

Quiz 55 Pot-Luck 25

Answers - see page 293

Level 3

1 Which explorer's last words were," I have not told half of what I saw"?
2 Who became known as "Darwin's bulldog"?
3 Which English composer wrote a Sea Symphony?
4 Who read "The Gift Outright" at President Kennedy's inauguration?
5 Which machine is used to manufacture paper industrially?
6 Which French brothers patented their cinematograph in 1895?
7 What is Griffith's film about the aftermath of the Civil War called?
8 What is the name of the body at the tip of a stamen?
9 How many pecks are there in a bushel?
10 Under what name did Nicholas Henty Dodd find fame as a DJ and TV personality?
11 What is the name given to the technique of measuring at a distance?
12 The existence of which civilization was confirmed by Arthur Evans' excavations on Crete?
13 In which year did the space shuttle Challenger explode?
14 What was set up after the Bretton Woods Conference.in 1944?
15 How did the car manufacturer, Charles Stewart Rolls, die?
16 In which war was the Battle of Shiloh?
17 Which body ensures the purity of the French language?
18 What is the name of the metal discs set in the rim of a tambourine?
19 Which French zoologist is associated with the concept that acquired characteristics can be inherited?
20 What is the United States' largest oil concern?
21 Who recorded under the aliases of Hector Grant, Charles Handy and Will Strong?
22 What does the ringing of eight bells mean on board a ship?
23 What is the earliest US military award for service beyond the call of duty?
24 At which place does the ship bringing Dracula to England land?
25 How many humps does a newborn camel have?
26 What is the most successful song written by Alex North and Hy Zaret?
27 Where were the first European coffee houses opened?
28 From 1933 to 1947 how was the Hoover Dam on the Colorado known ?
29 Who wrote "Out of Africa"?
30 Which prime minister of South Africa was assassinated in 1966?

Answers

Pot-Luck 24 (see Quiz 53) **1** Lady Godiva. **2** Eric Clapton. **3** Akira Kurosawa. **4** Greenbank. **5** Hawk. **6** Nitrate. **7** They secrete insulin. **8** Halibut. **9** Vladivostok. **10** Edwin Lutyens. **11** The Great Leap Forward. **12** Plutonium. **13** Friedrich Nietzsche. **14** Rabindranath Tagore. **15** She threw herself under the king's horse at the Derby. **16** Manhattan Project. **17** Jupiter. **18** Louis XIV. **19** La Manche. **20** Fishing. **21** Architect. **22** Both have the same letters reading forwards or backwards. **23** The crown jewels. **24** Aurora Australis. **25** Manganese. **26** Vanilla Ice. **27** Cosmogony. **28** Pointillism. **29** Don Gemmell. **30** January.

1   Against what is Hemingway's "For Whom the Bell Tolls" set?
2   Which US-born novelist lived much of his life in France and England and became a British citizen in 1915?
3   Who wrote,"Who's Afraid of Virginia Woolf?"?
4   In which Arthur Miller play do you meet Willy Loman?
5   What is a novel by Herman Melville and an opera by Benjamin Britten?
6   Where are most of Pearl S. Buck's novels set?
7   Who wrote the short story "I Robot" in 1950?
8   Who died at the age of 44 with his novel "The Last Tycoon" unfinished?
9   Who wrote the "Leatherstocking" tales of frontier life with their hero Natty Bumpo?
10   "A Farewell to Arms" is based on Hemingway's own experience as what in World War I?
11   Where were Robert Frost's poems first published?
12   Which character appears in all nine of Raymond Chandler's novels?
13   Who wrote "The Maltese Falcon"?
14   Holden Caulfield appears in which, once controversial, novel?
15   Which Norman Mailer novel is based on a protest march?
16   Whose novels are about social conditions in his native California?
17   Which dramatist wrote "Long Day's Journey Into Night"?
18   What is the setting for Hemingway's "The Old Man and the Sea"?
19   What is L. Frank Baum's most famous story?
20   Which US poet married Ted Hughes, later poet laureate?
21   Which Arthur Miller play is a comment on McCarthyism?
22   Which screenplay did Miller write for his wife Marilyn Monroe?
23   Who wrote plays with a political theme such as "The Little Foxes"?
24   Which poet spent time in a US mental hospital after supporting Mussolini and the Fascists in World War II?
25   Whose real name was Samuel Langhorne Clemens?
26   Who coined the phrase "the lost generations"?
27   In which Tennessee Williams play do you meet Big Daddy?
28   Who wrote the story of Rip van Winkle?
29   What type of writing is Paul Theroux associated with other than novels?
30   Whose most famous novel is "The Carpetbaggers"?

Quiz 57 Pot-Luck 26

Answers - see page 299

Level 3

1 Who was the first person to successfully climb the Matterhorn?
2 What was the name of the eldest of the Railway Children?
3 Whom did David Steel succeed as leader of the Liberal Party?
4 NaOH is the chemical formula for what?
5 What is the term for a group of monkeys?
6 Who conducted the Three Tenors concert?
7 In which month of the year did King Canute die?
8 What pigment comes from the cuttlefish?
9 In which country is the Napa Valley?
10 Who narrated the Paddington cartoon series?
11 Whose victory over the Danes is celebrated in Wiltshire's White Horse?
12 Which is the largest lake in the United Kingdom?
13 Which planet other than Venus does not have moons?
14 Which two people created "EastEnders"?
15 Which two words does the word modem come from?
16 In films how is Betty Joan Perske better known?
17 Which gaol made the mistake of installing door locks on the inside of the new visitors' waiting rooms?
18 Which record label did Jesus and Mary Chain first record on?
19 Which element has the symbol P?
20 Who said,"I want to be the white man's brother, not his brother-in-law"?
21 In what year was the first soccer World Cup broadcast on British TV in colour?
22 What's the link between Maria von Trapp of "The Sound Of Music" and Patrick Troughton of "Dr Who" fame?
23 Who designed the Spitfire?
24 When did the EEC become the EC?
25 Which pope occupied the Holy See for only two days?
26 Which 007 was once the "Big Fry" man in TV adverts?
27 The names of British racehorses are limited to how many letters?
28 Beverley Isherwood and Kathy Hynter were both on which programme?
29 Which river forms part of the frontier between Spain and Portugal?
30 Of which country did Leonid Kravchuk become President in 1991?

Answers

Pot-Luck 27 (see Quiz 59)
1 John Osborne. 2 Dorincourt. 3 Sir Geoffrey Howe. 4 Dry ice. 5 A skulk. 6 Dave Allen. 7 A seahorse. 8 Port. 9 Bedfordshire. 10 Adultery. 11 Stevie Wonder. 12 Horse. 13 1931. 14 Hazel. 15 Oxford Committee for Famine Relief. 16 Westminster Abbey. 17 Borstal, near Rochester, Kent. 18 The Kingston Trio. 19 Stalagmites. 20 Margaret Thatcher. 21 The turkey. 22 Carletonville, South Africa. 23 Tony Hancock. 24 The Soviet Union. 25 1959. 26 Johnny Cash. 27 George II. 28 Silkworms. 29 Pope John Paul II. 30 Please Please Me.

1 Which comedian performed stunts in "Just Nuts" and "The Freshman"?
2 Who produced the "Keystone Kops" films?
3 Which actress starred in "Modern Times"?
4 About which actress did Kenneth Tynan say, "What one sees in other women drunk, one sees in her sober"?
5 Who was directed by D. W. Griffith in "Birth of a Nation" in 1916?
6 In which film does Rudolph Valentino play a father and his son?
7 Who directed the 1923 version of "The Ten Commandments"?
8 Which 1920 film with Douglas Fairbanks was based on the novel "The Curse of Capistrano"?
9 Who was the star of "The Paleface" in 1922?
10 In which year was the first version of "Ben Hur" made?
11 Which memorabilia were sold at Christie's in 1987 for £82,500?
12 Who was the "It" girl?
13 Who was the only woman in the quartet who founded United Artists?
14 What is Rudolph Valentino's job in "Blood and Sand"?
15 Which 1925 film starred John Gilbert as an American in the war in 1917?
16 Which 1926 film was remade in 1952 with James Cagney and Dan Dailey?
17 Although a silent movie, what did "Way Down East" contain?
18 Who played opposite Chaplin in "The Tramp"?
19 Which actress stars opposite Mack Sennett in "Mack and Mabel"?
20 Who asked D. W. Griffith to make the film "Hearts of the World"?
21 Who was Gaston de Tolignac, screenwriter of "Hearts of the World"?
22 Which English actor/playwright starred in "Hearts of the World"?
23 Who wrote and starred in the 1922 version of "Robin Hood"?
24 Which film about early aviation starred Clara Bow and Gary Cooper?
25 What nationality was the hero Valentino played in "The Four Horsemen of the Apocalypse"?
26 Which two roles did Mary Pickford play in "Little Lord Fauntleroy"?
27 What was Fatty Arbuckle's real first name?
28 Who played the title role in the 1928 version of "Sadie Thompson"?
29 Who won the first-ever Oscar for best actress for "Seventh Heaven"?
30 Where does the action of Buster Keaton's "The Navigator" take place?

Answers

Golf (see Quiz 60)
1 Tom Watson. 2 Augusta, Georgia. 3 Bobby Locke. 4 Ted Ray. 5 Gary Player (South Africa). 6 Ben Hogan. 7 Ian Baker-Finch. 8 Tony Jacklin. 9 Supermex. 10 Cricket (Rod Marsh). 11 Byron Nelson. 12 Southport. 13 Wentworth. 14 Jack Nicklaus. 15 Portugal. 16 Newport, Rhode Island. 17 Muirfield. 18 Great Britain and Ireland. 19 Nick Faldo. 20 Curtis Cup. 21 British Open. 22 Ted Dexter. 23 Bobby Jones. 24 Amateurs. 25 Lee Trevino. 26 Richard Burton. 27 Christy O'Connor. 28 Bernard Gallacher. 29 Peter Oosterhuis. 30 Dwight D Eisenhower.

Quiz 59 Pot-Luck 27

Answers - see page 297

1 Who wrote the play "Look Back In Anger"?
2 Little Lord Fauntleroy's grandfather was the Earl of what?
3 Who was Margaret Thatcher's first chancellor of the exchequer?
4 What is solid carbon dioxide commonly called?
5 What is the collective name for a group of foxes?
6 How is David O'Mahoney better known?
7 What is the only male creature to carry and hatch eggs?
8 In polite circles, which drink should be passed to the left?
9 In which county is Woburn Abbey?
10 What shall you not commit according to the seventh commandment?
11 Who played every instrument on Cliff Richard's "She's So Beautiful"?
12 A centaur was a mythical creature half way between a man and what?
13 When was the gold standard finally abandoned in Britain?
14 Which tree has the alternative name of "cob"?
15 What name was OXFAM originally registered as?
16 Where is the Jacobean playwright Ben Jonson buried?
17 Where was the first borstal in Britain?
18 In folk music how were Dave Guard, Nick Reynolds and Bob Shane better known?
19 Which limestone formation found in caves grows upwards?
20 Who was turned down for a job at ICI in 1948 and later became a prominent politician ?
21 Which bird did Benjamin Franklin want to be the US emblem?
22 Where is the world's largest mine?
23 Which comedian was known as 'the lad himself'?
24 In 1920, which was the first country to legalize abortion?
25 In which year did the M1 motorway open?
26 Who started his career with the Tennessee Two?
27 Who was the last English monarch to be born abroad?
28 What do you breed if you are a sericulturist?
29 Who is the author of "Crossing the Threshold of Hope"?
30 What was the Beatles' first LP called in 1963?

Answers

Pot-Luck 26 (see Quiz 57)
1 Edward Whymper. 2 Roberta or Bobbie. 3 Jeremy Thorpe. 4 Caustic soda.
5 A troop. 6 Zubin Mehta. 7 November. 8 Sepia. 9 United States. 10
Michael Hordern. 11 Alfred the Great. 12 Lough Neagh, Northern Ireland.
13 Mercury. 14 Julia Smith, Tony Holland. 15 Modulate, demodulate. 16
Lauren Bacall. 17 Reading. 18 Blanco y negro. 19 Phosphorus. 20 Martin
Luther King. 21 1970. 22 They died on the same day (March 30th, 1987).
23 Reginald Joseph Mitchell. 24 1965. 25 Stephen II. 26 George Lazenby.
27 18 letters and spaces. 28 Countdown. 29 The Guadiana. 30 Ukraine.

1 Which American won the British Open Golf championship five times between 1975 and 1983?
2 Where is the US Masters held?
3 Which South African won the British Open in 1949, 1950, 1952 and 1957?
4 Which comedian took his name from the 1912 British Open?
5 Who was the first non-American postwar winner of the US Masters?
6 Which American played in the British Open only once and won it?
7 Faldo won the British Open in 1990 and 1092. Who won in 1991?
8 Who was the first Englishman to win the US Open after World War II?
9 What is Lee Trevino's nickname?
10 For which sport is Graham Marsh's brother famous?
11 Which US golfer had 11 successive tournament wins in 1945?
12 In which town is Royal Birkdale golf course?
13 Over which course is the World Matchplay Championship played?
14 Who won the US Masters in 1986 for a record sixth time?
15 In which country is Penina golf course?
16 Where was the first-ever US Open played in 1895?
17 What name did Jack Nicklaus give to his own golf course in honour of his favourite British course?
18 Who opposed the US in the Ryder Cup between 1973 and 1977?
19 Who won the English Amateur Championship in 1975 aged 18?
20 Which trophy is played for by women golfers from the United States in competition with Britain and Ireland?
21 Which is the oldest open championship in the world?
22 Which England cricket captain is an amateur golf champion?
23 Which golfer was responsible for the the US Masters?
24 What is the status of competitors in the Walker Cup?
25 In 1971 who won the US Open, the Canadian Open and the British Open?
26 Which actor shared his name with the winner of the 1939 British Open?
27 Which Irish golfer played in ten successive Ryder Cup teams?
28 Who captained the European team to victory in the 1995 Ryder Cup?
29 Who headed the European Order of Merit between 1971 and 1974?
30 Which US president's home was alongside the course on which the US Masters is played?

Answers

The Movies: Silent Cinema (see Quiz 58)
1 Harold Lloyd. 2 Mack Sennett. 3 Paulette Goddard. 4 Garbo. 5 Lillian Gish. 6 Son of the Sheikh. 7 Cecil B. de Mille. 8 The Mark of Zorro. 9 Buster Keaton. 10 1926. 11 Chaplin's hat and cane. 12 Clara Bow. 13 Mary Pickford. 14 Matador. 15 The Big Parade. 16 What Price Glory? 17 A colour sequence. 18 Edna Purviance. 19 Mabel Normand. 20 British government. 21 D. W. Griffith. 22 Noel Coward. 23 Douglas Fairbanks. 24 Wings. 25 Argentinian. 26 Young Cedric and his mother. 27 Roscoe. 28 Gloria Swanson. 29 Janet Gaynor. 30 Transatlantic liners.

Quiz 61 Pot-Luck 28

Level 3

Answers - see page 303

1 Where were the 1952 Olympic Games held?
2 What colour was Rupert Bear's face in early books and annuals?
3 Where did the world's first controlled nuclear reaction take place in 1942?
4 What is the collective name for a group of bears?
5 In our solar system which planet is farthest from the Sun?
6 "Mastermind" participants are never known as contestants. What are they known as?
7 Which big cat has the proper name *Acinonyx jubatus*?
8 Who ordered the building of the Pavilion at Brighton ?
9 What is the side away from the wind called on a ship?
10 What was Robin's real name in the Batman TV series?
11 Which fish walks on land?
12 What does the musical term *Vivace* mean?
13 What was the real title of the painting called "The Laughing Cavalier"?
14 Which king was known as "Silly Billy"?
15 Who designed the first mechanical adding machine in 1641?
16 In which country did a cultural revolution take place during 1966–69?
17 Who drew the Katzenjammer Kids for the "New York Journal" in 1910?
18 Who was the first Irish athlete to win gold in the European Championships?
19 Which scale measures the effects of an earthquake at a particular place?
20 What is the vitamin riboflavin?
21 Which is the second largest island in the world after Australia?
22 Who was Jan Ludvik Hoch better known as?
23 What was the surname of soul musician Booker T.?
24 Which country has finished second most times in the Eurovision Song Contest?
25 In which Alpine range is the Swiss mountain, Jungfrau?
26 What nationality was the first non-US, non-Soviet spaceman?
27 Which treaty, signed by 32 countries, agreed to peaceful scientific research?
28 Where in Italy was Mussolini executed?
29 Which doctor searches for a one-armed man in "The Fugitive"?
30 What was the surname of the Windsors before they changed it?

Pot-Luck 29 (see Quiz 63)
1 Train á Grande Vitesse. 2 Giant Squid. 3 Edgar Degas. 4 Glasgow.
5 Mount of Olives. 6 Lincoln. 7 Marbles. 8 A fox. 9 Bull & Finch. 10
John Hinckley. 11 Happiness. 12 A knight in armour. 13 Rowland Hill.
14 Stanley Baldwin. 15 Charlie Chaplin. 16 Cherries. 17 The nine of
diamonds. 18 Tent stitch. 19 Barbados. 20 Shetland Islands. 21 A tax to
buy off the Danish invaders. 22 The typewriter. 23 Education. 24 The
Pearl Fishers. 25 St Giles High Street. 26 Nose bleed. 27 Dow Jones Index.
28 Henry Hall. 29 Somnus. 30 Wells.

Answers

Quiz 62 Pop: No 1s

Answers - see page 304

Level 3 ▮▮▮

1 What were Jimmy Young's two successive No 1s in 1955?
2 What was John Lennon's second No 1 hit, a month after his first?
3 Which was the first record to hit No 1 on two different occasions?
4 What was Anthony Newley's 1960 No 1?
5 Which title was a No 1 for Kylie Minogue and Johnny Nash?
6 Elton John's first hit was in 1971. When was his first solo No 1?
7 Who had three No 1s 11 years after first entering the charts solo?
8 With which two groups did Gerry Marsden have the same No 1?
9 Who is the only person to have a No 1 in each of five decades?
10 What novelty record, by an Australian, was the first No 1 single of the 70s?
11 What were Art Garfunkel's first two hits at No 1?
12 Who took their first three hits to No 1 in 1984?
13 Which solo artist has had most weeks at No 1?
14 Who is the oldest person to have a No 1?
15 Who is runner-up to Madonna as female star with most weeks at No 1?
16 Who were the two different backing groups which accompanied Cliff Richard on two No 1 versions of "Livin' Doll"?
17 In 1954 "Oh Mein Papa" and "Oh! My Pa Pa" were recorded by different men with the same christian name, what is it?
18 Mother and son, Hilda and Rob Woodward, reached No 1 as what?
19 Who is the youngest person to have topped the charts?
20 What were Rod Stewart's first two No 1 hits?
21 How many consecutive No 1s did The Beatles have between 1963 and 1966?
22 What were Abba's three consecutive No 1s in 1975–76?
23 Which No 1, later a hit for Robson and Jerome, was at the top spot for 18 weeks?
24 Who has David Bowie had No 1 records with?
25 What were Adam Faith's two No 1s?
26 What was the Boomtown Rats' first No 1?
27 Who were the two acts who had No 1s with "Without You"?
28 Which No 1 links Elvis Presley and UB40?
29 Who sang with UB40 on their No 1 "I Got You Babe"?
30 Which song was a No 1 for Joe Cocker and Wet, Wet, Wet?

Behind the Iron Curtain (see Quiz 64) **1** Churchill. **2** Pravda. **3** Union of Soviet Socialist Republics. **4** Glasnost. **5** COMECON (Council for Mutual Economic Assistance). **6** Warsaw Pact. **7** Albania. **8** German Democratic Republic. **9** Yugoslavia. **10** Hungary. **11** Khrushchev. **12** Prague Spring. **13** Jaruzelski. **14** Human rights. **15** 1961. **16** Cold War. **17** Perestroika. **18** Erich Honecker. **19** Shipyards. **20** Committee for State Security. **21** 1958. **22** Brezhnev. **23** Milan Kundera. **24** Gerald Ford. **25** East Germany. **26** Walter Ulbricht. **27** Ronald Reagan. **28** Leningrad. **29** Shevardnadze. **30** Each country to construct foreign policy on a "my way" basis.

302

Quiz 63 Pot-Luck 29

Level 3

1 In France what do the initials TGV mean?
2 What is the largest living invertebrate?
3 Which French artist is known for his paintings of the ballet and dancers?
4 Which city comes from two Gaelic words and means "the place in the green hollow"?
5 Which hill marks the traditional site of the Ascension in the Bible?
6 Which is the third-largest cathedral in England?
7 Which competition is held on Good Friday at Tinsley Green, Sussex?
8 What type of animal was J. Worthington Foulfellow?
9 Exterior shots in "Cheers" featured a real bar. What was its name ?
10 Who shot Ronald Reagan in March 1981?
11 Of what is the bluebird a symbol?
12 Who would have worn a gorget, pauldron, beaver and greave?
13 Who instituted the penny post in England?
14 Who was the British prime minister when Edward VIII abdicated?
15 Which film star had his feet insured for $150,000?
16 With what is the Belgian beer Kriek flavoured?
17 Which playing card is referred to as the "curse of Scotland"?
18 In needlework, which stitch may be described as "petit point"?
19 Which paradise holiday island is the most easterly of the West Indies?
20 On which islands is the ceremony of Uphellya celebrated?
21 What, in English history, was the Danegeld?
22 With which invention of 1801 is the Italian, Pellegrine Tarri, credited?
23 Before he became party leader what was Neil Kinnock's shadow post?
24 In which work do Nadir and Zurga appear?
25 Which London street was the site of a former leper colony?
26 What is epistaxis, a common complaint, the medical term for?
27 What is the US equivalent of the Financial Times Index?
28 Whose autobiography was entitled "Here's to The Next Time"?
29 What was the name of the Roman god of sleep?
30 Which is England's smallest city?

Quiz 64 Behind the Iron Curtain (Level 3)

Answers - see page 302

1 Who first popularized the expression "Iron Curtain"?
2 Which newspaper used "Iron Curtain" earlier in the sense of protection?
3 What was the official name of the Soviet Union?
4 What was the name given to Gorbachev's foreign relations programme?
5 What was the communist economic association called?
6 Which treaty organization was set up as a counterpart to NATO?
7 Which eastern European country maintained close relations with China?
8 What was East Germany's official name?
9 Which communist country remained outside the military alliance of eastern bloc countries in 1955?
10 In which country were the AVF the security police?
11 Who succeeded Stalin as Communist Party leader?
12 What was the period of liberalization in Czechoslovakia in 1968 called?
13 Which general introduced martial law in Poland in 1981?
14 What was the Czech Charter 77 protesting about in 1977?
15 In which year was the Berlin Wall built?
16 What name was given to the state of tension between the communist states and the west after World War II?
17 What name was given to the reform programme initiated by Gorbachev?
18 Who was East Germany's last Chairman of the Council of State?
19 Where in Gdansk was Solidarity founded?
20 What were the KGB in the Soviet Union?
21 When was the Hungarian uprising?
22 Who was the first Soviet statesman to hold the posts of general secretary and president simultaneously?
23 Which exiled Czech wrote "The Joke"?
24 Which US president said in a TV interview in 1976, "There is no Soviet domination of Eastern Europe."?
25 Which communist state was ruled by the Volkskammer?
26 Who was the leading statesman of East Germany in the 1950s and 1960s?
27 Who described the Soviet Union as "The Evil Empire"?
28 What was St Petersburg called during communist rule?
29 Which Soviet foreign minister formulated the Sinatra doctrine?
30 Why was the Sinatra doctrine so called?

Quiz 65 Pot-Luck 30

Answers - see page 307

1 Where are the painted lakes?
2 What name is given to a young hawk taken from its nest for training?
3 Where in London would you find the sculpture of Prospero and Ariel?
4 Under which king was the Royal Observatory at Greenwich built?
5 Who, according to the Book of Samuel in the Bible, was born in Gath?
6 Which is the largest Gothic church in northern Europe?
7 What names are given to the old and new styles of calendar?
8 Musky Muskrat was the sidekick of which cartoon lawman?
9 What are Micmac, Cree and Ojibwa?
10 Which signal replaced the CQD signal in 1906?
11 What is the botanical emblem of Australia?
12 Who would wear an orphrey, morse and cope and carry a crozier?
13 What did the Polish oculist Dr L. Zamenhof invent?
14 Who was elected the first woman Lord Mayor of London in 1983?
15 Who gained an honorary Oscar in 1985 for 50 years of performing?
16 Which Scandinavian alcoholic spirit is made from potatoes?
17 In which country did the card game bridge originate?
18 Which residential university college was founded in 1899 for working people?
19 What are the Tonga Islands otherwise known as?
20 From which tower of the New Palace of Westminster does the Union Jack fly by day?
21 Which English king invented a candle clock?
22 What Latin word is used to express the meaning "word for word"?
23 What did the American Hamilton Smith invent in 1858?
24 Where was the last battle between Britain and the United States?
25 In which London street is Hamley's toy shop?
26 What is the common name for the disease called trismus?
27 What is the French equivalent of the Stock Exchange?
28 Who composed the Symphony No 7, known as "the Leningrad"?
29 Who was the Greek goddess of victory?
30 Where are the birthplace and statue of King Alfred the Great?

Answers **Pot-Luck 31** (see Quiz 67)
1 Victoria Falls. 2 Chlorophyll. 3 Iolanthe. 4 The Vedas. 5 Princess of Wales. 6 St Matthew. 7 Lactose. 8 Hong Kong harbour. 9 Lloyd George. 10 Morris Garages. 11 Lord Scarman. 12 A glider. 13 China. 14 Bud Flanagan. 15 1967. 16 Wedge. 17 Connecticut. 18 Gynocracy. 19 Barnum. 20 The Althing. 21 Jesuits. 22 Gypsy Rose Lee. 23 The kukri. 24 A dance. 25 Canada. 26 Touchstone. 27 Goering. 28 Caves. 29 The Atholl Highlanders. 30 Alpenstock.

1 Which hero is Beethoven's "Eroica" Symphony said to be named after?
2 Who were J. S. Bach's two sons?
3 What is the nationality of composer Isaac Albéniz?
4 On which instrument is Handel's "Harmonious Blacksmith" played?
5 What type of horns feature in Haydn's Symphony No 31 in D?
6 Whose ebony clarinet was Stravinsky's Clarinet Concerto written for, thus giving it the nickname "Ebony"?
7 In which country was Greek composer Iannis Xenakis actually born?
8 What was Vivaldi's profession aside from violinist and composer?
9 What type of works did John Wilbye compose?
10 To which composer is Bruckner's Symphony No 3 in D minor dedicated?
11 Who was Britten's Simple Symphony written for?
12 Which Gilbert and Sullivan opera has the subtitle "Flowers of Progress"?
13 Who wrote the tone poem "Tintagel"?
14 Which keyboard instrument did John Bull specialize in?
15 Which American folk hero is the title of a ballet by Aaron Copland?
16 What is Debussy's dreamlike music often called?
17 What type of work is Elgar's "Dream of Gerontius"?
18 Which honorary degree was Haydn receiving when his Oxford Symphony was first performed?
19 Which modern English composer wrote the opera "Punch and Judy"?
20 Which two Russian revolutions does Shostakovich commemorate in his 11th and 12th symphonies?
21 What is the "joke" which gives Haydn's String Quartet in E flat its name?
22 Which Soviet republic did Khachaturian come from?
23 For which musical instrument were Liszt's "Liebesträume" written?
24 How many major symphonies did Mahler write?
25 What was Mussorgsky's first name?
26 Including interval time, how long does a performance of Richard Wagner's "Gotterdämmerung" last?
27 Which rival of Mozart has been accused, falsely, of poisoning him?
28 Who wrote "The Snow Maiden" and "The Golden Cockerel"?
29 What is the "Miracle" which gave Haydn's Symphony No 96 its name?
30 What were Johann Stamitz's "Mannheim rockets"?

1 What is the biggest tourist attraction in Zambia?
2 What name is given to the green colouring matter found in plants?
3 What was Reginald Perrin's middle name in the sit com with Leonard Rossiter?
4 What name is given to the four holy books of the Hindus?
5 Who represented the Queen at the funeral of Princess Grace in 1982?
6 Who is the patron saint of tax collectors?
7 What is the name of the sugar found in milk?
8 Where did the passenger liner "Queen Elizabeth" catch fire in 1972?
9 Who was the first prime minister to occupy Chequers?
10 What do the initials MG stand for on a sports car?
11 Who headed the inquiry into the Brixton Riots in 1981?
12 What kind of aircraft was the World War II Horsa?
13 Where did the Boxer Rising take place between 1898 and 1900?
14 What was the stage name of the British comedian Robert Winthrop?
15 In which year did the British breathalyzer law come into force?
16 In golf what is the traditional name for the number ten iron?
17 Which US state is called the Nutmeg state?
18 What name is given to a government ruled by women?
19 Which show became in 1981 the most heavily insured in British theatre?
20 What is the Icelandic parliament called?
21 What were the names of the followers of Ignatius Loyola?
22 How is Rose Louise Hovick better known?
23 What name is given to the knife which the Gurkha soldiers use?
24 What is a saraband?
25 In which country would you find the Laurentian Mountains?
26 What was the name of the jester in "As You Like It"?
27 Who created the German Luftwaffe?
28 What does a speleologist study?
29 What is the name of Britain's only private army?
30 What is the name of the long staff with an iron tip used in mountaineering ?

Quiz 68 Natural Phenomena

Answers - see page 306

1 What fell in Coffeyville, Kansas, the size of a melon, in September 1970?
2 What is the highest standard cloud formation called?
3 Where is the most thundery place on earth?
4 What occurred in the Kalahari Desert on September 1st, 1981?
5 Where did the longest-lasting rainbow glow for three hours?
6 What name is given to the bending of the winds caused by the Earth spinning on its axis?
7 Which volcanic eruption gave the loudest sound ever recorded?
8 Where is the wettest place in England?
9 What is the name given to the lightning which clings to ships' masts?
10 What are the seven colours of the rainbow in their correct order?
11 What is the name for a column of swiftly spinning air?
12 What name is given to the phenomenon of bright lights in the atmosphere caused by the solar wind entering the ionosphere?
13 What are caused by changes in the level of the ocean floor?
14 What occurs when the central zone of the Sun is covered?
15 What are the "Ring of Fire" and "Alpine Belt"?
16 Which patrol group keeps track of all icebergs?
17 Which is the largest active volcano on Earth?
18 What forms when a tornado runs over water?
19 Which lake is the deepest in the world?
20 Which island emerged from the sea off the coast of Iceland in 1963?
21 Which Greek philosopher was responsible for 5th-century BC studies in vulcanology?
22 Where did the strongest earthquake ever recorded take place in 1960?
23 Which is the only active volcano in Antarctica?
24 What is a vent in the Earth's crust that spouts a fountain of boiling water?
25 Which volcanic rock is so strongly charged with gas that it appears frothy and floats on water?
26 What occurs when a lunar eclipse take place?
27 What is a rising air current caused by heating from below called?
28 What are Tugela and the Buyoma?
29 What name is given to a volcanic opening that gives out gas and steam?
30 What scale, other than the Richter, measures earthquakes?

Classical Music (see Quiz 66)
1 Napoleon I. 2 Carl Philip Emanuel, Johann Christian. 3 Spanish. 4 Harpsichord. 5 Hunting horns. 6 Woody Herman. 7 Romania. 8 Priest. 9 Madrigals. 10 Wagner. 11 Young people. 12 Utopia Limited. 13 Sir Arnold Bax. 14 Virginals. 15 Billy the Kid. 16 Musical impressionism. 17 Oratorio. 18 Doctorate. 19 Harrison Birtwhistle. 20 1905, 1917. 21 Several false endings. 22 Armenia. 23 Piano. 24 Nine. 25 Modest. 26 Six hours. 27 Antonio Salieri. 28 Rimsky-Korsakov. 29 Chandelier said to have fallen, but injured no one. 30 Brilliant scale passages.

Quiz 69   Pot-Luck 32

Answers - see page 311

1 What, in computer terminology, do the initials COBOL stand for?
2 What are the two types of camel?
3 Which character announced "I'm not here" in times of crisis in "Drop the Dead Donkey"?
4 What name is given to the highest point of the heavens?
5 Who replaced Gilly Coman as Aveline in "Bread"?
6 In which city was the first boy scout troop registered?
7 On which date does International Labour Day fall?
8 Who created the popular 1920s cartoon character Felix the Cat?
9 Leap-Frog, The Gallant Hussar and Ampleforth are all types of what?
10 By what nickname was the criminal Albert De Salvo better known?
11 How many points has a Star of David?
12 What is the lace scarf worn over the head by Spanish women called?
13 Which Frenchman discovered the St Lawrence River?
14 Who was the BBC's principal TV commentator during the Queen's coronation?
15 Who became an overnight sex symbol when she made the film "10"?
16 Which drink do you associate with Holy Island in Northumberland?
17 Which English king reigned the longest?
18 In bridge, what jargon word describes "holding no trumps"?
19 What was the title of the first women's magazine ever published, in 1693?
20 What name is given to a whirling tornado-like cloud at sea?
21 Of which island republic is Antananarivo the capital?
22 The first of what was appropriately called "The Original"?
23 With which invention is William Le Baron Jenny of the United States credited?
24 What was the title of John Wayne's final film?
25 Which stretch of water separates Sicily from Italy?
26 What is the Japanese word for goodbye?
27 Who was the author of "Carrie's War"?
28 Which musical instrument do you associate with Dizzy Gillespie?
29 By what name is Portuguese West Africa now known?
30 Which early film star was widely known as the "world's sweetheart"?

Level 3

1 Who played for Doncaster Rovers at football and Leicestershire at cricket in September 1975?
2 Which Young Player of the Year in 1951 was the first to captain England?
3 Who was the last England captain to play South Africa before the ban?
4 Who won the county championships in every season from 1951 to 1958?
5 Where in the West Indies did Brian Lara score his record-breaking 375?
6 Who was the first player to make over 1,000 catches in first-class cricket?
7 What did ICC stand for before 1965?
8 Who were the first winners of the Women's World Cup in 1973?
9 What is Bob Willis's middle name?
10 Which England batsmen each scored double centuries against India in 1985 in the same innings?
11 Who was the first batsman to score 10,000 runs in Test cricket?
12 In which country are the first-class sides United Bank and National Bank?
13 Who were the first three members of the ICC?
14 What was the Nat West Trophy previously called?
15 In the 1986 season who was the youngest player to do over 2,000 runs?
16 Who kept wicket for Yorkshire in 412 consecutive county championships?
17 Who succeeded Mike Brearley as England cricket captain?
18 Who scored 322 runs against Warwickshire in less than a day in 1985?
19 In which country do first-class teams compete for the Plunkett Shield?
20 Who did a former England manager turn professional with to play football in 1956?
21 What is the trophy played for by first-class inter-state sides in India?
22 Who captained England during the "bodyline" series?
23 Who was the first bowler to take 300 Test wickets?
24 Which batsman's nickname was 'The Barnacle'?
25 What has South Africa's Currie Cup been renamed?
26 Who said, "The bowler's Holding, the batsman's Willey"?
27 In 1986 what record was set by Indian Test player Aggarwahl?
28 Which two cricketers were BBC Sports Personality of the Year between 1956 and 1981?
29 In what way does Sobers still hold a record with 365 runs?
30 Which cup succeeded the Shell Shield in the West Indies?

Quiz 71 Pot-Luck 33

Level 3

1 Whose final opera was called "Death in Venice"?
2 Which Greek mountain is consecrated to the muses?
3 Whose secret service code names are Potus and Flotus?
4 Which bird is sometimes called the windhover?
5 What is the national flower of Mexico?
6 Who lives at Number 12 Downing Street?
7 Which was the first British newspaper to issue a colour supplement?
8 Which religious sect was founded by J. N. Darby and E. Cronin?
9 Which British king was the first to own and drive a motor car?
10 Who is the patron saint of wine growers?
11 What name is given to an alloy of mercury?
12 In which shipyards were the "Queen Mary" and "QE2" built?
13 What is the traditional name for the number 3 wood in golf?
14 By what name is the Russian, Nicolai Poliakoff, better known?
15 Who wrote the classic Irish play "Cock-a-Doodle Dandy"?
16 Who won the '96 Oscar for Best Actress?
17 What name is given to the study of the paths taken by projectiles?
18 Which year saw the deaths of James Hunt and Les Dawson?
19 Which city in Ontario is known as Steel City of Canada?
20 What do maiden, mother-of-all and footman have in common?
21 Which British city is served by Aldergrove airport?
22 In tennis, what name is given to the women's World Cup?
23 Which royal estate was bought by Prince Albert for £31,000?
24 Divali, or the Festival of Lights, is a celebration in which religion?
25 Who was president of the United States during the Wall Street crash of 1929?
26 What is the name given to the female reproductive organ of a flower?
27 To which group of birds does the capercaillie belong?
28 Who was the "dancing chancellor" during Queen Elizabeth I's reign?
29 What was the name of the pub in "Minder"?
30 Who was the king of Sparta who was husband to Helen of Troy?

Quiz 72 Animals

Answers - see page 310

Level 3

1 In which London borough was Cruft's first held?
2 Which is the only snake to be found regularly north of the Arctic Circle?
3 Which breed of setter is named after an English duke?
4 What is a dik-dik?
5 Which animal is the symbol of the US Republican party?
6 What are goannas and anoles?
7 Which breed of dog is a cross between an Irish wolfhound and a greyhound?
8 What general name is given to manatees and dugongs?
9 Of which family is the linsang a member?
10 What is unusual about a chameleon's eyes?
11 What region is the arrow-poison frog a native of?
12 What group of insects include German, American and common?
13 Which animal might be Siberian or Caspian?
14 What do entomophagous animals eat?
15 What are the five groups of vertebrates?
16 What are oviparous animals?
17 What do horse, snake and scorpion have in common?
18 Which largest rodent became a serious pest in East Anglia?
19 What are the tail fins of a whale called?
20 Which is the largest of all the animal phyla?
21 What are stag, rhinoceros and tiger other than animals in their own right?
22 What sort of animal is a fennec?
23 Where are the ayaye the remaining endangered animals?
24 What does an impala do when frightened?
25 What country are Père David's deer native to?
26 What name is given to a mammal which bears live young?
27 What is a group of hedgehogs called?
28 What is another name for an Old English terrier?
29 What is a sand mason?
30 What is a Clydesdale?

Answers

Cricket (see Quiz 70)
1 Chris Balderstone. 2 Peter May. 3 M.. J. K. Smith. 4 Surrey. 5 Antigua.
6 Frank Woolley. 7 Imperial Cricket Conference. 8 England. 9 Dylan. 10 Mike Gatting, Graeme Fowler. 11 Sunil Gavaskar. 12 Pakistan. 13 England, Australia, South Africa. 14 Gillette Cup. 15 Graeme Hick. 16 Jimmy Binks. 17 Ian Botham. 18 Ian Botham. 19 New Zealand. 20 Charlton. 21 Ranji Trophy. 22 Douglas Jardine, Surrey. 23 Fred Trueman. 24 Trevor Bailey. 25 Castle Currie Cup. 26 Brian Johnston. 27 Her 190 was a world women's Test record. 28 Jim Laker, Ian Botham. 29 Not out. 30 Red Stripe Cup.

Quiz 73 Pot-Luck 34

Level 3

Answers - see page 315

1 The Plains of Abraham overlook which city?
2 What were Vince's parents called in "Just Good Friends"?
3 Which French painter and sculptor created "The Pink Nude"?
4 By what other name is the constellation Pyxis known?
5 What is majolica?
6 Where is Santiago de Compostela?
7 To which family of flowers does the pimpernel belong?
8 What does the "M" stand for in Richard M. Nixon's name?
9 Whose final words were, "So little done, so much to do"?
10 Which is the smallest Canadian province?
11 What are the other three Christian names of Prince Charles?
12 The Three Stars is the national ice-hockey team of which country?
13 What was the name of the bar in "Dallas"?
14 Which is the only English city whose ancient walls are complete?
15 The Sam Maguire Trophy is the major competition in which sport?
16 What is the stage name of Carol Bongiovi's rock star son?
17 Which US actress was known as "the sweater girl"?
18 What is General Sherman in the Sequoia National Park?
19 Who along with Sitting Bull led the Native Americans at the Battle of Little Big Horn?
20 The Pindus are the principal mountain range of which country?
21 In boxing, who was known as the 'Ghost with the hammer in his hand'?
22 In yachting, what is a metal mike?
23 Who was the first Australian cricketer to be knighted?
24 What caused Prince Albert's death in 1861?
25 Who in 1989 said, "The Communist party has no God-given right to rule"?
26 What is a basenji?
27 Which planet did Mariner 9 photograph in 1971–72?
28 "Vision of a Knight" was the work of which Florentine painter?
29 What type of animal is a bariroussa?
30 By what other name do we know the Somers Islands?

Pot-Luck 35 (see Quiz 75) **Answers** 1 Missile Defence Alarm System. 2 A wild goat. 3 The Inland Revenue. 4 They are meteorites. 5 Exodus. 6 A minaret. 7 Pickpocket. 8 A distress signal. 9 Prince Henry of Portugal. 10 Glen Miller, Chattanooga Choo Choo. 11 Nelson Mandela and F. W. de Klerk. 12 Joan Crawford. 13 Pikelets. 14 The Sorbonne, Paris. 15 Mexico. 16 Perth. 17 Launching missiles or stones. 18 Fidel Castro. 19 All are types of wine glass. 20 India. 21 Burt Reynolds. 22 Paraguay. 23 Ludicrus Sextus. 24 The Weir of Hermiston. 25 Marie Lloyd. 26 Shoulder blade. 27 Hungarian. 28 A single horse hair. 29 John Dryden. 30 Bamboo.

Quiz 74 TV: Memorable Moments (Level 3) ▮▮▮

Answers - see page 316

1 Which TV personality had government minister John Nott walk out on him during an interview in 1983?

2 Whom did Malcolm Ryder try to poison so as to claim insurance?

3 Which EastEnder received a marriage proposal from Benny Bloom?

4 How did camerawoman Lee Lyon die whilst filming "Survival"?

5 Who appeared on TV in 1974 as she held up a bank in San Francisco?

6 What feature was dropped from "The Great Egg Race" in 1981?

7 Whom did Connie Hall stab in 1988 in Dallas?

8 Who sat on a protesting lesbian during the 6 o'clock news in 1988 and who continued to read the news?

9 Which series ended when Tara King sent the main character into space?

10 Which soap saw Jason Gioberti die in its first episode?

11 Who rescued Bet when the Rovers Return caught fire?

12 Who presented the first British TV programme of birds in their natural habitat?

13 In addition to the "Blue Peter" team, who took part in the 1971 safari?

14 Who was ditched by Dame Edna for being boring?

15 How many people died in the Crossroads motel fire?

16 Who admitted that her face erupted when she first used Camay soap?

17 Who was the first British politician to have a televised state funeral?

18 Which sporting event was the first programme to be in colour?

19 What did Brian Connell have that no other newsreader had?

20 Which soap's first death was May Hardman on December 31st, 1960?

21 In which year were subtitles first included in the Queen's speech?

22 Which newsreader's drugs for epilepsy made him appear to be drunk?

23 What TV first did Gareth Jones achieve during a live transmission?

24 Whose was the first televised royal funeral?

25 Which "Blue Peter" team member was knocked out by a flying marrow?

26 What did Stephanie Rahn do in the "Sun" in 1970 to find herself on TV?

27 Which news programme was first to enter the Top 10 ratings in 1967?

28 Who stopped an interview when asked about the money he had made from his memoirs?

29 Which DJ hosted "First AIDS", which gave condoms to the audience?

30 Who was the first British newsreader to lose an earring on television?

Pop: DJs (see Quiz 76)

Answers

1 Jimmy Young. 2 David Hamilton. 3 Liz Kershaw. 4 Terry Wogan. 5 Anthea Turner. 6 Tony Blackburn. 7 David Jacobs. 8 Gloria Hunniford. 9 Pat and Mick. 10 Anne Nightingale. 11 News reader. 12 Chris Evans. 13 Steve Wright. 14 Simon Mayo. 15 Ray Moore. 16 Jimmy Savile. 17 David "Kid" Jensen. 18 Tony Prince. 19 Rosko. 20 Ken Bruce. 21 Fabulous 208. 22 Mike Smith. 23 Princess of Wales' brother, Earl Spencer. 24 Mike Read. 25 Paul Gambaccini. 26 Radio 1 DJ Posse. 27 Alan Freeman. 28 Kenny Everett. 29 Dave Lee Travis. 30 Janice Long.

Quiz 75 Pot-Luck 35

Answers - see page 313

1 What is the meaning of the acronym MIDAS?
2 What type of animal is a markhor?
3 In "The Darling Buds of May" who did Charley work for?
4 What do Hoba, Baruberito and Williamette have in common?
5 In which Book of the Bible is found the story of the birth of Moses?
6 What is the high tower of a Muslim mosque called?
7 What type of person could have been referred as a cutpurse?
8 What does it mean if the Union Jack is flown upside down from a ship?
9 Which European prince was known as "the Navigator"?
10 Who received the first gold disc and for which song?
11 Which two men were awarded the Nobel peace prize in 1993?
12 Which actress's story was portrayed in the 1983 film "Mommie Dearest"?
13 What is the north-country name for crumpets?
14 Which is the oldest of the European universities?
15 In which country is the volcanic mountain called Popocétapetl?
16 By what name is St Johnstown in Scotland now known?
17 In medieval times, what was a mangonel used for?
18 Who was the chief figure in the "26th of July" movement?
19 What do tulip, balloon and flute have in common?
20 Which country has the peacock as its national bird?
21 Who directed himself in "Sharky's Machine"?
22 Of which country is Asunción the capital city?
23 Who was Frankie Howerd's master in "Up Pompeii"?
24 What was the name of Robert Louis Stevenson's last and unfinished novel?
25 How is Matilda Alice Victoria Wood better known?
26 What is the other name for the scapula?
27 What nationality was the composer Bartók?
28 In Greek mythology what was the Sword of Damocles suspended by?
29 Who was nicknamed "Glorious John"?
30 What is the world's tallest-growing grass?

Quiz 76 Pop: DJs

Level 3

Answers - see page 314

1 Who had a hit with "Miss You" in 1963?
2 Whose nickname was "Diddy"?
3 Who sang "It Takes Two" with Bruno Brookes?
4 Which DJ invited listeners to "fight the flab"?
5 Who is former DJ Peter Powell married to?
6 Which DJ was the first voice on Radio 1?
7 Which former Radio 2 DJ has the initials DJ?
8 Who presented a weekday afternoon show on Radio 2 from 1982 to 1995?
9 Which DJ duo had a Top Ten hit with "I haven't stopped dancing yet"?
10 Who was the first regular woman DJ on Radio 1?
11 What was Noel Edmonds' first job on Radio Luxembourg?
12 Who once called himself "Noddy No-Level"?
13 Which Radio 1 DJ had a posse on his afternoon show and then on his breakfast programme?
14 Which Radio 1 DJ read out "Confessions"?
15 Which late DJ had a Top 30 hit with "My Father Had a Rabbit"?
16 Who formed the "Under the Bedclothes Club" on Radio Luxembourg?
17 Which Canadian has been a DJ on Luxembourg, Capital, Radio One, Radio Four and Radio Trent?
18 Who used to announce himself as "Your royal ruler, I wouldn't fool ya, nothin' could be cooler"?
19 Which DJ was an "Emperor"?
20 Who replaced Terry Wogan on the breakfast show?
21 Which 1960s pop magazine promoted Radio Luxembourg DJs as stars?
22 Who was the Sony DJ of the year in 1986 and went on to present the "Late Late Breakfast Show" with Noel Edmonds?
23 Who was involved in a row with Tony Blackburn in a restaurant?
24 Who refused to play Frankie Goes to Hollywood's "Relax" on his show?
25 Which Radio 1 DJ went on to host a morning show on Radio 3?
26 Who backed Bruno and Liz on "Let's Dance"?
27 Who was DJ on "Pick of the Pops" which featured the Top Twenty?
28 Whose real name was Maurice Cole?
29 Who resigned from Radio 1 on air?
30 Which radio DJ is Keith Chegwin's sister?

Answers

TV: Memorable Moments (see Quiz 74)
1 Sir Robin Day. 2 Meg Mortimer. 3 Ethel Skinner. 4 Charged by an elephant. 5 Patty Hearst. 6 The actual egg race. 7 Ray Krebbs. 8 Nicholas Witchell and Sue Lawley. 9 The Avengers. 10 Falcon Crest. 11 Kevin Webster. 12 Sir Peter Scott. 13 Princess Anne. 14 Sir Cliff Richard. 15 One. 16 Katie Boyle. 17 Sir Winston Churchill. 18 Wimbledon. 19 A beard. 20 Coronation Street. 21 1981. 22 Reginald Bosanquet. 23 He died. 24 George VI's. 25 John Noakes. 26 Became the first topless page 3 girl. 27 News at Ten. 28 Harold Wilson. 29 Mike Smith. 30 Angela Rippon.

1 What do the initials NASA stand for?
2 What is a palmiped?
3 In which city would you find the house of the painter Rubens?
4 Whose catchphrase was "I've arrived and, to prove it, I'm here"?
5 What is the last Book of the Bible?
6 Which buildings did Don Quixote mistake for evil giants?
7 What do Romney Marsh, Suffolk, Clun and Forest have in common?
8 Who was the singer on the radio classic "Take It From Here"?
9 What is the colour of the ribbon of the Victoria Cross?
10 In "Dad's Army" what was the occupation of Private Frazer?
11 What was Casanova's occupation at the time of his death?
12 Who was known by the nickname "The Great Commoner"?
13 Which swimmer starred in the film "Bathing Beauty"?
14 Which organization was founded in Ontario, Canada, by Mrs Hoodless in 1897?
15 What is the British equivalent to the US trademark Plexiglas?
16 Monte Marmolada is the highest peak of which mountain range?
17 Where in Britain would you find Roedean Girls' School?
18 Of what ancient empire was Persepolis the ceremonial centre?
19 What was referred to as Black Forty-Seven?
20 Where in the world would you find a vicuna and an alpaca?
21 What are Prince Andrew's three other first names?
22 Concord is the capital of which US state?
23 What is the opposite of oriental?
24 Which of Charles Dickens' novels was left unfinished in 1870?
25 Which Scottish mathematician invented logarithms?
26 What is the longest bone in the human body?
27 Who wrote "Anything Goes" and "Can Can"?
28 In Greek legend, which prophetess was the foreteller of doom?
29 Who was nicknamed "The Beard" by the US intelligence service?
30 The carnation is the national flower of which country?

Quiz 78 Around England

Level 3

1 Which English county has the longest coastline?
2 Who is responsible for the blue plaques in London?
3 In which London borough are there the most blue plaques?
4 What was Marble Arch originally designed to be?
5 What is the stately home owned by the Spencer family in Northamptonshire called?
6 What are Grimes Graves and where are they?
7 Where is England's largest castle?
8 Which two English cathedrals have three spires each?
9 Which county used to be divided into Parts?
10 Which dukes are associated with Woburn Abbey?
11 Where would you go to watch a Furry dance?
12 Where are St Agnes, St Martin's and Bryher?
13 Which English county bordering the sea has the shortest coastline?
14 What is the eastern strait between the Isle of Wight and the English mainland called?
15 What is the main type of rock forming the North Downs?
16 Dunkery Beacon is the highest point where?
17 On which lake does Keswick stand?
18 Which part of England is associated with the novels of Arnold Bennett?
19 Under which London landmark are buried a razor, cigars and a portrait of Queen Victoria?
20 Where is there a Nelson's column other than the one in London ?
21 What is England's smallest mainland county?
22 Which stately home in Britain is the home of the Marquess of Bath?
23 In which city is Whip-ma-Whop-ma Gate?
24 How many parishes does Greater London have?
25 In which county is there a village called Middle Wallop?
26 Which Derbyshire village lost most of its population to plague in 1665 but prevented the spread of the disease?
27 Where would you find the Bell Harry tower?
28 Which English county has the smallest perimeter?
29 What are the chalk cliff headlands between Eastbourne and Seaford?
30 Where are trees laid out in the form of troops at a famous battle?

1 Who was the first black actor to win an Oscar?
2 What would you fear if you had apiphobia?
3 In which year was the Festival of Britain?
4 What is the name of the Queen's bodyguard in Scotland?
5 In which country do the Monteneros guerrillas operate?
6 What is a person who collects coins called?
7 What was John Glenn's Mercury capsule called when he became the first American to orbit the Earth?
8 Under what name was Erich Weiss (1874–1926) better known?
9 With what sport is Bisley in Surrey associated?
10 If you were studying coleoptera what would you be examining?
11 In dyeing, what name is given to the substance used to fix the colour?
12 When is St Sylvester's night?
13 Where was the main residence of British sovereigns from 1698 to 1837?
14 What was the first newspaper to have a "Personal Column" on its front page?
15 Which game was patented under the name Sphairistike?
16 Which American founded the Jehovah's Witnesses?
17 Which club was founded by Paul Harris and others in Chicago in 1905?
18 Which two cities were the first two capitals to have a telephone link?
19 What was the final episode of M*A*S*H called?
20 Which actor was born Joe Yule Jnr in 1920?
21 What is the name of the Russian triangular guitar?
22 What name is given to a dry watercourse in a desert?
23 What is the common name for the illness pertussis?
24 Where is the Gulf of Carpentaria?
25 In which sport are the Triffus, Miller and Rudolf moves performed?
26 Which famous castle is the country seat of the Duke of Norfolk?
27 Adélie Land is a French territory on the coast of which continent?
28 How would the music of Vivaldi, Purcell and Handel be classified?
29 Which British politician became leader of the Liberal party in 1956?
30 Who shared flats at different times with Sandra Hutchinson, first of all at Huskisson Road, Liverpool?

1 Who set up the Society of British Gastronomes?
2 Which couple had a TV show called "Gourmet Ireland"?
3 Which food expert presents "The Food Programme" on Radio 4?
4 At which London hotels did Auguste Escoffier gain his reputation?
5 Which chef is associated with the world-class "Waterside Inn" at Bray?
6 Whose cookery book is called "Food of the Sun"?
7 What type of food does Valentina Harris specialize in?
8 Who is the chef/proprietor of "Le Manoir aux Quat' Saisons"?
9 Vatcharin Bhumichitr has written about the taste of which country?
10 Which writer, raconteur and food expert is a former Liberal MP for Ely?
11 What sort of food is a speciality at Rick Stein's restaurant?
12 Which chef is the restaurant "Bibendum" associated with?
13 Which cook and writer produced a "Cook's Tour of France"?
14 Which expert on Indian cooking is also an accomplished actress?
15 Who founded a School of Food and Wine and was instrumental in improving British Rail sandwiches?
16 Where was Gary Rhodes chef when he shot to fame on TV?
17 Which TV cook is a native of New Zealand?
18 Which cook is a founder of Classic FM?
19 Who wrote the foreword to the collection of recipes in book form Delia Smith compiled as a response to Live Aid?
20 Who is chef/patron of the Miller Howe, Windermere?
21 Where did Delia Smith have a cookery column before achieving fame on TV?
22 What type of cuisine does Sarah Brown specialize in?
23 Which cook has been married to the founder of "Habitat"?
24 Who produced the "Food Lover's Guide to Britain"?
25 What was the name of the chef played by Lenny Henry?
26 What was the first name of Sophie Grigson's mother?
27 Who founded the magazine where Mrs Beeton's articles were printed?
28 Which TV programme consists of chefs producing a dish from a limited list of ingredients against the clock?
29 Which team wrote the Daily Telegraph's "Bon Viveur" column?
30 Who wrote "Man in the Kitchen" and was a TV cookery pioneer?

Quiz 81 Pot-Luck 38

Level 3

Answers - see page 323

1 Aluminium is extracted from which ore?
2 Which US statesman defined the "four freedoms"?
3 What caused the fire in the "Rovers' Return" in 1986?
4 Which word, meaning "I forbid" in Latin, means the right to prevent a law being enacted or an action being taken?
5 Which American humorist invented the town of Lake Wobegon?
6 After Earth, which planet was orbited first by a man-made object?
7 Which instrument did Albert Schweitzer play?
8 Whom did Neil Kinnock describe as "the most courteous man in the western world"?
9 In cricket, who is the fielder who patrols the boundary behind the slips?
10 Who was the last emperor of the Incas?
11 Which gland in the body produces luteinizing hormone?
12 Who was the tightrope walker who repeatedly crossed Niagara Falls?
13 Which Australian cricketer needed to score only four in his final test innings to average 100, yet only got a duck?
14 Which theory compares the Earth to a living organism?
15 Which Italian opera composer said, "In the theatre the public will stand for anything except boredom"?
16 When did the Big Bang take place?
17 Which painting medium uses egg yolk and water?
18 In the Sikh religion what is kesh?
19 Which twins are represented by the zodiacal sign Gemini?
20 Who said there are "lies, damned lies and statistics"?
21 Who is known as the founding father of eugenics?
22 What was the occupation of the "Wicked Lady" in the film?
23 Whose "guest" was six-year-old Stuart Lockwood in August 1990?
24 What sort of people was a Nansen passport issued to?
25 In how many films did James Dean appear?
26 What was the name of the landlord in "The Young Ones"?
27 What was Jim Hacker's wife called in "Yes Minister"?
28 What is the earliest known unit of length?
29 What causes Down's syndrome?
30 What is an astrolabe?

Answers

Pot-Luck 39 (see Quiz 83)
1 1922. 2 Tsunami. 3 Household management. 4 Ferdinand Porsche. 5 1941. 6 She was born a man. 7 Hammond organ. 8 Donna. 9 So that he could eat without leaving the gaming table. 10 Akihito. 11 T. S. Eliot. 12 White. 13 Insects. 14 Nitrogen oxides. 15 Medulla oblongata. 16 Turmeric. 17 Charles II and James II. 18 Iron. 19 Chord. 20 Kemal Ataturk. 21 Crow. 22 He wraps them. 23 About 1.5 light years. 24 A violin bow. 25 Charlemagne. 26 He lost his sword arm. 27 Gabriel Garcia Márquez. 28 Female. 29 P. T. Barnum's. 30 Patrick White.

Level 3

1 Which horse gave Lester Piggott his first Royal Ascot winner?
2 Why was the 1955 Royal Ascot meeting postponed for a month?
3 When were women first elected to membership of the Jockey Club?
4 As the Knavesmire is to York, so the Carholme was to which course?
5 Which was the first horse to win two Grand Nationals?
6 Who owned triple Grand National winner Red Rum?
7 Which Grand National winner of the 80s was named after a lighthouse?
8 Who was the first woman to ride in the Cheltenham Gold Cup in 1984?
9 Over which racecourse is the Greenham Stakes run?
10 Which horse was the first to win both the Derby and the St Leger?
11 Who was the first National Hunt jockey to ride more than 1,000 winners in Britain?
12 In which year was the Derby first run?
13 Where in Doncaster did the St Leger take place before it was transferred to Town Moor?
14 Who won the flat racing jockeys' championship 26 times?
15 Who was the first trainer to turn out winners of more than £1 million in one flat racing season in Britain in 1985?
16 Which jockey won the 1970 St Leger on Nijinsky?
17 Over which racecourse is the Ebor Handicap run?
18 Which European flat race is run annually on the first Sunday in October?
19 In which years did Red Rum win the Grand National?
20 Who was the first woman to ride in the Grand National in 1977?
21 Which trainer, who died in 1983 aged 95, saddled 13 Classic winners?
22 Who was the first jockey to win both the Epsom and Kentucky Derbies?
23 Over which flat racing course is the Welsh Derby run?
24 When is a racehorse's official birthday south of the equator?
25 What kind of a race is a "Bumper"?
26 Which race is known as "The Publicans' Derby"?
27 The Hambleton Cup, first run in 1612, is still run at which course?
28 Where did Jonjo O'Neill break his leg so badly that amputation was considered?
29 Which trainer's autobiography was called "The Glorious Uncertainty"?
30 Who is the St Leger named after?

1 When did Howard Carter and Lord Carnarvon find Tut's tomb?
2 What is the proper name for a tidal wave?
3 What does the word "economy" mean in the original Greek?
4 Who designed the Volkswagen Beetle?
5 In which year did the Japanese attack Pearl Harbor?
6 Why did the European court refuse to allow Caroline Cossey to marry in 1990?
7 What was the electric tone-wheel organ invented in 1934?
8 What was the name of Kathy Beale's long-lost daughter in "EastEnders"?
9 Why did Lord Sandwich invent the sandwich?
10 Who succeeded Hirohito as emperor of Japan?
11 Who wrote "The Four Quartets"?
12 What colour is the cross of the Greek flag?
13 In which animals would you find compound eyes?
14 Which emissions from cars are acidic?
15 Which part of the brain controls the heart rate?
16 Which member of the ginger family is used to colour curries?
17 Who are the only two English sovereigns from whom Prince Charles is not descended?
18 What metallic element is found in fool's gold?
19 What name is given to the line which joins any two points on a circle?
20 Who in 1934 took the name meaning "Father of the Turks"?
21 What can be a bird or a North American Indian tribe?
22 What does the sculptor Christo do to things?
23 How far does the Sun's gravitational influence extend?
24 What did the baton replace for conducting an orchestra?
25 Who was crowned the first Holy Roman emperor in AD 800?
26 What injury did Lord Raglan, after whom the Raglan sleeve is named, sustain in battle?
27 Who wrote "100 Years of Solitude"?
28 Which gender of earwig has straight rather than curved pincers?
29 Whose circus did General Tom Thumb join at the age of five in 1843?
30 Which Australian writer, the author of the "The Tree of Man" and "Voss", won the Nobel Prize for Literature in 1973?

Quiz 84 Modern History: US Politics (Level 3) ▮▮▮

Answers - see page 322

1 The name of which US president is Bill Clinton's middle name?
2 Which US statesman won the Nobel Peace Prize in 1973, although the man he shared it with declined his award?
3 Which state did Robert Dole become senator for in 1968?
4 Under whose presidency was racial discrimination made illegal?
5 Which US president was born Leslie Lynch King?
6 Who is the only US president to have been divorced?
7 Who was the first US president to resign office?
8 Which First Lady was nicknamed the "Steel Magnolia"?
9 Which president initiated his "Great Society" programme?
10 Who was John F. Kennedy's attorney general?
11 Which American ambassador is the mother of Winston Churchill MP?
12 Which president other than John F. Kennedy was killed this century?
13 Which secretary of state announced to the world that he was in charge after the assassination attempt on Ronald Reagan?
14 What is Al Gore's wife called?
15 Which president ordered the dropping of the atomic bombs on Hiroshima and Nagasaki?
16 Which president's foreign policy was to "speak softly with a big stick"?
17 Whose memoirs were called "Mandate for Change" and "Waging Peace"?
18 Which president was a former director of the CIA?
19 Which Democrat founded what he called his "Rainbow Coalition"?
20 What was the official name of the so-called "Star Wars" programme?
21 What was the cause of Franklin D. Roosevelt's paralysis?
22 Which two journalists broke the story of the Watergate burglary and which paper did they work for?
23 Which leaders did Carter bring to Camp David to sign a peace treaty?
24 Whom did George Bush defeat to become president in 1988?
25 Which post did Joseph Kennedy hold at the outbreak of World War II?
26 Whose death at Chappaquiddick stopped Ted Kennedy's ambitions?
27 Which First Lady was nicknamed the "Iron Butterfly"?
28 Who was Richard Nixon's first vice-president?
29 Where did Martin Luther King make his "I have a dream" speech?
30 What was the full name of George Bush's vice-president?

Quiz 85 Pot-Luck 40

Level 3

1 Marble is formed by the metamorphosis of which rock?
2 In which country was the playwright Tom Stoppard born?
3 Which constellation is named after the mother of Andromeda?
4 Where was Europe's first hard-paste porcelain made?
5 What kind of coolant is used in a fast reactor?
6 Who is told the tales of "The Thousand and One Nights"?
7 What was Queen Victoria first "not amused" by?
8 Who gave his name to the absolute scale of temperature?
9 Which country is the world's largest consumer of champagne?
10 Who was Wyatt Earp's brother who, with Doc Holliday, fought the Clanton gang at the OK Corral?
11 What name is given to the technology of creating and reading codes?
12 Who replaced Geoffrey Howe as foreign secretary in 1989?
13 Who was the only US president whose terms of office were not consecutive?
14 Whom did James Callaghan describe as "the sexiest woman on TV"?
15 What is the smallest unit of time?
16 Beriberi results from a lack of which vitamin?
17 Where does the Lhasa Apso dog originate?
18 What did Charles Dawson "discover" in the early 20th century that was proved a fake 40 years later?
19 In which year did the "Titanic" sink?
20 Who wrote "The Wealth of Nations"?
21 In which country did the first organized motor race take place?
22 How many time zones does mainland USA have?
23 Pidgin English originally evolved for trade between Britain and where?
24 How many reeds does an oboe have?
25 Which member of the "Gang of Four" was Mao Tse Tung's third wife?
26 What is the world's most heavily funded art gallery?
27 In the international Code of Signals what does "Oscar" signify?
28 About which soap did Jasper Carrott say that when the cast went on strike they were threatened with rehearsal?
29 In which Wilkie Collins novel does the villain, Count Fosco, appear?
30 Where would you go to find a wild vampire bat?

Answers **Pot-Luck 41** (see Quiz 87)
1 Stratosphere. 2 Renal artery. 3 Sicily. 4 Dolly and Cissy. 5 Marcus Garvey. 6 Amritsar. 7 Lead. 8 Harry Lauder. 9 Iran. 10 Electoral college. 11 Sylvia and Christabel. 12 Neptune. 13 Sydney University. 14 Norway. 15 Wrestling. 16 A spore-producing body in a fern. 17 Dr Crippen. 18 Prison officer about the Strangeways riots. 19 Cricket St Thomas. 20 Neil Simon. 21 A rapidly rotating neutron star. 22 Edward Hopper. 23 Ivana Trump. 24 78. 25 Mae West. 26 Archie Bunker. 27 Belshazzar. 28 Red and yellow. 29 Hyperbole. 30 Gus Grissom.

Quiz 86 Pop: All Girl Groups

Level 3 ▮▮▮

Answers - see page 328

1 What were the Supremes originally called?
2 What was the family relationship of the three Ronettes?
3 Which Ronettes hit was Phil Spector's only Grammy award?
4 What occupations did Martha Reeves, Rosalind Ashford and Annette Sterling have before they were Martha and the Vandellas?
5 Who sang "Stay" in 1993?
6 What does "TSOP" stand for in the 1974 Three Degrees song?
7 Which 1960s group were named after a football pools company?
8 Which quartet consisted of Susanna Hoffs, Annette Zilinskas and Debbi and Vicki Peterson?
9 Which group were "...in the Mood for Dancing" in 1979?
10 Which duo's only hit was "You Don't Have to be a Baby to Cry"?
11 What was Patricia Holt known as and what was her backing group?
12 Which singer replaced Florence Ballard in The Supremes?
13 What was The Crystals first UK Top Ten hit?
14 Who were Babs, Teddy and Joy?
15 Whose hit "We Are Family" became an anthem for gay rights and the Pittsburgh Pirates baseball team?
16 Whose "Fairytale" was a pop and country hit in 1974?
17 Which line goes before "Keeps a telling me no" in the Paper Dolls hit?
18 What was unusual about The Crystals' hit "He's a Rebel"?
19 Who was Frank on the Kaye Sisters' hit "Gotta Have Something in the Bank Frank"?
20 Which Broadway show was based on the life of The Supremes?
21 Who recorded "Rhumboogie" and "The Booglie Wooglie Piggie"?
22 Which duo were "Respectable" in 1987?
23 What was the real first name of Ronnie Spector, formerly Bennett?
24 Who led Hot Gossip on "I Lost my Heart to a Starship Trooper"?
25 What was it raining according to The Weather Girls in 1984?
26 Who rejected "Baby Love" which was later a hit for The Supremes?
27 Which actor is waiting in the title of the Bananarama hit?
28 Who married Dave Stewart and formed Shakespear's Sister?
29 Who backed Reparata on "Captain of Your Ship"?
30 Who had a 1960s hit with "Sweet Talkin' Guy"?

Answers

The Movies: Best of British (see Quiz 88) **1** Robert Downey Jnr. **2** Lion in Winter. **3** Cheryl Campbell. **4** Brigitte Bardot. **5** Mike Newell. **6** Kind Hearts and Coronets. **7** Killing Fields. **8** Talbot Rothwell. **9** Prime of Miss Jean Brodie. **10** Don't Lose Your Head. **11** Lavender Hill Mob. **12** Room with a View. **13** I'm All Right Jack. **14** Oliver. **15** Lewis Gilbert. **16** Third Man. **17** Turin. **18** Harmonica. **19** Christy Brown. **20** Martita Hunt. **21** 84 Charing Cross Road. **22** Gordon John Sinclair. **23** Italy, China. **24** Oh, Mr Porter! **25** Richard Briers. **26** Lauri Peters. **27** Peter Finch, Glenda Jackson, Murray Head. **28** How I Learned to Stop Worrying and Love the Bomb. **29** Albert Finney. **30** Gandhi.

1 In which part of the atmosphere is the ozone layer?
2 Which artery supplies the kidney with blood?
3 Which Italian region is the source of Marsala?
4 In "Dad's Army" what were Godfrey's two sisters called?
5 Who was the founder of the Back to Africa movement who largely inspired Rastafarianism?
6 In which Indian city did British troops open fire without warning on a crowd of 10,000 in 1919?
7 Which element gains its symbol from the Latin word "plumbum"?
8 Which music hall singer's real name was Hugh MacLennan?
9 In which country did polo originate?
10 What is the name of the system by which the president of the US is elected?
11 What were Mrs Pankhurst's two suffragette daughters called?
12 Which planet has a Great Dark Spot?
13 Where was Enoch Powell a professor of Greek at the age of 25?
14 Which country's parliament is called the Storting?
15 Which sport has two main styles, called freestyle and Greco-Roman?
16 What is a "sorus"?
17 Who was the first criminal captured by radio after a message to a ship?
18 Who said about what, "If they don't come down by midnight we are going to play Des O'Connor records"?
19 In which village was Penelope Keith "To the Manor Born"?
20 Which playwright wrote "Barefoot in the Park" and "The Odd Couple"?
21 What is a pulsar?
22 Which painter caught the loneliness of city life in the 1930s and 1940s?
23 Who on the break-up of her marriage said "Gimme the Plaza, the jet and 150 million dollars"?
24 How many cards are there in a tarot pack?
25 Who said, "I used to be Snow White, but I drifted"?
26 What was the Alf Garnett character called in "All in the Family"?
27 In the Bible, which king of Babylon saw his own death prophesied?
28 What two colours are on a semaphore flag?
29 What is the deliberate use of exaggeration for emphasis called?
30 Who was the first man to go into space twice?

Quiz 88 The Movies: Best of British

Answers - see page 326

1 Who played "Chaplin" in the film directed by Richard Attenborough?
2 For which film did Katharine Hepburn win the first best actress BAFTA?
3 Who played Eric Liddell's sister in "Chariots of Fire"?
4 Who played opposite Dirk Bogarde in "Doctor at Sea"?
5 Who directed "Four Weddings and a Funeral"?
6 Which Ealing comedy was based on Roy Horniman's "Noblesse Oblige"?
7 Which 1984 film was based on "The Death and Life of Dith Pran"?
8 Who was the most prolific writer of "Carry On" scripts?
9 In which film did Maggie Smith call her girls "The créme de la créme"?
10 Which Carry On film was (very) loosely based on The Scarlet Pimpernel?
11 In which Alec Guiness film does a bank clerk carry out a bullion robbery?
12 Which 1986 film had "O Mio Babbino Caro" as its theme?
13 In which Boulting Brothers film did Ian Carmichael star as a graduate who starts work in a factory and causes a national strike?
14 Which musical was "the most non-U subject ever to be given a U certificate"?
15 Who directed "Educating Rita" and "Shirley Valentine"?
16 Which British film was the first non-French film to win the prestigious Palme d'Or at the Cannes Film Festival in 1949?
17 In which city does "The Italian Job" take place?
18 On what instrument is the music for the film "Genevieve" played?
19 Who was played by Daniel Day-Lewis in "My Left Foot"?
20 Who played Miss Haversham in David Lean's "Great Expectations"?
21 In which film was Anne Bancroft writing to a London bookseller?
22 What is John Gordon Sinclair called in the credits to "Gregory's Girl"?
23 "The Last Emperor" was a collaboration on film between Britain and which two other countries?
24 In which Will Hay movie does he play a haunted stationmaster?
25 Who plays Peter's father in Kenneth Branagh's "Peter's Friends"?
26 Who starred opposite Cliff Richard in "Summer Holiday"?
27 Which three actors made up the love triangle in "Sunday Bloody Sunday"?
28 What was the alternative title of "Dr Strangelove"?
29 Who turned down the role of T. E. Lawrence in "Lawrence of Arabia"?
30 Which film opens with the dedication "No man's life can be encompassed in one telling"?

1 What did Australian company Merino Wool Harvesting develop the prototype of in 1991?
2 What does RAM stand for?
3 What do we call human-like robots?
4 What do the black bars and white spaces of bar codes represent?
5 What are optical fibres made from?
6 Who invented the mouse?
7 Which device converts chemical energy into electrical energy?
8 What was the name of the first communications satellite?
9 What does "laser" stand for?
10 Which separate companies invented and promoted the CD-ROM?
11 Which company developed the first electronic pocket calculator?
12 What device enables computers to send data down a telephone line?
13 Which software program was launched in 1982 by Lotus?
14 What name is given to a computer screen which responds to touch?
15 What does BASIC stand for?
16 What is the study of automated communication and control mechanisms in machines and humans called?
17 What do we call the wafer of silicon that carries miniaturized circuits?
18 What did the US company Diablo invent for use on typewriters?
19 How many bits or binary elements has a byte?
20 What is the largest bulletin board system (BBS) in the world?
21 What was the name of the first working electromechanical computer?
22 Which highly insoluble substance is opaque to X-rays?
23 Who marketed the first dot matrix printers in 1957?
24 In digital communication terms what does MIME stand for?
25 What phrase applies to graphics programs which interact with people?
26 What was ARPANET a forerunner of?
27 What was launched in November 1985 by Microsoft?
28 Who invented the first calculating machine in 1642?
29 What term is given to part of a computer's memory that has its program permanently fixed?
30 Who developed the laser printer?

Quiz 90 Pot-Luck 42

Answers - see page 332

Level 3

1 Where was the Canadian goldrush which began in 1896?
2 Parsley belongs to which family?
3 Radioactivity is measured in which units?
4 What initials are used to describe chronic fatigue syndrome?
5 What device was originally used to explore the depths of an ocean?
6 What type of burial mounds date from the the early Bronze Age?
7 Which cricketer said about his autobiography, "I can honestly say that I've written one more book than I've read."?
8 In which year was the European Economic Community established?
9 After Ettore Bugatti's death in 1947, which company took over Bugatti?
10 During which battle did the charge of the Light Brigade take place?
11 RP is the standard form of English accent – what do the letters stand for?
12 Who had a CD called "But Seriously"?
13 From which boat did Jacques Cousteau conduct his underwater research?
14 Which coin ceased to be legal tender from January 1st, 1991?
15 What is the feast of the Purification of the Virgin Mary?
16 From what colour rock is the Jordanian city of Petra carved?
17 In "Rising Damp" what is Rigsby's cat called?
18 What is the term for the energy obtained from hot underground rocks?
19 Where do the Graafian follicles develop?
20 What does "lager" literally mean in German?
21 Where in the world can you see two bridges linking one continent with another?
22 What are crosses between bulldogs and terriers called?
23 Which element was used in the manufacture of the first florin?
24 To which Anglican movement did Newman, Pusey and Keble belong?
25 Which society was founded in London in 1884 to promote socialist ideas peacefully and to establish a socialist state in Britain?
26 Who was the French soldier whose constant drilling made his name a byword for strict discipline?
27 Which space probes failed to find life on Mars?
28 What was Beethoven's only opera?
29 Who regularly joins Roy Hudd for "The News Huddlines"?
30 Where does the Australian Open Tennis Championship take place?

Pot-Luck 43 (see Quiz 92)
Answers
1 Spike Milligan. 2 Samuel Goldwyn. 3 Troposphere. 4 Canucks. 5 Mass.
6 Man Ray. 7 Brookfield. 8 Baron Munchhausen. 9 The Rubicon.
10 Carbolic acid. 11 Pluto. 12 Yvonne, Phoebe. 13 Intermediate technology. 14 24. 15 Meriwether Lewis and William Clark. 16 Orchid.
17 Korea. 18 Staphylococcus. 19 Fleur. 20 Etruscan. 21 Hindenburg.
22 John Stuart Mill. 23 Citroën. 24 Holly. 25 Farsi. 26 Cremona. 27 Descent of Man. 28 Fred Quimby. 29 The pressure of fluids. 30 Harrison.

Quiz 91 Foreign Literature

Level 3 ▮▮▮

Answers - see page 329

1 Which Czech dramatist became president after the fall of communism?
2 Which German poet was prime minister to the Duke of Saxe-Weimar?
3 Which Russian dramatist married one of the actresses in his company?
4 Which French philosopher and writer was imprisoned in the Bastille and also wrote the fable "Candide"?
5 Which Italian dramatist wrote "Can't Pay, Won't Pay" in 1974?
6 Who wrote the novel Eugene Onegin?
7 In which war was "War and Peace" author Tolstoy on active service?
8 Before success as a writer what did Hans Christian Andersen do?
9 Which Russian novelist was sentenced to hard labour in Siberia in 1849 for printing socialist propaganda?
10 Franz Kafka wrote in German but what nationality was he?
11 What were the first names of the brothers Grimm?
12 In which Eugéne Ionescu play do the characters turn into animals?
13 Which famous film is Heinrich Mann's "Professor Unrat" based on?
14 Who wrote a sequence of 94 novels under the title "La Comédie Humaine"?
15 Which French playwright's real name was Jean Baptiste Poquelin?
16 Which Iranian poet's most famous translator was Edward Fitzgerald?
17 Which Russian dissident's memoirs were called "The Oak and the Calf"?
18 What was the nationality of "Maigret" creator Georges Simenon?
19 What is Cervantes' parody of chivalric literature called?
20 Which Russian declined the 1958 Nobel prize after his novel about his mother country was published in Italy?
21 Who wrote "A la Recherche du Temps Perdu"?
22 What was the occupation of the author of "Le Petit Prince"?
23 What is the French title of Baudelaire's "The Flowers of Evil"?
24 Which French novelist's real name was Marie Henri Beyle?
25 Which Brecht play presents a dilemma about motherhood?
26 Whom was Zola defending in his open letter "J'accuse"?
27 What is the nationality of short-story writer Jorge Luis Borges?
28 Which French feminist writer wrote "The Second Sex"?
29 Which World War II member of the French resistance wrote "Nausea"?
30 How is Amandine Aurore Lucie Dupin better known?

Hi Tech (see Quiz 89) **1** Robot sheep shearers. **2** Random access memory. **3** Androids. **4** Binary numbers. **5** Pure glass. **6** Douglas Engelbart. **7** Battery. **8** Telstar. **9** Light amplification by stimulated emission of radiation. **10** Philips invented, Sony promoted. **11** Texas Instruments. **12** Modem. **13** 1-2-3. **14** Tactile screen. **15** Beginners All-purpose Symbolic Instruction Code. **16** Cybernetics. **17** Silicon chip. **18** Daisy wheel printer. **19** 8. **20** CompuServe. **21** Coloccus. **22** Barium. **23** IBM. **24** Multipurpose Internet Mail Extension. **25** Virtual reality. **26** Internet. **27** Windows. **28** Pascal. **29** Read Only Memory. **30** Canon.

Quiz 92 Pot-Luck 43

Answers - see page 330

1 Who played the part of Eccles in "The Goon Show"?
2 Which film mogul said, "include me out"?
3 Which layer of the atmosphere is closest to the surface of the Earth?
4 What is the slang term for Canadians?
5 In the general theory of relativity what causes space-time to be modified?
6 How was the Parisian photographer Emmanuel Rudnitsky better known?
7 In "The Archers", at which farm do Phil and Jill Archer live?
8 Which 18th-century German soldier was famous for his exaggerated accounts of his adventures?
9 On crossing which river did Julius Caesar say, "The die is cast"?
10 What did Lister use to improve the hygiene of surgical operations?
11 What did the astronomer Clyde Tombaugh discover in 1930?
12 Who were Gary's 90s wife and 40s girlfriend in "Goodnight Sweetheart"?
13 What is it called when technology is adapted for developing countries?
14 In a standard cine film how many frames are shown each second?
15 Which two explorers did Jefferson send to find a land route to the Pacific?
16 Which type of flower has pods which are a source of vanilla?
17 Where does the martial art taekwondo originate?
18 Which bacterium causes toxic shock syndrome?
19 In "May to December" what was Alec and Zoe's baby called?
20 Excavating the tombs of which civilization revealed lively paintings showing feasting, dancing and swimming?
21 Which airship exploded in New Jersey in 1937?
22 Which English economist sat as a Radical in Parliament during 1865–68 and urged votes for women?
23 Who made history with the 1st front-wheel drive vehicle in 1934?
24 In "Red Dwarf" what was the spaceship's computer called?
25 What is the official language of Iran?
26 In which Italian city did Antonio Stradivari and Niccolò Amati make their violins?
27 Which book by Darwin discussed human evolution?
28 Who was the producer of the Tom and Jerry cartoons until 1956?
29 What does a manometer measure?
30 What surname did the 9th and 23rd presidents of the US share?

Answers

Pot-Luck 42 (see Quiz 90)
1 Yukon. 2 Carrot family. 3 Becquerels. 4 ME. 5 A bathyscaph. 6 Round barrows. 7 Merv Hughes. 8 1957. 9 Hispano Suiza. 10 Balaclava. 11 Received pronunciation. 12 Phil Collins. 13 Calypso. 14 5p pieces, which were the old shilling. 15 Candlemas. 16 Red. 17 Vienna. 18 Geothermal energy. 19 Ovaries. 20 Store. 21 Bosporus. 22 Boston terriers. 23 Gold. 24 The Oxford Movement. 25 Fabian Society. 26 Jean Martinet. 27 Viking probes. 28 Fidelio. 29 June Whitfield and Chris Emmet. 30 Flinders Park, Melbourne.

Quiz 93 Capital Punishment

Answers - see page 335

1 Which British dependent territory has a capital called The Valley?
2 The name of the capital of which country means "good air"?
3 Other than in Scotland, where is there a capital called Edinburgh?
4 What is the capital of Venezuela?
5 Which capital's "Spring" was shattered by Soviet tanks?
6 What is the capital of the largest country in Europe after Russia?
7 Which US state's capital is the name of a lively 1920s' dance?
8 "One Night" in where is the name of a song from the musical "Chess"?
9 Oranjestad is the capital of Aruba but to whom does it belong?
10 Which fabric was originally made in Syria's capital?
11 In which US state's capital is the headquarters of the Mormon Church?
12 Which island's capital is Flying Fish Cove?
13 Which US state capital has the longest name?
14 In which capital was Gordon besieged for 10 months and then murdered?
15 Which African capital was sold to Italy in 1905?
16 What is the name of Greenland's capital, formerly Godthab?
17 Which country's capital is the end of a motor rally from Paris?
18 What shape is the Kremlin in Russia's capital, Moscow?
19 Which capital is linked to Almada by a bridge over the River Tagus?
20 Which US state capital is the name of the man credited with "discovering" America?
21 Which capital city has a state within it?
22 Which Arab capital's name is the name of a sweet dessert wine?
23 What did Abuja replace as Nigeria's capital?
24 Why is the Government Building in Wellington so notable?
25 Which Mexican state's name and state capital are also the name of a breed of small dog?
26 Which capital was founded in 1566 by the Knights of St John?
27 What is the capital of Malawi?
28 Which African capital's name was the name of a hit song by Tommy Steele in 1958?
29 "They Came to" which Middle Eastern capital in the title of a mystery by Agatha Christie?
30 Who sang about the capital of Catalonia in 1992?

Answers

Sports Bag (see Quiz 95)
1 Troon. 2 Geoff Howarth. 3 David Bryant. 4 Bradford. 5 Greyhound Racing Association. 6 Walter Swinburn. 7 1979. 8 Susan Brown. 9 Johnny Weissmuller. 10 Pat Smythe. 11 Curling. 12 Terry Griffiths. 13 Wimbledon. 14 Ayr. 15 Paavo Nurmi. 16 Brough Scott. 17 100-metre breaststroke. 18 The Cresta Run. 19 Basketball. 20 Sonny Liston. 21 Parc des Princes. 22 Notts County. 23 Heather McKay. 24 Sandy Lyle. 25 Argentinian. 26 Doug Mountjoy. 27 Everton. 28 Hurst Park. 29 Joe Davis and his brother Fred. 30 Sydney, Australia.

Quiz 94 Pot-Luck 44

Answers - see page 336

Level 3

1 What dye is named after a battle fought near Milan in 1859?
2 Which group of insects includes a hairstreak?
3 What component of CFCs causes destruction of ozone?
4 Which part of the gut absorbs water from the food?
5 Which plant-sucking insect caused huge disruption to the wine industry of Europe in the 19th century?
6 The mother and son of which king of England were both beheaded?
7 Which element is used in the preparation of light-sensitive film?
8 The Digambaras and the Swetambaras are sects of which religion?
9 What word for unthinking patriotism is derived from the name of one of Napoleon's admirers?
10 What metal is used for the filament in a light bulb?
11 Which planet has the lowest density?
12 Who was Millie, whose book was on the US bestsellers' list in 1990?
13 Who played Marty Hopkirk in "Randall and Hopkirk (Deceased)"?
14 Which type of bond is most common in organic molecules?
15 Whose children were called Bernie and Gash?
16 Which actress was the original choice for Alexis in "Dynasty"?
17 Who converted the Louvre from a palace to an art gallery?
18 Which Marx brother was the piano player?
19 With which civilization did the legend of the phoenix begin?
20 Which comedian said that a bank will lend money to those who can prove they don't need it?
21 Whose theories of population growth helped Darwin form his theory?
22 What did social reformer George Williams found in 1844?
23 Whose plays include "Anna Christie" and "Mourning Becomes Elektra"?
24 In which battle were the British commander, Wolfe, and the French commander, Montcalm, both killed?
25 What is it called when the length of day controls the start of flowering?
26 Who wrote bad verse about the Tay Bridge disaster of 1879?
27 Who were the first to use tear gas in warfare and against whom?
28 Whose first film as a director was "Ordinary People"?
29 After a crash at Le Mans who stopped motor racing for over 30 years?
30 Which modern instrument was developed from the sackbut?

Answers

Pop: The Rolling Stones (see Quiz 96) 1 Andrew Loog Oldham.
2 Lennon and McCartney. 3 The Last Time. 4 Alexis Korner's.
5 Aftermath. 6 Sitar. 7 Drowned in pool. 8 Jean-Luc Godard. 9 Ned Kelly.
10 Jade. 11 Andy Warhol. 12 Jamaica. 13 Undercover. 14 Je suis un
rock star. 15 David Bowie. 16 Willie and the Poor Boys. 17 Freejack. 18
Chuck Berry. 19 X-Pensive Winos. 20 Virgin. 21 Ian Stewart. 22 Muddy
Waters. 23 Charlie Watts. 24 As Tears Go By. 25 Jeff Beck. 26 Have You
Seen Your Mother Baby Standing in the Shadow? 27 Let's Spend the Night
Together. 28 Brown Sugar. 29 Rolling Stones No 2. 30 Michael Jackson.

Quiz 95 Sports Bag

Level 3 ▮▮▮

Answers - see page 333

1 On which British golf course is the hole called the "postage stamp"?
2 Which New Zealand cricket captain also captained Surrey?
3 Who was the first world champion at bowls in 1966?
4 Which is the home town of Joe Johnson, the snooker player?
5 Which sport's governing body carries the initials GRA?
6 Which jockey rode Shergar when it won the 1981 Derby?
7 When did Seve Ballesteros win the first of his Open championships?
8 Who was the first woman to compete in the Boat Race?
9 Which Olympic swimmer played the film role of Tarzan?
10 Who won the British Show Jumping Association Ladies' championship eight times?
11 The Air Canada Silver Broom is won in which sport?
12 Which Welshman won the world snooker championship in his first season as a professional?
13 At which course is the greyhound racing classic, The Laurels, run?
14 Over which course is the Scottish Grand National run?
15 Whose statue is outside the Olympic Stadium in Helsinki?
16 Which TV racing journalist rode more than 100 National Hunt winners?
17 At which event did Duncan Goodhew win an individual gold at the 1980 Moscow Olympics?
18 The St Moritz Tobogganing Club stages which famous race?
19 What is the modern name of "Pok-ta-Pok", which originated in Mexico?
20 Whom did Muhammad Ali beat to win the World Heavyweight boxing championship in 1964?
21 On which ground does France play its home rugby union matches?
22 Which is the oldest club in the Football League, founded in 1862?
23 Which woman squash player was unbeaten for 16 years from 1962?
24 Who became the first British golfer to win the European Open in 1979?
25 What nationality is lawn tennis player Gabriela Sabatini?
26 Whom did Steve Davis defeat in his first world snooker title final in 1981?
27 Which club reached the FA Cup Final in 1984, 1885 and 1986?
28 Which racecourse used to be alongside the Thames near Hampton Court?
29 Who were the first two world champions in snooker and billiards?
30 Where is Randwick racecourse situated?

Quiz 96 Pop: The Rolling Stones

Level 3 ▮▮▮

Answers - see page 334

1 Who was The Rolling Stones' manager in the 1960s?
2 Who wrote their first Top Twenty hit?
3 Which was their first No 1 to be written by Jagger and Richard?
4 In which blues band did both Mick Jagger and Charlie Watts perform?
5 From which album was the US chart entry "Mother's Little Helper"?
6 Which instrument did Brian Jones play, other than guitar, on "Their Satanic Majesties Request"?
7 How did Brian Jones die?
8 Which French director made The Stones film "One Plus One"?
9 Which Australian outlaw did Mick Jagger play on film?
10 What is the name of Mick Jagger's daughter by his first wife, Bianca?
11 Who designed the sleeve and logo on "Sticky Fingers"?
12 Where did they record the album "Goat's Head Soup"?
13 Which 1983 video for the title track was banned?
14 Which record was a hit for Bill Wyman in 1983?
15 Who did Mick Jagger sing "Dancing in the Street" with at Live Aid?
16 What was the name of Bill Wyman's group that performed charity gigs?
17 Which sci-fi thriller did Mick Jagger appear in in 1992?
18 Who was the subject of the film "Hail Hail Rock 'n' Roll", for which Keith Richards directed the music?
19 Who were Keith Richards' band on "At the Hollywood Palladium"?
20 For which record label did The Stones sign a deal in 1991?
21 Who was dropped from the group in its early days because "he looked too normal"?
22 Whose song were The Rolling Stones named after?
23 Which Stone described his career as "five years of playing and 20 of hanging about"?
24 Which Jagger-Richard song was Marianne Faithfull's first hit?
25 Which famous guitarist played on Jagger's album "She's the Boss"?
26 Which 1960s Stones' hit had the longest title?
27 What was on the other side of "Ruby Tuesday"?
28 What was their first hit on their own Rolling Stones record label?
29 What was The Rolling Stones' second album called?
30 Who did Jagger share vocals with on the song "State of Shock" in 1984?

Quiz 97 Pot-Luck 45

Answers - see page 339

1 Huntingdon is the birthplace of which ruler of England?
2 To whom is the Dunmow Flitch awarded each year?
3 About whom did Otto Preminger say, "Directing her was like directing Lassie. You need 14 takes to get each one of them right"?
4 The characters from which sit com appeared in a sequel called "It Sticks out Half a Mile"?
5 Which "Professionals" were played by Lewis Collins and Martin Shaw?
6 What is the profession of country singer Hank Wangford?
7 Besides Hadrian, which Roman emperor had a wall built across Britain?
8 How are train robbers Parker and Longbaugh better known?
9 What are the Christian names of the two brothers who formed Bros?
10 On which show did Les Dawson say, "The prizes are so bad, some people leave them in the foyer"?
11 In which year did the ten-shilling note cease to be legal tender?
12 In "The Odyssey", into what did the witch Circe change the sailors?
13 In heraldry, what colour is gules?
14 Rolf Harris was once Australian Junior Champion at what?
15 Which country won the soccer World Cup in 1982?
16 In Scotland what is or was a tawse?
17 Instead of Palin, who was originally to go round the world in 80 days?
18 Holi is a spring religious festival. In which religion?
19 Who wrote the poems "Ozymandias" and "Ode to the West Wind"?
20 What does a psephologist study?
21 Which large island is said to have been discovered by Eric the Red?
22 Which comedy drama had the theme song "That's Living Alright"?
23 In mythology which riddle was solved by Oedipus?
24 Which novelist wrote the book "Westward Ho!"?
25 Who was once a hostess on "Double Your Money" and became a "Coronation Street" regular in 1988?
26 Which character did Amanda Burton play in "Brookside"?
27 Who directed Mia Farrow in "Rosemary's Baby"?
28 If someone is lachrymose, what do they do a lot?
29 Who appoints the BBC's board of governors?
30 Between which towns was the railway for Stephenson's first locomotive?

Answers

Pot-Luck 46 (see Quiz 99)
1 Their shorthand could not be deciphered. 2 All Gas and Gaiters. 3 The Decameron. 4 Red and green. 5 Carol Drinkwater. 6 Vostok 1. 7 Battle of Actium. 8 12. 9 James Hanratty. 10 Dien Bien Phu. 11 Bill of Rights. 12 Albania. 13 Saturn. 14 Michael Jackson. 15 Yalta. 16 Sonja Henie. 17 Paraguay. 18 Six. 19 Amelia Earhart. 20 Indians. 21 Methane. 22 Serious Money. 23 Barbara Hepworth. 24 Romania. 25 Gertrude Stein. 26 Edward Teller. 27 Noriega. 28 Printing. 29 The Empire Strikes Back. 30 Bovine spongiform encephalopathy.

Quiz 98 Hollywood Heyday

Answers - see page 340

Level 3

1 Which studio had a lion as its symbol?
2 Why didn't some of the cast of "Gone With the Wind" see its premiere?
3 Whose roles included characters called McLain, McLintock and McQ?
4 Which future politician was beaten by Elizabeth Taylor for the role of Velvet Brown in "National Velvet"?
5 Who starred with Bergman and Grant in "Notorious"?
6 In which film did Bette Davis play Margo Channingt?
7 How was Ronald Reagan overlooked for a cinematic "White House"?
8 For which film were live leeches imported to Africa?
9 Which artist devised the dream sequence in "Spellbound"?
10 Who was voted king of Hollywood in 1937?
11 Which Astaire-Rogers film had the Oscar-winner "Cheek to Cheek"?
12 What was the first film co-starring Humphrey Bogart and Lauren Bacall?
13 In 1933 who choreographed "42nd Street" in which Ginger Rogers had a lesser role as Anytime Annie?
14 In which film did James Cagney play vaudevillian George M Cohan?
15 Who was "The Hunchback of Notre Dame"in 1923?
16 Which classic was based on "The Tin Star" by John W Cunningham?
17 In which movie did Gary Cooper play a farmer who became a war hero?
18 Who played "Mildred Pierce"?
19 Which 1948 classic was described as "Greed, gold and gunplay on a Mexican mountain of malice"?
20 What was Citizen Kane's real first name?
21 What was shown at the beginning of Paramount pictures?
22 Which John Wayne western was described as "'Grand Hotel' on wheels"?
23 What was Cary Grant's real name?
24 Which musical was the first to pair Mickey Rooney and Judy Garland?
25 What were the names of the four Warner Brothers?
26 What is the name of the drunk played by James Stewart in "Harvey"?
27 What did Cary Grant donate his salary from "The Philadelphia Story" to?
28 Which film star's real name was Reginald Truscott-Jones?
29 Which western hero is the subject of "My Darling Clementine?
30 Which film opens with an office memo including the words "I killed Dietrichson. Me. Walter Neff, insurance salesman, 35 years old..."?

Answers

Culture Vulture: Bestsellers (see Quiz 100) 1 Mao's Little Red Book. 2 Agatha Christie. 3 Webster's Dictionary. 4 Harper Lee. 5 Frederick Warne. 6 Thirteen and three-quarters. 7 Catch 22. 8 Guinness Book of Records. 9 Mickey Spillane. 10 The Remains of the Day. 11 Hold the Dream. 12 Catherine Cookson. 13 Cranberries. 14 Joan Collins'. 15 Nelson Mandela. 16 Jacqueline Susann's (Valley of the Dolls). 17 Peter Benchley. 18 Jung Chang. 19 Miss Smilla. 20 Delia Smith. 21 Wales. 22 Lady Chatterley's Lover. 23 Riders. 24 Kate Hannigan. 25 Alistair MacLean. 26 Ruth Rendell. 27 Danielle Steel. 28 Ian McEwan. 29 Mary Wesley. 30 Dr Benjamin Spock.

338

Quiz 99 Pot-Luck 46

Level 3

Answers - see page 337

1   Why were Samuel Pepys' diaries not published until after 1825?
2   Which sit com was set in and around St Ogg's Cathedral?
3   What was the name of Boccaccio's collection of stories?
4   Which two colours are mixed in a television to produce yellow?
5   Whom did Lynda Bellingham replace as Helen Herriot?
6   What was Yuri Gagarin's spacecraft called?
7   In which battle did Rome defeat the forces of Antony and Cleopatra?
8   What is the atomic number for magnesium?
9   Who was hanged for the A6 murder?
10 In which 1954 battle did the Vietminh defeat the French and end their influence in Indochina?
11 What name is given to the first ten amendments to the US constitution?
12 Zog was king of which country from 1928 to 1939?
13 Which planet has the largest number of moons?
14 Whose first solo hit was "Got to Be There"?
15 Where did Roosevelt, Churchill and Stalin meet in 1945?
16 Which Norwegian Olympic skating champion featured in many Hollywood films in the 1930s and 1940s?
17 Which country's currency is the guaraní?
18 How many carbon atoms are there in the phenol molecule?
19 In 1937 which woman flyer vanished without trace over the Pacific?
20 In Fiji ethnic Fijians are outnumbered by which people?
21 What is the main constituent of natural gas?
22 Which 1987 play by Caryl Churchill satirized London's brash young financial brokers?
23 Which English sculptress exhibited her "Mother and Child" in 1930?
24 Which country had a secret police called Securitate, banned in 1990?
25 Who said, "Rose is a rose is a rose is a rose"?
26 Who worked on the Manhattan Project and later testified against its director, Robert Oppenheimer?
27 Which Central American dictator had the nickname "Pineapple Face"?
28 Which industry uses the gravure method?
29 Which was the second of the Star Wars films?
30 Often known as mad cow disease, what do the initials BSE stand for?

Answers

Pot-Luck 45 (see Quiz 97)
1 Oliver Cromwell. 2 The year's happiest newlywed couple. 3 Marilyn Monroe. 4 Dad's Army. 5 Bodie and Doyle. 6 Gynaecologist. 7 Antoninus. 8 Butch Cassidy and the Sundance Kid. 9 Matt and Luke. 10 Blankety Blank. 11 1970. 12 Pigs. 13 Red. 14 Swimming (backstroke). 15 Italy. 16 Strap, leather belt. 17 Alan Whicker. 18 Hinduism. 19 Shelley. 20 Elections, how people vote. 21 Greenland. 22 Auf Wiedersehen Pet. 23 The Riddle of the Sphinx. 24 Charles Kingsley. 25 Amanda Barrie. 26 Heather Haversham. 27 Roman Polanski. 28 Cry. 29 The Queen. 30 Stockton and Darlington.

Quiz 100 Bestsellers

Answers - see page 338

Level 3

1 Which book had, by law, to be owned by every member of the population of the country between 1966 and 1971?

2 Which author said, "An archaeologist is the best husband a woman can have; the older she gets, the more interested he becomes in her"?

3 According to the Bob Hope/Bing Crosby song, which bestseller is Morocco bound as they were they were in the Road film?

4 Who wrote "To Kill a Mockingbird"?

5 Who has published Beatrix Potter's "Tale of Peter Rabbit" since 1902?

6 How old was Adrian Mole when he started writing his autobiography?

7 Which Joseph Heller book describes a "no win" situation?

8 Which book is the bestselling contemporary book of recent years?

9 Who created the detective Mike Hammer?

10 Which prize-winning novel by Kazuo Ishiguro became a successful film?

11 What was the second in Barbara Taylor Bradford's Emma Harte series?

12 Who holds the record as the novelist most borrowed from libraries?

13 Which fruit appears on the cover of Delia Smith's "Winter Collection"?

14 Whose sister wrote "Hollywood Wives"?

15 Whose autobiography was called "Long Walk to Freedom"?

16 Whose novel is said to be the bestseller of all time?

17 Who wrote the book on which the film "Jaws" was based?

18 Who wrote "Wild Swans"?

19 Who had a feeling for snow?

20 Who cooked through the four seasons?

21 In the books about Inspector Morse where does Lewis come from?

22 About which book did a judge once ask if it was the sort of thing you would want your wife or servant to read?

23 Which book's hero is Rupert Campbell-Black and Jake his main rival?

24 What was Catherine Cookson's first novel?

25 Who wrote 30 books, with 28 of them selling a million in Britain?

26 Who sets her detective novels in Kingsmarkham?

27 Whose novels include "Lightning", "Accident" and "The Gift"?

28 Whose first novel was called "The Cement Garden"?

29 Whose first novel, "Jumping the Queue", came out when she was 70?

30 Who wrote a multi-million bestseller about child care in 1946?

Answers

Hollywood Heyday (see Quiz 98)
1 MGM. 2 All-white cinema. 3 John Wayne. 4 Shirley Williams. 5 Claude Rains. 6 All About Eve. 7 Rejected for Rick in Casablanca, (White House). 8 The African Queen. 9 Salvador Dali. 10 Clark Gable. 11 Top Hat. 12 To Have and to Have Not. 13 42nd Street. 14 Yankee Doodle Dandy. 15 Lon Chaney. 16 High Noon. 17 Sergeant York. 18 Joan Crawford. 19 Treasure of the Sierra Madre. 20 Charles (Foster). 21 Mountain. 22 Stagecoach. 23 Archie Leach. 24 Babes in Arms. 25 Jack, Harry, Samuel, Albert. 26 Elwood. 27 War relief. 28 Ray Milland. 29 Wyatt Earp. 30 Double Indemnity.

Quiz 101 Pot-Luck 47

Level 3

Answers - see page 345

1 In which country did Eddi Cochrane die?
2 What does the South African secretary bird kill and eat?
3 In Venice, what links the Ducal Palace with the state prison?
4 The African and French marigolds are both natives of which country?
5 In which speech did President Lincoln state that American government was "of the people, by the people, for the people"?
6 What the poodle called at the Queen Vic in "EastEnders"?
7 Who stood against Margaret Thatcher for the Tory leadership in 1989?
8 Whose 1968 slogan was "You're either part of the solution or part of the problem"?
9 Which monarch had as one of his titles "The Lion of Judah"?
10 Which football team did Wolfie of "Citizen Smith" support?
11 Which forbidden river can no pure Hindu pass?
12 Who was known as Madame Deficit?
13 Who is the patron saint of grave diggers?
14 In which part of the body is pepsin produced?
15 Bell metal is an alloy of which two metals?
16 Who wrote "Guy Mannering"?
17 What descriptive term is applied to Force 11 on the Beaufort scale?
18 Which Sunday paper was launched in January 1990?
19 What does the letter A stand for in QUANGO?
20 Who was the second Pope?
21 In which year was the first Wembley FA Cup Final to need a replay?
22 What did Del Boy in have written on the side of his car?
23 Who was the founder in 1945 of the Theatre Workshop, which moved to Stratford in east London in 1953?
24 The term "veteran" refers to cars made up to the end of which year?
25 What did the Germans codename "Operation Barbarossa"?
26 Which English king was nicknamed "The Hammer of the Scots"?
27 The marbimba is an African form of which instrument?
28 What name is given to the art of telling fortunes by cards?
29 In "The Archers" what is the name of the church in Ambridge?
30 Whom did Stephen Hendry beat to become the youngest-ever world snooker champion in 1990?

Answers

Pubs (see Quiz 104) **1** Isle of Man TT course. **2** The Nutshell. **3** X. **4** Grand Stand Bar. **5** Grace Neill's Bar. **6** The Fighting Cocks. **7** North Yorkshire. **8** The George Inn. **9** The Horse Shoe. **10** Crown Liquor Saloon. **11** Medieval farmhouse. **12** The Dove. **13** Stalybridge. **14** Brazen Head Inn. **15** Earl Grey. **16** Woolpack, Malt Shovel. **17** Southport. **18** Coach & Horses. **19** Chichester. **20** Downham Tavern. **21** Lovejoy. **22** Olde Trip to Jerusalem **23** The Dove, Hammersmith **24** Recruitment centre for the Napoleonic Wars. **25** Blue Peter. **26** Munich. **27** Holland. **28** The B.B.C.. **29** The Snowdon Summit Bar. **30** Red Lion.

Quiz 102 Pop: Writers

Answers - see page 346

Level 3

1 Who wrote "Wichita Lineman" and "By the Time I Get to Phoenix"?
2 Who co-wrote Eurovision "Puppet on a String" with Bill Martin?
3 Which songwriting pair penned hits in the rock 'n' roll era such as "Teenager in Love" and "Save the Last Dance for Me"?
4 Who won an Oscar for their writing of the title song of "Born Free"?
5 Who wrote a song about Buddy Holly's?
6 Which Small Faces hit was co-written by Kenny Lynch?
7 Who wrote "Sailing", recorded by Rod Stewart?
8 Who replaced Bernie Taupin as Elton John's lyricist in 1979?
9 Who wrote the satirical "Dedicated Follower of Fashion"?
10 Which Neil Diamond song was The Monkees' first No 1?
11 What product was advertised in the Cook & Greenaway hit of 1971?
12 Who wrote Chris Farlowe's No 1 hit "Out of Time"?
13 Which singer sold more than 15 million records of the songs of Bacharach and David between 1962 and 1970?
14 Who wrote "It's Not Unusual" for Tom Jones?
15 Which songwriting trio established the Invictus and Hot Wax labels?
16 Which classical pianist became a pop writer with Howard Greenfield?
17 Which songwriting pair wrote "The Locomotion" for Little Eva?
18 Which 10CC member wrote "For Your Love" for The Yardbirds?
19 Which Lennon and McCartney song was Cilla Black's first single ?
20 Who was named "Officer of Arts and Letters" by the France 1993?
21 Which group was Stephen Stills with before Crosby, Stills, Nash and Young?
22 Which songwriting team, who wrote for Presley, the Isley Brothers and many more, often used the pseudonym Mark Marwell?
23 Who wrote Cliff Richard's first cart topper "Livin' Doll"?
24 Who wrote "Georgy Girl" and "I'll Never Find Another You"?
25 Who wrote the song which begins "I feel it in my fingers…"?
26 Who wrote the lyrics for Cliff Richard's "Heathcliff" musical?
27 Who wrote "If Not For You", a hit for Olivia Newton-John in 1971?
28 Who wrote the biggest-ever selling soundtrack album of its day in 1978?
29 Which songwriters had individually belonged to The Hep Stars and the Hootenanny Singers?
30 Which member of Fleetwood Mac wrote "Albatross"?

1 What is Muckle Flugga?
2 Which Flemish painter produced "Adoration of the Kings"?
3 Who was described by the "Radio Times" as "The scummiest toerag in the great laundry basket of English history"?
4 Which French engineer conceived the idea of the Suez Canal?
5 On which day is Canada's Dominion Day or Canada Day celebrated?
6 What was the "Gluckauf" the first of its kind?
7 Who was the criminal who used a violin case for carrying his tools?
8 In which country is Newt Gingrich an eminent politician?
9 In which needlecraft is honeycomb stitch worked?
10 Which two surveyors drew a line to set the boundary of Pennsylvania and Maryland?
11 What was the occupation of Mary Read and Anne Bonny?
12 Italian dictator Benito Mussolini previously had which two jobs?
13 Which US film director's work includes "Taxi Driver" and "Raging Bull"?
14 Who was the principal female dancer in "The Red Shoes"?
15 On whose novel was the film "Lassie Come Home" based?
16 Which film was considered to be the first of the spaghetti westerns?
17 What name is given to the small chunk of wood, on which short actors stand to bring them up to the correct height for their role?
18 Which film of 1934 gained an Oscar for the song "The Continental"?
19 By what nickname was the silent actor GM Anderson was known?
20 What is the German term printed on labels of a high-quality wine?
21 What type of soup is Dubarry?
22 Which society requires a belief in the Great Architect of the Universe?
23 When was the radio-only licence fee abolished?
24 Who joined French and Saunders in the quartet of "Girls on Top"?
25 In canasta, how many playing cards are needed?
26 Where would you find Amsterdam Island, Kerguelen and Crozet Island?
27 What is the Australian name for a kind of long, narrow lake?
28 Where would you find a canal in a national park in Britain?
29 For what is Peter the Hermit particularly known historically?
30 Why was Aberdeen's win over Celtic in the 1990 Scottish Cup Final a famous first?

Quiz 104 Pubs

Level 3

Answers - see page 341

1 On which famous course is the Sulby Glen Hotel?
2 What is the name of the tiny pub in Bury St Edmunds?
3 What was the previous name of the "Merry Harrier" in Devon which gave it the shortest pub name in the country?
4 What's the bar Galway Racecourse which is 210 feet long called?
5 What is said to be the oldest pub in Northern Ireland?
6 Which pub in St Albans is an 11th-century building?
7 In which county is the elevated Tan Hill Inn?
8 Which pub in Southwark is mentioned by Dickens in "Little Dorritt"?
9 Which pub in Drury Street, Glasgow, has one of the longest bars in Britain?
10 Which Belfast pub in Great Victoria Street is owned by the National Trust?
11 What was The Fleece Inn in Evesham before it became a licensed house?
12 What is the name of the pub, with the smallest bar room, in Upper Mall Chiswick?
13 Where is "The Old Thirteenth Century Cheshire Astley Volunteer Rifleman Corps Inn"?
14 What is the name of the 17th century pub in Lower Bridge Street, Dublin?
15 Which Gloucestershire pub with a small bar room shares its name with a type of tea?
16 Which two pubs feature in the soap "Emmerdale"?
17 Where will you find "The Lakeside Inn" reputed to be Britain's smallest?
18 Which Soho pub was Jeffrey Barnard's regular haunt?
19 Where is the Gribble Inn which makes its own Black Adder II?
20 Which pub in Bromley, built in 1930, is said to be the country's largest?
21 Which antique dealer might you have met at the Butt & Oyster in Suffolk?
22 Which East Midlands pub served soldiers prior to going to fight the Crusades?
23 In which Hammersmith pub was 'Rule Britaina' written?
24 Why is "The Napoleon" in Boscastle, Cornwall, so called?
25 Which pub in Polperro, Cornwall, shares its name with a TV programme?
26 In which city is the largest beer-selling establishment in the world?
27 In which country would you find the 't IJ Proeflokaal pub?
28 The George in Great Portland Street, London is which Auntie's local?
29 Where is the highest place you can buy beer in Wales?
30 What is the commonest name for a pub?

Answers

Pot-Luck 50 (see Quiz 107)

1 Monza, Italy. 2 Elias. 3 Gold centre, then red, blue, black, white. 4 Tennis, anyone? 5 Amanda Barrie. 6 Victoria and Euston. 7 Admiral John Jellicoe. 8 Aeroflot. 9 Highest point of the city. 10 Silk screen painting. 11 Scampo. 12 3-tined fork. 13 A mollusc. 14 Chelsea. 15 Lizard. 16 American Indians in the United States. 17 Graham Sutherland. 18 The Coach. 19 Andromeda. 20 A mess of pottage. 21 Stained glass. 22 March 15th. 23 All are varieties of roses. 24 Clock face. 25 Dermot. 26 A large hat. 27 Wales. 28 Woodrow Wilson. 29 Lou Costello. 30 Tony Warren, creator of "Coronation Street".

1 What illness is caused by the Epstein-Barr virus?
2 What does "hors d'oeuvre" mean on a menu?
3 Which fictional detective was known as the female James Bond?
4 In which of Graham Greene's novels does Pinkie appear?
5 What was Mickey Mouse first called?
6 What title is held by Shakespeare's "Cymbeline"?
7 Which cemetery is the resting place of Thackeray and Trollope?
8 Which organ of the body is affected by Bright's Disease?
9 How did the word "exchequer" come into being?
10 In 1919 which pianist was elected prime minister of Poland?
11 What is the nickname of Haydn's Symphony No 101 in D major?
12 Which mezzo-soprano created the role of Auntie in "Peter Grimes"?
13 On which river is the rocky cliff of the Lorelei located?
14 What was Calamity Jane's married name?
15 What was "The Times" first known as, in 1785?
16 Who was nicknamed "Impeesa", meaning "The Wolf who Never Sleeps", by the Matabele tribe?
17 How many islands make up the Calendar Islands in Casco Bay?
18 By what name is the mavis better known?
19 Who wrote the song known in English as "If You Go Away"?
20 Of which country is the Easter lily a native?
21 What is BT's videotext information service called?
22 Which British playwright said, "Never trust a man with short legs – brains too near their bottoms"?
23 Who kills the bull in a bullfight?
24 Which sisterhood established at Assisi around 1212 adopted the Franciscan rule and habit?
25 Which US politician shares his name with with Duke Ellington?
26 Nossa Senhora da Aparecida is the patron saint of which country?
27 What would be measured with an anemometer?
28 To five years either way, in what year did Francis Drake begin his voyage around the world?
29 Whom did Hitler choose to head the SS in 1929?
30 In "Birds of a Feather" what is Dorien's husband called?

Answers

Pot-Luck 47 (see Quiz 101)
1 England. 2 Snakes. 3 The Bridge of Sighs. 4 Mexico. 5 Gettysburg Address. 6 Roly. 7 Sir Anthony Meyer. 8 Eldridge Cleaver. 9 The emperor of Ethiopia. 10 Fulham. 11 Attock. 12 Marie Antoinette (wife of Louis XVI). 13 St Anthony. 14 Stomach. 15 Copper and tin. 16 Sir Walter Scott. 17 Storm. 18 The Independent on Sunday. 19 Autonomous. 20 Saint Linus. 21 1970. 22 Trotter's Independent Trading Company. 23 Joan Littlewood. 24 1918. 25 The invasion of the Soviet Union. 26 Edward I. 27 Xylophone. 28 Cartomancy. 29 St Stephen's. 30 Jimmy White.

1 Which former Liverpool player's middle name was Everton?
2 Who were the first country to win the World Cup four times?
3 What is Scotland's oldest club?
4 Who captained Arsenal when they won the League and Cup in 1970–71?
5 Which Scottish side's nickname is "The Blue Brazil"?
6 Which club, formed in 1863, won their first trophy 109 years later?
7 Which was the first Welsh side to win the FA Cup?
8 Which football commentator used to play for Corinthian Casuals?
9 What was the England World Cup Squad's No 1 hit in 1970?
10 Which two England internationals captained on "A Question of Sport"?
11 Which football club folded in 1992 after 66 years in the League?
12 Which soccer player advertised "Brut" in the 1980s?
13 Who was the first Scot to make 100 appearances for his country?
14 Who were the first club this century to win the FA Cup and the FA Amateur Cup?
15 With whom did Alan Ball begin his playing career?
16 Who was the first soccer manager to manage all three Birmingham clubs – Aston Villa, Birmingham and West Brom?
17 Who or what is Alexandra in Crewe Alexandra?
18 In 1971 what was England's first commercially sponsored tournament?
19 Which England captain was sent off when captaining the side in 1986?
20 Who won the European Cup in the first five seasons from 1955 to 1960?
21 Which Football League club went from the fourth to the first division in five seasons in the 60s?
22 Which was the first 3rd division side to reach FA Cup semis?
23 What did goalkeeper Gordon Banks reputedly put on his hands to improve his grip?
24 In which language does 1980s Irish winger Tony Galvin have a degree?
25 Who said on supporting Birmingham, "You lose some, you draw some"?
26 Which manager said he'd been in more courts than Bjorn Borg?
27 Which stadium hosted its first FA Cup semifinal in 1991?
28 Which team first won an FA Cup semifinal on a penalty shoot-out?
29 Who was the first Footballer of the Year in England and Scotland?
30 Who were Asia's two representatives in the 1990 World Cup Finals?

Level 3

1 Pit Straight, Lesmo Bend and Roggia Bend are parts of what?
2 What was Australina cricketer Patsy Hendren's real first name?
3 Starting at the centre, what are the five colours of an archery target?
4 What was the only line that Humphrey Bogart had in his first play?
5 How is Shirley Ann Broadbent better known?
6 Name the first railway hotels opened in London in September 1839?
7 Who was the commander of the British fleet at the Battle of Jutland?
8 Which airline was originally called Dobrolet?
9 What is the literal meaning of acropolis ?
10 What is the common name for the craft known as serigraphy?
11 What is the singular of scampi?
12 What is a runcible spoon?
13 The shipworm is not a worm. What is it?
14 What is Bill and Hillary Clinton's daughter called?
15 What is a chuckwalla?
16 Marlon Brando refused to accept his Oscar for "The Godfather" because of the oppression of which people?
17 Who painted the 80th-birthday portrait of Sir Winston Churchill?
18 In "Cheers" what was Ernie Pantouso's nickname?
19 Which constellation represents a princess in Greek mythology?
20 In the Book of Genesis, what did Esau get in return for his birthrigh?
21 Chartres cathedral in France is famed for what particular feature?
22 Julius Caesar was murdered on the Ides of March. What date was this?
23 What do Paddy McCready, Elizabeth of Glamis and Dorothy Perkins have in common?
24 In "Safety Last" where is stunt actor Harold Lloyd seen hanging from?
25 Who did Harry Enfield play in "Men Behaving Badly"?
26 What kind of clothing is a dolly varden?
27 In which country was the explorer HM Stanley born?
28 Who was in office as president of the United States when the decision was taken to declare war on Germany during World War I?
29 Which American comedian's last words were, "That was the best ice-cream soda I ever tasted"?
30 Whose autobiography was called "I Was Ena Sharples' Father"?

Answers

Pot-Luck 48 (see Quiz 103)
1 The rock & lighthouse on Uist. 2 Brueghel. 3 Black Adder. 4 de Lesseps. 5 July 1st. 6 Custom-built oil tanker. 7 Charles Peace. 8 United States. 9 Smocking. 10 Mason and Dixon. 11 Pirates. 12 Teaching, journalism. 13 Martin Scorsese. 14 Moira Shearer. 15 Eric Knight's. 16 A Fistful of Dollars. 17 Pancake. 18 The Gay Divorcée. 19 Bronco Billy. 20 Kabinett. 21 Cream of cauliflower. 22 Freemasons. 23 1971. 24 Tracey Ullman, Ruby Wax 25 108, two packs and four jokers. 26 Indian Ocean. 27 Billabong. 28 Brecon Beacons. 29 Led the First Crusade. 30 Decided on a penalty shoot-out.

HOW TO SET UP YOUR OWN
PUB QUIZ

It isn't easy, get that right from the start. This isn't going to be easy.
Think instead of words like; 'difficult', 'taxing', 'infuriating' consider
yourself with damp palms and a dry throat and then, when you have
concentrated on that, put it out of your mind and think of the
recognition you will receive down the local, imagine all the regulars
lifting you high upon their shoulders dancing and weaving their way
around the pub. It won't help but it's good to dream every once in a
while.

What you will need:

- A good selection of biros (never be tempted to give your own pen up, not even to family members)
- A copy of *The Best Pub Quiz Book Ever*
- A set of answer sheets photocopied from the back of the book
- A good speaking voice and possibly a microphone and an amp
- A pub
- At least one pint inside you
- At least one more on your table
- A table

What to do:

Choose your local to start with, there is no need to get halfway
through your first quiz and decide you weren't cut out for all this and
then find yourself in the roughest pub in Christendom 30 miles and a
long run from home.

Chat it through with the landlord and agree on whether you will
be charging or not, if you don't then there is little chance of a prize
for the winners other than a free pint each and this is obviously at the

landlord's discretion – if you pack his pub to bursting then five free pints won't worry him, but if it's only you and a two others then he may be less than unwilling, as publicans tend to be.

If you decide on a payment entry keep it reasonable, you don't want to take the fun out of the quiz; some people will be well aware that they have very little hope of winning and will be reluctant to celebrate the fact by mortgaging their house.

Once location and prize are all sorted then advertising the event is paramount, get people's attention, sell sell, sell or, alternatively, stick up a gaudy looking poster on the door of the bogs. Be sure to specify all the details, time, prize and so on – remember you are selling to people whose tiny attention span is being whittled down to nothing by alcohol.

After this it is time for the big night, if you are holding the event in the 'snug' which seats ten or so you can rely on your voice, if not you should get hold of a good microphone and an amplifier so that you can boom out your questions and enunciate the length and breadth of the pub (once again, clear this with the landlord and don't let liquid anywhere near the electrical equipment). Make sure to practice, and get comfortable with the sound of your own voice and relax as much as possible, try not to rely on alcohol too much or "round one" will be followed by "rown' too" which will eventually give way to "runfree". Relax with your voice so that you can handle any queries from the teams, and any venomous abuse from the 'lively' bar area.

When you enter the pub make sure you take everything listed above. Also, make sure you have a set of tie-break questions and that you instruct everybody who is taking part of the rules – and be firm. It will only upset people if you start handing out impromptu solutions and let's face it the wisdom of Solomon is not needed when you are talking pub quiz rules; 'no cheating' is a perfectly healthy stance to start with.

Finally, keep the teams to a maximum of five members, hand out your answer papers and pens and, when everybody is good and settled, start the quiz. It might not be easy and it might not propel you to international stardom or pay for a life of luxury but you will enjoy yourself. No, really.

ANSWERS   Part One

1 _____

2 _____

3 _____

4 _____

5 _____

6 _____

7 _____

8 _____

9 _____

10 _____

11 _____

12 _____

13 _____

14 _____

15 _____

16 _____

17 _____

18 _____

19 _____

20 _____

21 _____

22 _____

23 _____

24 _____

25 _____

26 _____

27 _____

28 _____

29 _____

30 _____

ANSWERS

Part Two

1 _____	**16** _____
2 _____	**17** _____
3 _____	**18** _____
4 _____	**19** _____
5 _____	**20** _____
6 _____	**21** _____
7 _____	**22** _____
8 _____	**23** _____
9 _____	**24** _____
10 _____	**25** _____
11 _____	**26** _____
12 _____	**27** _____
13 _____	**28** _____
14 _____	**29** _____
15 _____	**30** _____

ANSWERS

Part Three

1 _____	16 _____
2 _____	17 _____
3 _____	18 _____
4 _____	19 _____
5 _____	20 _____
6 _____	21 _____
7 _____	22 _____
8 _____	23 _____
9 _____	24 _____
10 _____	25 _____
11 _____	26 _____
12 _____	27 _____
13 _____	28 _____
14 _____	29 _____
15 _____	30 _____